Bob!! :)

Not a BBQ!

but at least in English!! :)

[signature]

JUDICIAL REVIEW IN NORWAY

Outside the United States, Norway's 1814 Constitution is the oldest still in force. Constitutional judicial review has been a part of Norwegian court decision-making for most of these 200 years. Since the 1990s, Norway has also exercised review under the European Convention of Human Rights. Judicial review of legislation can be controversial: having unelected judges overruling popularly elected majorities seems undemocratic. Yet Norway remains one of the most democratic countries in the world. How does Norway manage the balance between democracy and judicial oversight? *Judicial Review in Norway* tells the story of Norwegian constitutionalism from 1814 to today through the lens of judicial review debates and cases. This study adds important insights into the social and political justifications for an active judicial review component in a constitutional democracy. Anine Kierulf argues that the Norwegian model of judicial review provides a useful perspective on the dichotomy of American and European constitutionalism.

Anine Kierulf is Research Director at the Norwegian National Human Rights Institution.

COMPARATIVE CONSTITUTIONAL LAW AND POLICY

Series Editors

Comparative constitutional law is an intellectually vibrant field that encompasses an increasingly broad array of approaches and methodologies. This series collects analytically innovative and empirically grounded work from scholars of comparative constitutionalism across academic disciplines. Books in the series include theoretically informed studies of single constitutional jurisdictions, comparative studies of constitutional law and institutions, and edited collections of original essays that respond to challenging theoretical and empirical questions in the field.

Judicial Review in Norway

A BICENTENNIAL DEBATE

ANINE KIERULF

Norwegian National Human Rights Institution

CAMBRIDGE
UNIVERSITY PRESS

CAMBRIDGE
UNIVERSITY PRESS

University Printing House, Cambridge CB2 8BS, United Kingdom

One Liberty Plaza, 20th Floor, New York, NY 10006, USA

477 Williamstown Road, Port Melbourne, VIC 3207, Australia

314–321, 3rd Floor, Plot 3, Splendor Forum, Jasola District Centre, New Delhi – 110025, India

79 Anson Road, #06–04/06, Singapore 079906

Cambridge University Press is part of the University of Cambridge.

It furthers the University's mission by disseminating knowledge in the pursuit of education, learning, and research at the highest international levels of excellence.

www.cambridge.org
Information on this title: www.cambridge.org/9781108426688
DOI: 10.1017/9781108617727

First published 2018

Printed and bound in Great Britain by Clays Ltd, Elcograf S.p.A.

A catalogue record for this publication is available from the British Library.

Library of Congress Cataloging-in-Publication Data
NAMES: Kierulf, Anine, 1974– author.
TITLE: Judicial review in Norway / Anine Kierulf.
DESCRIPTION: Cambridge [UK] ; New York : Cambridge University Press, 2018. | Series: Comparative constitutional law and policy | Includes bibliographical references and index.
IDENTIFIERS: LCCN 2017055358 | ISBN 9781108426688 (hardback)
SUBJECTS: LCSH: Judicial review – Norway. | Constitutional law – Norway.
CLASSIFICATION: LCC KKN2650 .K54 2018 | DDC 347.481/012–dc23
LC record available at https://lccn.loc.gov/2017055358

ISBN 978-1-108-42668-8 Hardback

For Rune and Richard

Contents

Abbreviations

Arbeiderdemokratene	Norwegian Radical Liberal Labor Party (1911–1940)
Arbeiderpartiet	Norwegian Labor Party (1887)
CoE	Council of Europe
ECA	Norwegian Expropriation Compensation Act 1973
ECHR	European Convention of Human Rights
ECtHR	European Court of Human Rights
Fremskrittspartiet	Norwegian Right-wing Progress Party (est. 1973)
Frisinnede Venstre	Norwegian Conservative Liberal Party (1909–1936)
HRA	Norwegian Human Rights Act 1999
Høyre	Norwegian Conservative Party (est. 1884)
Kristelig Folkeparti	Norwegian Christian Democrat Party (est. 1933)
MoFA	Norwegian Ministry of Foreign Affairs
MoJ	Norwegian Ministry of Justice
MOF	Norwegian Ministry of Finance
NC	Norwegian Constitution 1814
NOU	Norwegian Official Reports [Norges Offentlige Utredninger]
NPC 1902	Norwegian Penal Code 1902
NPC 2005	Norwegian Penal Code 2005
NSCt	Norwegian Supreme Court
OVF	Norwegian Church Endowment Foundation [Opplysningsvesenets fond]
PLI	Norwegian Property Lease Instruction 2007
Power Study	Norwegian Study on Power and Democracy (1998–2003)
Rt.	Norwegian Supreme Court Reporter [Retstidende], ex: "Rt. 1976 s. 1"
Sosialistisk Venstre	Socialist Left Party (est. 1975)

Senterpartiet	Agrarian Center Party (est. 1920)
Socialdemokratisk Arbeiderparti	Moderate Labor Party (1921–1927)
Stortinget	Norwegian Parliament
USSCt.	Supreme Court of the United States
Venstre	Norwegian Liberal Left (est. 1884)

Table of Cases

CASE LAW

The Norwegian Supreme Court

Supreme Court Decision 1.11.1866
Rt. 1890 s. 455
Rt. 1894 s. 753
Rt. 1902 s. 684
Rt. 1908 s. 481
Rt. 1910 s. 100
Rt. 1913 s. 449
Rt. 1914 s. 208
Rt. 1914 s. 289
Rt. 1914 s. 881
Rt. 1915 s. 1041
Rt. 1916 s. 648
Rt. 1918 s. 403
Rt. 1922 s. 41
Rt. 1922 s. 624
Rt. 1945 s. 2
Rt. 1946 s. 196
Rt. 1946 s. 198
Rt. 1950 s. 831
Rt. 1952 s. 1089
Rt. 1952 s. 1281
Rt. 1955 s. 439
Rt. 1956 s. 952
Rt. 1961 s. 1350

Rt. 1962 s. 369
Rt. 1966 s. 476
Rt. 1970 s. 67
Rt. 1974 s. 935
Rt. 1976 s. 1
Rt. 1979 s. 727
Rt. 1982 s. 24
Rt. 1982 s. 241
Rt. 1983 s. 998
Rt. 1983 s. 1004
Rt. 1984 s. 1175
Rt. 1984 s. 1359
Rt. 1985 s. 22
Rt. 1985 s. 1421
Rt. 1985 s. 1444
Rt. 1987 s. 612
Rt. 1987 s. 1058
Rt. 1987 s. 1285
Rt. 1988 s. 314
Rt. 1988 s. 476
Rt. 1990 s. 257
Rt. 1991 s. 1096
Rt. 1994 s. 610
Rt. 1994 s. 1244
Rt. 1996 s. 1415
Rt. 1997 s. 580
Rt. 1997 s. 1019
Rt. 1999 s. 1742
Rt. 2000 s. 996
Rt. 2001 s. 603
Rt. 2001 s. 1006
Rt. 2001 s. 1720
Rt. 2002 s. 764
Rt. 2003 s. 301
Rt. 2003 s. 593
Rt. 2003 s. 914
Rt. 2003 s. 928
Rt. 2003 s. 1190
Rt. 2004 s. 1483
Rt. 2004 s. 1737

Rt. 2005 s. 833
Rt. 2005 s. 1677
Rt. 2006 s. 293
Rt. 2007 s. 1281
Rt. 2007 s. 1306
Rt. 2007 s. 1308
Rt. 2008 s. 1089
Rt. 2010 s. 143
Rt. 2010 s. 535
Rt. 2010 s. 1445
Rt. 2011 s. 304
Rt. 2013 s. 374
Rt. 2013 s. 1345
HR-2014–445-A
Rt. 2014 s. 1045
Rt. 2014 s. 1105
Rt. 2014 s. 1292
Rt. 2015 s. 93
HR-2016–304-S
HR-2016–2554-P
HR-2016–2591-A
HR-2016–2171-A

Norwegian Lower Courts

Borgarting Court of Appeals	LB-2009–24039
Oslo City Court	TOSLO-2008–18985
Oslo City Court	TOSLO-2008–182790

The European Court of Human Rights

A and others v. *United Kingdom*, Application no. 3455/05, 19.2.2009 (GC).
A. v. *Norway*, Application no. 28070/06, 9.4.2009.
Animal Defenders International v. *the United Kingdom*, Application no. 48876/08, 22.4.2013.
AS Dagbladet v. *Norway*, Application no. 60715/14, 20.03.2018.
Avisa Nordland AS v. *Norway Application*, no. 30563/15, 20.03.2018.
Axel Springer AG v. *Germany*, Application no. 39954/08, 7.2.2012 (GC).
Bergens Tidende and others v. *Norway*, Application no. 26132/95, 2.5.2000.

Bladet Tromsø and Stensaaas v. *Norway*, Application no. 21980/93 20.5.1999.
Case of Lawless v. *Ireland (No. 3)*, Application no. 332/57, 1.7.1961.
Chauvy and others v. *France*, Application no. 64915/01, 24.6.2004.
Christine Goodwin v. *the United Kingdom*, Application no. 28957/95, 11.7.2002.
Cumpănă and Mazăre v. *Romania*, Application no. 33348/96, 17.12.2004 (GC).
Dahlab v. *Switzerland*, Application no. 42393/98, 15.2.2001.
Dudgeon v. *the United Kingdom*, Application no. 7525/76, 22.10.1981.
EON v. *France*, Application no. 26118/10, 14.3.2013.
Janowski v. *Poland*, Application no. 25716/94, 21.1.1999.
Jersild v. *Denmark*, Application no. 15890/89, 23.9.1994.
Lautsi v. *Italy*, Application no. 30814/06, 3.11.2009.
Lautsi v. *Italy*, Application no. 30814/06, 18.3.2011 (GC).
Lillo-Stenberg and Sæther v. *Norway*, Application no. 13258/09, 16.1.2014.
Lindheim and others v. *Norway*, Application no. 13221/08.
Lindon, Otchakovsky-Laurens and July v. *France*, Applications nos. 21279/02 and 36448/02, 22.10.2007 (GC).
Lingens v. *Austria*, Application no. 9815/82, 8.7.1986.
Murphy v. *Ireland*, Application no. 44179/98, 10.7.2003.
Nilsen and Johnsen v. *Norway*, Application no. 23118/93, 25.11.1999.
Osmanoglu and Kocabas v. *Switzerland*, Application no. 29086/12, 10.01.2017.
Otegi Mondragon v. *Spain*, Application no. 2034/07, 15.3.2011.
Pedersen and Baadsgaard v. *Denmark*, Application no. 49017/99, 17.12.2004 (GC).
Radio France and others v. *France*, Application no. 53984/00, 3.3.2004.
Ruokanen and others v. *Finland*, Application no. 45130/06, 4.10.2010.
Salem v. *Denmark*, Application no. 77036/11, 1.12.2016.
Scoppola v. *Italy (no.2)*, Application no. 10249/03, 17.9.2009.
Selistö v. *Finland*, Application no. 56767/00, 16.11.2004.
TV Vest AS & Rogaland Pensjonistparti v. *Norway*, Application no. 21132/05, 11.12.2008.
Tyrer v. *the United Kingdom*, Application no. 5856/72, 25.4.1978.
Tønsberg Blad AS and Marit Haukom v. *Norway*, Application no. 510/04, 1.3.2007.
VgT Verein Tierfabriken v. *Switzerland*, Application no. 24699/94, 28.6.2001.
Von Hannover v. *Germany*, Application no. 59320/00, 24.6.2004.
Von Hannover v. *Germany (no. 2)*, Applications nos. 40660/08 and 60641/08, 7.2.2012 (GC).
Wemhoff v. *Germany*, Application no. 2122/64, 27.6.1968.
White v. *Sweden*, Application no. 42435/02, 19.9.2006.

I v. *Norway*, Decision by the Commission, 17.12.1963.

The Supreme Court of the United States

Abrams v. *United States* 250 U.S. 616 (1919).
Chaplinsky v. *New Hampshire* 315 U.S. 568 (1942).
Fletcher v. *Peck* 10 U.S. 87 (1810).
Lochner v. *New York*, 198 U.S. 45 (1905).
Marbury v. *Madison* 5. U.S. 137 (1803).
New York Times v. *Sullivan* 376 U.S. 254 (1964).
Roe v. *Wade* 410 U.S. 113 (1973).
Truax v. *Corrigan* 257 U.S. 312 (1921).
United States v. *Carolene Products Co.*, 304 U.S. 144 (1938).
West Coast Hotel Co. v. *Parrish*, 300 U.S. 379 (1937).
Whitney v. *California*, 274 U.S. 357 (1927).

United Kingdom House of Lords Decisions

Ullah, R (on the Application of) v. *Special Adjudicator* [2004] UKHL 26 (June 17, 2004).

LEGAL AUTHORITY AND PUBLIC DOCUMENTS

Norwegian Statutes

Lov angaaende Forbrydelser af 20. august 1842.
Lov om Rettergangsmaaden i Straffesager av 7. januar 1887 nr. 5.
Almindelig borgerlig Straffelov av 22. mai 1902 nr. 10.
Lov av 13. august 1915 nr. 5 om domstolene (domstolloven).
Lov av 13. august 1915 nr. 6 om rettergangsmåten for tvistemål (tvistemålsloven).
Lov av 25. juni 1926 nr. 2 om forandring i lovgivningen om Høiesterett (plenumsloven).
Lov av 15. desember 1950 nr. 7 om særlige rådgjerder under krig, krigsfare og liknende forhold (beredskapsloven).
Lov av 13. Juni 1969 nr. 26 om skadeserstatning.
Lov av 26. januar 1973 nr. 4 om erstatning ved ekspropriasjon av fast eiendom.
Lov av 22. mai 1981 nr. 25 om rettergangsmåten i straffesaker (straffeprosessloven).
Lov av 6. april 1984 nr. 17 om vederlag ved oreigning av fast eigedom (ekspropriasjonserstatningslova).

Lov av 27. november 1992 nr. 109 om gjennomføring i norsk rett av hoveddelen i avtale om Det europeiske økonomiske samarbeidsområde (EØS) m.v.
Lov av 4. desember 1992 nr. 127 om kringkasting og audiovisuelle bestillingstjenester.
Lov av 7. juni 1996 nr. 33 om Opplysningsvesenets fond.
Lov av 13. juni 1997 nr. 44 om aksjeselskaper (aksjeloven).
Lov av 21. mai 1999 nr. 30 om styrking av menneskerettighetenes stilling i norsk rett (menneskerettsloven).
Lov av 2. juli 1999 nr. 62 om etablering og gjennomføring av psykisk helsevern (psykisk helsevernloven).
Lov av 20. mai 2005 nr. 28 om straff (straffeloven).
Lov av 17. juni 2005 nr. 90 om mekling og rettergang i sivile tvister (tvisteloven).
Lov av 28. november 2008 nr. 81 om endring i lov 7. juni 1996 nr. 33 om Opplysningsvesenets fond.
Lov av 7. mars 2008 nr. 4 om endringer i straffeloven 20. mai 2005 nr. 28 mv. (skjerpende og formildende omstendigheter, folkemord, rikets selvstendighet, terrorhandlinger, ro, orden og sikkerhet, og offentlig myndighet).
Lov av 15. januar 2010 nr. 2 om endringar i domstolloven mv. (sidegjeremål for dommarar m.m.).

Norwegian Administrative and Parliamentary Documents

NOU 1988:8 Lov om psykisk helsevern uten eget samtykke.
NOU 1992:29 Lov om aksjeselskaper.
NOU 1993:18 Lovgivning om menneskerettigheter.
NOU 1995:10 Reformer innen injurielovgivningen.
NOU 1996:3 Ny aksjelovgivning.
NOU 1999:19 Domstolene i samfunnet.
NOU 1999:27 "Ytringsfrihed bør finde Sted."
NOU 2001:32 Rett på sak. Lov om tvisteløsning (tvisteloven).
NOU 2002:4 Ny straffelov. Straffelovkommisjonens delutredning VII.
NOU 2003:19 Makt og demokrati.
NOU 2004:25 Penger teller, men stemmer avgjør. Om partifinansiering, åpenhet og partipolitisk fjernsynsreklame.
NOU 2009:1 Individ og integritet. Personvern i det digitale samfunnet.
NOU 2012:2 Innenfor og utenfor.
NOU 2012:14 Rapport fra 22. juli-kommisjonen.
Dokument nr. 10 (1945), Stortinget etter valget i 1945.

Dokument 8:164 S (2009–2010), Representantforslag fra stortingsrepresentantene Bente Thorsen, Dagrun Eriksen, Trine Skei Grande og Svein Harberg om konsekvenser av Høyesteretts dom i favør av Kirkelig arbeidsgiver- og interesseorganisasjon i saken om Opplysningsvesenets fond.

Dokument 12:12 (2011–2012), Grunnlovsforslag fra Sverre Myrli, Gerd Janne Kristoffersen og Steinar Gullvåg om endring av Grunnloven § 106 (forvaltning av geistlighetens benefiserte gods Opplysningsvesenets fond).

Dokument 8:120 S (2012–2013), Representantforslag fra stortingsrepresentantene Anders Anundsen, Ulf Erik Knudsen og Øyvind Vaksdal om egen lovrådgiver for Stortinget.

Dokument 12:30 (2011–2012), Grunnlovsforslag fra Per-Kristian Foss, Martin Kolberg, Marit Nybakk, Jette F. Christensen, Anders Anundsen, Hallgeir H. Langeland, Per Olaf Lundteigen, Geir Jørgen Bekkevold og Trine Skei Grande om grunnlovfesting av sivile og politiske menneskerettigheter.

Dokument 12:31 (2011–2012), Grunnlovsforslag fra Per-Kristian Foss, Martin Kolberg, Marit Nybakk, Jette F. Christensen, Hallgeir H. Langeland, Per Olaf Lundteigen, Geir Jørgen Bekkevold og Trine Skei Grande om grunnlovfesting av økonomiske, sosiale og kulturelle menneskerettigheter.

Dokument 12:36 (2011–2012), Grunnlovsforslag fra Per-Kristian Foss, Martin Kolberg, Marit Nybakk, Jette F. Christensen, Hallgeir H. Langeland og Per Olaf Lundteigen om endring i Grunnloven § 97 (unntak fra tilbakevirkningsforbudet for handlinger som var straffbare etter folkeretten).

Dokument nr. 15 (1995–1996), Rapport til Stortinget fra kommisjonen som ble oppnevnt av Stortinget for å granske påstander om ulovlig overvåking av norske borgere ("Lund-rapporten").

Dokument nr. 15:1 (2010–2011), Spørsmål til skriftlig besvarelse med svar.

Dokument nr. 15:3 (2012–2013), Spørsmål til skriftlig besvarelse med svar.

Dokument 16 (2011–2012), Rapport til Stortingets presidentskap fra Menneskerettighetsutvalget om menneskerettigheter i Grunnloven.

Ot. forh. 13.7.1909.

Ot. forh. 11.1.1973.

Ot. forh. 13.4.1999.

Ot. forh. 23.10.2008.

Ot. forh. 9.7.1909.

Ot. forh. 22.3.1984.

Ot. prp. nr. 78 (1950).

Ot. prp. nr. 23 (1996–1997), *Om lov om aksjeselskaper (aksjeloven) og lov om allmennaksjeselskaper (allmennaksjeloven).*

Ot. prp. nr. 3 (1998–1999), *Om lov om styrking av menneskerettighetenes stilling i norsk rett (menneskerettsloven).*

Ot. prp. nr. 1 (2007–2008), *Skatte- og avgiftsopplegget 2008 – lovendringer.*

Ot. prp. nr. 8 (2007–2008), *Om lov om endringer i straffeloven 20. mai 2005 nr. 28 mv. (skjerpende og formildende omstendigheter, folkemord, rikets selvstendighet, terrorhandlinger, ro, orden og sikkerhet, og offentlig myndighet).*

Ot. prp. nr. 26 (1974–1975), *Om lov om skattelegging av undersjøiske petroliumsforekomster m.v.*

Ot. prp. nr. 28 1926, *Om forandring i lovgivningen om Høiesterett.*

Ot. prp. nr. 41 (1980–1981), *Om lov om endringer i rettergangslovgivningen.*

Ot. prp. nr. 58 (1998–1999), *Om lov om endringer i lov 4 desember 1992 nr 127 om kringkasting m.m.*

Ot. prp. nr. 22 (2008–2009), *Om lov om endringer i straffeloven 20. mai 2005 nr. 28 (siste delproposisjon – sluttføring av spesiell del og tilpasning av annen lovgivning).*

Ot. prp. nr. 102 (2008–2009), *Om lov om endringar i domstolloven mv. (godkjenning av sidegjeremål for dommarar mv.).*

Ot. prp. nr. 41 (2003–2004) *Om lov om endringer i lov 20. desember 1996 nr. 106 om tomtefeste.*

Ot. prp.nr.3 (1998–1999), *Om lov om styrking av menneskerettighetenes stilling i norsk rett (menneskerettsloven).*

Ot. prp.nr.11 (1998–1999), *Om lov om etablering og gjennomføring av psykisk helsevern (psykiatriloven).*

Ot. prp.nr.44 (2000–2001), *Om lov om endringer i domstolloven m.m. (den sentrale domstoladministrasjon og dommernes arbeidsrettslige stilling).*

Ot. prp.nr. 56 (1970–1971), *Erstatning ved ekspropriasjon av fast eiendom.*

Innstilling fra Husaasutvalget (1969), Innstilling om skjønnsordningen og om erstatningsutmåling ved ekspropriasjon.

Innst. O. XXI (1971–1972), Innstilling fra Justiskomiteen om lov om erstatning ved ekspropriasjon av fast eiendom.

Innst. O. nr. 27 (1983–1984), Innstilling frå justiskomitéen om lov om vederlag ved oreigning av fast eiendom.

Innst. O. nr. 81 (1995–1996), Innstilling fra finanskomiteen om endringer i skipsfartsbeskatningen.

Innst. O. nr. 51 (1998–1999), Innstilling frå justiskomiteen om lov om styrking av menneskerettane si stilling i norsk rett (menneskerettsloven).

Innst. O. nr. 1 (2007–2008), Innstilling fra finanskomiteen om skatte- og avgiftsopplegget 2008 – lovendringer.

Innst. O. nr. 29 (2007–2008), Innstilling fra justiskomiteen om lov om endringer i straffeloven 20. mai 2005 nr. 28 mv. (skjerpende og formildende omstendigheter, folkemord, rikets selvstendighet, terrorhandlinger, ro, orden og sikkerhet, og offentlig myndighet).

Innst. O. nr. 79 (2007–2008), Innstilling fra kirke-, utdannings- og forskningskomiteen om lov om endring i lov 7. juni 1996 nr. 33 om Opplysningsvesenets fond.

Innst. O. nr. 73 (2008–2009), Innstilling fra justiskomiteen om lov om endringer i straffeloven 20. mai 2005 nr. 28 mv. (siste delproposisjon – sluttføring av spesiell del og tilpasning av annen lovgivning).

Innst. S. LXXIV 1923, Innstilling fra konstitusjonskomiteen angående forslag til ophevelse eller forandring av grunnlovens §§ 81, 97, 105 og 112.

Innst. S. nr. 142 1926, Indstilling fra Utenriks- og Konstitusjonskomiteen angaaende Forslag til Forandring i Grundlovens §§ 88, 90 og 91.

Innst. S. nr. 113 1929, Innstilling fra utenriks- og konstitusjonskomiteen angående forslag fra J. Castberg, H. Arstad m-fl. til forandring i grunnlovens §§ 88, 89, 90 og 91.

Innst. S. nr. 147 1932, Innst. S. nr. 147 1932 Indstilling fra utenriks- og konstitusjonskomiteen angaaende forslag til forandring i grundlovens §§ 89, 90, 91 og 97.

Innst. S. nr. 121 1934, Innst. S. nr. 121 1934 Innstilling fra utenriks- og konstitusjonskomiteen angående forslag fra T. Haavardstad, K. Bergsvik og B. Olsen-Hagen om ny § 82 i grunnloven.

Innst. S. nr. 270 (2003–2004), Innstilling fra kontroll- og konstitusjonskomiteen om endring av Grunnloven § 100, forslag fra Gunnar Skaug, Carl I. Hagen, Einar Steensnæs, Jan Petersen, Kristin Halvorsen og Lars Sponheim om endring av Grunnloven § 100. (Ytringsfrihet) og forslag fra Gunnar Kvassheim og Lars Sponheim om ny § 100 a i Grunnloven. (Offentlighetsprinsippet).

Innst. S. nr. 252 (2004–2005), Innstilling fra Den særskilte komité nedsatt av Stortinget 18. mars 2005 for behandling av St.meld. nr. 17 (2004–2005) Makt og demokrati.

Innst. S. nr. 254 (2007–2008), Innstilling fra kontroll- og konstitusjonskomiteen om med hjemmel i Grunnloven § 83 å be om Høyesteretts betenkning om hvorvidt tomtefesteinstruksen fastsatt ved kgl.res. 14. september 2007 og forslag til endring i § 5 i lov 7. juni 1996 nr. 33 om Opplysningsvesenets fond, jf. Ot. prp.nr.60 (2007–2008), er i samsvar med Grunnloven § 106 første punktum.

Innst. S. nr. 237 (2008–2009), Innstilling til Stortinget fra familie- og kulturkomiteen.

Innst. 351 L (2009–2010), Innstilling fra finanskomiteen om endringer i skatte- og avgiftslovgivningen mv.

Innst. 491 S (2012–2013), Innstilling fra Stortingets presidentskap om representantforslag fra stortingsrepresentantene Anders Anundsen, Ulf Erik Knudsen og Øyvind Vaksdal om egen lovrådgiver for Stortinget.

Lt. forh. 3.11.2008.
Prop.106 S (2011–2012) Samtykke til ratifikasjon av FN-konvensjonen av 13. desember 2006 om rettighetene til mennesker med nedsatt funksjonsevne.
Prop. 81 L (2010–2011) Endringer i gravferdsloven og enkelte andre lover.
Prop. 126 LS (2009–2010) Endringar i skatte- og avgiftsreglane mv.
St. forh. des. 1815–16.
St. forh. 18.6.1869.
St. forh. 17.10 1923.
St. forh. 2.6.1926.
St. forh. 2.7.1926.
St. forh. 20.3.1929.
St. forh. 7.6.1929.
St. forh. 25.6.1932.
St. forh. 5.6.1934.
St. forh. 30.5.1962.
St. forh. 27.2.1963.
St. forh. 16.4.1964.
St. forh. 1.6 1977.
St. forh. 8.2.1989.
St. forh. 22.11.2007.
St. forh. 26.5.2010.
St. forh. 14.6.2010.
St. forh. 17.6.2010.
St. forh. 20.6.2013.
St. forh. 1920 Dok. nr. 35. nr. 17 fra representantene Fridtjov Hegge og Ludvig Enge til forandring i grunnlovens §§ 81, 97, 105 og 112.
St. forh. 1923 Dok. nr. 19 nr.19 fra N. Skaar, H. Aarstad, O. Mjelde m. fl. til forandring i grunnlovens §§ 88, 89, 90, og 91.
St. forh. 1926 Dok. nr. 20 nr. 14 fra J. Castberg, H. Aarstad, O. Mjelde til forandring i grunnlovens §§ 88, 89, 90 og 91.
St. forh. 1929 Dok. nr. 14 nr. 5 fra Alfred Madsen og Chr. Hornsrud og Henrik Ameln til forandring i grunnlovens §§ 49, 50, 63, 66, 74, 75 f, 76, 77, 82, 90 og 105 samt opphevelse av §§ 52 litr. a, 81, 97 og 109.
St. forh. 1932 Dok. 12 nr. 2 fra Torvald Haavardstad, K. Bergsvik og B. Olsen-Hagen til forandring i grunnlovens §§ 25, 50 1ste ledd, 57, 58, 61, 63 1ste ledd, 66, 74, 76 3dje ledd, 77, 80, ny § 82, 97 og 105 samt opphevelse av §§ 52 litr. a, 78, 79, 81.
St. forh. 1935 Dok. 23 nr. 13 fra Chr. Hornsrud, Sverre Støstad, Anton Alvestad og B. Olsen-Hagen til opphevelse av grunnlovens § 97.

St.meld. nr. 42 (1999–2000) Om endring av Grunnloven § 100.
St.meld. nr. 23 (2000–2001) Førsteinstansdomstolene i fremtiden.
St.meld. nr. 26 (2003–2004) Om endring av Grunnloven § 100.
St.meld. nr. 17 (2004–2005) Makt og demokrati.
St. prp. nr. 83 (1951) Om innhentelse av Stortingets samtykke til at Norge tiltrer Europarådets konvensjon om beskyttelse av menneskerettighetene og de grunnleggende friheter.
St. prp. nr. 104 (1955) Om innhentelse av Stortingets samtykke til at Norge anerkjenner den europeiske menneskerettighetskommisjons kompetanse til å motta klager fra enkeltpersoner, ikke-statlige organisasjoner eller grupper av enkeltpersoner over krenkelser av bestemmelsene i Europarådets konvensjon om beskyttelse av menneskerettighetene og de grunnleggende friheter.
St. prp. nr. 112 (1963–1964) Om samtykke til at Norge anerkjenner Den europeiske menneskerettighetsdomstols myndighet.

International Authority

Convention concerning Freedom of Association and Protection of the Right to Organise (Entry into force: July 4, 1950).
Convention concerning the Application of the Principles of the Right to Organise and to Bargain Collectively (Entry into force: July 18, 1951).
Convention concerning the Social Repercussions of New Methods of Cargo Handling in Docks (Entry into force: July 24, 1975), ETS No.163.
General Comment No. 1 (2014) [GC-2014–1-CRPD] part III, "Obligations of States Parties."
ICCPR, International Covenant on Civil and Political Rights, 999 UNTS 171 (1966).
ICESCR, Economic, Social and Cultural Rights, 993 UNTS 3 (1966).
ECHR, Convention for the Protection of Human Rights and Fundamental Freedoms, ETS no. 5 (1950).
ECHR Protocol No. 11, Protocol No. 11 to the Convention for the Protection of Human Rights and Fundamental Freedoms, ETS no. 155 (1998).
ECHR Protocol No. 14, Protocol No. 14 to the Convention for the Protection of Human Rights and Fundamental Freedoms, amending the control system of the Convention, CETS no. 194 (2004).
ECHR Protocol No. 15, amending the Convention for the Protection of Human Rights and Fundamental Freedoms.

Preliminary Opinion of the Court in preparation for the Brighton Conference www.coe.int/t/dgi/brighton-conference/documents/Court-Preliminary-opinion_en.pdf (2012).
UDHR, Universal Declaration of Human Rights, UNGA Res 217 A(III) (1948).
VCLT, Vienna Convention on the Law of Treaties, 1155 UNTS 331 (1969).

1

Introduction

1.1 BACKGROUND AND CONTEXT

Judicial review of democratically enacted legislation under constitutional norms has long been seen to present a "countermajoritarian difficulty":[1] If the central basis for legitimate public power is popular majorities, how may unelected judges justifiably set aside the democratically enacted legislation of these majorities? And if the legislative and executive branches of power are the ones democratically designated and legitimated to make the laws, how may the judicial branch decide on constitutional questions in ways affecting and narrowing the scope for future democratic law-making? These are, essentially, questions of the ideals of democracy and rule of law that are emphasized – which, how and why.

Traditionally, the countermajoritarian difficulty plagued primarily US legal and political scholarship.[2] As judicial review of legislation has spread outside the United States,[3] so has the difficulty. Following this, review is debated also within those other nation states and constitutional democracies that practice judicial review. The national debates vary with the political and legal arrangements in the systems they address, particularly with the *form* of review practiced. The degree of difficulty is lower where courts' constitutional

[1] A phrase introduced in Bickel, *The least dangerous branch* (1968), the first edition was published in 1962.

[2] See i.a. Friedman, The history of the countermajoritarian difficulty, part one: The road to judicial supremacy, (1998), The history of the countermajoritarian difficulty, part two: Reconstruction's political court (2002), The history of the countermajoritarian difficulty, part three: The lesson Of Lochner (2001), The history of the countermajoritarian difficulty, part four: Law's politics (2000), The birth of an academic obsession: The history of the countermajoritarian difficulty, part five (2002); Graber, The nonmajoritarian difficulty: Legislative deference to the judiciary (1993); Somin, Political ignorance and the countermajoritarian difficulty: A new perspective on the central obsession of constitutional theory (2004).

[3] Law and Versteeg, The declining influence of the United States constitution (2012).

decisions may be altered relatively easily by subsequent political decision-making, and higher where courts actually have the last word on constitutional questions, without much room for political alterations afterwards. *Weak forms* of review, such as in some Commonwealth countries, exist where parliaments retain broad formal power to override court decisions, so that the legislature or executive can reject constitutional rulings by the judiciary.[4] The most comprehensive or *strong forms* of review occur where courts have the power to set aside or even nullify unconstitutional legislation, and where the procedures for subsequent legislative alterations of constitutional provisions are more cumbersome than normal legislation – or close to impossible, either formally or in practice.

With the emergence of supernational courts the questions of review legitimacy spread also to the international level. There, the bases for review are not constitutions, but conventions, regional or international agreements between sovereign states. While different in structure, origin, democratic input and enforcement, such conventions too may be adjudicated in ways that make them also function constitutionally – such as by protecting individual or group rights in ways that limit the scope for political decision-making. Conventions may have their own enforcement mechanisms or courts – such as the Europan Court of Human Rights (ECtHR) – which have the last say over the interpretation of the European Convention on Human Rights (ECHR). Jurisdictions in which the ECHR apply are then left with review on two levels: national courts reviewing national legislation under the ECHR; and the ECtHR doing the same, but on a different level, in those cases that end up before it. This too, has caused significant debate over review legitimacy. Compared to national debates, debates of supernational review are complicated by parallel and multilevel judiciaries and political institutions, and actors structured and legitimized differently than those in nation states.

Perhaps curiously, even absent a representative, democratic character, judicial review is an institution in which people seem to have relatively high confidence, sometimes even higher than that in elected bodies.[5] Indeed, also outside the judicial sphere, a number of substantial decisions affecting a great number of people are made without the demos being able to influence them,

4 See Tushnet, *Weak courts, strong rights* (2009). While weak-form review is in principle less democratically troublesome, it may still seldom result in legislatures overruling judicial decisions of constitutional questions; see Dixon, Weak-form judicial review and American exceptionalism (2012).

5 See Zürn, Autorität und Legitimität in der postnationalen Konstellation (2012), with further references; and Grødeland, *Perceptions of European supranational courts: The legal insiders' and outsiders' perspective* (2012).

in any direct meaning of the word "influence." Central examples of such are decisions made by the "European Institutions": the European Central Bank, the European Commission and the Presidency of the Council of the EU, that make decisions with little, if any, degree of actual, popular input. This arguably makes the authority wielded by these decision-making bodies undemocratic. Still, perhaps due to the (perceived) necessity of their continued work, the relative distance to the people whose lives they affect and the lack of a European public sphere for discussion of concerns, they have, at least until recently, been subject to few accusations of perceived illegitimacy claims by their constituents.[6]

It could be thought, then, that the relatively lesser amount of authority wielded by courts through judicial review would not give rise to much concern, whether it be carried out on the national or supernational level, whether as a matter of normative, political-institutional desirability of review in itself or as a question of what is the right way to exercise review authority, particularly when the values protected by such review are human rights, the fundamental significance of which most affected parties agree upon. Yet claims that judicial rights review is undemocratic or in other ways illegitimate, and that this is, in fact, a problem, persist. This persistence is one reason to continue thematizing review legitimacy in general. The real-world contingencies at play when assessing the legitimacy of this institution make for a better understanding of the way it is justified and understood in a variety of specific settings.

In this book, I introduce the case of Norway into the general debates over review legitimacy. I do this by looking into review debates as they have developed from 1814 until today, a period of just over 200 years. This bicentennial debate analysis looks to discussions of review among the popularly elected, the legal community and, where accessible, public opinion.

Under the 1814 Norwegian Constitution, general courts have the competence of the strong form review of legislation, a tradition practiced since the early 1800s. Since the 1990s, this national constitutional basis for review has been supplied with courts' competency of review under the central international human rights instruments, most notably the ECHR. Since then, Norwegian courts have reviewed legislation under both the Constitution and the ECHR. Following the most fundamental constitutional reform in Norwegian history, several of what had until then been convention-based human rights were constitutionalized in 2014, thus enhancing the formal constitutional protection of rights in the country. And in 2015, what had

[6] Habermas, Democracy, solidarity and the European crisis (2013).

until then been customary law-based foundations for judicial review were amended to the written Constitution.

The existence of a dual basis for judicial review is not unique to Norway; many European countries have courts exercising some form of review under their national constitutions – and in various forms under ECHR and EU law as well, following incorporating acts or other legal instruments. What sets Norway apart is that its combination of review bases and forms, as well as its historical development and political endorsement of rights and review, seem to present a case contradicting some general, theoretical assumptions about review legitimacy.

One such assumption is that *strong form* judicial review has a substantial democracy-compromising potential. Another is that the broader the bases for strong form judicial review, the greater the undemocratic potential: constitutions with few rights provisions in theory leave less power to courts than do bases for review containing more, or more open-ended, rights provisions. A third assumption is that international conventions, based on compromises between a number of sovereign states, have less of a democratic input than national constitutions, so that review under such instruments is potentially even less democratic still than review under national constitutions.

Norwegian courts have had strong form review powers for more than 150 years under the 1814 Norwegian Constitution. The Constitution did not, however, originally, have many rights provisions. When, in 1999 Norway incorporated international human rights in a way that gave them legal preference before Norwegian law in cases of norm conflict, the scope of the constitutional and "semi-constitutional" basis for judicial review in Norway was substantially widened. Following the 2014 constitutional reform, several international rights were also constitutionalized. This has left Norwegian courts with the authority and duty to exercise a strong form review of legislation under a substantial amount of rights provisions, many of which are based on international conventions, which have less democratic input than those in the Norwegian Constitution. With the democracy-undermining potential of this dual source of strong court power, one might think Norway would suffer from some democratic deficit. Yet, Norway tends to be ranked as one of the most democratic countries in the world.[7]

How did this alternative review story develop? One explanation may be the historical legacy of a collectively focused and consensus-oriented society,

[7] See i.a. The Economist Intelligence Unit Democracy Index https://infographics.economist.com/2017/DemocracyIndex/, ranking Norway as number one in 2016; Democracy Ranking http://democracyranking.org/wordpress/?page_id=679 doing the same (both assessed May 2017).

combined with a lasting, underlying current of liberal rule-of-law principles – one possibly stronger in Norway than in the other Nordic countries. The persistence of liberal ideas may be observed in the various historical periods analyzed in this book. The analyses look at how the institution of judicial review – as one exponent of this tenet – has been discussed in Norway through its working history, and what arguments have been brought for and against it – both in its original constitutional form, and its international human rights-revitalized form.

The arguments traced in this bicentennial debate concern how judicial decision-making relates to ideals essential to democracy and rule of law. Central to the countermajoritarian difficulty is a sense that review is in some way undemocratic, as a core feature of democracy is some form of popular majority rule. A core feature of rule of law is, however, that courts are *not* to be guided by popular majority opinion. And the point of rights review is often to protect minorities or individuals *against* popular majority decisions.

Review debates are often based on various assertions or arguments as to why review is or is not *legitimate*. What people mean when they use this word differs, often because of how they emphasize the different societal ideals underlying democracy and rule of law, due to the potential paradox that a constitutional democracy represents. To structure the arguments in this bicentennial debate analysis, I find the following conceptualizations and elements of legitimacy relevant.

Legitimacy is a term hinting at something right, just or good, in some sense of those terms. Defining for legitimate practices is that their consequences in concrete cases are *accepted* or viewed as *acceptable*, even when one does not agree with one or several of the concrete outcomes. Legitimacy is not the same as legality,[8] although legality may be a source of legitimacy. But legitimacy is a thicker concept than legality, one that can be conceptualized in a number of ways.[9] One main distinction is drawn between normative and social or historical-political legitimacy. Normative legitimacy exists where there are good reasons to respect an exercise of public power, if it is respect-*worthy*;[10] social or historical legitimacy exists where the exercise is, in fact, respected.[11]

8 d'Entreves, Legality and legitimacy (1963); Dyzenhaus, *Legality and legitimacy – Carl Schmitt, Hans Kelsen, and Hermann Heller in Weimar* (1997); Schmitt, *Legality and legitimacy* (2004); Ashenden and Thornhill, *Legality and legitimacy – normative and sociological approaches* (2010).

9 See i.a. Peter, *Political legitimacy* (2010); Solum, *Legitimacy* (2010).

10 Rawls, *Political liberalism* (1993), 233; Michelman, Ida's Way: Constructing the respect-worthy governmental system (2003).

11 Weber and Parsons, *The theory of social and economic organization* (1964), 382.

Central to discussions of legitimacy is a distinction between the *input to* and *outcome of* a particular institution or decision-making process.[12] The input perspective looks at what contributions do or at which should be incorporated into an institution or system to make it respected or respect-worthy. Outcome arguments focus on whether review produces good results. A plurality of opinions exists about what does, in fact, represent substantially "good" results – one may like or dislike the outcome of particular review cases or such a practice in general. Some thus argue that the only way to ensure the legitimacy of outcomes is by agreeing upon what is a fair *process* for establishing authority and resolving disagreement,[13] or, in the case of review, for ensuring the procedural due process to assure majority governance while protecting minority rights.[14]

From the side of *input legitimacy*, a central component is popular consent in the form of procedural mechanisms for popular majority rule or deliberative democratic involvement. Courts and their review authority may enjoy such consent through a written constitution, or through the development of customary law, or other forms of democratically enacted legislation defining court powers. Depending on democratic theory, the *size* of a popular majority going into such an establishment is relevant. An input factor relevant from a deliberative point of view may be that of the traditionally developed or "organic nature" of norms or institutions: the more they are rooted in tradition, or can be seen to have "grown out of the people" themselves, the more legitimate they are. Even without a democratically authoritative basis for review, the absence of democratic movements to abolish review already in existence – or attempts at abolishment with little popular support – may provide a negative variety of such input.

The input perspective to review legitimacy may also include the derived (or posterior) variety of *accountability*; the procedural and formal ease with which elected representatives may override the effects of review by altering the constitutional basis for it. On the supernational level, exit possibilities from treaties are relevant to this end. In national review regimes based on constitutions that are hard to alter, the degree of constitutional rigidity, formally and in practice, is an important factor for assessing input legitimacy from both an aggregative and a deliberative democratic point of view.

12 Scharpf, *Governing in Europe – effective and democratic* (1999).

13 Dahl, *A preface to democratic theory* (1956), Gaus in Bohman and Rehg, *Deliberative democracy – essays on reason and politics* (1997), 205ff. As the concept of fairness is also open to debate, however, procedural perspectives are also to some extent substantial, Michelman, *Brennan and democracy* (1999).

14 Ely, *Democracy and distrust* (1980).

An important factor on the input side of legitimacy is the ideal of particular *knowledge*. Knowledge represents expertise that may be necessary, but is sometimes found wanting in the political process. Carrying a different basis and logic for decision-making than that of popular support, differing forms of knowledge are also elements grounding the ideal of *division of powers*. Particular expertise may be recognized as a desirable foundation for decision-making, and the unease of leaving too much power in the hands of one state branch may make desirable the counterbalancing decision-making powers of another. Adding to the latter is the differing form in which different institutions function. A classic ideal of judicial review in this respect is the "sober, second thought," as represented by courts, in the words of Alexander Bickel in 1963.[15]

"Their insulation and the marvelous mystery of time give courts the capacity to appeal to men's better natures, to call forth their aspirations, which may have been forgotten in the moment's hue and cry."[16] But are courts a trustworthy forum of principle, or unaccountable, unrealistic philosopher-kings?[17] Judges are not politicians, and are instead set to employ "neutral principles" to resolve constitutional disputes.[18] If they are suspected of being but political actors, they must still *appear* neutral, and are thus forced to preserve neutrality in a different way from politicians.[19] As democracy needs transparent justifications obtainable only in concrete cases through questioning or "Socratic contestation," courts may be seen as the Socrates inviting politicians to deliver such justifications.[20]

From this knowledge-based, institutional perspective, the independence and impartiality of courts are important. These factors are influenced by the structuring and funding of courts, the appointment procedures and professional quality of judges and courts' formal and actual independence – both in their establishment and in their independence of later instructions or other

15 Bickel, *The least dangerous branch* (1986), with further reference to Stone, The common law in the United States (1936). See also Vermeule, Second opinions (2011).

16 Bickel, *The least dangerous branch* (1962), 26.

17 Dworkin, *A matter of principle* (1985) ch 2.

18 See Wechsler, Toward neutral principles of constitutional law (1959), 17, defending judicial review to the extent it is based on neutral principles: "[I]s not the relative compulsion of the language of the Constitution, of history and precedent – where they do not combine to make an answer clear – itself a matter to be judged, so far as possible, by neutral principles – by standards that transcend the case at hand?"

19 Shapiro, The Supreme Court and constitutional adjudication: Of politics and neutral principles (1963).

20 Kumm, The idea of Socratic contestation and the right to justification: The point of rights-based proportionality review (2010).

influences from outside. To these ends, the salary, privileges and immunities of judges, their tenure, nonremovability and the transparency of court financing, are also factors to be considered.[21] Other elements concerning the *process* under which courts conduct review may be ensured by the democratically enacted framework for courts' decision-making. To these factors belongs the composition of courts: how many judges are sitting to decide, and whether they are life tenured, term limited or ad hoc. Relevant are also to what extent judicial proceedings are adversarial, what the rules of evidence allow parties to present and how publicly transparent and challengeable written and other proceedings are. Differing systems regulate differently depending on whether arguments are based on written statements or oral presentations allowing for direct deliberation in court. Variations also exist as to how internal court disagreements may be settled – by majority vote, weighing votes of senior judges more on the basis that they have more experience or of junior judges because they are likely to better represent popular opinion,[22] and as to what extent unprofessional or otherwise delinquent judges may be held accountable.

Central to the *outcome* ideals of review legitimacy is the liberal ideal of protecting individuals or minorities; it serves as a guarantee against the tyranny of the majority and a check against political usurpation of state power. Given the fact of plurality – that different individuals have different conceptions of a good life and a fair society – outcome ideals for review often differ: Did the court strike the right balance between collective and individual interest in this or that case? Differing ideas of "good" outcomes entail the whole enigma of what law *is* and how adjudicators – not only courts – "find" the law, as well as what constitutes "good" law. Such differences notwithstanding, some outcome ideals are more generally regarded as necessary for adjudication to be considered legitimate: Judges' attempts at best interpretation and application as measured by a certain set of norms – i.a. linguistic, teleological and rhetorical, and an internally consistent and predictable interpretative practice conforming to what the relevant "legal community" accepts as methods for application. Outcome factors delegitimizing adjudication are illogical or inconsistent argumentation, selective or unrepresentative reading and presentation of legal authority, untenable analogies and justification seriously undermining the possibility of predictability in later cases.

Also significant for assessments of "good" court results is whether they contribute to the central judicial role of problem-solving, and to what extent they follow established adjudicative patterns or readily introduce new ones.

[21] Venice Commission CDL(2012)035.

[22] The latter example is from Dworkin, *Justice for hedgehogs* (2011), 483, fn. 9.

From a *deliberative* point of view they can be measured by what further deliberation they produce, and how they pave the way for institutional dialogue – either within traditional institutional levels or toward and within new ones. Courts' review may stir up popular debate. While all debate is not necessarily good debate, court decisions may, to the effect of debate, be more conducive the more controversial the issue decided by the review decision.[23] Controversial decisions may thwart constructive debate by deciding them "once and for all," but may also promote it – through popular debate and institutional dialogue between the branches of government, by pushing forth issues of importance. Review decisions may thus inspire legislatures to address difficult issues, possibly even in a constitutionally principled manner.[24] Review decisions may also implement popular deliberation through supplying their legal assessment of conflicts at hand also with that of public opinion,[25] or indeed through harmonizing constitutional provisions with prevalent democratic influences, thus modernizing constitutionalism with the help of public opinion.[26]

The degree to which premises or justifications are of a type understandable and acceptable to most is important to further the rule of law ideals sustaining review legitimacy. So too is the extent to which review practice is generally in accordance with Rawls' "liberal principle of legitimacy" – namely, founded on a constitutional or conventional basis, "the essentials of which are of a kind all citizens may reasonably be expected to endorse in the light of principles and ideals acceptable to them as reasonable and rational."[27]

The inherent logic of review is conservative – not in a meaning corresponding to a left–right political or ideological axis, but in that the very dynamic of review is aimed at preserving some "old" provision already embedded in a constitution, to the potential detriment of some more "modern" provision in a statute. While the constitutional provision may lead to review cases coming out in favor of some more progressive or unconservative result in the *political* sense – e.g. criminals cannot be punished as harshly as some factions of the contemporary conservative political majority wants because of constitutional bans on nonretroactive laws – minority segregation is untenable under equal protection clauses, for instance; review cases may for this reason still be perceived as conservative.

23 Post and Siegel, Roe rage: Democratic constitutionalism and backlash (2007).
24 Friedman, Dialogue and Judicial Review (1993).
25 Friedman, *The will of the people: How public opinion has influenced the Supreme Court and shaped the meaning of the constitution* (2009).
26 Strauss, The modernizing mission of judicial review (2009).
27 Rawls, *Political liberalism* (1993), 217.

Continuing the outcome perspective, the degree of authority or power wielded is another important factor. Strong form review is more in need of solid legitimation than weak-form review – and enforceable review decisions more than nonenforceable ones. Considering this factor, however, may imply something of a paradox: Judicial decisions are made transparent and, to the extent possible, verifiable through explaining how and why premises lead to conclusions; how and why what appears as deduction is supplied with legal discretion. Consequently, the *justificatory* parts of cases exercising judicial review seem to be a central outcome-legitimating factor. The better, more comprehensive and more transparent the justification, the greater the potential for legitimacy.[28] The more reasoned a decision is, however, the greater is its potential for law-making – and the greater the authority wielded, thus the greater the legitimacy required. Its contribution to the law outside the case at hand also increases with the level of detailed explanation of the principles employed and the moments relevant for balancing them toward a concrete decision – the narrower the rule created, the lesser the authority wielded. So, the better reasoned a decision is, the more legitimate it may be seen to be, yet the more "rule" or public authority it wields, and the more legitimacy it needs. This is one of several areas in which review confronts two potentially conflicting ideals of legitimacy.

These distinctions between normative and descriptive or historically embedded ideals, and between input and outcome factors, clarify some of the concerns we have about review legitimacy. Due to their internal interdependency, however, they are more challenging to trace in any stringent manner when assessing actual debates. Normative legitimacy is hard to conceive sans descriptive, historic or doctrinal embeddedness of norms and institutions, outside a particular historic context and set of linguistic conventions and justificatory structures.[29]

One blurring of such distinctions prevalent in the Norwegian debates, perhaps in all debates over review legitimacy, is what could be termed the *input–outcome entanglement*: What is formed as critique of the institution of review, based on some lacking *input* factor such as democracy or accountability, is instead critique of certain *outcomes* of review. Or, praise of review as a decision-making mechanism as such is not necessarily based on the

[28] See i.a. Forst, *The right to justification* (2012). A convincing argument for judicial *minimalism* is given in Sunstein, *One case at a time* (1999); see, however, Sunstein, Beyond judicial minimalism (2008).

[29] Hurrell, Legitimacy and the use of force: Can the circle be squared? (2005), 29; Bodansky, Legitimacy in international law and international relations (2013).

input of original intent or constitutional text, but on agreement with its *outcomes* during a particular historical or political period. Both input and outcome factors are central for assessing review legitimacy: an institution set up and conducted in a manner worthy of respect, producing some outcomes that few agreed with, could still be considered legitimate. If, however, *all* outcomes produced were perceived as immoral or unjust in other ways, it would probably not be considered legitimate, even in spite of spotless input legitimacy. And, conversely, even though an institution lacked some input legitimacy, such as judicial review may be perceived to lack democratic input, it may still be considered legitimate, if producing only, or mostly, outcomes that are normatively or socially perceived as respect-worthy, good or just.[30] Assuming the legitimacy of review needs to be viewed institutionally, if the institution itself is legitimate, it remains legitimate, even though it produces (some) outcomes with which some or many disagree. Consequently, discussions of the institutional legitimacy of judicial review cannot be done solely with reference to one or a few of its particular outcomes. Judicial review is not legitimated by producing one outstanding judgment that everyone agrees with, nor is it illegitimate due to an equally contested terrible one. Only to the extent that judicial review on a theoretical or empirical level is, on aggregate, liable to produce reasonably "good" or "bad" outcomes by some standard, does the actual outcome become valuable as a legitimating factor. In addition to the claim of input illegitimacy – that judicial review is undemocratically countermajoritarian – arguments against review are tied to output illegitimacy – that courts do not necessarily produce better *decisions or outcomes* than do ordinary, majority politics. This is hard to measure on the whole. While single cases may lead to valid critique or applause of those decisions, unless they are somehow seen to be representative, evaluating the *institution* or practice of review as a whole seems less persuasive. Still, it seems we are likely to cheer for the *institution* of judicial review if and when courts decide what we, for various reasons, like them to – and vice versa.

The interdependency and blurring of assessment factors notwithstanding, when looking at the debates of Norwegian review practice, it is possible to recognize arguments as more or less tied to the various ideals. I seek to trace

[30] Illustrative of the input–output connection are two central theories on review: While review does not conform with Jürgen Habermas' procedural and deliberative view of what input is needed to ensure democratic legitimacy, this does not preclude the institution of judicial review from legitimacy in his theory: Habermas, *Between facts and norms* (1996), 244. And, conversely, Ronald Dworkin's substantive conception of democracy does not necessitate such an institution of review: Dworkin, *Justice in robes* (2006), 71.

the ideals underlying various normative claims of review (il)legitimacy by searching out historical arguments about judicial review. It may be possible to analyze judicial review purely normatively, "uncluttered by discussions of particular decisions or the history of its emergence in particular systems of constitutional law,"[31] but purely normative assessments risk neglecting the impact and explanatory force of constitutional culture.[32] The Norwegian contradiction of general theoretical assumptions about the democracy-threatening effects of judicial review suggests that assessing the legal and societal ideals underlying review discussions purely by use of normative theory is insufficient.

I have based this study instead on the premise that evaluation of embedded practices in existing systems requires tying such normative assumptions to politically and historically situated inquiries. As has been noted, "[t]he concept of rational justification ... is essentially historical. To justify is to narrate how the argument has gone so far."[33] This book provides one such narrative of the Norwegian story.

1.2 NORWAY IN A NUTSHELL

Norwegian history bears early marks of the democracy and of rule-of-law principles the tension between which judicial review exemplifies. Norway's independence from Denmark in 1814 was established through one of the most radically democratic constitutions of its time.

Enfranchising a comparatively substantial part of the population, it also contained central constitutional principles: it divided powers between the legislative, the executive and the judicial branch, and it contained some fundamental rights and rule of law elements, such as the principle of legality, the protection of free speech and property and bans on retroactive legislation and unwarranted searches.

Outside the US 1789 constitution, Norway's from 1814 is the oldest one still in force. Despite having been changed about 300 times since, it has proven particularly durable.[34] Moreover, outside the United States, Norway is the country that has practiced judicial review the longest: Recognized soon after

31 See Waldron, The core of the case against judicial review (2006), abstract, 1346.

32 See e.g. Ginsburg and Melton, *Does the constitutional amendment rule matter at all? Amendment cultures and the challenges of measuring amendment difficulty* (2014)

33 MacIntyre, *Whose justice? Which rationality?* (1988), 8.

34 Ginsburg, The virtues of evolution in an age of revolution: Norway's enduring constitution in comparative perspective (2014)

the constitutional enactment, it was practiced soon after 1814, if only explicitly thematized and ascertained by the Supreme Court in 1866.[35]

Norway also developed a parliamentary system relatively early; it was definitely established in 1884. Around this time the exercise of review intensified, a development leading historians to connect the two phenomena: Judicial review was developed, it was held, as a means of reclaiming influence for the high state officials losing ground to popular power.[36] Later studies have proven this theory wrong.[37] The persistence of the liberal *motif* central to a rule-of-law state based on autonomous rights and law has been seen as a defensive strategy against an unchecked monarchy. At the same time, the rule of law state opened for a "revolutionary" social and democratic development.[38] Norway's is the history of a small country where these two institutionalizations of public power – one democratic, one rule-of-law-based – originated quite early, to a degreee paving the way for a relationship of separation, yet cooperation of powers.

The 1814 Norwegian independence was short-lived; in the fall of 1814 the country was unionized by Sweden. It retained, however, a relative autonomy – and its own constitution. The union with Sweden notwithstanding, Norway developed quite differently than its unionizer. Sweden never developed general courts with judicial review competences; its judiciary resembles the traditional continental-European specialization of courts into different branches. Compared to Sweden, Norway was also democratized earlier, a development formative for the further trajectory of the Norwegian balance between collective and individual impulses in political thinking.[39] The role that this early democratization later played for the modernization of the Norwegian welfare state has been emphasized as a unique feature of the Norwegian strain of the Nordic model.[40] Another influential Norwegian feature, setting Norway out from the sometimes paternalistic tendencies of the Swedish "Folkhemmet," as well as from formative, but more structured tendencies in the other Nordic countries, is an "anarchistic" element. In the geographically scattered Norwegian population, this has been seen to cause a certain skepticism from the more peripheral and rural parts of Norwegian society against national centralization.[41] This co-existence of cultures and countercultures may be one important background against which to

35 See Section 3.3. 36 Seip, Den norske Høyesterett som politisk organ (1964) 113.

37 Slagstad, Prøvingsretten i det norske system (1989).

38 Sejersted, *Demokrati og Rettsstat* (2001) 289.

39 Sejersted, *The age of social democracy* (2011), 11. 40 Ibid. 2.

41 Rokkan, Geography, religion and social class: Crosscutting cleavages in Norwegian politics (1967).

understand the particular Norwegian combination of early – and continued – tension and interdependence between the collective and the individual defining the historically shifting democracy and rule-of-law balancing inherent in judicial review discussions.

The Norwegian welfare state was built by means of legal regulations. Social reform through legal reformism started in the 1800s and intensified under the regulatory state in the early 1900s and later in the emerging social democracy.[42] The Norwegian welfare state may be described as a culture relying on a strong ideal of equality and social integration, one that has developed in tandem with a strong state. What separates the Norwegian and Scandinavian versions of this socialist model from those of the former Eastern Europe is that the existence of, and reliance on, a strong state has been combined with real liberal rights guarantees for the individual.[43]

The persistence of the liberal potential in the emerging regulatory state has varied in historical periods. The two themes have historically corresponded roughly to political party lines: Simplified, the political narrative of Norway is one of a Conservative Party that has historically represented the defendant of liberal rule-of-law institutions, whereas the liberal, moderate and radical left, particularly the long-dominant Labor Party, have been the proponents of increasing interventions into constitutional rights, and regulations of individual freedoms for the sake of the common good. This division is central to what positions have been adopted toward the institution of judicial review, but also for ideological views of liberal rights more generally. In the period between WWI and WWII, the intense regulatory needs emerging from industrial and other developments, combined with economic recession, made constitutional limits to state regulations particularly unwelcome. In this period various Left- and Labor Party coalitions tried to abolish judicial review (as well as the troublesome constitutional provisions safeguarding private property) several times. They never got the required majority to succeed.

The Labor Party has played a central role in the development of the Norwegian welfare state, particularly after WWII. In this period, this party reigned continuously for about twenty years and headed the broad political-consensus-based postwar national rebuilding project. In this period, the Labor Party dominance was often inattentive to liberal, constitutional arguments. The task of arguing for these positions was left to the opposing Conservative Party. A central manifestation of this positioning was the 1976 Supreme Court

42 Slagstad, Shifting knowledge regimes: The metamorphoses of Norwegian reformism (2004)

43 Sejersted, *The age of social democracy* (2011), 7–8.

Kløfta case[44] and the debates leading up to and following this decision, which was seen as a re-emergence of the then long-dormant institution of judicial review. The case occurred more or less simultaneously with the break-up of the social democratic regime and the end of the decade-long political dominance of Labor Party governments in 1981. As one among many driving forces, hereunder the increasing European rights-thinking and economic liberalization of the 1980s, this contributed to a revitalization of institutional and professional debates on constitutional questions.

In this period, the foundation of the modern Norwegian economy was established, following the first oil discovery in 1969. In the early 1900s, the national natural resources of waterfalls and hydroelectric power had been subject to strict state regulatory regimes. This common view of resources continued in the oil era: Oil resources were state-owned. Private companies could obtain time- and place-restricted concessions to explore for and extract oil on Norwegian territory. A substantial part of these concessions were allocated to national oil companies, most notably the state oil company Statoil. Oil politics had the aim of gradual development and extraction – and national control. Around this time, fostering some focus on sovereignty and skepticism toward foreign capital, came the first referendum over Norwegian EU (EEC) membership. The people voted no by a small margin in 1972, a result replicated in 1994.[45] Norway thus has remained a nonmember to the EU, but became party to the European Economic Area (EEA) in 1992.[46] Following agreements with the EU, in addition to the basic EU principles, more than 170 statutes and 1,000 administrative regulations were incorporated into Norwegian law in the period 1992–2011.[47] This makes EU law the most influential example of foreign law reception in Norwegian history. The absence of EU membership renders Norway with less procedural and deliberative democratic input leverage into the decision-making processes of the EU – processes that even for member states are criticized for suffering from a democratic deficit.

44 Rt. 1976 s. 1 45 53.5 percent in 1972 and 52.2 percent in 1994.

46 The EEA agreement allows the EFTA states to participate in the EU Internal Market without being members of the EU. It was incorporated into Norwegian law in 1992 by Lov av 27. november 1992 nr. 109 om gjennomføring i norsk rett av hoveddelen i avtale om Det europeiske økonomiske samarbeidsområde (EØS) m.v. Its § 2 gives relevant EU legislation prevalence before Norwegian law in cases of conflict. While not a full membership, it incorporates the basic treaty principles with respect to the internal market. About 70 percent of EU directives are also relevant to Norway under the EEA agreement, NOU 2012:2, 25.3.3 In addition to the influence of the directives and other EU regulations come the decisions of the EU and EFTA courts.

47 NOU 2012:2 at 7.1.

The other central line of international legal development adding to the rights-thinking in the 1990–2000s came from international human rights, particularly the ECHR. Following an official 2003 report on power and democracy in Norway holding human rights to erode national democracy by shifting decision-making power from the Parliament to the courts,[48] questions of rights and judicialization of politics were widely debated. The study's conclusions were not shared by Parliament: In 2014 it amended several of the central human rights to the constitution in order to better safeguard their position in Norway. In 2015, Parliament also constitutionalized what had until then been the customary law of judicial review. The study's conclusions do, however, contribute to the Norwegian chapter of a much larger story: one about how rule of law affects the relation between a state and its citizens; one of variations over the counter-majoritarian difficulty immanent in constitutionalism; one concerning the democratic role of the judiciary. The scene for this story has traditionally been that of the nation state. In today's postnational constellation, the national scene is but one in a developing theater, an expansion revitalizing old, but also raising new questions about democracy, constitutionalism and judicial review as phenomena transgressing nation-state frameworks.

1.3 REVIEW UNDER THE CONSTITUTION AND UNDER THE ECHR

1.3.1 *Debates on Review*

What have been the formative arguments – within the legal and political communities – for and against review in the varying historical periods in which it has worked? What were they when the principle of constitutional review was established as a legal norm? What were its constitutionally enabling conditions, within the legal community and for the courts? What have been the formative case and debates?

I seek to cast light on some of these questions in the coming historical chapters – as they arise first under the Constitution, then both under it and the ECHR. Norwegian review dates back more than 150 years – and so do political and legal discussions about it. They revolve around only the perceived tension inherent in the constitutional paradox. They used to be concerned mainly with how two constitutional provisions – one for the protection of property, and one prohibiting nonretroactivity – were to be construed, and by whom.

[48] December 11, 1997. A group of social scientists was established by Royal Decree March 13, 1998.

From around 1990 onward, they have increasingly come to add to the tension between political and judicial decision-making powers the tension between national sovereignty and international decision-making institutions. Driving this study are analyses of how review arguments have played out in historical practice, and how the institution of review has contributed to and functioned in society in differing historical periods. My hope is to shed light on Norwegian constitutional history through the prism of review debates.

A particularity of Norwegian thought is the extent to which it relies on the work of its institutions. Rather than through academic theory-building, central features of Norwegian political thought have emerged through institutional practice – a way of informal institutional dialogue.[49] As, by the traditional narrative of review illegitimacy, the institution primarily challenged by review is the legislative, I keep my main focus of the historical analyses on the arguments of the popularly elected, as presented both inside and outside of parliamentary debates. To contextualize these, and to follow the legal understanding and assessments of judicial review, arguments from central actors within the legal community are also sought. I trace these back to review emergence in the 1800s, and here expose the particular liberal undercurrent that sets Norway apart from other Nordic countries, and that re-emerges in later historical and political periods. While these later periods – around 1918, 1976 and 2010 – are well-described legally and historically, they have not been subjected to analyses structured around actors' arguments concerning the institution of review. The latest period, that of constitutional reform in 2014, has not been studied before.

The historical chapters on review under the Norwegian Constitution are followed by and juxtaposed with a similar approach to Norwegian ECHR review. Tracing the arguments in the ECHR debates from the acceptance of ECtHR jurisdiction in 1964 toward the 1995 constitutional amendment mandating respect for the ECHR, and the 1999 Human Rights Act, it demonstrates the similarity of arguments between ECHR-related debates with the historical discussions of national review.

In the late 1970s and early 1980s, Norway saw a revitalization of institutional and professional debates on constitutional questions alongside the departure from the Labor Party government period that dominated the decades following WWII. Through its recollection of review discussions in these years, the book shows how the Norwegian social democratic drive at this time even lay ahead of the tendency later described by Tony Judt as the progressives'

[49] Slagstad, Høyesteretts institusjonelle egenart (2015).

rediscovery and use of rights in political rhetoric and work.[50] This exposes the persistency of the latent liberal position from a perspective not formerly examined in Norwegian and English studies of this period.

The analysis of arguments preceding the 2010 period confirms the traditional positioning with the Conservative Party as the constitutional rule-of-law defender and the Labor Party less so inclined. Analyses of the 2014 constitutional reform, however, do not: Toward, and during, this reform, the two major parties, somewhat surprisingly, switched sides. The initiative and driving force for the rights reform was the Labor Party. While the actual reform work was led by a prominent member of the Conservative Party, on several issues this party marked itself by reluctance and even resistance to the reform. A particularly unexpected element in this resistance was the Conservative Party arguments for parts of this period against the constitutionalization of judicial review. These led to the review amendment being left out of the 2014 reform altogether – and then amended only after substantial debate in 2015. The Conservative Party's longstanding historical role as guardian of this Norwegian institution was instead defended by one faction of the Labor Party: then Parliamentary President Thorbjørn Jagland (Labor) was the driving force in 2009 to establish the Lønning Committee which got the mandate to "strengthen the position that human rights have in Norwegian law by ensuring central human rights were protected at the constitutional level."[51] This was the last national political act of Jagland before he became Secretary General of the Council of Europe later that same year. Toward the 2014 constitutional reform, MPs Martin Kolberg and Jette F. Christensen (both Labor) were central actors in arguing for both civil and political and socioeconomic rights. They were also instrumental to the amendment constitutionalizing judicial review that was voted in a year later. Central in opposing the socioeconomic parts of the reform, as well as the review amendment, were representatives of the right-wing Progressive Party and the agrarian Center Party, but also Michael Tetzschner from the Conservative Party. This process may be an indication of the attentiveness in parts of the Labor Party to the specific Norwegian national adaptation of the universal element in the idea of socialism or social democracy that has also defined its earlier periods of governing reign: At a time when the formerly statute-based rights-thinking had long since come to be seen as a new form of constitutionalism, and one in

50 Judt, *Postwar. A history of Europe since 1945* (2007). See also Madsen, From Cold War instrument to Supreme European Court: The European Court of Human Rights at the crossroads of international and national law and politics (2007).

51 Dok 16 (2011–2012), 1.1.

practice denationalized with an external final say (in the ECtHR), it was renationalized as a new form of Labor Party embraced constitutionalism.

1.3.2 *The Constitutional Debates*

Debates of judicial review co-emerging with its origins in the 1800s have been formative to Norwegian review debates ever since. The positions in the early debates represented the classical dichotomy: on the one hand, that judicial review was a democratically illegitimate usurpation of political power; and, on the other, that it was an important, nonpolitical guarantee for individual rights and rule of law. This view of the constitutional theme was continued primarily by historians, sociologists and political scientists in the 1960s and beyond.[52]

For a long time, a Supreme Court case from 1890 was held up as the precedent for the customary law of judicial review.[53] In the 1890 accounts, review breakthrough is linked to the breakthrough of Norwegian parliamentarism in 1884: The period from 1814 to 1884 was marked by a power struggle between Parliament and the Swedish–Norwegian king, particularly revolving around the king's power to veto constitutional amendments from Parliament (suspending their effect), Parliament's taxing and spending power (keeping the king in check) and the king's right to elect his own cabinet which did not have to answer to Parliament. Following an 1884 impeachment case against the cabinet for thrice refusing to effectuate a constitutional amendment obliging cabinet members to present themselves in Parliament, the king was forced to appoint Johan Sverdrup, who was supported by the majority in Parliament, as prime minster. As part of this struggle, 1884 was also the year in which was founded what were then the two main opposing parties: the Liberal Left and the Conservative Party.

Both earlier and later legal and historical studies do, however, date both the idea and the practice of review much further back than 1890. Some legal studies particularly dealing with the possible existence and justifications for and against review were written during the 1800s and in the early 1900s. The review theme was, however, revitalized by a historical study in 1964,

52 See Sejersted, *The age of social democracy* (2011) 456ff., with reference to Sejersted, *Ideal, teori og virkelighet* (1973); Elster, *Ulysses and the Sirens* (1979); Slagstad, *Rett og politikk: et liberalt tema med variasjoner* (1987); Elster, *Constitutionalism and democracy* (1988). An important legal contributor to this debate was E. Smith: see i.a. Smith, *Høyesterett og folkestyret* (1993) and Smith, *Constitutional justice under old constitutions* (1995).

53 See i.a. Eckhoff in Lejman, *Festskrift tillägnad professor, juris doktor Karl Olivecrona vid hans avgång från professorsämbetet den 30 juni 1964* (1964), stating that "There are no instances of courts disregarding statutes on review prior to 1890." The case concerned was Rt. 1890 s. 455.

wherein the institution of review was portrayed as one "made to be used in the political game," a "spanner deliberately thrown in the works of democracy, behind the back of Parliament, by the dethroned high state officials."[54] This reconstruction led to vigorous opposition and fruitful debate on the legal and democratic ideals and over the relationship between politics and law. Cases from 1822 and 1841 were held out as earlier examples of review, and documentation was presented to support that judicial review was also an accepted legal institution several decades earlier than 1890, and was even explicitly stated in a case from 1866.[55]

Prior to 1864, the written reasoning behind Supreme Court case conclusions was not published.[56] While Supreme Court precedent was the directive for the reasoning in the Supreme Court, the effect of the justifications as a foundation for understanding Supreme Court reasoning as well as serving as a way to understand precedent outside the Supreme Court itself became stronger following this shift.[57]

In recent decades, review debate has been revitalized both politically and within the legal community, following three different, but interconnected phenomena: The first is the increase in international bases for judicial review from around 2000, and how these have affected and continue to affect Norwegian law through the case law of Norwegian courts. The second is a revitalization of "traditional" review under the Constitution, likely inspired by just the same international review revival, peaking in three much-debated cases of Supreme Court review in 2010. The third is the process leading to the expansion of the Constitution, where central human rights – as well as the thitherto customary law tradition of judicial review one year later, were added to the Constitution in time for its 200-year anniversary in 2014.[58]

Norwegian review debates have, however, to scant degree been connected with the review discourse in other countries or on the supernational level.[59]

54 Seip, Jus og politikk (1965), 407.

55 The case is mentioned, among others, by Andenæs, Høyesterett som politisk organ (1965), 31 fn 9, and Eckhoff, Høyesterett som grunnlovens vokter (1976), but its position as the first in which a statute is found unconstitutional by explicit discussion of judicial review powers and implications is established by Slagstad, Prøvingsretten i det norske system (1989), 337 (in English, see Slagstad, Breakthrough of judicial review in Norway [1995]).

56 Prior to 1864 the reasoning of Supreme Court decisions was not publicized; this was altered by lov av April 11, 1863, see Østlid, Hvordan offentlige voteringer ble gjennomført i Norges Høyesterett (1955), 200ff.

57 Michalsen, Ny og gammel rettskildelære (1994), 227.

58 See Chapter 9

59 See i.a. Elster and Slagstad, *Constitutionalism and democracy* (1988), where the Norwegian and US perspectives concentrate on constitutionalism, but not on the question of review legitimacy.

Central in this discourse historically is the difference between US and European models of constitutionalism.[60] Contrary to traditional review forms in Europe,[61] the US method of review is via the concrete and strong form.[62] Where European review (either preceding or posterior) was often in the abstract and not authoritative in a way barring a consecutive different interpretation by the legislator, US review takes place after legislation has been enacted, following a concrete case before the courts, and is regarded as binding on other departments of government unless and until revised either by judicial decision or by constitutional amendment. To this duality, the example of Norway has been seen to represent a third way:[63] It resembles US review both in time of origin and way of development,[64] it is European, yet strong form; and it has mainly worked in ways substantially less challenging to the other branches of government than those of US review.

1.3.3 *The Constitutional Debates Internationalized*

"It is certainly a good question, on principle, whether seven judges from Strasbourg – from Azerbaijan and six other countries – know better about free speech, than does the Norwegian majority in 'Stortinget' [the Norwegian parliament]."[65] This good question was raised by then Norwegian Minister of Culture, Trond Giske (Labor), in the wake of a 2008 decision from the ECtHR finding Norway in breach of the ECHR.[66] His question reflected what had since WWII become the traditional Labor skepticism toward judicial review, only now applied to an internationalized variety of review. Parliament had enacted a total ban on the use of the TV medium for political advertising. It saw such a regulation to be but a question of how to ensure a well-functioning democratic process.[67] The Norwegian Supreme Court enforced

60 Nolte, *European and US constitutionalism* (2005).

61 Kelsen, Judicial review of legislation – a comparative study of the Austrian and the American constitution (1942).

62 Tushnet, Alternative forms of judicial review (2003).

63 Hirschl, The Nordic counternarrative: Democracy, human development and judicial review (2011).

64 Holmøyvik, Årsaker til utviklinga av prøvingsretten i Noreg og Danmark (2007), chapter 2.4, tracing the influence of *Marbury* v. *Madison* 5 US (1 Cranch) 137 (1803), the Federalist papers, Story, Commentaries on the Constitution of the United States; with a preliminary review of the constitutional history of the colonies and states, before the adoption of the Constitution (1833), see Tocqueville, *De la démocratie en Amérique* (1835).

65 Minister of Culture, Trond Giske, on the TV newshour "RedaksjonEN" (National Broadcasting station "NRK"), April 15, 2009.

66 *TV Vest AS & Rogaland Pensjonistparti* v. *Norway* (2008).

67 Lov av 4. desember 1992 nr. 127 om kringkasting og audiovisuelle bestillingstjenester, § 3.

the ban unhindered by the free speech provisions in the Constitution and the ECHR for the same reason. The ECtHR, however, held political TV advertising to be a form of expression protected as a fundamental right. A total ban on such expression needed a principled and proportional justification, which the ECtHR did not find in the Norwegian ban as it was applied.

Taken literally, Minister Giske's opening question is based on a view of democracy in which the national legislature, compounded by popularly elected representatives, is seen as representing the will of the people, and on which the majority of this legislature is the only legitimate decision maker. On such a view, there is little scope for legitimate limitations on the representative majority will – whether they be national or international. A central tenet of an international human rights society, particularly the structured European version of such, does, however, serve as such a limitation – namely, fundamental, individual rights. ECHR rights define the scope of what national legislatures may legally and legitimately enact. Since the 1990s, the formerly national question of Norwegian review has been affected and actualized by two phenomena. First, an increasing rights-thinking as part of a general juridification and *judicialization* of politics: While initiated and continued by political choice as answers to ever-more complex societal challenges, juridification causes a number of areas formerly subject to political deliberation to now be tied up in legal regulations. Some of these regulations leave little scope of action for either political or judicial evaluations. Others, however, such as the rights central here, by virtue of their necessarily open-ended structure, leave ample room for interpretation – and differences of interpretation – in all governmental branches.

The second phenomenon is increasing *globalization*, contributing further to the complexity of societal regulation and posing new challenges to previously nation-focused legal systems. The most significant shift of power due to the internationalization of law in Norway follows from Norway's agreements with the European Union (EU). In Europe, the influence of EU law, including court-made EU law, is significant even in associated nonmember states such as Norway. The pressing questions concerning legitimate exercises of authority following the EU–EEA influence are, however, not the subject of this study. It instead focuses on legitimacy questions following another external influence more resembling the one represented by individual rights as set out in the Constitution, namely the ECHR.[68]

68 There is broad, international debate on the work of international courts, notably the EU Court: see i.a. Rasmussen, *On law and policy in the European Court of Justice* (1986); Gibson and Caldeira, The legitimacy of transnational legal institutions: Compliance, support, and

One dissimilarity between EU and ECHR influences, which is significant particularly in the way it makes the two systems operate and appear differently to the public, is the way the two have been incorporated into and given effect in the Norwegian legal system. While the EU Court decisions are certainly influential for the understanding of EU law,[69] the substantial part of EU law enters Norway through a steady flow of directives or other EU legal acts that are "translated" into Norwegian law by *legislative acts*. The difference from a traditional, Norwegian law-making process is that the laws and regulations enacted, rather than having extensive *travaux* prepared by Norwegian administrative agencies,[70] now instead are prepared by EU organs. This, of course, is a substantial difference, but one that is more pressing on and visible to the national bureaucracy than the general public.

While ECHR law was also sanctioned by Parliament through the Human Rights Act of 1999 (HRA 1999), and while ECtHR law is attracting increasing attention in the legislative process, Parliament did not go through existing law to evaluate its compliance with ECHR norms upon the HRA enactment. Instead, potential conflicts and harmonizations were left to be brought forth in individual cases to be solved through court practice – preferably by Norwegian courts; if not, by the ECtHR. While there are many good reasons for incorporating the ECHR in this way, the chosen solution has led to the influence of ECHR law both being and appearing more "court-made" than EU law, even considering the significant influence of the EU Court on EU law.

the European Court of Justice (1995); Weiler, *The constitution of Europe* (1999); Weiler, The geology of international law: governance, democracy and legitimacy (2004); Lindseth, *Power and legitimacy: reconciling Europe and the nation-state* (2010). Debates over human rights adjudicative bodies such as the ECtHR have increased in the last 10–15 years: see i.a. Lord Sumption, *The limits of law (the 27th Sultan Azlan Shah Lecture)* (2013); Hoffman, The universality of human rights (2009); Bjørge, The status of the ECHR in Norway: Should Norwegian courts interpret the convention dynamically? (2010); Bruch et al., The legitimacy of the ECHR: The view from the ground (2011); Føllesdal, The legitimacy of international human rights review: The case of the European Court of Human Rights (2009). Particular concerns with regards to these courts are the lack of parliamentary influence on the international level, the more cumbersome processes to amend or re-regulate legal developments as produced by courts on the international level – both in principle and in practice – and what is perceived as a different methodological approach to rights protection than what have been the traditions in various member states – the particularly problematic type of adjudication being that of relying on "dynamic interpretation."

69 EU law, through the Norwegian EEA agreement, may also influence the interpretation of rights protection, but this perspective is not further pursued here. For an intake to this, see Fredriksen, Betydningen av EUs pakt om grunnleggende rettigheter for EØS-retten (2013).

70 Platou, *Forelæsninger over retskildernes theori* (1915), ch. 1; Augdahl, *Rettskilder* (1961) ch. 8–11; Eckhoff and Helgesen, *Rettskildelære* (2001), ch. 2–3; Backer, *Loven – hvordan blir den til?* (2013).

The idea of "unelected elites" making law is what fundamentally triggers the countermajoritarian difficulty. This makes the authority exercised through review under the ECHR resemble in an interesting way that of review under the Constitution. Rights need to be interpreted to be applied – they cannot, conceptually or factually, be regulated with finality in a way either obviating or minimizing the need for concrete assessment in cases where the scope of rights is questioned.[71] So, retaining the effectuation of rights primarily with the legislator really is no viable alternative to subsequent interpretation for application. The more general or abstract the convention, constitutional or legislative regulation, such as those set out to protect fundamental rights often are the less precise and unambiguous their protective scope, and the greater the room for – and the need for – adjudicative interpretation in particular cases.

As interpretation and application of individual rights are carried out by a governmental branch other than the legislative branch, rights legislation entails a shift of power away from Parliament and toward the courts adjudicating cases concerning such rights. When these rights stem from ordinary legislation, the limits as defined by the courts may be redefined or reversed by ordinary legislation. Other forms of rights legislation and codification through other legal instruments do, however, complicate such redefinition through the popularly elected majority of Parliament: rights protected by some higher-ranked norm than ordinary legislation, such as the Constitution – and the international human rights conventions to which Norway is a party.

A recent official thematization of the relationship between democracy and judicial review was the aforementioned Norwegian Study on Power and Democracy from 2003 ("the Power Study"). Holding democracy first and foremost to be procedural – a "formal system of decision-making through majority decisions and popularly elected representatives"– the study maintained that democracy perceived as (individual) rights, deliberation or values amounts to "additional forms of democracy" that may "supplement" but never "replace" the procedural "main" democracy.[72] Based on this conception of democracy, the Power Study conclusions as to the state of democracy in Norway were rather bleak: "The parliamentary chain of government is weakened in every link; parties and elections are less mobilizing; minority governments imply that the connection between election results and policy formation is broken; and elected assemblies have been suffering a notable

[71] Kant, *Critique of pure reason* (1982), 59; Kelsen, *La garantie juridictionnelle de la Constitution* (1928), 221ff.

[72] NOU 2003:19, 13.1.

loss of domain."[73] One of the culprits of this unhappy development was to be found in the role of courts, and particularly international courts: "Norwegian law is increasingly internationalized. This development has augmented judicial power to the detriment of the representative elected government."[74] Parliament did not share the report assessment of democracy as a primarily procedural, but instead held democracy to be both popular majority rule and human rights together.[75]

1.4 BOOK STRUCTURE AND TERMINOLOGY

The aim of this book is to provide one insight into Norwegian constitutionalism by looking into political and legal-historical discussions of judicial review. A general assessment of courts' review of *administrative actions* falls outside its scope; the focus is on the review of parliamentary laws under constitutional norms. Such review of legislation is occasionally called "constitutional review," but this term is sometimes understood as review undertaken by any government institution. As the focus of the book is on the role of Norwegian courts and the ECtHR, "judicial review" meaning "review undertaken by courts as part of litigation" seems more descriptive.

"Judicial review" is used in the wide sense encompassing all adjudication under rights instruments, such as national constitutions or international rights conventions, that potentially affect the scope for legitimate law application or law-making. This is done because all such cases in principle, if not always directly, have some bearing on the understanding of the constitutional right in question. It thus also affects the scope of potential future political action – as well, ultimately, as the relationship between the state and its citizens. I view all cases where individual rights protected in a way that in principle actualizes their function as substantive limits on legislative power, as cases of human rights review. The outcome of the decision – whether some legislative act or action is found unconstitutional or not – is of interest to the analysis, but not determinative for what is considered judicial review cases.

The term "ECHR judicial review" is used to describe review under the ECHR, but one undertaken by all courts competent of such review. In Norway, ordinary courts have general jurisdiction; in principle and in practice, therefore, ECHR judicial review is practiced on all levels, from the district courts to the Supreme Court – before eventually also in the ECtHR.

73 Østerud and Selle, Power and democracy in Norway: The transformation of Norwegian politics (2006), 25.

74 NOU 2003:19, 6.3.

75 Innst. S. nr. 252 (2004–2005), 3.7.

ECHR judicial review may be seen as one example of "international judicial review." This term, however, is sometimes reserved for review undertaken by international organs, such as the ECtHR. I will use the term "ECHR judicial review" or just "ECHR review" for adjudication by all courts exercising review under the convention, and "ECtHR review" for review undertaken by the ECtHR.

Structuring this story about Norwegian judicial review are central Supreme Court review cases and formative debates of "constitutional cases." These are used as the main means for periodizing the chronology: seven historical chapters that sometimes overlap in time tell a story starting out in 1814 and ending in 2017. Chapter 2 outlines the institutional design of the Norwegian review models under both the Constitution and the ECHR, as well as the institutional and doctrinal particulars of the Norwegian legal system. Chapters 3 through 9 focus on the debate history. The first of these (Chapters 3–5) study debates on review under the Norwegian Constitution. Chapter 3 focuses on the formative 1800s, where review cases arose from legislation infringing upon the constitutional privileges of high state officials, and the legal and political foundations for review were established. Chapter 4, set in the early 1900s, with its increasing tension between the constitutional protection of property on the one hand, and the societal need for economic and welfare regulations on the other, has a central review case of 1918 as its main focus. The period following WWII and leading up to 1976 in which judicial review – then a long-established practice, but one dormant for about fifty years – had a rather surprising revival, which is analyzed in Chapter 5. Chapter 6 takes a step back in history to recollect the years leading up to Norway's ratification of the ECHR and recognition of ECtHR jurisdiction from around 1950 to 1964, and follows debates under this form of review through the 1970s–1990s and the work toward the 1999 HRA. Having established the foundations for the two forms of review, Chapter 7, concerning the historical period 2000–2010, looks into two free speech cases that serve as illustrations of how dual review of free speech – one of the rights protected by both the Constitution and the ECHR – functions. Free speech is a necessary precondition for all conceptions of democracy and rule of law, and is a right that has been substantially altered,[76] and become subject to a more principled protection due to the ECHR influence – a development

[76] See i.a. Eggen, Journalistisk formidling av ærekrenkende ytringer – med særlig vekt på betydningen av Menneskerettighetsdomstolens avgjørelse i Tromsøsaken (1999); Schiøtz and Strømme, Paradigmeskifte i injurieretten (2002); Kierulf and Strømme, Tolkning og injurier (2004); Wessel-Aas in Dahl, *Norsk presses historie* (2010).

primarily brought forth by *courts*. As such, the case of free speech development provides an example of the democratizing prospect of judicial review.[77] Norwegian free speech protection before 2000 serves as one example that judicial review is not enough in itself to protect individual rights, and that the impact that such review may have can be dependent on revitalization by an external review dynamic. Following a decade of ECHR-dominated rights review, 2010 marked a revitalization of "traditional" review under the Constitution, by presenting three plenary Supreme Court review cases all leading the court to a different constitutional interpretation than the legislature. These, and the discussions following them, are covered in Chapter 8. Chapter 9 concludes the historical analysis by looking into the movement toward constitutionalizing central human rights in 2014, thus potentially fusing the two bases for review – as well as the 2014–2015 parliamentary discussions leading up to the customary law practice of review being formalized and amended into the written constitution. Chapter 10 reflects upon contemporary and future review challenges.

[77] As outlined in Kierulf, Rettsstatens overnasjonale vending: den andre prøvingsretten (2009).

2

Legal Foundations and Doctrinal Specifics

2.1 INTRODUCTION

The debates of review in this book take place within the framework of the Norwegian constitutional and legal system. Debates of Norwegian constitutional review may be easier to follow with a basic understanding of the form and basis of such review, as well as some legal cultural and methodological specifics of the Norwegian legal system. Reflections upon Norwegian review under the ECHR also presuppose some knowledge of ECHR foundations and of the scope and method of ECtHR review: The ECtHR way of review functions as a doctrinal model for domestic review, and case law from the ECtHR serves as a guiding, sometimes authoritative precedent for Norwegian legal practitioners attempting to establish relevant requirements under the ECHR. Also, assertions about ECHR review (il)legitimacy, as practiced by both the Norwegian Supreme Court and the ECtHR – i.e. that the ECHR is interpreted in a way too protective of rights or too deferential to state interference – make apposite some background knowledge of ECHR history and the ECtHR method of interpretation. Central to discussions of constitutional and ECHR review legitimacy alike is a foundational understanding of the Norwegian Supreme Court. For those unfamiliar with either of these systems or institutions, this chapter provides a brief outline.

2.2 THE NORWEGIAN SUPREME COURT

As the third leg of the division of powers underlying the 1814 Constitution, the judiciary is constitutionally a branch independent from the legislative and executive ones. This independence has not been seen as a hindrance to having courts be dependent on the other branches, financially or organizationally.[1] The Norwegian Supreme Court was established in 1815.[2]

As Norway is a civil law country, the main legal authorities are parliamentary enacted statutes and their subsequent administrative regulations, and, in review cases, the Constitution. Court decisions, however, also represent a significant legal authority. The position of case law in Norwegian history is quite particular, as expounded in Section 2.3.2.

A supreme court is presupposed in the 1814 Constitution (§ 88), and Supreme Court decisions cannot, as a general rule, be altered by other authorities (§§ 88 and 90). The "last word" in legal decisions lies with the Supreme Court (cf. § 88), and decisions from the Supreme Court are inappealable (§ 90). In addition to resolving disputes brought before them, court decisions influence the law on a more general level. Through the Norwegian version of the doctrine of precedence or *stare decisis*, the Supreme Court also has a legislative function in that its decisions affect the way comparable legal questions are later handled. Thus, court decisions influence the ways in which courts – both lower instance courts and the Supreme Court itself – handle subsequent cases. They also influence the way in which legal norms are interpreted by the general public, legal practitioners and other branches of government.

Norwegian courts have general jurisdiction; with few exceptions, all courts are competent to handle all cases – criminal, civil, administrative and constitutional ones.[3] As such, the courts may suffer from a shortage of detailed insights into very specialized fields of law, an aspect sometimes thematized.[4] What they lack in specialized expertise, however, they gain in generalist competence. The benefits of this are that courts of general jurisdiction are better equipped to get an overall perspective and avoid "tunnel vision," and thus ensure one of the main judicial goals as presupposed in the civil and criminal procedure acts: to establish a unified and uniform legal application.[5]

The Norwegian Supreme Court today consists of twenty ordinary justices and one Chief Justice. Individual Supreme Court cases are heard by five

1 Indeed, the independence of courts was seen to have been strengthened between the early 1900s and 1960; see Dahl Jacobsen and Eckhoff, *Rationality and responsibility in administrative and judicial decision-making* (1960), 37.

2 Kierulf and Slagstad, Høyesteretts dommere (2015).

3 Exceptions are i.a. *Trygderetten* (the Social Security Tribunal) and *Arbeidsretten* (the Labor Court).

4 See i.a. St.meld. nr. 23 (2000–2001), 7, Norges Juristforbund, *Strid om spesialdomstoler* (2013).

5 NOU 1999:19, 12.5.2.1.

justices, and the court works in two parallel divisions. In some instances cases are heard in Grand Chamber by eleven justices or by all of the justices in plenary sessions. Review cases are always tried by such strengthened chambers, when of particular importance or impact, in plenary.[6] The justices rotate between chambers and the Appeals Selection Committee. This committee decides on nonconcluding orders and decisions from lower courts, and selects what appeals are significant enough (either because of the matter at hand, or the possible effects outside the case of a Supreme Court decision) to be brought before the Supreme Court. Which justices work in chambers and in the Committee is based on a regular rotation, based only on a principle of randomness, to avoid particular justices sitting or not sitting in cases they have a particular expertise or professional interest in.

As a rule, all decisions must be justified by explicit, judicial reasoning.[7] The composition of Norwegian Supreme Court decisions is comparatively long and thorough, reciting the reasoned claims of the parties and with transparent and accessible reasoning for the court's assessment. The importance of accessible reasoning and justification is emphasized as "obvious" in the *travaux préparatoires*, which explicate the underlying justification for such a rule as "courts as state organs need to justify its exercise of public power in order for it to be rational and legitimate."[8] The transparency ensured

> provides the possibility for control and access to the functioning of the courts and strengthens confidence in them. It further ensures that the decision is thoroughly pondered by the judge both as concerns the assessment of evidence and of law. This reinforces the quality of the decision. … The justification, and particularly the explication of reasons for the assessment of law is required in order that the decision can contribute to [*rettsavklaring*] clarification of law and [*rettsutvikling*] development of law … A precondition for the abovementioned effects is that the reasoning is good and convincing. Conversely, a poor reasoning will have a number of negative effects and at times be more destructive than no reasoning at all.[9]

Norwegian courts handle only cases brought before them; they generally have no abstract or prelegislative competence. Formally, however, the Constitution § 83 opens for such prelegislative or advisory review, under it,

6 The Court's Act 1915 *Lov av 13.august 1915 nr. 5 om domstolene (domstolloven)* § 5.

7 The Criminal Procedure Act 1981, *Lov av 22. mai 1981 nr. 25 om rettergangsmåten i straffesaker (Straffeprosessloven)* § 39, The Civil Procedure Act, *Lov av 17. juni 2005 nr 90 om mekling og rettergang i sivile tvister (tvisteloven) lov om mekling og rettergang i sivile saker* § 19–6.

8 NOU 2001: 32, 21.8.4.3.

9 Ibid., 21.8.4.3.

Parliament may call upon the Supreme Court to opine on legal questions (in the early 1800s, the executive too called for opinions under § 83).[10] Primarily, § 83 has been used in questions of legislation about courts in general and the Supreme Court in particular, and only rarely. From time to time, some minority in Parliament suggests that prelegislative review under § 83 should be obtained from the Supreme Court. The main argument against this form of review, particularly as regards questions of constitutionality of legislation, is that being tied up by a previous opinion could compromise the independence of the Supreme Court, by influencing how it decides later cases that are brought before it. As with other questions handled by courts, the initiative to have the legal matter at hand assessed under § 83 lies outside the court itself, not with the parties to a concrete case ex post, but with Parliament ex ante.

The role of the Supreme Court is to ensure "*Rettsenhet, rettsavklaring, rettsutvikling*,"[11] which means uniform legal application, clarification of the more specific content of legal rules and the development of law. Although development of law has long been recognized as one function of court practice, it has periodically been quite controversial. Skepticism about courts' role in *developing* the law, not only *applying* it, has much in common with the arguments for limiting or even opposing judicial review: that of courts being but the mouth of the law, the normative stance that legal development is the department of the legislature, not the courts. The argument is that courts – by developing the law – engage in partisan politics rather than independent legal analysis, and that such political activity (or activism) is something the administration and legislator are better equipped to prepare and decide – and more legitimized in so doing. A central turn, if not in the awareness of this tension, then at least for developing an open debate about the legal development of courts, came with a lecture held at the annual judges meeting in 1974.[12] Carsten Smith, at the time a professor of law, later Chief Justice of the Supreme Court (1991–2002), advocated for a more active role for the Supreme Court in the development of the law, which should, in his view, hold as its primary role not that of solving individual cases, but of staking out directions for the future.[13]

One challenge to the "rettsavklaring" aim of courts is the existence of *dissenting opinions*. While such dissent may merely expose different

10 See Hiorthøi in *Den Europeiske menneskerettskonvensjon og Norge* (1963), 458ff.

11 Ot. prp. nr. 41 (1980–81) 4, 7, NOU 2001:32, 13.1.

12 The 7th ordinary judges meeting in Tromsø, June 28, 1974, printed as Smith, Domstolene og rettsutviklingen (1975).

13 Ibid., 318.

interpretations within the permissible room of legal discretion, the more dissent, the less clarity about what the law "really" is, particularly the closer the size of the minority and majority factions (3–2 in ordinary cases, 6–5 in Grand Chamber, 10–9 in plenary cases.) Studies of dissent cases in the Supreme Court (in general, not only in review cases) show, however, that the amount of dissenting opinion has not changed much in the period from 1965–2009. In this period, the overall percentage of dissent was 11.3 percent; or 21.2 percent in civil and 7.7 percent in criminal cases.[14] This has been seen as within the methodologically permissible room of legal discretion.[15] The tendency toward civil dissents within this period is a dip from a high of 29 percent in the 1965–1969 period to a low of 13 percent in 1985–1989, rising to 23 percent in 1995–2005, and sinking slightly to 20 percent in 2005–2009. The tendency in criminal cases is generally a rise throughout the period, from 5 percent in 1965–1969 to 17 percent in 2005–2009.[16]

Following 1995, the general rule was altered so that the Supreme Court generally refused appeal in criminal cases.[17] Up until this year it had treated all, and after 1986 most,[18] such cases.[19] Following changes in the Civil Procedure Act in 1960 and 1981, civil cases refused appeal increased from 44 percent in 1959 to 78 percent in 2005.[20] The increasing refusal of appeals leaves the Supreme Court with working room to decide only, or mostly, cases concerning interesting principles, or cases the decisions in which may influence other cases to the betterment of "*rettsenhet, rettsavklaring and rettsutvikling*." While having improved, finding the right balance between what cases count as significant enough for Supreme Court judgment is an issue of ongoing discussion.[21] The average length of Supreme Court decisions has increased steadily from 1970 to 2010.[22] This plausibly reflects the increasing complexity of and amount of relevant legal sources, i.a. following EU and ECHR influence, yet also suggests the Supreme Court takes the ideals underlying justifying its exercise of authority seriously.

14 Sunde, Dissenting votes in the Norwegian Supreme Court 1965–2009: A legal cultural analysis (2012), 63.

15 Ibid., 63. 16 Ibid., 63ff.

17 Lov av 22. mai 1981 nr. 25 om rettergangsmåten i straffesaker (Straffeprosessloven) § 323.

18 Ibid. § 349. 19 Lov om Rettergangsmaaden i Straffesager av 7.1. 1887 nr. 5 § 387.

20 Aasland, Argumentasjonsmønsteret i nyere høyesterettspraksis (2006), 389.

21 Arnstad, Høyesterett konsentrerer seg om det prinsipielle (2013); Høyesterett, Norges Høyesterett Årsmelding 2013 (2014).

22 Sunde, Dissenting votes in the Norwegian Supreme Court 1965–2009: A legal cultural analysis (2012), 71.

Judges and justices are formally appointed by the Government (the king in Council), as set out in the Constitution § 21.[23] Their independence is ensured i.a. through their being "embedsmenn" (high state officials; cf. the Constitution § 22), who cannot be dismissed absent court proceedings. Supreme Court justices are protected by the Constitution against liability cases concerning their professional work. Alleged breaches of Supreme Court justice professional duties under the constitution are only legally actionable through impeachment proceedings as set out in the Constitution §§ 86 and 87. This serves to enforce the legitimacy ideal of individual independence of justices.[24] Judges and Justices are appointed for life, i.e. until mandatory retirement at seventy. While formally "democratically" appointed, justices cannot be held politically accountable – their tenure is only dependent on their upholding their constitutional duties; unconstitutional actions are to be pursued through impeachment proceedings following the Constitution §§ 86 and 87.

In the Courts Act 1915, several rules are set out to further ensure both institutional and individual independence of courts and justices from the other branches of government. Up until 2002 courts were administered by the Ministry of Justice, and have consequently been within the Minister of Justice's realm of responsibility. The desirability of such a system was questioned prior to the work toward the 2002 changes. In 1967, a committee was established to assess this model of organization. This work originated with judges as driving forces, based on a desire for judges, who knew the challenges within the court system from the inside, to have more influence on the part of justice administration concerning courts.[25] By statute, judicial appointments now take place following the recommendation of an independent advisory board.[26] This board, administered by the independent Court Administration sitting on four-year terms, is composed of three representatives from the judiciary, one private and one public lawyer, and two members from outside the legal profession.[27] Ordinary administrative law applies to the appointment proceeding, so that the list of applicants and the council nomination reasoning are public,[28] thus ensuring impartiality and transparency in appointment proceedings. The council nomination is sent to the king (in practice, the government and the Ministry of Justice), and, when this is done, the Supreme Court Chief Justice in writing or orally presents a statement to the Ministry of

[23] The following presentation relies on a more extensive analysis of Supreme Court Justices 1815–2015 in Kierulf and Slagstad, Høyesteretts dommere (2015).

[24] NOU 1999:19 7.5.4.

[25] Wold, Domstolenes deltakelse i justisforvaltningen (1964).

[26] The Court Act (1915) § 55 a.

[27] Lov av 13.august 1915 nr. 5 om domstolene (domstolloven) § 55, § 55a, 1.

[28] Ibid., § 55i.

Justice based on the council nomination.[29] Political affiliations are not discussed on the independent appointment board, in the internal discussions of the Supreme Court or in the conference between the Chief Justice and the Minister of Justice. Prior to appointment, the Chief Justice advises the Minister about whom of the nominees the Supreme Court ranks highest. In practice, the Chief Justice's advice has not diverged from the independent board recommendation, and the Minister of Justice has not appointed anyone else but the top recommendation of the board. In the absence of parliamentary hearings, judicial appointments have drawn little public attention, and have traditionally been unpoliticized.

Candidates for Supreme Court positions must satisfy high professional and personal requirements, and the aim that justices represent varied professional backgrounds is now in the Court Act.[30] From the perspective of expertise or knowledge-based input legitimacy, the professionalism of justices is important. Although hard to measure in any precise manner, the professional quality of Supreme Court justices seems very high.[31] Formally, since 1915 they have had to meet the requirement of (some) life experience – being a minimum of thirty years of age, and, until 2010,[32] having graduated with the highest honors. While this requirement is no longer explicated in the Court Act,[33] the emphasis on examination grades is not supposed to be of any less significance.[34] In practice, only highly qualified and experienced lawyers become Supreme Court justices.[35]

Supreme Court justices are obviously not popularly representative – they need to be lawyers, and qualified ones at that. For a number of years justices were primarily recruited from lawyers and, if not from Oslo, then at least with their formative experience gained there. Moreover, this experience was often developed through working in some part of the central administration, such as the Ministry of Justice legal department or the Attorney General for Civil Affairs. To the extent that this was too prominent, it could add to an imbalance for justices' understanding of state interests to the detriment of individual rights, ostensibly weakening the legitimacy ideals of representativity and diversity of justices.[36] Any significant imbalance is, however, hard

29 Ibid., § 55b. 30 Ibid., § 55.

31 See i.a. Hiorthøy in Nissen, et al., *Den dømmende makt* (1967); Andenæs, Høyesterett som politisk organ (1965); Sunde, Dissenting votes in the Norwegian Supreme Court 1965–2009: A legal cultural analysis (2012).

32 Lov av 15.januar 2010 nr. 2 om endringar i domstolloven mv. (sidegjeremål for dommarar m.m.).

33 Due to numerous reforms of law studies also influencing the grading system.

34 Ot. prp. nr. 102 (2008–2009), 9. 35 Schei, Har Høyesterett en politisk funksjon? (2011).

36 Kjønstad, Er Høyesterett statsvennlig? (1999).

to find when examining justices' backgrounds in differing historical periods.[37] Upon the reorganization of the judicial nomination process leading up to new procedures effective from 2004, the mandate and policy for the Court Administration nomination board is centrally focused on ensuring a broader basis for recruitment.[38] This has led to an increased representativity of justices, as regards diversity between the sexes, geographical origin and practical background experience. As of May 2017, out of twenty justices, seven are women; five are younger than fifty-five years of age; and eight were born outside Oslo. While many still have formative experience from some part of the central administration or the criminal prosecutor, eleven justices have five or more years in private practice.[39] This suggests a fairly high degree of diversity.

2.3 THE FORM OF AND BASIS FOR CONSTITUTIONAL REVIEW

2.3.1 *Constitutional Judicial Review*

Constitutionalism is sometimes divided into a US and a European variety.[40] This distinction is generally informative,[41] but has little eye for the Nordic countries as part of Europe.[42] In the Nordic region, at least some countries employ review models that in origin and institutional design lie closer to the US than the European model, yet are practiced very differently than in the US. While a part of Europe, Norway lies closer to the US model of constitutionalism: The Supreme Court has the final word in constitutional questions. If the legislature wants the Constitution to mean something other than what follows from a decision by the Supreme Court, it has to alter the Constitution, by the procedures for constitutional amendment. This feature distinguishes Norway from traditional, continental-European systems where administrative and/or constitutional questions are handled by special courts, and review is often done in the abstract, and prior to statutory

37 Kierulf and Slagstad, Høyesteretts dommere (2015).

38 See NOU 1999:19, 7.3.1.3. I Ot. prp. nr. 44 (2000–2001) pkt. 8.1.7, and Policy Memo 2006: www.domstol.no/globalassets/upload/da/internett/domstol.no/om-domstolene/innstillingsradet/dokumenter/pp-notat_mars-2017.pdf.

39 www.domstol.no/no/Enkelt-domstol/-Norges-Hoyesterett/Om-Hoyesterett/Personalia/Dommere/.

40 Nolte, *European and US Constitutionalism* (2005).

41 See, however, Gardbaum, The new Commonwealth model of constitutionalism (2001).

42 See Hirschl, The Nordic counternarrative: Democracy, human development and judicial review (2011).

enactments.[43] While the unitary states of Denmark, Iceland and Norway lack the federal element central to US constitutionalism and judicial review, they all (in principle) vest the competence of review ex post in general jurisdiction courts. Further, these powers do not traditionally stem from any constitutional codification, but have grown out of court practice. Review is undertaken ex post, and regardless of whether claims of unconstitutionality are brought by the parties (*iura novit curia*).[44] The formal effect of review finding regulations unconstitutional is not that they are voided, but that they are disregarded or interpreted so as not to be in conflict with the Constitution in the case at hand. Very seldom is a statute explicitly found to be unconstitutional; more often, courts interpret the statute in a way so that it accords with the constitution. This harmonizing process may happen openly, in that the potential tension is recognized, but the more constitutional of alternative interpretations is chosen; or, it may take on the form of harmonization at earlier cognitive steps of the interpretative process, in the balancing and interpreting of the various sources of law along the way to a final, interpretative result.

Prior to the constitutional reform in 2014–2015, there was no constitutional provision mandating judicial review in Norway.[45] From a formal input perspective, Norwegian constitutional review is thus marked by a lack of formal legality and procedural democratic input – all the way up until the review constitutionalization in 2015. This, however, mirrors how the "democratic counterpart" to review – namely, parliamentarism – has grown from an institution of customary law into its formal status: Breaking through in the 1880s, the parliamentary system has been adhered to since, but did not find its formal constitutionalization before 2007. Viewed in the negative, no constitutional amendment has been enacted to bar review even though several proposals to this effect were suggested in the 1920s and 1930s. Not constituting any lasting supermajority against review, these proposals were all rejected, albeit by decreasing majorities. Formally, the proposed amendments were all presented according to the constitutional amendment procedure, thus at least

43 For a foundational study of the two systems, see Kelsen, Judicial review of legislation – a comparative study of the Austrian and the American constitution (1942).

44 See i.a. Lov av 17. juni 2005 nr 90 om mekling og rettergang i sivile tvister (tvisteloven) § 11–3.

45 None of the constitutional sources of inspirations explicitly mandated review either, so the Constitution was no anomaly to its constitutional period in this respect: see Holmøyvik, Dommernes uavhengighet og forholdet til de øvrige statsmakter (2012), 123. In newer constitutions, explicit mandates for review are quite normal, ranked as number sixteen of the sixty most used provisions in modern constitutions: see Law and Versteeg, The declining influence of the United States constitution (2012), 774. An explicit provision mandating review was also proposed as part of the 2014 constitutional human rights revision: see Dokument 12:30 (2011–2012), § 114.

formally opening for direct popular election input on this question. As an argument for democratic input into the institution of review, however, this negative approval is not very convincing, as the threshold for abolishing embedded institutions is a lot higher than deciding not to institute them in the first place.[46]

On an informal level of input, as will become evident from the historical debates, judicial review has enjoyed popular acceptance over time. It has also gradually developed within an otherwise emerging and functioning democracy, perhaps as an answer to needs and interests in historical, political and cultural contexts, as legitimated because of their "natural" or organic growth, out of the people, so to speak – a source of legitimacy stressed by representatives of the legal community in the late 1800s and early 1900s. The gradual emergence and acceptance of review fits such a perspective quite well. It is further underlined by the 1976 *Kløfta* case, which only appeared after a long period of nonreview, yet was followed by little debate. An informal development providing a historical argument against review legitimacy is, however, that of the turn to parliamentarism. Emphasized by the Special Committee of 1927, this shift from a system of divided powers to one of unification of powers leaves no room for limiting institutions outside Parliament and the government. As considered in Section 4.6, however, this argument implies that there is no room for any constitutional limitation to popular majority rule, a view that has had little support historically.

Only the dispute between the parties to the case is settled by a review decision. Due to the doctrine of *stare decisis*, however, the general justification for a concrete decision may also have implications for later cases. This is important for this book in two respects: first, that court holdings may limit future legislation based on the same constitutional interpretation found untenable in a previous review case; and second, that the review decision may effectively function as legislation by courts, in being an authoritative source of law in other comparable cases. In practice, thus, the effect of review is that the unconstitutional part of the regulation is no longer enforced.

The consequence of these courts finding a statute unconstitutional is not that it is voided. It remains valid; it will, however, subsequently be interpreted with the limitations resulting from the initial review, due to the precedent created. To the extent that the legislature wishes to effectuate the legal regulations of a statute found unconstitutional or to have the constitutional limits changed, this requires constitutional amendment. Norwegian constitutional review is practiced within a system fitting all four criteria of "strong

46 Kahneman et al., Anomalies: The endowment effect, loss aversion, and status quo bias (1991).

constitutionalism":[47] First, the Constitution is one of significant rigidity – legislative amendments to it require not only a two-thirds supermajority, but also popular participation through an intermediary election. While formally rigid,[48] the Constitution has, however, been altered informally several times, and also as concerns foundational constitutional questions – most notably, by the introduction of parliamentarism in the late 1800s, an alteration not formally amended until 2007. This modification to formal rigidity, however, has not resulted in any informal legislative overruling of courts' constitutional interpretations. Consequently, it is not a modification of institutional design relevant to an assessment of review legitimacy. Second, it may be argued that this rigidity is of a counter-majoritarian nature. While opening for amendments due to shifting historical needs, alterations cannot run counter to the spirit and principles of the Constitution. Third, through longstanding legal practice, and as formalized in 2015, the Norwegian system is one of judicial review – the judiciary is not only competent, but committed to interpreting the Constitution. And fourth, this competence and commitment also implies that it is courts that are the final arbiters of how the Constitution is to be interpreted. If Parliament wants a different conclusion than one reached by the Supreme Court, it must amend the Constitution.

In review cases, the Supreme Court may be strengthened, either by Grand Chamber or Plenary compositions. Court proceedings ensure thoroughness of legal and factual presentation through the writs of the parties. In the Supreme Court there are, however, no direct hearings of witnesses or other evidence, as is central in the lower courts. This removes Supreme Court processes one step away from direct factual evaluations, but keeps these evaluations within the court system. Contradiction and nuancing is ensured through substantial spoken hearings; by the principle of oral proceedings, all arguments relevant

47 Martí Mármol, The sources of legitimacy of political decisions: Between procedure and substance (2005).

48 While satisfying parameters for a rigid constitution, the Constitution is not so rigid that it has not been formally amended a number of times; in fact, most Constitution provisions have been altered in some way since 1814. A study shows the Constitution has been formally amended 287 times from 1814–2011; of these, 233 amendments were made in the period 1905–2011: cited in Sejersted, Det elastiske panser (2013), 60 with further references. In addition, in practice, the Constitution can – and has – also been altered a number of times in less formal ways, through interpretation and customary law. These two ways of constitutional alternation sometimes also interact. A significant example of this is the introduction of the parliamentary system into the (until then) 1814 constitutional monarchy. Through practice it became a foundational part of Norwegian constitutional law following the impeachment case (Riksretten) in 1884, but only as customary law. Having been a central and unchallenged part of our constitutional order since, it became formally added to the Constitution in 2007.

to the case decision must be verbalized in open court. These hearings also enforce the transparency and possible verifiability essential to popular confidence through being open to the public.

The great majority of cases throughout the Norwegian review history concern only two constitutional provisions: the general ban on retroactive legislation in § 97, and the protection of property and due compensation for expropriation in § 105. As is further explored in Chapter 7, § 100 has been used as an interpretative standard, but has never led to any legislative regulation being disregarded on review.

With some historic variations, for significant periods Norwegian courts have been deferential to how the other branches of government have handled constitutional questions. Even when reviewing legislative acts that clearly challenge the Constitution, individual guarantees such as the principle of legality and the nonretroactivity of laws, the Supreme Court has often been loyal to legislative provisions – or, even more often, the perceived legislative intent.[49] Review intensity has varied with the constitutional provision at hand – a variance explicated in case law in the 1950s–1970s. While the scope and intensity of review has not been generally established, provisions to the protection of individual freedom or security have been seen to require intense review, whereas review of provisions regulating the competencies of governmental branches less so. In these latter matters, it has been assumed that courts should pay more respect to the view taken on constitutionality by Parliament. While certainly also concerning individual freedom – i.a. of property – economic regulations have been seen to "place themselves in an intermediary position."[50] A study of what number of review cases have been tried, measured by cases in which the Constitution is not only mentioned, but has played a role of some significance for the decision at hand, showed the following percentages of the total Supreme Court caseload: 1945–1954: 0.69 percent, 1955–1964: 0.87 percent, 1965–1974: 0.35 percent, 1975–1984: 0.88 percent.[51] It also argued that judicial review had a renaissance in the years from the mid 1970s to around 1990. An estimate of the following years, based on related criteria for what counts as review cases, indicates, however, that the upswing in review cases does not really come before around 2000, and even then the increase is not dramatic. An average of 0.57 percent (45 cases) of the total Supreme Court caseload in the years 1990–1999 concerned the Constitution, based on

49 Rt. 1946 s. 196, Rt. 1955 s. 439, Rt. 1982 s. 241.

50 Rt. 1976 s. 1, 5. For a critique of this devaluation of economic rights, see Smith, *Høyesterett og folkestyret* (1993), 255ff.

51 Smith, *Høyesterett og folkestyret* (1993), 203ff.

a total of 7,900 cases.[52] Of these forty-five cases, six had the effect of rendering legislation to be interpreted differently because of the Constitution. In the years 2000–2009 some 4,832 cases total were decided, of which fifty-nine cases [a yearly average of 1.22 percent; one covering variations from 0.62 percent (2009) to 2.54 percent (2002)] concerned the Constitution in some way, whereas the Constitution in fourteen cases led to a different interpretation. In the years 2010–2013, twenty-three cases out of 2,131 in total concerned the Constitution (1.08 percent), while the number of cases leading to different interpretations was nine. In 2014 and 2015, Parliament constitutionalized central human rights and the customary law of judicial review, i.a. with the aim of revitalizing the Constitution as a workable legal-political foundation. This reform led to a substantial increase in the Supreme Court's *mentioning* and *use* of constitutional provisions in the years 2014–2016. The use of such provisions in ways leading to substantially different interpretation has, however, remained as it was prior to the reform, with about one such case per year.

2.3.2 *Some Legal, Cultural and Methodological Features*

Central to understanding Norwegian judicial review are some Norwegian legal doctrinal particularities. As mentioned, review has traditionally had no positive foundations in the Constitution or other written legislative sources. The reliance on court-made case law does not have such foundations either; in fact, the Constitution positively vests the legislative power in Parliament,[53] and presupposes a detailed civil and criminal code. The role of court-made law has, however, been a central feature of the Norwegian legal system since the constitutional enactment in 1814. One reason for this is that there simply was no legislation to apply in the early years of the Norwegian nation; another reason is that jurists were accustomed to customary law as a legal source;[54] a third is the relatively late emergence and expansion of a Norwegian legal science to supply case law as a source of legal argument.[55] Compared to the doctrine of *stare decisis* in British or US law, the Norwegian doctrine of precedent is relatively relaxed:

[52] Percentage of total caseload in the Supreme Court based on reasoned decisions in civil and criminal cases as counted by the Lovdata database, omitting decisions without reasons.

[53] The Constitution, § 49.

[54] Aubert, *Om den dømmende Magts Virksomhed som Kilde til Udviklingen af vor Ret ved Siden af Lovgivningsvirksomheden* (1865).

[55] Sunde, Dissenting votes in the Norwegian Supreme Court 1965–2009: A legal cultural analysis (2012), 60.

Precedent is not binding, and the extent to which even rather recent precedent is in fact followed by the Supreme Court itself varies in different historical periods.[56]

Other central specifics of Norwegian law important to note when trying to grasp parts of the broader background under which judicial review fluctuations have developed are its reliance on *travaux préparatoires* and the role of *pragmatism* in doctrine and legal adjudication. The ideal of representative democracy through parliamentary power has been particularly strong in Scandinavia. One consequence of this is a reliance on preparatory works – *travaux préparatoires* – in statutory interpretation. Rather than formulating the statutory provisions in an overly detailed manner, explanations for what more general formulations are enacted can be found in the expert reports, the preparations of these reports by the governmental departments and administrative agencies, and the discussions of the proposed statutes as based on these preparations in the Parliamentary committees and in Parliament. While challenging rule-of-law principles such as legality and predictability, the reliance on various *travaux*, notably often those from the Ministry of Justice legal department, has been seen to strengthen the centrality of the perceived will of the people and forms an integral part of Scandinavian adjudicative tradition.[57]

Since the 1920s and '30s, Norwegian legal doctrine has been influenced by the Scandinavian legal realist challenge to both legal positivism and natural law. Scandinavian legal realism had the same critical motivation as American legal realism. But, while the latter extended the progressivist view that law was infused with power as a reaction to the politically conservative "legal science," Scandinavian legal realism bore the similarity to legal positivism, seeking a strict separation between law and politics and law and morality in order to "demystify" law, and remove it from its aristocratic, and metaphysic, undemocratic tendencies.[58] The theoretical foundations for Scandinavian legal realism, however, emphasized the ontological claim that everything that exists is to be found within the philosophical framework of logical empiricism.

56 Smith, Domstolene og rettsutviklingen (1975), Eng, *The doctrine of precedent in English and Norwegian law* (1993), Holmøyvik, Årsaker til utviklinga av prøvingsretten i Noreg og Danmark (2007).

57 Eckhoff and Helgesen, *Rettskildelære* (2001) ch. 3. Documenting the increase of this tendency, see Bergo, *Høyesteretts forarbeidsbruk* (2000), 90.

58 Alexander, Comparing the two legal realisms – American and Scandinavian (2002). For an account of Alf Ross's legal realism, see Blandhol, *Juridisk ideologi* (1999); Slagstad, Norsk rettsrealisme etter 1945 (1987).

Although this rather radical antinormative position extensively marked Scandinavian legal thinking, it further influenced legal thinking and practice following WWII, with the legal scholar Torstein Eckhoff as its primary driving force.[59] Improbably, in light of the leading realist Alf Ross' knowledge/evaluation dichotomy, the impact of legal realism survived through a renewed version of pragmatism, a position Ross had discarded as "methodless pear gruel."[60]

Modifying the realist view with elements of utilitarianism, Eckhoff continued the realist rejection of the metaphysical aspects of natural law. From a more pragmatic position, however, he explained the method of jurisprudence as a *balancing model* where a certain set of legal authorities (Eckhoff listed seven such authorities or "legal sources") are considered *relevant*, and where the various factors are interpreted separately and in conjunction, and then balanced against each other in order to establish a norm. Particularly through introducing judicial discretion as a factor of its own, by the term "real considerations" (*reelle hensyn*), he meant to open up judicial reasoning to expose what "really went on." While aiming at a more open judicial reasoning, the use of "real considerations" has, however, also had the opposite effect. Rather than describing *what* real consideration – as in what actual argument – weighs for or against an interpretative choice, unspecified references to "real considerations" and what this unspecified source dictate have sometimes blurred actual justifications. Viewed as a methodological principle, however, the way the introduction opens legal reasoning both formally and in practice for the explication of discretion at all steps of the interpretative/balancing process brings Eckhoff's realism close to a *pragmatist* position.[61] A feature of such a pragmatic approach to the law is its view of the consequences of the various legal interpretative alternatives; and, as such, to interpret a textual foundation so as to best realize its (assumed) purpose – and not necessarily the original purpose of the time the constitution or statute was written, but as much its assumed purpose at the time of interpretation. As explored further in the historical debates over review, what this pragmatic approach lacks in stringency and foreseeability, it gains in political flexibility.

59 Eckhoff, *Rettsvesen og rettsvitenskap i USA* (1953).

60 Ross, *Retskilde- og Metodelære i realistisk Belysning* (1931), 245.

61 Blandhol, *Pragmatismens aktualitet i rettsvitenskap og rettsanvendelse* (2004). This position, Blandhol argues, is not an Eckhoffian invention, but rather a continuation of a historical tradition central to Scandinavian legal systems.

2.4 THE BASIS FOR ECHR REVIEW

2.4.1 *Foundation and Scope of ECHR and ECtHR Review*

2.4.1.1 Background

The first steps toward the ECHR were taken in the Hague Congress in 1949, where parliamentarians from twelve Western European nations discussed a European human rights instrument with a court to enforce it. The Hague Congress gave the initiative to the Council of Europe (CoE), which continued to work out what would become the ECHR, established in 1950 and entering into force in 1953. It was inspired by the Universal Declaration of Human Rights (1948), and can be seen as a direct, European response by the Allied Powers to the atrocities committed during WWII; one of ECHR's central goals was to prevent such grave human rights violations in the future. Together with the growth of Communism in Eastern Europe, this historical experience served as a driving force toward an instrument protecting Europe against the development of authoritarian regimes.[62]

From the ECHR preamble it is clear that it aims to secure and to further realize some of the rights set out in the Universal Declaration of Human Rights, and that this aim is seen as a means to unite the CoE member states and reinforce democracy and human rights in Europe.[63]Although there were discussions over which rights to protect, and how to protect them, it seems clear, i.a. from the aim to create the ECtHR, that the parties were in agreement that the ECHR should be a *legal* instrument, rather than a political declaration. One consequence of this was the inclusion of monitoring bodies in the ECHR, an institutional feature setting it apart from contemporary international human rights instruments. Together with a Commission deciding on the admissibility and examining the merits of complaints, the ECtHR was mandated through art. 19 of the ECHR to supervise member states' observance of the convention.[64] The ECtHR, in the form of

62 This brief presentation of the ECHR historical background is inspired by Jacobs et al., *The European Convention on Human Rights* (2010), Dijk, et al., *Theory and practice of the European Convention on Human Rights* (2006), ch. 1; Nicol, Original intent and the European Convention on Human Rights (2005); Madsen, From Cold War instrument to Supreme European Court: The European Court of Human Rights at the crossroads of international and national law and politics (2007).

63 Convention for the Protection of Human Rights and Fundamental Freedoms, ETS no. 5 (1950), preamble.

64 On the role of the ECtHR in also enabling agreement on the ECHR, see Simpson, Hersch Lauterpacht and the genesis of the age of human rights (2004), 49ff.

a nonpermanent organ deciding through chambers of nine judges, was established on January 21, 1959, and pronounced its first decision in 1960.[65] The jurisdiction of the ECtHR has been recognized by all ECHR member states.

One central line of disagreement during the preparations of the ECHR is relevant to the theme of this book: the division into what may simply be seen as two "camps" – one viewing the convention and court as instruments serving to preserve the human rights already protected by the solid democracies of Europe; the other aiming for a more ambitious project of furtherance and development of the human rights protected by the various member states. It seems clear that while some member states, with British representatives in the lead, primarily wanted the ECHR to become an instrument preventing the descent into dictatorship presented by a fascist revival or a Communist coup,[66] others saw the centralized instruments for consistent human rights protection as sowing one seed to grow a tighter European integration alongside the economic and political integrative projects in Brussels.[67]

From the *Travaux Préparatoires* of the ECHR, a group of negotiating members made very clear that they were concerned that too open-ended rights formulations would open for "a thousand and one interpretations." Not wanting the ECHR to interfere with cases even of injustice if they occurred within functioning democracies, it was held forth as "of the utmost importance that we should confine ourselves to the essential rights to secure that the [states] remain democratic states."[68] The other camp, parts of which would also have economic, ethnic and gender equality protected by the convention, contended that the ECHR necessarily had to be "a living instrument" in order to be a "means to helping one another to watch and nip in the beginning any of that undermining process,"[69] as "democracies do not become Nazi countries in one day."[70]

What may be inferred from the *Travaux Préparatoires* is that there was no consensus either on the purely minimalist or the very broad federalist views on what the ECHR should be. This renders the *Travaux* a source of limited value when it comes to establishing *the* intention of the ECHR founders. From a legal perspective, preparatory material for conventions is also but

65 *Case of Lawless* v. *Ireland (No. 3)* (1961).

66 Nicol, Original intent and the European Convention on Human Rights (2005), 155.

67 Madsen, From Cold War instrument to Supreme European Court: The European Court of Human Rights at the crossroads of international and national law and politics, 143.

68 Council of Europe, Collected edition of the "travaux préparatoires" of the European Convention on Human Rights (1975), II, 60–62.

69 Ibid., II, 52.

70 Ibid., I, 292.

a supplementary means of interpretation.[71] For the purpose of this book, however, it is helpful to understand that the disagreement between a minimalism/restricted jurisdiction and a living and dynamic instrument view of the ECHR has followed the convention and its legal and institutional development since its very foundation.

2.4.1.2 Central Features of the ECHR and ECtHR

The ECtHR has states as parties, but with the possibility for citizens of these states to seek the court's jurisdiction. While the ECtHR also has jurisdiction over, and on rare occasions does try, interstate cases, these raise different kinds of legitimacy questions than do the cases that have become its main function: review of applications for redress of alleged state violations of individuals' human rights. In these individual complaints, the state–individual focus is central. Complaints are made in writing and registered with the Court. If admissible and referred to a Chamber (consisting of seven judges), the case is sent to the responding state for comments, before on some occasions brief oral hearings are held.

Decisions from the ECtHR are reasoned in writing, and its decisions present case facts, domestic proceedings, party arguments, relevant domestic law, relevant ECHR case law guiding the legal question to be decided and the court's own assessment and application of the guiding principles. To the extent that states are found to have violated the ECHR, the ECtHR may award damages, but may also serve as an effective remedy to the convention breach in itself by declaring the state was in violation. Findings of violations do not lead to annulment of domestic laws or administrative practices; it is up to the member states to alter legislation, interpretation or practices to the extent necessary to have them accord with the convention. And while the CoE Committee of Ministers supervises the execution of the Court's judgments, neither it nor the court has any enforcement mechanisms. Decisions by the ECtHR are legally binding on member states, and are usually complied with. This compliance rests, however, on the authority and continued acceptance of the court, not on any hard power.

Protocol 14[72] strengthened the Court's filtering capacity to deal with clearly inadmissible applications, i.a. through single-judge decision competence in admissibility cases, a new admissibility criterion concerning cases in which the applicant has not suffered a significant disadvantage and measures for

[71] VCLT art. 32.

[72] Protocol No. 14 to the Convention for the Protection of Human Rights and Fundamental Freedoms, amending the control system of the Convention, CETS no. 194 (2004).

dealing more efficiently with repetitive cases. It was adopted by the CoE Committee of Ministers in 2004, but did not enter into force until June 2010 due to opposition from some member states. Increasingly after 2000, legal, political and public debate intensified over whether the ECtHR struck the right balance between interfering too little or too much into the national legal-political affairs of ECHR member states. As of spring 2013, the structured discussions leading up to the 2010 Interlaken, 2011 Izmir and 2012 Brighton Declarations led to draft Protocols 15 and 16.[73] Protocol 15 aims i.a. to clarify the principle of subsidiarity, the margin of appreciation and the continued supervisory function of the ECtHR through a reformulation of the ECHR preamble; to lower the age limit for judge candidates; and to shorten the deadline for complaints from six to four months. Protocol 16 is an optional protocol opening for requests for advisory opinions from member-state high courts.

Of the various reforms, ECHR Protocol 11 has been of particular significance: It abolished the original two-tier system of a Commission and a Court,[74] merging their competences into the ECtHR as a permanent court to which all alleged violations were to be referred directly. Under Protocol 11, individuals may petition the ECtHR directly, after having exhausted national remedies, without having complaints treated by the Commission first. It also created the Grand Chamber – a Court-internal instance of appeal consisting of seventeen judges and deciding on exceptional cases referred by a screening panel.

The composition of the ECtHR is representative to the extent that each member state elects one judge, and there is always a judge from the state at trial in chamber. Following the 2010 Protocol 14 judges serve single terms of nine years. Three prospective judges are nominated by their member states, and one of these is appointed by the Parliamentary Assembly.[75] As for the independency of judges, ECHR art. 51 guarantees the privileges and immunities of judges. The independence, or appearance of independence, of ECtHR judges has, however, been subject to criticism,[76] as has the procedure for selecting and electing judges to the Court, the quality of and the experience of those judges.[77] This led to a series of recommendations for reform of

73 Steering Committee for Human Rights (CDDH) (2012) R76 Addenda III and V.

74 Convention for the Protection of Human Rights and Fundamental Freedoms, ETS no. 5 (1950) art 19 (before 1998).

75 Ibid. art. 22.

76 Miller, *The European Court of Human Rights: The election of judges* (2011), Hoffman, *The universality of human rights* (2009).

77 Interights, *Judicial independence: Law and practice of appointments to the European Court of Human Rights* (2003), 4.

the election process aimed at ensuring the quality of judges, and making the process more transparent.[78] Appointment procedures are not perfect, but reforms have enhanced the quality and independence of judges.[79] A 2011 study on attitudes toward the ECtHR shows that some countries – the United Kingdom, Ireland and Germany – are of the opinion that the Court could further improve the selection processes of judges at the domestic level.[80]

2.4.1.3 ECtHR Interpretative Method

Article 32 § 1 of the ECHR provides that the ECtHR's jurisdiction extends to all matters concerning the *interpretation* and *application* of the ECHR. The interpretation of the ECHR has been guided by the Vienna Convention on the Law of Treaties (VCLT) arts. 31 and 32, which mandate a purposive or teleological interpretation prioritizing an effectuation of the object and purpose of treaties and which includes the treaty preambles as integral to the context for its interpretation. As set out above, the ECHR preamble states interpretation of the convention should be aimed at "maintenance" and "further realization of Human Rights and Fundamental Freedoms." These two notions carry what have been termed the "evolutive" or "living instrument" interpretations of the ECHR, an interpretative style adopted early in the ECtHR case law which aims to "realize the aim and achieve the object of the treaty, not [to] restrict to the greatest possible degree the obligation undertaken by the Parties,"[81] and which see human rights treaties as "living instruments, whose interpretation must consider the changes over time and, in particular, present-day conditions."[82] "It is of crucial importance that the Convention is interpreted and applied in a manner which renders its rights practical and effective, not theoretical and illusory."[83] If the ECHR's rights are to be safeguarded according to its object and purpose, and neither the literal meaning of the words nor the intention of the drafters pose any clear limits to it, such an evolutive interpretation method seems a reasonable strategy. Still, the ECtHR is aware of the challenge inherent in this interpretative approach – the risk of interfering "too much," whatever that may encompass, into the sovereign rule of the member states.[84]

78 Summed up in ECtHR – Procedure for electing judges (2010).
79 Letsas, *Intentionalism and the interpretation of the ECHR* (2010).
80 Bruch et al., *The legitimacy of the ECHR: The view from the ground* (2011), 36.
81 *Wemhoff* v. *Germany* (1968), para. 8, series A no. 7.
82 *Tyrer* v. *the United Kingdom* (1978). 83 *Scoppola* v. *Italy (no. 2)* (2009).
84 European Court of Human Rights, *Dialogue between judges* (2011)

Balancing the effectuation of the ECHR against state sovereignty poses a continual challenge, one which has less to do with the ECtHR than with the dual aim of the convention. This dualism is closely related to that of the constitutional paradox: to protect the foundational rights of the member states' citizens, while at the same time keeping within the "constitutional" mandate given by states that remain sovereign, through their initial ratification and acceptance, and through the tacit consent of their remaining members of the evolving convention. This balancing remains a challenge because ECHR rights are open-ended. This, again, makes ample room for application to a number of such particular instantiations, even ones that were not envisaged in the first place. A number of cases exemplify this approach by applying the ECHR to situations not contemplated by its framers, yet still covered by the language of the convention, such as homosexuals enjoying the same protection for their private life and private expressions of their sexuality under ECHR art. 8 as heterosexuals,[85] or that judicial birching amounts to inhuman and degrading treatment as prohibited under ECHR art. 3,[86] to name but two examples. When not just one, but a very large number of instantiations under a right occur – as with the ECtHR caseload – the effects of ECtHR case law represent a significant exercise of power, simply through mapping out the details of already existing norms – norms that apply to all member states. While adopted, incorporated and repeatedly recognized by member states, this means the ECtHR continuously exists in a balancing position between effectuation of individual rights and respect for national sovereignty.

The abovementioned Brighton Declaration invited the Court to strengthen the *principle of subsidiarity* and the *margin of appreciation*.[87] These are two concepts central to the ECHR method of adjudication, concepts guiding the emphasis on respect for national sovereignty of the member states. The principle of subsidiarity carries the foundational notion that it is the member states that have the primary responsibility to safeguard the rights set out in the ECHR – either through legislative means, or as applied by administrative and judicial bodies on a national level. Recourse to the ECtHR by means of complaints is but a supplementary (subsidiary) means of ensuring that ECHR rights are in fact protected, if or when member states themselves fail to do so. Together with the *fourth-instance doctrine*, this principle may guide the ECtHR not to interfere in cases where it simply functions as another

85 *Dudgeon* v. *the United Kingdom* (1981). 86 *Tyrer* v. *the United Kingdom* (1978).

87 High Level Conference on the Future of the European Court of Human Rights, Interlaken Declaration, 19.22010; Council of Europe, High Level Conference on the Future of the European Court of Human Rights, Brighton Declaration, April 20, 2012.

appeals court; it will, however, accept and decide cases where national courts have not properly applied or balanced factors decisive under ECtHR case law. The margin of appreciation refers to the space for maneuvering that the ECtHR grants national authorities in satisfying their duties under the ECHR. Due to the heterogeneity of member states' cultural and legal systems, they enjoy a certain margin within which they can seek to fulfil their obligations under the convention – a margin which, if not overstepped, may lead the ECtHR to abstain from reviewing their national decisions. A central reason for this margin is the foundational value of state sovereignty and the significance of sovereign state consent to ECHR and ECtHR legitimacy. This issue – the balance between respecting state sovereignty while at the same time ensuring the most effective impact of the ECHR – continues to be a central task for the ECtHR. Thus serving both legal and political values, the margin remains a legal instrument resisting definitions of any doctrinal finality.

Following a general European revitalization of the idea of rights in the 1980s,[88] and particularly as a consequence of the accession of new member states after the fall of the Berlin wall in 1989, the ECHR system saw a sharp increase in the number of complaints in the decades leading up to 2000. To meet the challenges posed by this increase, several proposals were put forward with the aim of making the convention supervisory mechanisms more efficient. One of these, a work toward reform starting in 1993, led to the entry into force of Protocol 11 to the ECHR in 1998. This in many ways revolutionized the ECtHR as a practical institution of European law: While making the ECHR a much more efficient instrument for redress of human rights violations in the member states, rather than lowering the amount of complaints, it led to an increase. More than 91 percent of the ECtHR total decisions from 1959 through 2011 have been delivered since 1998.[89] Both the rise in the number of member states and the right to individual petition led to an explosive increase of cases.

In 1999, the number of pending applications was 12,600; in 2009 it had increased to 119,300. In 2012, for the first time since 1998, the stock of allocated applications pending before the Court decreased over the year, by 16 percent from 151,600 to 128,100.[90] As of June 30, 2017, this number is down to 80,300.

[88] Judt, *Postwar – A History of Europe since 1945* (2007), 564. See also Madsen, From Cold War instrument to Supreme European Court: The European Court of Human Rights at the crossroads of international and national law and politics.

[89] European Court of Human Rights, 4. Now more than 50,000 complaints are lodged every year, and there is ongoing work to reform aspects of complaint handling in order to make the system more efficient in filtering out less important cases, while still ensuring that those dealing with serious breaches or questions of principled interest are not overlooked.

[90] European Court of Human Rights, 4 (10.3.2013).

The main culprits – the caseload overflow – are clearly inadmissible cases (more than 90 percent of complaints) and repetitive cases stemming from the same flawed member-state systems (e.g. Italian lack of efficient court systems to meet the requirement that cases be tried within reasonable time as set out in ECHR art. 6). More than half of the pending caseload stems from former Eastern Bloc countries. As of 2017, the top three states in terms of pending cases are Ukraine, Turkey and Hungary.

Several reforms were brought about to meet the 1999–2011 caseload increase, both within the ECtHR itself and through additional protocols and other member-state initiatives. The most notable of these are the aforementioned Protocol 14 and the Interlaken Declaration in 2010, and the Brighton Declaration in 2012, enacting procedural reforms and producing action plans for a long-term reform process of the ECtHR. The Brighton Declaration did not go uncontested.[91] Early drafts were heavily criticized by several member states and NGOs, for threatening to weaken the ECtHR.[92] This led to several modifications of the original declaration proposal. In discussion of the modified proposal, then ECtHR president Bratza stated that

> The principal characteristic of a court in a system governed by the rule of law is its independence. In order to fulfill its role the European Court must not only be independent; it must also be seen to be independent. That is why we are, I have to say, uncomfortable with the idea that Governments can in some way dictate to the Court how its case-law should evolve or how it should carry out the judicial functions conferred to it. I would respectfully submit that these elements must be borne in mind in any discussion of proposals for reform. Convention amendment must be consistent with the object and purpose of the treaty and must satisfy the rule of law principles, notably that of judicial independence. The true test of any proposed amendment is the extent to which it will actually help the Court cope more easily with the challenges facing it.[93]

How exactly the measures following the Brighton Declaration will solve a problem which is primarily caused by the 90 percent of clearly inadmissible

91 An account presented by Rui, The Interlaken, Izmir and Brighton Declarations: – Towards a Paradigm Shift in the Strasbourg Court's Interpretation of the European Convention of Human Rights? (2013), who is critical of the legitimacy of the measures.

92 Amnesty International, the AIRE Centre, the European Human Rights Advocacy Centre (EHRAC), Interights, the International Commission of Jurists (ICJ), the Helsinki Foundation for Human Rights (HFHR), Human Rights Watch, JUSTICE and Liberty https://www.opensocietyfoundations.org/press-releases/joint-statement-strengthening-protection-human-rights-europe-0 (16.3.2013).

93 Address by Sir Nicolas by Bratza Friday 27 January 2012, 3; available at https://www.echr.coe.int/Documents/Speech_20120127_Bratza_JY_ENG.pdf).

complaints and repetitive cases is unclear.[94] What it signaled, however, was a national reaction, from at least some influential countries, to ECtHR judicial review in the internal sense – how the court interprets the ECHR. As foreshadowed above, a central dividing line in the history of member states' guiding legitimacy ideals between those wishing for the ECtHR mainly to prevent authoritarian regimes and those seeing it as a living, integrative instrument, has thus received a formal continuation. The last few years seem to show a tendency in ECtHR case law suggesting a shift toward an "operationalization of the principle of subsidiarity and the margin of appreciation," removing the Court from an inner, material control of national authorities to an outer, procedural control.[95] By this development, the focus of the ECtHR seems to emphasize more the legislative or judicial justifications in the member states: To the extent they have assessed and balanced the criteria relevant under ECtHR case law, the ECtHR will be more hesitant to conclude differently than the member states judicial bodies have done,[96] and thus to honor the principle of subsidiarity.

2.4.2 *Outline of ECHR Review in Norway*

Since the Norwegian acceptance of the ECtHR in 1964, both the ECHR and decisions from the ECtHR have sporadically been drawn into Norwegian legal practice. While very few cases mentioned or used the convention in any way up until around 1980, from then on such cases gradually came to occur more frequently. Searches in the Norwegian legal database "Lovdata" show a steady rise of ECHR mentions in Supreme Court case law between 1990 and 2000, from 9 to 56 cases in which the ECHR is mentioned. The respective numbers for mentions of the ECtHR – an indication that the ECHR has been discussed in some detail in the decision – is 0 and 4. The rise continues along a flattened curve from 2000–2013, giving an average of 75.9 and 18.6 cases per year mentioning the ECHR and the ECtHR respectively. The average number of cases decided in total per year in this latter period is around 500.

Norway is a *dualist* legal system; international conventions ratified by Norway do not become an integral part of national law absent some active

94 A point discussed also by Wessel-Aas, Effektivisering av subsidiaritet i EMK – En replikk til Marius Emberland (2013); Emberland, Effektivisering av subsidiaritet i EMK, ibid.

95 Rui, The Interlaken, Izmir and Brighton Declarations: – Towards a paradigm shift in the Strasbourg Court's interpretation of the European Convention of Human Rights? (2013), 54.

96 See i.a. *Lillo-Stenberg and Sæther* v. *Norway* (2014), *Salem* v. *Denmark* (2016), *Osmanoglu and Kocabas* v. *Switzerland* (2017).

implementation through transformation or incorporation. This dualist approach to international law is modified by a "principle of presumption" – a customary law principle of interpretation stipulating that Norwegian law is presumed to be in conformity with international law. This principle served as an interpretative review standard leading Norwegian courts to interpret some Norwegian rules differently from how they would have been without the unincorporated international rule. One early example of this is from 1966, when a 1956 regulation proscribing compulsory civil service for dentists was seen to be in accordance with ECHR art. 4.[97] And in 1984, the Supreme Court relied on ECHR art. 5 when concluding that a committed psychiatric patient had an actionable cause to have his forced commitment tried in court.[98] In certain areas, there were statutory regulations of precedence of international law, notably in the Civil Procedure Act (1915) § 36 a, and Criminal Procedure Act (1981) § 4.

The principle of presumption was modified by a "doctrine of clarity" under which rules derived from international legal obligations must be "sufficiently clear and precise" for Norwegian courts to rely on them, rather than decide the case based on established domestic law.

Concern about the ECHR position in Norwegian law was articulated in legal theory from the 1950s–1960s, with the later leader of the Human Rights Committee and Supreme Court Chief Justice Carsten Smith as one leading voice.[99] Law professor Torkel Opsahl held that the incorporation of human rights conventions into national law was the Alpha and Omega of actual and effective human rights protection. Gradually, and due to the unclear position and inconsistent use of the ECHR in Norwegian law, work toward incorporation started in 1989 and ended up as the Human Rights Act of 1999 ("the act on strengthening the position of human rights"). Under its § 3, it stated that "The provisions of the conventions and protocols mentioned in section 2 [hereunder the ECHR] shall take precedence over any other legislative provisions that conflict with them."

97 The case was dismissed from the Supreme Court in Rt. 1961 s. 1350, and the plaintiff brought it before the ECHR Commission. The Commission (by 6–4) found the regulation to be in accordance with the convention in 1963, but only after an extensive assessment under ECHR art. 4. It was thus upheld also in the Supreme Court, but only after a substantial assessment of the ECHR, see Rt. 1966 s. 476.

98 Rt. 1984 s. 1175.

99 Smith, Den internasjonale rettens innvirkning på den nasjonale retten (1962); Smith, Folkerettens stilling ved norske domstoler (1964). For an early analysis, see also Helgesen, *Teorier om Folkerettens stilling i norsk rett* (1982).

On the international level, the HRA almost coincided in time with Protocol 11 to the ECHR.[100] Norway signed this protocol upon its opening, and ratified it on July 24, 1995.[101] These two phenomena, which occurred closely related in time, have served as the two main driving forces for domestic Norwegian ECHR review since.

The ECtHR required that the national authorities "applied standards which were in conformity with the principles embodied in [the relevant ECHR article]" and that they "based themselves on an acceptable assessment of the relevant facts."[102] The Norwegian civil and criminal procedural systems generally meet the procedural requirements as set out in ECHR arts. 13, 35 and 41.

The total number of ECtHR decisions concerning Norway is modest. Of the forty-two total cases against Norway reaching judgment in the years 1959–2016, violations were found in twenty-eight cases.[103] These numbers are on par with or modest compared to those of the other Nordic countries,[104] and low compared to some other established democracies, even adjusted for population. This suggests that Norway, to a substantial degree, manages to live by the principle of subsidiarity and protect convention rights at the national level.

In 2000, the implications of the HRA for Norwegian courts' scope of review were clarified.[105] In interpreting the HRA provision of preference, the Supreme Court stated:

> Even though Norwegian courts are to employ the interpretative method of ECtHR when applying the ECHR, further development of the ECHR is for the ECtHR ... To the extent the case at hand mandates a balancing of conflicting interests or values, it must also be acceptable – within the method employed by the ECtHR – for Norwegian courts to rely on traditional Norwegian value prioritizations [*verdiprioriteringer*].[106] Particularly this must be the case where the Norwegian legislator has taken the ECHR into

100 ETS No. 155, opened for ratification on May 11, 1994, entering into force on November 1, 1998.

101 CoE Treaty Office, http://tinyurl.com/cjuayjg.

102 See i.a. *Jersild* v. *Denmark* (1994) § 31.

103 European Court of Human Rights Violation by Article and By State 1959–2016.

104 Ibid., showing that Finland and Sweden top the Nordic statistics with 139 violations of 186 cases in total, and 16 of 149 cases in total respectively, whereas Denmark has 15 violations of 46 cases in total.

105 Rt. 2000 s. 996, 1007–1008.

106 The expression "traditional Norwegian value prioritizations" is said to have come into the Supreme Court reasoning due to a discussion of the differing views of the biological principle in cases concerning child custody cases in Northern and Southern Europe. It has been argued that the reference to such traditional national values has not led to any less openness toward the ECHR in later Supreme Court case law – rather, the opposite: see Andenæs and Kravik, Norske verdier og EMK (2010).

> consideration and found no conflict. . . . Based on this, I am of the opinion that Norwegian courts, when in doubt about how to interpret the ECHR, are not to employ an interpretational method that is too dynamic. As a general rule, they are neither to interpret the ECHR in a way safeguarding against ECtHR decisions against Norway. Based on ECtHR practice and the values and traditions upon which our society is built, Norwegian courts must seek to appreciate how the ECHR is to be understood.[107]

Some aspects of the review-scope clarification found in this case have been challenged in later cases.[108] However, it still constitutes the basic guideline for Norwegian courts' review strategy under the ECHR.

Norwegian ECHR review relies on an institutional design that diverges from that of constitutional review in many respects. First, there is no formal constitutional rigidity. Where the ECHR itself is rigid (verging on the unalterable), Norwegian ECHR dependence is formally no more rigid than other legislative regulations. The HRA may be formally abolished through an ordinary legislative decision, thus voiding the superiority both of the ECHR and of ECtHR case law. And under Norwegian law, termination of Norwegian CoE-membership and ECHR ratification can be done without referenda and supermajorities.[109] What it lacks in formal rigidity, however, Norwegian ECHR review gains in countermajoritarian nature. While possibly considered less relevant as a check on developed democracies, and more as one on countries in greater need of such checks, acceptance of this nature was one part of the rationale for ratifying the ECHR, accepting the jurisdiction of the ECtHR and for incorporating the ECHR with the § 3 preference clause. While the supremacy of the judiciary lies with the ECtHR rather than the Supreme Court, it is still clear that there is a judicial, rather than legislative supremacy in Norwegian ECHR enforcement. The legal questions arising under the ECHR are decided with finality by a judicial not a representative body.

The lack of formal rigidity might void procedural, democratic skepticism toward ECHR review. A significant rigidity exists, however, through informal mechanisms. It is, at least presently, politically hard to envisage an abolishment or even significant modification of the HRA. Arguments calling for abolishment of ECHR membership, such as seen in the UK,[110] are rare.

107 Rt. 2000 s. 996. 108 Notably Rt. 2005 s. 833.

109 Constitution § 26 cf. § 28, and subject to the requirements set out in ECHR art. 58.

110 As by UK Prime Minister Theresa May https://www.theguardian.com/politics/2016/apr/25/uk-must-leave-european-convention-on-human-rights-theresamay-eu-referendum. See also Justice Secretary Liz Truss's call to repeal the UK Human Rights Act, which incorporates the ECHR in UK law: www.telegraph.co.uk/news/2016/08/22/new-british-bill-of-rights-will-not-be-scrapped-insists-liz-trus/.

Even if political winds were to change on this point, a 2014 constitutional reform amending central human rights provisions to the Constitution makes the consequences of such abolishment pointedly less significant: Ensuring central human rights the even stronger formal protection of being constitutionalized, the reform was also based on the premise that the new constitutional rights were to be construed in light of their international counterparts. This interpretative strategy is now established also by steady Supreme Court precedence.

3

Foundations Reviewed
The Formative 1800s

3.1 OUTLINE OF A NATION CONSTITUTED

An historical outline of Norway as a constitutional democracy has its fulcrum in 1814, a year in which more than 400 years of Norwegian union with Denmark ended and Norway adopted its own constitution.[1] The independence gained did not last long. Denmark had promised Norway to the Swedes under the Treaty of Kiel in 1814. Rather than agreeing to the new union arrangement, however, the Norwegians mustered opposition, and enacted their own constitution on May 17, 1814, electing the Danish Prince Christian Frederik, the resident viceroy in Norway, as their new king. The parties to the Treaty of Kiel did not accept this treaty breach, and over the summer of 1814 the Swedes effectively struck down the opposition, paving the way for a settlement between the two peoples: The Norwegian Constitution would, with the alterations necessary to have Norway become part of a Swedish–Norwegian union, remain in force, provided the Norwegians accepted becoming unionized. King Christian Frederik abdicated, and the Swedish–Norwegian union, which was to last until 1905, was established.[2]

The 1814 Constitution was inspired by the American Constitution of 1787, the French Constitution of 1791, models for division of powers and Kant's ideas of the centrality of the individual,[3] and established Norway as a constitutional monarchy. The royal power was to be limited through a division of powers between

[1] The following reconstructive outline relies on several works on Norwegian constitutional history, among them Holmøyvik, *Maktfordeling og 1814* (2011), Michalsen, *Rett. En internasjonal historie* (2011), Seip, *Utsikt over Norges historie* (2002), Slagstad, *De nasjonale strateger* (1998).

[2] See Mestad in Mestad and Michalsen, *Rett, nasjon, union* (2005).

[3] Among others; for further accounts and references, see Helgadóttir, *The influence of American theories of judicial review on Nordic constitutional law* (2006), 4, and Holmøyvik, *Maktfordeling og 1814* (2012).

three branches: the legislative, the executive (consisting of the King and his Norwegian ministers) and the judiciary. In addition to the separation of powers, the inspiration from John Locke's idea of a social contract under which the people retain their natural rights may be seen in the protection of some basic civil rights, such as the principle of legality, the prohibition of arbitrary punishment and retroactive laws and the protection of freedom of expression and of property.

The significance of the popular will is central also to the existence and durability of the Constitution. One expression of this can be found in the provision setting out the procedures for constitutional amendment in the amendment clause (then § 112): Alterations are premised on the recommendation of one Parliament, and then the adoption by two-thirds of the next Parliament following an intermediary election. In addition to the safeguards represented by the two-Parliament slow-down requirement and the two-thirds supermajority, the people also have a direct opportunity to influence the constitutional amendments by their ballot.

The Constitution has been considered radical; although balanced by mechanisms such as suspensive executive veto-power, power resided with the people, in contrast to the absolutist rule of the Danish monarchy.[4] This aspect of the Constitution was visible in the competencies apportioned to Parliament in the Constitution § 49. Approximately 10 percent of the total population were enfranchised, and about 40 percent of men above 25 years, a number significantly higher than that of other constitutional states at the time.[5] Throughout the 1800s, particularly toward the end of the century and in the first decades of the 1900s, the constitutional state slowly turned into a more democratic state. The electorate expanded in 1898 to enfranchise men in general, and in 1913 women were given the vote. Parliament was an important arena for public debates, particularly following its 1869 expansion of activities from its previous triennial to annual meetings.

Political and societal discussions followed the prevalent ideological ideas of the time: conservatism and liberalism. In comparison with most other European nations, including the Nordic countries, from early on liberal currents were influential in Norway. Theories of natural law were prevalent in the years leading up to and following the enactment of the NC.[6] Its founding fathers,

4 The Constitution marked some clear differences to the former Danish rule. For an account of elements from this legal period paving the way for the foundational constitutional ideas, including the development of judicial review, see Sunde in Michalsen, *Forfatningsteori møter 1814* (2008), 215ff.

5 Michalsen, *Rett. En internasjonal historie* (2011), 314.

6 See i.a. Mestad and Michalsen, *Frihetens forskole: professor Schlegel og eidsvollsmennenes læretid i København* (2013).

who were high state officials, had a strong position in Norwegian society throughout the 1800s, being centrally placed in executive, legislative and judicial posts, as well as taking on professorates in the formative years of the University of Oslo, established in 1811.

3.2 COURTS, LAWYERS AND BACKGROUND FOR JUDICIAL REVIEW

The 1814 Constitution contained no provision establishing the institution of judicial review.[7] When this practice nevertheless became a part of Norwegian constitutional law in the 1800s, as we shall see most formatively around the 1850–1860s, it came as a gradual development in the interaction between legal scholars' and courts' practice, as well as lawyers using constitutional provisions, and arguing their preferred position, as part of their litigation.

The 1814 Constitution protected some individual rights. Central were the protection against takings without due compensation (§ 105), the protection against retroactive legislation (§ 97), the principle of *nulla poena sine lege* (§ 96), the protection against house searches (§ 102) and the protection of free speech (§ 100). Of these provisions, relatively few have been frequently adjudicated. The ones provoking debate of judicial review have most often been (§§ 97 and 105).[8] The Constitution is formally rigid, as it can be amended only through political procedures that are more complex than those required for the enactment and repeal of ordinary legislation.

Courts are regulated under chapter D of the Constitution. Apart from provisions setting out the Court of Impeachment, the only provisions concerning courts are about the Supreme Court. By § 88, the Supreme Court is the last instance court ("has the last word"), and its decisions are, under § 90, nonappealable. The organization, funding, further competencies and setting up of lower courts are all left either to legislative regulation or development through case law.

An operative court system requires a functioning framework and sufficient capacity in the form of judges and funding. Throughout the 1800s and particularly the first decades of the 1900s, there were extensive debates on these questions – the courts needed funds to maintain efficiency and quality

7 No provision establishes explicitly the institution of administrative review either, yet the Supreme Court had exercised such review already in 1818. Administrative review is not further thematized here; for an account of its history, see Halvorsen, Schweigaard, Aschehoug og prøvingsretten som forsvant: bidrag til utviklingen av læren om prøving av skjønnsmessige forvaltningsvedtak (2011).

8 A full list is given in Dokument 16 (2011–2012), 4.3.

with an ever-increasing caseload, whereas the government and Parliament resisted, sometimes simply because there were no funds, at other times possibly also motivated by the opportunity to exercise some court control through allocating only temporary positions.[9] A study from 1988 notes that there were fewer judges at that time than in 1814 relative to the population at large, whereas the size of the administrative branch expanded by approximately seventy times from 1814 to 1988.[10]

With few exceptions, European constitutions in the first half of the 1800s had their main functions as political documents or declarations of popular will, rather than functional legal instruments.[11] The Norwegian Constitution, however, was from quite early on regarded not only as a legal document, but also as part of the positive law of the land. In this respect, it resembles the US Constitution. This quite unique feature of the Constitution is an important premise for the development of judicial review, which presupposes the existence of a (potentially) higher-ranked norm against which ordinary legislation may be reviewed.

The organization and early drafts of the Constitution support the view that the courts were meant to be subordinate to the other branches of government, and that the main aim for thoughts on division of powers was to balance the king against the people. As the Constitution was considered to be positive law, it did, however, leave the courts with an active, constitutional role.[12] The most obvious reason why the Constitution was considered positive and operative law was the scarcity of formal legislation in the first years immediately following 1814. The constitutional plan of enacting a general civil and criminal code did not come about,[13] and, pending this reform, very few civil laws were enacted during the decades immediately following 1814.[14] A substantial part of the early legal system was consequently left to the courts to develop, and they did this by looking to what legal sources they had for support.

9 Kierulf and Slagstad, Høyesteretts dommere (2015).

10 Eckhoff and Smith, Forvaltningsrett (1997), 87.

11 The following recollection relies on Holmøyvik, Årsaker til utviklinga av prøvingsretten i Noreg og Danmark (2007); Seip, *Tanke og handling i norsk historie* (1968); E. Smith, *Høyesterett og folkestyret* (1993). English publications on the subject include Slagstad in E. Smith, *Constitutional justice under old constitutions* (1995), and C. Smith, Judicial review of parliamentary legislation: Norway as a European pioneer (2000). See also Helgadóttir, *The influence of American theories of judicial review on Nordic constitutional law* (2006) and Kári á, *West-Nordic constitutional judicial review* (2013).

12 Holmøyvik, Årsaker til utviklinga av prøvingsretten i Noreg og Danmark (2007).

13 The first Criminal Act came in 1842 [Lov angaaende Forbrydelser af August 20, 1842].

14 Aubert, *Om den dømmende Magts Virksomhed som Kilde til Udviklingen af vor Ret ved Siden af Lovgivningsvirksomheden* (1865), 73, see also Sandvik and Michalsen, *Kodifikasjon og konstitusjon: Grunnloven § 94s krav til lovbøker i norsk historie* (2013).

The Constitution was not only seen as positive law, but also regarded as *lex superior*; § 94 of the Constitution stated that existing laws were only to be followed to the extent they were in conformity with the Constitution.

While contributing to clarify why the Constitution was considered positive law, several other historic and cultural aspects have been seen to play a part in explaining the particular Norwegian development of judicial review. The circumstances under which the Constitution was adopted seem important. As outlined, it represented an anchoring of the welcome, but very brief Norwegian independence in the spring of 1814 – thus rendering it a constitutional document heavily laden with national pride and a rare symbol of Norwegian sovereignty, which was possibly reinforced by the union period that lasted to 1905. The Constitutional protection of individual rights represented something new compared to the absolutist Danish monarchic rule, making it an encouraging source for anchoring the gradually emerging democratic and liberal ideas. And while the Constitution certainly created a new legal situation in the constitutional state of Norway, one important feature of the earlier Danish–Norwegian legal system resembled, and potentially created, a familiarity with the structure of higher-ranked norms trumping even enacted laws if contrary to equity or some vaguer notion of justice: During the 1700s, natural law not only supplemented positive law, but had also, at times, suppressed it, so that enacted legislation was set aside due to natural law norms.[15] Regarding natural law norms as part of positive law was thus an established possibility even before the enactment of and adjudication under the Constitution.[16] And the backdrop of natural law thinking as an integrated part of the legal system persisted. While natural law gradually became less influential in other European countries, and was depreciated by central legal scholars such as A. M. Schweigaard and (partly) F. Stang, in various forms it remained influential in Norway, defended on differing grounds by legal scholars H. Steenbuch, F. G. Lerche and T. H. Aschehoug.[17] This background may be one contributing factor to the legal community's arguments for and courts' development of judicial review.

Judicial review under the Constitution developed regardless of a reigning *departmentalist* view that each branch of government defined its own

[15] Sunde, "Ansees Hævet" – Føresetandar for utviklinga av den norske prøvingsretten på 1800-talet (2008).

[16] See, however, on the Kantian natural law scholar J. F. W. Schlegel and his influence on the Constitution founders, Mestad in Michalsen, *Forfatningsteori møter 1814* (2008), 31 f. and Mestad, *Frihetens forskole* (2013).

[17] Slagstad, *Rettens ironi* (2011), 49–57, Aubert, *Om den dømmende Magts Virksomhed som Kilde til Udviklingen af vor Ret ved Siden af Lovgivningsvirksomheden* (1865).

competencies.[18] There was certainly disagreement on both the existence and the scope of judicial review. Indeed, it was questioned whether the courts should even be considered a self-administered governmental branch. Consistent with French constitutional theory, influential Norwegian scholars argued that as Parliament enacted legislation and the executive appointed judges, the courts did not have a will of their own.[19] In addition to being disregarded by the courts, who from the early years acted very much as an independent branch, the theory of departmentalism was refuted by later scholars. L. M. B. Aubert pointed to how "without hesitation" the courts had tried acts of the other branches of government against the Constitution,[20] and T. H. Aschehoug, relying on case law and liberal theories of constitutional limits for the exercise of governmental power, held that the theory of departmentalism was simply "wrong."[21]

An important feature of Norwegian law developing at this time was that of *judicial precedent*. While closer to a civil law than common law tradition, there existed a dual view of adjudicative law in Norway: that which appeared to the judge at hand, and that existing in previous case law.[22] Accepting the effect of precedents implies accepting that courts not only *find* or *pronounce*, but also contribute to *expounding* or *constructing* law. There is, however, a jurisprudential difference between systems using precedents as an inspiration and those seeing it as a binding or more authoritative guideline. While precedent seems generally to have been agreed to be binding for later practice in the early 1800s, the more precise meaning of "binding" was not further theorized until the later 1800s, and in case law the view of precedents remained more pragmatic than formalistic.

In a central 1864 lecture, three drivers are held out as having contributed to the establishment of a Norwegian doctrine of precedent: The relative scarcity of legislation, leaving the courts to find the law, and to follow its own practice when appropriate; the increasing theoretical focus on this aspect of court practice; and the implications that the courts' own use of precedent had for other legal practitioners.[23] The discussions toward, and the 1863 legislation to

18 On Stang's position in 1833, and Aschehoug's later rejection of it, see Section 3.6; on the opposing views of Nellemann and Lasson in the 1860s, see Holmøyvik, Årsaker til utviklinga av prøvingsretten i Noreg og Danmark (2007), 743ff.

19 Ibid., 725, referring to Stang, *Systematisk Fremstilling af Kongeriget Norges constitutionelle eller grundlovbestemte Ret* (1833),67–68, and Falsen, *Norges Grundlov* (1818), 141–152.

20 Aubert, *Om den dømmende Magts Virksomhed som Kilde til Udviklingen af vor Ret ved Siden af Lovgivningsvirksomheden* (1865), 77.

21 Aschehoug, *Norges nuværende Statsforfatning III* (1893), 350.

22 Michalsen in Hagstrøm, *Ånd og rett – festskrift til Birger Stuevold Lassen* (1997).

23 See i.a. Ørsted, Haandbog over den danske og norske Lovkyndighed (1822), Lasson and Hurtigkarl, *Haandbog i den norske Processes første Deel* (1843), Brandt, *Repertorium for praktisk*

the effect that courts had to write down and make public the *deliberations* and *reasons* for their decisions, allowed for a normative effect not only of the conclusions in court decisions, but also of the reasoning *behind* these conclusions. The effect of precedent is important, in that the Supreme Court relied on its earlier use of the Constitution and reasoning based on similar arguments as those of review present in this earlier case law when developing the doctrine of judicial review. Indeed, the development of judicial review was in 1864 viewed as one of the clearest examples of Norwegian judge-made law.[24]

As documented in Holmøyvik's 2012 study on 1814 and the separation of powers, the Constitution and the early understanding of it was, to a much greater extent than in other European and Nordic countries, influenced by the idea of *liberal constitutionalism*. The ideas of individual rights protected from state intervention and of the constitution as the supreme law of the land from which all other valid legislation emanated were at this time foreign to both continental-European and British constitutional law. It was, however, central to theoretical and judicial writings on the US Constitution. Whether inspired by it, or originating in parallel due to similar understandings of constitutionalism, it may be noted that both the case of *Marbury* v. *Madison* and the commentaries of Joseph Story seem to have been known to central Norwegian jurists.[25]

> On the 19th of May, 1814, two days after the new Norwegian independence was realized by the election of Prince Christian Frederik to the throne of Norway, Christian Magnus Falsen, "the Father of the Constitution," became the father of a son. He was christened George Benjamin, George in honor of Washington, Benjamin in honor of Franklin. This is remarkable evidence of what the American example meant to this generation of Norwegians in their work and struggle for Norwegian freedom and independence.[26]

Not quite conclusive evidence, this story about one of the central figures behind the Norwegian Constitution, C. M. Falsen, foreshadows one important feature of Norwegian constitutional law, namely the US influence on the Constitution and on how it came to be viewed and used. References to the United States increased throughout the 1800s,[27] but were also visible at

Lovkyndighed (1855), Aubert, *Om den dømmende Magts Virksomhed som Kilde til Udviklingen af vor Ret ved Siden af Lovgivningsvirksomheden* (1865).

24 Aubert, *Om den dømmende Magts Virksomhed som Kilde til Udviklingen af vor Ret ved Siden af Lovgivningsvirksomheden* (1865).

25 Story, *Commentaries on the Constitution of the United States* (1833); see Holmøyvik, Årsaker til utviklinga av prøvingsretten i Noreg og Danmark (2007).

26 Castberg, *Norway and the western powers* (1957), 12.

27 For the later half of the 1800s, see Helgadóttir, *The influence of American theories of judicial review on Nordic constitutional law* (2006).

the time of the Constitution enactment. The historical and legal cultures of the common law in the US and the civil law in Norway are quite different, and Norway is also a unitary state. Under a federal structure judicial review is one means to maintain a unity of the many, like it was in one of the few other early European countries developing judicial review, Switzerland.[28] Norway had no such need for developing a review tradition. Still, the Norwegian development of judicial review resembles that of the United States in several aspects: judicial review is concrete and posterior to the enactment of legislation, it is initiated by parties outside the courts, comes about as part of the court's solving of actual conflicts, and the review competency rests with ordinary courts where hard cases are ultimately decided by one supreme court.

3.3 ON NOT LOSING SIGHT OF (SOME) INDIVIDUALS

The US influence was not limited to the theoretical legal debates. In the first Norwegian Supreme Court case to explicate judicial review in 1866, the formulation of the reasoning behind review so markedly resembles that made by Justice Marshall in *Marbury* v. *Madison* in 1803 that it has been seen to indicate quite clearly that Chief Justice Lasson knew of the Madison case and reflected its reasoning. This 1866 case, and the review debates preceding and following it, are the subject of the present chapter.

While the 1866 case was the first case to explain judicial review, examples of cases based on the same hierarchical logic as that underlying judicial review date back as far as the enactment of the Constitution.[29] Most of the review case law in the 1800s concerns questions of the privileges guaranteed to high state officials in the Constitution, which were affected by legislation emerging through the century. A case from 1822 has been held up as the first case in which the Supreme Court practiced judicial review:[30] The case concerned a claim for compensation from a high state official following new regulations that deprived him of some of the monetary privileges that he had expected upon assuming his position. While the regulation was not set aside as unconstitutional, the majority held that its negative effects must be compensated.

28 Cappelletti, Judicial review of legislation: European antecedents and adaptations (1966).

29 See generally Aschehoug, *Norges nuværende Statsforfatning III* (1893); Lie, *Betenkning angående grunnlovens §§97 og 105 og om domstolenes myndighet til å prøve loves indre gyldighet* (1923); Eckhoff, Høyesterett som grunnlovens vokter (1975); Andenæs, Høyesterett som politisk organ (1965); Slagstad, Prøvingsretten i det norske system (1989); Smith, *Høyesterett og folkestyret* (1993); Holmøyvik, Årsaker til utviklinga av prøvingsretten i Noreg og Danmark (2007).

30 Decision of December 10, 1822, discussed by i.a. Aschehoug, *Norges nuværende Statsforfatning III* (1893), 355–356.

Reference was made both to "general fairness" and to §§ 97 and 105 of the Constitution, under which retroactive laws are forbidden and takings of property cannot be done without compensation.[31]

Later legal theory has disagreed about whether judicial review was established as legal doctrine starting from the 1822 case itself, gradually in between,[32] in 1866,[33] or after the breakthrough of parliamentarism in 1884.[34] With regard to the period between 1822 and 1866, these differences are likely caused by differing views of what constitutes review (the mere use of the Constitution as a *lex superior* norm or the use of such a norm to the detriment of a legislative act or to differently interpret such an act) and of what it takes for legal decisions to become precedence of a kind establishing customary law. When this chapter focuses on the 1866 case, this is because it was the first in which the Court explicitly discussed its own review competencies,[35] and from which broader debate about judicial review arose.

3.4 REVIEW DISCUSSIONS PRIOR TO THE 1866 CASE

The question of review was discussed prior to the enactment of the Constitution. In the central constitutional draft of Adler and Falsen, review powers were in fact explicitly banned.[36] This draft provision was, however, not enacted. C. M. Falsen, a central founding father, later held that it was quite misleading to call courts "a judicial power," as the only branch of power in society was "the one enacting and executing laws."[37] Falsen also left out courts as arbiters of potential conflict between the legislative and the executive of a statute's constitutionality in his discussion of royal veto powers in 1924.[38]

31 As has been noted, there was hardly any contradiction between referring to fairness and the written Constitution alike, as the two types of norms – natural law and written constitutional law – were more closely tied together for the jurists of the time. Smith, *Høyesterett og folkestyret* (1993), 134–135.

32 Smith, *Høyesterett og folkestyret* (1993), 158, dates its establishment to the 1840s

33 Slagstad, Prøvingsretten i det norske system (1989). Slagstad's conclusion is motivated by a refutation of Seip's claim that review was only established as a politically motivated legal answer to the breakthrough of parliamentarism.

34 Rt. 1890 s. 455, held out by Eckhoff as the "first clear example of the Supreme Court setting aside a law as unconstitutional"; Eckhoff, Høyesterett som grunnlovens vokter (1975). As for the 1960s, Eckhoff held that while judicial review was no "foreign thought" to "some of the Supreme Court justices," there was not yet any general acceptance of this view. See also Seip, Den norske Høyesterett som politisk organ (1965).

35 Slagstad, *Rettens ironi* (2011), 358.

36 The Adler and Falsen draft for the Constitution, § 148.

37 Falsen, *Norges Grundlov, gjennemgaaet i Spørgsmaal og Svar* (1816), 148.

38 Falsen, *Bemærkninger i Anledning af Constitutions-Forslaget om Kongens Veto* (1824), 18.

In contrast to this, the first ordinary Parliament in 1815–1816 seems to have supposed judicial review competences as disregarding unconstitutional statutes.[39] An early opponent to Falsen's view was also the first professor of law at the University of Oslo, H. Steenbuch. While avidly defending the allocation of popular power to Parliament, he held there were some limits to this popular power: "No one . . . can be obliged to obey by an act of parliament to the extent that it is incompatible with the Constitution, a question the courts must decide with absolute judicial effect."[40]

A formative textbook on constitutional law in this period was written by then Assistant Professor F. Stang in 1833. He shared Falsen's view on the role of the courts, and consequently on judicial review: it was a competence he did not view courts as having unless a state power had *willfully* acted against a constitutional provision.[41] To subordinate the interpretation made by the legislative branch to that of the courts would "run counter to all conceptions of an ordered society."[42]

A formative discussion often cited in later writings concerning judicial review[43] is an opinion by two law professors, A. M. Schweigaard and U. A. Motzfeldt, about whether the abolishment of bakers' guild privileges would make the state liable for damages.[44] They concluded that it would not. Two of the possible causes for action analyzed are §§ 97 and § 105 of the Constitution. Although none of these causes were found actionable in the case at hand, the analyses are premised on the assumption that legislative acts must be in accordance with the Constitution. If they are not, this may generate state liability: Any law depriving a citizen of part of his estate for the common good would necessarily need to be understood so that this taking should be compensated – "and even though the law clearly denied such compensation, he would still have to be awarded it, as the constitution is stronger than the law."[45] Having established that there was no right to compensation by analogy for rights not amounting to "movable or immovable property," they held that "if there be any occasion where the constitution must be exclusively decisive and one must solely rely on [the Constitution], it must be when the question arises

39 See St. forh. des. 1815–16 and Skeie, *Den norske civilproces* (1940) I, 37. It may be noted that Skeie does not make this point in the 1929 first edition of his treatise.

40 Steenbuch, *Svar paa det fra Lehmanns Bogtrykkerie udkomne Skrift: Nogle Ord om Kongens Veto* (1824) s. 5.

41 Stang, *Systematisk Fremstilling af Kongeriget Norges constitutionelle eller grundlovbestemte Ret* (1833), 548.

42 Ibid., 546.

43 See i.a. Andenæs, Høyesterett som politisk organ (1965).

44 Schweigaard and Motzfeldt, *Det juridiske Fakultets Betænkning af 18 Januar 1841 angaaende Ophævelsen af det bergenske Bagerlaugs Privilegier* (1841).

45 Ibid., 291.

whether a legislative act contradicts the constitution and for that reason must be assumed false and without effect whether to the detriment of the private party or not."[46]

Munch-Ræder in the Ministry of Justice held review competence to be part of constitutional law. Interestingly, he pointed to a challenge represented by a written constitution in combination with review competences and duty. The trouble was posed to courts not when constitutional provisions were ambiguous, but rather when they were *too explicit*. Section 97 of the Constitution states that:

> no law must be given retroactive effect; perhaps making a constitutional provision out of this that is in any just system an accredited and obvious maxim. By it [it being explicated in writing], it has ceased to be but a rule drifting before the eyes of the legislator and the judge while being adapted to the circumstances; and become an absolute, stringent regulation. As such it is often hard to adapt, and it can place the judge who has to obey by the public [constitutional] and private [ordinary] law in painful embarrassment.[47]

Following an 1854 Supreme Court case in which an estate court official succeeded in claiming compensation following an 1851 Act lowering such officials' right to compensation, the Attorney General for Civil Affairs, B. Dunker, published a series of newspaper articles called "Should Courts Obey the Laws?" In it, he thematized the courts' review of legislation under the Constitution as deeply troublesome and of the utmost importance for the Norwegian constitutional situation: "When courts would refuse to obey the laws enacted by the legislative, this would be to betray the just case they are set to protect. . . . [Through the 1854 case] the Supreme Court has given a decisive precedent that there are occasions where it is not for the King and Parliament to have their common will."[48]

Professor of law T. H. Aschehoug, who later was to give the most extensive discussion of and arguments for judicial review, provided a defense for judicial review also in a lecture series in 1862–1863. As Norway was a nation of divided power (contrary to e.g. England, with its parliamentary sovereignty), there was nothing unorderly about challenging whether something that was in fact a law was legal. "It has furthermore been assumed by our courts that they are competent to review the constitutionality of statutes . . . As courts are

46 Schweigaard and Motzfeldt, *Det juridiske Fakultets Betænkning af 18 Januar 1841 angaaende Ophævelsen af det bergenske Bagerlaugs Privilegier* (1841).

47 Munch-Ræder, *Den norske Statsforfatnings Historie og Væsen* (1841), 197.

48 Slagstad, *Rettens ironi* (2011), 372–373.

competent to solve antimonies between statutes, they must also be competent to solve antimonies between statutes and the Constitution."[49]

"[A] radical defendant of popular power,"[50] P. K. Gaarder, also saw the Supreme Court as the guardian of the Constitution in an 1845 commentary: to the extent a statute was applied to facts older than its enactment contrary to the ban on retroactive laws in § 97, "it would not be upheld by courts."[51] "The duty, as well as the competence to refuse loyalty to an act by one of the governmental powers is dependent upon its illegality, and the resolution of this question in the end rests with the courts."[52]

In an 1862 article, lawyer J. P. Andresen held that courts not only had the right, but also the duty to interpret the laws, and thus also had the opportunity for or necessity of deciding according to the constitution rather than the statutory law – courts were, as in the US, an equal power to the legislative and executive. Contrary to the "unity of statutes," courts were "representatives of the diversities in life."[53]

More skeptical toward the "preponderant position" the "democratic element" had achieved, C. Winter Hjelm in 1863 held to be vital the "utmost independence of the courts from both the monarchy and the democracy" in order for them to ensure the limits set out in the constitution.[54]

In his 1864 lecture qualifying for a professorate (*konkurranseforelesning*), "The Judicial Branch," L. M. B. Aubert accentuated that the judiciary had in no way presented itself as a judicial *power* when acting as constitutional guardian. Conceding theoretical discussions had held controversial the question as to whether courts were competent to review the constitutionality of acts by the other branches of government, courts had "without further ado reviewed and found unconstitutional not only royal decrees and parliamentary plenary decisions, but also actual legislation." Giving examples of such review, he emphasized,

> it is also certain that the judicial branch is the guarantor for individuals' constitutional rights towards the other branches. Indirectly the judicial

[49] Slagstad, *Rett og politikk: et liberalt tema med variasjoner* (1987), 53; Aschehoug, *Norges nuværende Statsforfatning* (1875–1885).

[50] Slagstad, *Rettens ironi* (2011), 379.

[51] Gaarder, *Fortolkning over Grundloven og de øvrige Love, som danne Norges Riges offentlige Ret* (1845), 453.

[52] Gaarder, *Fortolkning over Grundloven og de øvrige Love, som danne Norges Riges offentlige Ret* (1845), 350.

[53] Andresen, *Norsk Folkeblad og Regjeringsadvokat Dunker om den dømmende Magt*, Aftenbladet March 30, 1869. See Slagstad, *Rettens ironi* (2001), 365.

[54] Hjelm, *Om Grundlovens Principer og den Aand, hvori de under gjensidig Begrændsning ere gjennomførte i dens enkelte Bestemmelser* (1863), 53.

> branch could, and has also had occasion to, be in the position to review the relationship between the other governmental branches, i.a. the King's privilege to establish courts, to levy taxes through awarding tax decisions from Parliament retroactive effect, or through temporary decree to raise customs duty.

The same would be the case where, for example, one wanted to sue a minister for damages for an unconstitutional act, the natural remedy for such acts to be impeachment.[55]

3.5 THE 1866 CASE

The 1866 case concerned an Act of 1857, following which naval officers (a type of high state official) could be called upon to lead recruitment commissions as part of their duty – without further payment. Captain Lieutenant Wedel-Jarlsberg sued the state, claiming the 1857 Act infringed on the privileges that the high state officials had under the Constitution § 22, which, in addition to stating that these officials could not be removed from office absent judicial decision, also protected them against being assigned burdens other than those taken on at the time of their appointment.

Following a central tradition in these early high-state official constitutional cases, the argument under § 22 was combined with a claim under the ban on retroactive laws in § 97. The reasoning in these cases was often combined explicitly or implicitly with the provision in § 105 protecting "property" in a wide sense, and mandating due compensation for any taking of such property. With this construction, legislation infringing on established privileges or adding additional burdens could be challenged as unconstitutional through a claim for *compensation* based on the unconstitutional actions, rather than as a claim that the unconstitutional acts and orders under them were void. The construction in these cases may be seen as a very concrete understanding of the social contract (between the state and these privileged citizens) – a contract of constitutional rank ordering compensation for certain types of contractual breach.

The Supreme Court, by a 4–3 vote, found for the plaintiff. Justice Løvenskiold held for the majority that high state officials were indeed protected against new burdens under the Constitution, and that the 1857 Act ran counter to this system. He referred to an 1854 case (the case that spurred the acting Attorney General for Civil Affairs Dunker's series of articles against

55 Aubert, *Om den dømmende Magts Virksomhed som Kilde til Udviklingen af vor Ret ved Siden af Lovgivningsvirksomheden* (1865), 77.

review mentioned earlier), and affirmed that case to be "well reasoned." He also affirmed an 1862 case in which the 1857 Act had been found unconstitutional, stating he did not doubt its reasoning, and with it would find for the plaintiff's claim in the current case. This did not, he emphasized, represent any disrespect for the legislative branch, which "like any human power may be in err." When it did err, and its error was clearly unconstitutional, such as in the present case, "the courts have a right to stride in."

Justice Blich for the minority agreed to this reasoning, but did not find the burdens added burdensome enough to mandate compensation.

In a concurring opinion acknowledged by Løvenskiold, Chief Justice Lasson joined the majority, but added i.a. the following reasoning to the principled question of judicial review: "What has the Supreme Court to do, when presented at the same time with the Constitution and a private statute? It has then, as far as I know constitutional law, been generally agreed that as one cannot place it upon the courts to uphold both these laws at once, they must necessarily give preference to the Constitution."[56] As this is done in the least offensive and most indirect way – by awarding compensation to the plaintiff rather than holding the statute to be void – this way of solving a dispute between a statute and the constitution appears "far more natural, and for the individual and the society far more becoming, than the holiness which the Attorney General views the legislative branch as, even when it legislates contrary to the constitution."

3.6 ARGUMENTS FOLLOWING 1866

The 1866 case was cited in later cases, although there were still disagreements and dissents in the Supreme Court, about both courts' review competences and the scope of review.

Whether caused or re-kindled by the 1866 case, vigorous public debate of review and the courts' role arose in the wake of it, particularly in 1869.[57] Chief Justice Lasson published a theoretical defense for judicial review in which he

56 Lasson's separate opinion in the majority of four. Cf. Justice Marshall's wording in *Marbury* v. *Madison* (1803): "So, if a law [e.g., a statute or treaty] be in opposition to the Constitution, if both the law and the Constitution apply to a particular case, so that the Court must either decide that case conformably to the law, disregarding the Constitution, or conformably to the Constitution, disregarding the law, the Court must determine which of these conflicting rules governs the case. This is of the very essence of judicial duty. If, then, the Courts are to regard the Constitution, and the Constitution is superior to any ordinary act of the Legislature, the Constitution, and not such ordinary act, must govern the case to which they both apply." (5 U.S. 137, 177–78).

57 As observed by Slagstad, *Rettens ironi* (2011), at 384ff.

concluded that the institution of review was indeed the "highest and final civil guarantee of a liberal society."[58] Where his colleague, Justice Løvenskiold, in the 1866 case had pointed to courts' *right* to review, Lasson argued that "[t]he Constitution is and remains the highest law of the land, and it must thus be the *duty* of the judiciary, in a dispute between the Constitution and the private laws to follow solely that law, the binding power of which is highest." This preference for the constitution would need to remain respected, whether the legislative overstepping of constitutional limits was intended or not.

The debate ensued in the papers. Author Bjørnstjerne Bjørnson commented on a proposal brought forth by Ole Richter (MP) to alter the conditions for becoming a high state official and to make possible alterations to their contracts without compensation. Bjørnson saw this as one potentially popular effort to counter the power arrogated by courts to the detriment of Parliament, an arrogation thrice criticized by Dunker, which could now possibly gain some help from the "popular opinion" awakened by Richter's proposal. This momentum preceded a debate between attorneys J. Ebbell and J. P. Andresen, who supported review, with reference i.a. to case law establishing precedent, and Dunker, who continued to argue against it.

Andresen argued that review competencies followed from courts being courts: "the ordinary competencies of legal interpretation as assigned to courts, applied to the Constitution,"[59] and emphasized the double function of courts as adjudicators of majority enacted laws as well as guarantors for individual rights. He contrasted this to the general focus of Parliament, which "even attended to with the utmost care" could lead Parliament to "lose sight of the right of the individual."[60] He also pointed to how the Supreme Court did not have the final word about the Constitution: Under its amendment clause, Supreme Court interpretations of the Constitution could be brought before the "Supreme tribunal of a free constitutional system: The sovereignty of the people."[61]

Ebbell underlined the argument from institutional difference by contrasting the diverging actual competences of the legislative and the judiciary: While "equipped with the highest degree of power, Parliament was composed per quite different criteria than that of legal professionalism."[62] Arguing that review was no novel Norwegian invention, he also referred to how review had

58 Ibid., with reference to Lasson, Supplement og Ord- eller Realregister til det i 1868 trykte Skrift om "Straffeprocessen i dens nyeste Skikkelse m. v." (1869).

59 Andresen, *Aftenbladet*, March 30, 1869.

60 Andresen *Aftenbladet*, April 3, 1869 (Stortinget, som "fra det alminneliges Standpunkt . . . selv med den største Omhu, kan tabe synet for den Enkeltes Ret").

61 Andresen, *Aftenbladet*, March 30, 1869.

62 Ebbell, *Aftenbladet*, March 13, 1869.

for decennia been exercised in the United States, "the most democratic system in the world."[63]

As opposed to his 1854 rejection of review, Dunker now conceded courts had this right to review, but questioned whether "this right" that "admittedly is the province of our courts" was also one to review a statute that "does not run counter to any constitutional provision, but solely to *some principle* of which one in the constitution may well find some limited expression of application, but which the courts would use outside those limits that the constitution has set for its application."[64] This timbre makes sense in light of Richter's proposal, which, contrary to Supreme Court precedent under § 22 of the Constitution, aimed at obliging high state officials to accept alterations to their contracts as established by later legislation, without being entitled to compensation.[65] To the extent judicial review was to have the effect that it represented the authoritative interpretation of constitutional limits, such a proposal could not have been made into law absent constitutional amendment altering § 22 pursuant to the amendment clause of the Constitution.

Some months later, Richter's proposal was debated in Parliament. Richter found it peculiar that the "legislative's competence to act within its own sphere" was repeatedly held in doubt as a subject for legal process and decision.[66] The guarantees awarded to officials ought to be sought "in something larger and stronger than the courts' mediation ... namely in the confidence that the branch in which the Constitution had vested legislative power would use and not abuse this power." It could not "interfere with the right of the individuals without endangering its own very existence." He had the support of representative Hammerstad, whose reasoning was that high state officials' privileges were unfair: "many laws have been given, of the highest inconvenience to private citizens, but he could not ask the state for compensation therefore."[67]

Representative Michelsen, conversely, held voting for the proposal to "infringe upon the Constitution" (and in this view he was followed by Schweigaard and Aschehoug).[68] He asserted they who believed that courts as a rule held for the high state officials in the cases brought before them were wrong, as he "had a list of cases decided documenting that the courts in the great majority of cases had *not* found for the high state officials."[69] Also against

63 Ebbell, *Aftenbladet*, March 13, 1869.

64 Dunker, *Aftenbladet*, April 24, 1869 (emphasis added. For a continuation of this argument, see Skeie's view of precedent under the Constitution § 97 in Section 4.3 and Fleischer's view of precedent under the Constitution § 105 in Section 5.5.

65 St. forh. 18. 06. 1869, 1200 ff. 66 Ibid., 1201. 67 Ibid., 1210. 68 Ibid., 1211–1213.

69 Ibid., 1211 (emphasis added).

the proposal was Vogt, who refuted the assertion that the privileges of the high state officials placed them in a different class than ordinary citizens under the Constitution, "as any citizen may call upon the Constitution against the law."[70]

In support of the proposal (and often cited in later studies critical of review[71]) was the leader of the opposition, J. Sverdrup: "Should a Supreme Court decision stand above the decisions of Parliament and the Government, the sovereign powers? Was there anyone, who dared say that those 7 gentlemen were wisdom incarnated, ranging above as providence for us to bow to? It would be crazy to assert such a thing." Conceding that court precedent indeed existed, Sverdrup held that "the Supreme Court in this had far exceeded its competences. It was therefore about time to set a limit for them [the courts] muscling in on what solely belonged with the sovereign branches."[72]

This view was countered by Aschehoug, who pointed out that this development was not particular to the Norwegian situation; it was indeed a central tenet of i.a. the US constitutional system. Further, "[o]ur Constitution §§ 97 and 105 rested on just the same assumptions, [73] that it was not impossible that the branches of government could happen to interfere with individual rights." Even though Sverdrup had claimed sovereignty to be solely in the hands of one authority, "this was not the view of the Norwegian Constitution." The Supreme Court was not there to "decide what was in the best interest of the state, but it was there to decide what was the law of the land, and it was no strange thought to the Constitution that the courts were the most competent authority in this province."[74] Schweigaard seconded this, and added that "an absolute sovereignty had the inevitable property of wanting to permeate everything; new evidence for this could be found in a party in the US that wanted to abolish courts' competence to review the constitutionality of congressional acts" – an "aggregation of sovereignty quite in conflict with the ideas of the founding fathers."[75]

In the 1880s, Aschehoug wrote extensively on courts' competences in his treatise on constitutional law. His thesis was that judicial review was part of

70 Ibid., 1205.

71 See i.a. Lie, *Betenkning angående grunnlovens §§97 og 105 og om domstolenes myndighet til å prøve loves indre gyldighet* (1923); Innst.S.nr 237 (2008–2009); Lejman, *Festskrift tillägnad professor, juris doktor Karl Olivecrona* (1964).

72 St. forh. 18.6.1869, 1212.

73 Aschehoug maintained that the USC had two provisions equaling § 97 of the Constitution. This is not correct: the USC contains no general ban on retroactive legislation, only on retroactive *criminal* legislation. See USC Article I, Section 9, Clause 3, directed to Congress; and Section 10, Clause 1, directed to the States.

74 St. forh. 18.6.1869 case no. 2, 1214.

75 Ibid., 1215.

Norwegian constitutional law. As a precursor to his argument on constitutional review on legislation, he considered – and refuted – the position of departmentalism, namely that "it is for every individual branch of government ultimately to decide its own competence . . . This assertion is not right."[76] Like citizens, governmental branches must interpret regulations relevant to their position *before* taking action. Solving the conflict arising following an act committed *pursuant* to such interpretation, which is then contested as wrong by someone, creates an entirely different situation: "There is no explanation of the concept judicial assessment which does not omit the former and include the latter part of this situation." Aschehoug presents four arguments for assigning this power of review to courts: They are, "by their nature," more *apt* to solve pure questions of law than are other authorities. Further, they are more *experienced* in following this "particular call." Courts are also in the particular governmental position of having only one goal to look after: "No other societal interest is designated to their care than that of rule of law." And, finally, the procedure by which courts work is particularly beneficial: The contradictory process is "more than any other well suited to bring about the multifaceted analysis necessary to assess a disputed question of law . . . These arguments speak nothing, however, about any superior position for courts; such superiority is a faulty assumption." For one, courts have no competence to review whether laws are appropriate, due or fair – merely whether they are right. And even this question they cannot consider on their own initiative, solely to the extent a question is brought before them, and then binding only upon the parties to the case at hand.[77]

Having established that the theory that every branch of government is the final guardian of its own competence lacks foundation and is not Norwegian law, Aschehoug opened his chapter on judicial review by listing two arguments against this competence: that of imbalance in the branches of government – if the courts could disregard legislation of which both Parliament and the King approved, it would place the courts above the two other branches, even though it was but one among them. This would, in turn represent a second challenge in that it would be unfair, disrupt the foreseeability of the legal system and obstruct the work of the other branches.[78] He explained these objections as being an argument that the legislative and executive branches are free to breach the constitution once they agree upon it, and rejected such a view as "an arbitrary refusal of the necessary consequences of the given premises": The founding fathers set out limits for governmental

[76] Aschehoug, *Norges nuværende Statsforfatning III* (1893), 350–351. [77] Ibid.

[78] Ibid., 362.

power not just to stipulate what was just and convenient, but precisely because they realized that power could possibly be abused. Granting the legislature a right to breach these limits would make it sovereign, which it is not in a constitutionally limited system. Rather than being the nation's sovereign in cases where it agrees with the King, in our system the legislature was instead to be regarded "the agent of society and the constitution its power of attorney."[79] Instances where "the constitution is disregarded by the other branches cannot free *courts* from their duty to follow the constitution. This is so, even if it is clear that the enacted law is representative for the legal opinion of a majority of the people."[80]

3.7 LIBERAL CONSTITUTIONALISM DEFINED

In the early legal debates, the main argument against review seems to have been the argument from the rule by *popular sovereignty* as emphasized by Stang, Dunker, Bjørnson, Richter, Sverdrup and others. Support for this conception of sovereignty was also based on a view of the proper balance between branches of power. A central premise for this argument was Falsen's and Stang's understanding of the division of powers as one primarily between the King and the people, and their consequential rejection of courts as a separate branch: The judiciary had no room for independent decision-making, but were merely there to apply the will of the people on the facts of the case. In addition to this is the *textualist* argument: Judicial review has no basis in the constitution. Powerfully voiced by Sverdrup are the *countermajoritarian difficulty* and the outcome skeptic *political* arguments: That there is no reason to believe that courts are any better at deciding political questions than is Parliament.

Apart from the legal argument of pointing to legal authority when established (or alleged established) through precedent, the central arguments for review in this period seem to be the *lex superior* argument,[81] by which courts must necessarily prefer the higher law before the lower, and the rule of law-aspect of *legality* (whether a law is really a law if it conflicts with the Constitution). In themselves, these arguments need support of an argument for why the higher law cannot simply be considered with finality by Parliament itself. Such are found either in the prevailing *division of powers/ power balance* argument or in the *legal questions for courts* argument.

79 Ibid., 364 ("ikke Samfundets uindskrænkede Herre, men dets Fuldmægtig og Grundloven dens Fuldmagt").

80 Ibid., 364. 81 Steenbuch 1824, Gaarder 1845, Winter Hjelm 1863, Aubert 1864.

The emphasis on courts' competencies points to the different logic and province in making general laws aiming forward, and applying these general rules in concrete cases. It seems to be deduced from one or more of the three following bases: The Constitution's chapter on courts competencies; the legal professionalism and courts' specific training in applying law in particular cases, and in resolving conflicts (and serving as safety valves) – and/or the institutional difference between Parliament and the courts: one aiming at regulations for the many, the other at upholding these collective regulations as well as protecting the individual.

The *constitutional* argument – that the constitution limits what political power could legally be exercised, is closely connected to the *liberal* argument of natural or inherent rights residing with the people (some more than others), following the social or constitutional contract.

A mediating argument seems to have been that of the particular *form* in which Norwegian review was effectuated, as emphasized by Chief Justice Lasson in the 1866 case: The law in question was not voided, courts merely awarded the plaintiff compensation for the constitutional breach. Another mediating argument was that it was not the courts, but Parliament who was in reality the *final arbiter* of the constitution: If unhappy with the Supreme Court's interpretation of the constitution, Parliament could choose to use its powers under the amendment clause to alter the Constitution. The debate surrounding Richters proposal suggests that the *final arbiter*-argument may not have been too central. This interpretation is supported by the proposal neither being presented nor discussed as anything mandating a constitutional amendment, even though many of Richter's opponents argue that his proposal runs counter to the Constitution. One possible reason for this is the relative novelty that the concept of review seems to have presented to several of the MPs when debated in 1869. Further, Dunker's arguments that it is the Constitution, not the Supreme Court interpretations of its provisions that places limits on the legislative scope, may have been shared by some. This view remained part of review debates in the 1900s, not least in the period leading up to the 1976 *Kløfta* case.[82]

As for the scope of review, apart from in cases of *intentional breach* of the constitution, judicial review would in Stang's view "run counter to the entire idea of an ordered society."[83] Where Stang reserved review competence for legislation willfully enacted as unconstitutional, Aschehoug held that courts

82 See Section 5.5.

83 Stang, *Systematisk Fremstilling af Kongeriget Norges constitutionelle eller grundlovbestemte Ret* (1833), 547.

have the *duty* to review also legislative "misunderstandings" of the constitution. Nevertheless, where the legislature had carefully considered an act to be constitutional, this was indeed a weighty argument against review, and courts should not reject legislation of this kind if they themselves were to find the unconstitutionality ambiguous.[84] This part of review doctrine has, as we shall see, to varying degrees remained central to the understanding of the scope of review up until today.

The *American* argument discussed by Schweigaard, Aschehoug and others, is used not only as proof that judicial review existed and worked elsewhere, but also as an argument against those skeptical that review could lead to abuse. There were safeguards against review abuse, Aschehoug maintained, such as legislative amendments to the constitution and impeachment of abusive justices. Citing Cooley,[85] Aschehoug pointed out that not only has the US Constitution never been altered to counter a judicial interpretation of it, also neither of the two instances of cases against a judge led to impeachment. He held the "about one hundred year long" US practice of judicial review to be one "with which one on the whole seems very satisfied." "The US experience proves that judicial review, far from creating the disorder and disadvantage feared by many European jurists, is instead one of the best guarantees for rule of law, albeit ostensibly not always entirely sufficient."[86] Although prevalent as an early line of *defense* for the legitimacy of judicial review, the American argument eventually turned into, and seems to have survived mainly as, a tool for those skeptical of review.

84 Aschehoug, *Norges nuværende Statsforfatning III* (1893), 370.

85 Cooley, *A treatise on the constitutional limitations which rest upon the legislative power of the States of the American union* (1868).

86 Aschehoug, *Norges nuværende Statsforfatning III* (1893), 364–365.

4

The Emerging Regulatory State and a Constitutional Watershed (Early 1900s)

4.1 CONSTITUTIONAL QUESTIONS ARISING – AND DISCUSSED

The period between 1909 and 1930 represents the most active period in the Supreme Court's exercise of judicial review – "a culmination of the Supreme Court's attempt to put on airs," as later formulated by historian J. A. Seip.[1] A shifting state–citizen balance, new regulatory regimes necessitated by an increasingly industrialized society and particularly the more intense debates on these issues following the 1905 independence from Sweden have been pointed out as likely drivers for this development.[2]

Following the growth of social regulations to benefit the common good, tensions between individual and common interests increased. Three constitutional questions came to be discussed as part of this tension of the emerging regulatory state: how to interpret the ban on retroactivity and protection of property clauses in the Constitution §§ 97 and 105 in general, and in relation to desired regulations; whether judicial review *existed*, and, if so, what its proper *scope* was; and, not least, whether undesired constitutional effects could be eliminated through altering or amending the Constitution. The constitutional amendment clause (then § 112) at the time read:

> If experience shows that any part of this Constitution of the Kingdom of Norway ought to be amended, the proposal to this effect shall be submitted to the first or second Parliament after a new General Election and be publicly announced by print. But it shall be left to the first or second Parliament after the following General Election to decide whether or not the proposed amendment shall be adopted. Such amendment must never, however,

[1] Seip, Høyesterett som politisk organ (1964).

[2] Slagstad, Prøvingsretten i det norske system (1989); see also Eckhoff, Høyesterett som grunnlovens vokter (1975) and Smith, *Høyesterett og folkestyret* (1993), 186 with further references.

contradict the principles embodied in this Constitution, but solely relate to modifications of particular provisions which do not alter the spirit of the Constitution, and such amendment requires that two thirds of the Parliament agree thereto.[3]

While the procedural requirements set out to ensure a supermajority and allow for popular participation through the intermediate election did not present much of an interpretative problem, legal and political opinions were divided on whether the "principles and spirit" that amendments could not contradict amounted to a *legal* limit, and, if so, what this limit implied in practice. To the extent Parliament wanted to alter or abolish §§ 97 and 105 – or, indeed, judicial review – could this be achieved without running counter to the material constitutional limits of constitutional amendment? This latter question primarily arose in connection with discussions of alternation/abolishment of §§ 97 and 105. The three issues – the scope of §§ 97, 105 and then 112, and the existence and scope of judicial review – arise in connection with each other. To some extent they also influence each other, particularly as the scope of judicial review may be decisive for the interpretation of §§ 97 and 105. Whilst attempting not to undercommunicate the interconnectedness between the scope of review under the two provisions and the question of judicial review in general, this chapter aims to focus on the latter.

In the following, examples are sought from judicial review debate as expressed in three fora: constitutional case law, legal opinions and parliamentary debates. These examples seem, in various ways, to be particularly representative for an analysis of the legal-professional and political attitude toward judicial review in Norway in this period. One constitutional case, Rt. 1918 s. 403, is analyzed and followed because it is the only case in this period in which the question of judicial review *existence* and *scope* is explicitly discussed.[4] It is also a case that has continued to be a reference point for discussions of judicial review since its decision. Surrounding the case are three legal opinions. These are central in that they represent prominent legal thoughts on the issue of judicial review in this period, because they remain influential in later scholarly writings on the issue and, most importantly, because they are formative for the parliamentary debates. Following the aforementioned tension created by the increasing social regulations, a number of legal opinions are commissioned and formulated in this period, mostly relating to the Constitution §§ 97 and 105.[5] Many of these at

3 The Constitution § 112, as amended on July 7, 1913.

4 It is not, however, the first case in which review is explicitly discussed, as claimed by Seip, *Tanke og handling i norsk historie* (1968), 100, as expounded in Chapter 3.

5 I.a. Rt. 1914 s. 208, Rt. 1914 s. 289, Rt. 1914 s. 881, Rt. 1915 s. 1041 (at this point in time, opinions were often printed in the case law legal reporter *Retstidende*; "Rt.," which remains the official citation for Supreme Court cases).

least indirectly touch upon the question of judicial review, as varying views on the standards and intensity of review influences the interpretation of the two constitutional provisions. Three of the opinions analyzed in this chapter are selected because they deal more directly with the question of review, whereas the one indirectly treating it (Jon Skeie, 1917) is included as it has become a later reference point in legal and political discourse.

The parliamentary debates in this period are the only historical instances of political proposals to abolish the institution of judicial review. Such institutionalized, political debate seems central to any assessment of judicial review legitimacy within a national setting, particularly given the underlying premise that it is indeed the parliament which is challenged by the exercise of review. The aim of the following analysis is to extract the arguments to be found – and, where pertinent, also to question their viability.

4.2 THE WATERFALL CASE

The formative case from this period, decided in 1918, concerns the Norwegian regime for the management of waterfalls.[6] It was part of a social reform strategy representing a significant building block in the emerging regulatory state, and the discussions related to this strategy brings out the tension between private and public interests quite clearly. It also presents a clarification of judicial competence under the constitution by being one of only a few cases explicitly discussing review. In addition to ascertaining the existence of and outlining the scope of judicial review, it exposes this institution to a wider public. The open acknowledgment of judicial review and the fact that the case was decided 4–3 again sparked legal and political debate concerning the desirability of this institution, which also brought about a parliamentary proposal to abolish judicial review by way of constitutional amendment. The case has become a reference point in historical and legal literature, both for the emerging welfare state regulations and for judicial review.[7] This chapter looks into the arguments it presents both for and against review.

The background for the 1918 case was the 1909 Act of Concessions, enacted following several temporary regulations aimed at protecting Norwegian natural resources by way of concessions and subsequent state ownership. As a consequence of the Norwegian mountainous topography, possibilities

6 Rt. 1918 s. 403.

7 Andenæs, Høyesterett som politisk organ (1965) Hiorthøy in Nissen, *Den dømmende makt* (1967), 147ff.; Kierulf, Historikeres fortellinger om juss (2012); Langeland, *Siste ord* (2005); Seip, *Tanke og handling i norsk historie* (1968).

for developing hydroelectric power were abundant. At the turn of the century, however, almost all regulated waterfalls were owned by foreign capital. In order to ensure continuation of the emerging industrialization while at the same time safeguarding national interests, rights to property, mining and waterfalls were regulated throughout the first decades of the 1900s. Central actors for the regulation were Prime Minister Gunnar Knudsen from the Liberal Left and Johan Castberg of the Radical Liberal Labor Party ("Arbeiderdemokratene"). One of the provisions in the 1909 Act set out a state "right of reversion": Waterfalls could only be acquired (traded) pursuant to a concession from the state, and the concessionary period could last no longer than 90 years. Upon termination of the concession, the waterfall and appurtenant power installations were "reversed" and became state property, without any compensation to the concessionaire.

In 1918, the Supreme Court was asked to decide whether the right of revision was in accordance with § 105 of the Constitution. The plaintiffs claimed that in reality it represented expropriation without compensation. The court found the provision to be constitutional, by a 4–3 vote, based on the reasoning that § 105 did not directly regulate anything but the actual expropriation of property, and that Parliament had substantial discretion to regulate property in order to balance the individual right to property against the collective needs following societal development. As one line of defense, lawyer A. Schjødt, serving as Attorney General at the time,[8] argued that courts had no competence to review the statute under the Constitution. Prompted by this assertion, preceding the assessment of § 105, the court explicitly discussed the existence and scope of judicial review.

The first observation of interest here is that all justices held judicial review to be an ingrained part of Norwegian law. Even Chief Justice Thinn, who maintained that in his personal view, the Constitution should serve as a guideline primarily for politicians, and that courts ought not to have the right of review, conceded that his view was not in accordance with "the common sense of justice, as follows from legal literature and case law." As to the scope of review, four positions were formulated.

Justice Backer presented a position of possible judicial restraint following *parliamentary debate*: Courts have both the right and the duty to ensure that legislative acts lie within the limits of the Constitution (lest the legislator has acted outside its competences under the Constitution). The intensity of such review cannot, however, be formulated as a general norm, but will vary

[8] The Office of the Attorney General was established in 1962. Before this, the Attorney General position was held by varying private attorneys.

according to circumstances. If Parliament has explicitly discussed the question of constitutionality and concluded that the act is constitutional, this could be a particular reason for judicial restraint.

Justice Mejdell's position was that of the *constitutionalist* and *textualist/original intent* approach: The principle of popular sovereignty is set out in the Constitution, but this sovereignty must be exercised within the limits of the Constitution. Neither the legislative nor the executive may dispense themselves from these constitutional limits. Courts have a duty to keep a parliamentarism extending beyond the Constitution within the constitutional limits. It is the written constitutional provisions, rather than any natural law conception, that constitute the framework for review, and the Constitution should be interpreted with the aim of establishing its historical meaning and the framers' intent, rather than what the framers would have thought about future legal or factual situations, had these been discernible to them at the time of enactment.

Justice Bjørn's *interpretivist* approach was that judicial review of legislation is a longstanding and well-established part of Norwegian law, and its scope is such that if, and to the extent, courts find an act to be in discordance with the Constitution as interpreted by the courts, courts have the competence to disregard the act.

Ad hoc Justice Berg advocated judicial restraint based on "*true meaning interpretation*"[9] That judicial review is to be employed only to the extent an act is "obviously or undoubtedly" unconstitutional, and not unless the court "with certainty" can establish the right interpretation.[10]

The reason for judicial restraint as advised by Justice Backer had, he stated, earlier been advanced in legal theory by T. H. Aschehoug.[11] It follows from the idea of respect for parliament as the primary source for the common will and relies on a view of the relationship between courts and legislature in which courts pay deference to reasonable legislative interpretations of the constitution. It is connected with the view expressed by Justice Berg and prevalent in some earlier case law and early theory – particularly that of Stang, more moderately joined by Aschehoug (see Section 3.4) – that only unreasonable

9 Berg was later Chief Justice (1929–1946).

10 In line e.g. with Justice Andresen, who in the 1866 case maintained the unconstitutionality had to be "indisputable and clear": UfL VI, 171, and later scholarly writings of Aschehoug, *Norges nuværende Statsforfatning* (1875–1885), III, 368. Compare also the scope for review during the earlier years of judicial review in the US as defined by Chief Justice Marshall in *Fletcher v. Peck* (1810), at 128: "The opposition between the constitution and the law should be such that the judge feels a clear and strong conviction of their incompatibility with each other."

11 Aschehoug, *Norges nuværende Statsforfatning* (1875–1885) III, ch. 63 § 20.

or obviously unconstitutionally legislation was to be disregarded under review. As observed, that this was a valid requirement at the time of the Waterfall case is not clear, not from contemporary case law nor from the fact that the decision on the waterfall regulation constitutionality was one on which the court split 4–3.[12] Although the question of what weight to accord to parliamentary discussions and conclusions on how an act relates to the Constitution has since been debated,[13] the relevance of such parliamentary assessments has remained part of legal doctrine outlining the scope for judicial review.[14]

The *political* debates concerning the waterfall regulations were long lasting and very heated, exposing fundamental ideological differences as to the state–citizen balance. This context is vital when attempting to understand the positions explicated – those skeptical of the new regulations could be likely to seek out the arguments they had to fight against such regulations; those in favor to diminish them. A strong card in the line of argument for private ownership and against the regulations was the constitutional protection of property. One of the many parliamentary debates about the right of revision and the Constitution § 105, an exchange illustrative for the political response to constitutional limits, took place between one of the main proponents for the Act of Concessions, Prime Minister Gunnar Knudsen (Liberal Left), and one of its opponents, Fredrik Stang (Conservative). Stang asked whether it could be the case that

> Parliament was meant to balance on the edge of § 105, as much on the edge as possible without falling into it? We lawyers use to say that when a man tries to balance on the edge of criminal fraud, he is likely to fall into it, and if one tries to balance on the edge of § 105 one might just fall into it.[15]

Prime Minister Gunnar Knudsen, rather than arguing against this view, claimed debates about the legal issues under the Constitution were not particularly pertinent to Parliament: "We have certainly heard a lot about the Constitution § 105. I myself have not been addressing it in the previous debates, for it was my opinion that discussions on § 105 could be left to the legal advisors."[16]

Knudsen's position is understandable under the circumstances. While certainly legally cumbersome, diminishing the political practicability of the Constitution and leaving the questions arising under it entirely to the lawyers does, however, seem like something of a political abdication from

[12] Hiorthøy in Nissen, et al., *Den dømmende makt* (1967), 146.
[13] References i.a. in Andenæs, *Statsforfatningen i Norge* (1990), 350ff.
[14] See i.a. Rt. 1976 s. 1 (see Section 5.6).
[15] Fredrik Stang d.y., Ot. forh. 9.7.1909, 696.
[16] Ot. forh. 13.7.1909, 800.

constitutional inquiries – indeed, from constitutional responsibility. To the extent that this position indicates something general about political attitudes toward constitutional questions, it would also be a tendency leaving the argument that courts should defer to or emphasize parliamentary conclusions on constitutional questions difficult to realize: In order for courts to rely on parliamentary discussions in review cases, such discussions must say something about the constitutional question at hand – about Parliament's interpretation of the Constitution, and about what it is that makes Parliament find a proposed act of legislation to be (un)constitutional. In light of Justice Backer's formulation in the Waterfall case, it is interesting to note that the Supreme Court in this case does not explicitly relate its § 105 reasoning to *any* concrete part of parliamentary discussions of the right of reversion constitutionality.

The Supreme Court has often been charged with acting in a "political" way in review cases. Such accusations have rarely, if ever, been substantiated as anything but political, legal or ideological disagreement with case outcomes. The Waterfall case does, however, represent a possible exception to this rule: At the time of the case, the caseload in the Supreme Court was often greater than the working capacity of the Court could handle. Rather than increasing the number of regular justices, the political branches held back such funding due to budgetary considerations,[17] and instead solved the problem by mandating the use of "extraordinary" justices.[18] Such extraordinary justices were appointed by the Government, and were often high state officials from the administrative agencies, notably the Ministry of Justice. They would keep their administrative positions upon returning from service as extraordinary justices. This arrangement had been a longstanding cause of tension between the political branches and the Supreme Court, the latter being of the opinion that it represented a threat to both efficient case handling and judicial independency: "It cannot be right that of the members of the highest Court of the land approximately half, or sometimes more than half are not permanent justices, but only for a short period of time appointed justices, who whenever it suits the Government may be replaced," as the Supreme Court noted in 1904.[19] The arrangement was also criticized for lacking constitutional support from the legal community, such as professor Morgenstierne in his treatise on constitutional law from 1900.[20] It continued, however, and was

17 See i.a. St.forh. 1908, 7, Tid., 394.

18 A historical outline of the arrangement is in Kierulf and Slagstad, Høyesteretts dommere (2015), 70ff.

19 See i.a. Nissen, *Den dømmende makt* (1967), 111

20 Morgenstierne, *Lærebog i den norske Statsforfatningsret* (1900), 315.

expanded following the splitting of the Supreme Court into two chambers in 1905; from 1908 there were twelve such extraordinary justices.

At the time of the Waterfall case the arrangement was such that the extraordinary justices appointed by the Government could be called in by the Chief Justice upon demand.[21] With increasing tension between the regulation-keen Liberal Left government and the Supreme Court serving as a brake on what the government saw to be necessary regulations, an interesting "renewal"[22] of the extraordinary justices taking place in 1913 may be noted: Gunnar Knudsen's Liberal Left government appointed three extraordinary justices – Paal Berg, Henrik Frisak and Halvard Heggen – "of which at least two were true Leftists."[23]

All three were called in for the case by Chief Justice Thinn, himself a supporter of the waterfall regulations. He also called as an extraordinary justice Birger Stuevold-Hansen, a Liberal Left MP who, in such capacity, had been party to a 1915 amendment to the Act of Concessions making stricter the requirements for attaining concessions. This backdrop made the plaintiff to the 1918 complain about his nonimpartiality, a complaint leading to the exclusion of Stuevold-Hansen.[24] Extraordinary Justice Berg, a person markedly on the radical wing of the Liberal Left party who became Social Secretary in Gunnar Knudsen's 1919 government, only reluctantly joined the exclusionary opinion. Although he did not dissent, he said there "really were no grounds on which the impartiality of Stuevold-Hansen as a justice could be questioned."[25] Extraordinary Justice Heggen joined Berg's opinion. Thinn, Berg and Heggen were three of the four justices finding the waterfall regulations constitutional, thus providing the Liberal Left regulation line with a Supreme Court stamp of approval.

According to the later historian Seip, the Waterfall case showed that the Supreme Court "did not have the courage to go against a decision made on the highest political level."[26] That is an odd interpretation of a decision by a Supreme Court composed so that it for once substantiated suspicions of a possible political motivation for its conclusion.[27]

Law professor Johs. Andenæs refused the idea of such a political motivation in 1965. He argued it was "improbable" as it would easily be noticed and then be grounds for strong criticism of the Chief Justice.[28] Andenæs substantiated this notion with reference to a conversation between then Chief Justice Paal

[21] The Court Act 1915 § 3, para. 2 as it read at the time.
[22] Formulation by Seip, *Tanke og handling i norsk historie* (1968), 101. [23] Ibid.
[24] Rt. 1918 s. 401. [25] Ibid. [26] Seip, *Tanke og handling i norsk historie* (1968), 101.
[27] Kierulf and Slagstad, Historikeres fortellinger om juss (2012), 437–438.
[28] Andenæs, Høyesterett som politisk organ (1965), s. 31 f.

Berg and Sverre Riisnæs, Justice Secretary in Vidkun Quisling's Nazi collaboration government, which took place in 1940.[29] Arguing against Riisnæs' plan to have the Supreme Court be comprised of justices "with the right political inclinations," Berg said that never in the 125 year history of the Supreme Court has the Chief Justice influenced the Court by composing it politically. Riisnæs had then pointed to the Waterfall case, arguing Thinn had just done that in that case. To this Berg replied that he had "sat with Thinn, and can assure you nothing could have been farther from his thoughts."[30]

As a refutation of a political interpretation of the Waterfall case, this passage seems unconvincing. It is at least possible to imagine other reasons why Berg may have answered Riisnæs like he did in just that situation, other than that there was nothing political about Thinn's thinking or the Court composition in 1918.[31]

4.3 LEGAL OPINIONS OF 1912 AND 1916

One of the works cited as a legal source in support of judicial review in the 1918 case is a lecture from 1912, later printed in the legal reporter "Retstidende,"[32] by Professor Bredo Morgenstierne.[33] It directly addressed the question of courts' competency to disregard unconstitutional statutory laws. Expanding on the view in his treatise on constitutional law from 1909,[34] Morgenstierne maintained that legal doctrine had "since the very birth of the constitution" held courts to have this competency; this "right and duty," and that clear precedent had later supported this assertion.[35] He held the arguments that this "best guard of citizens' liberty, a truly democratic legal protection" were to be considered "something disloyal . . . an undemocratic evasion of respecting the common will etc." was but an effect of political factors; "in particular the development of a sovereign Parliament which had gone to the head of some and led them to see any opinion but the one expressed by the majority in Parliament as crimen læsæ majestatis."[36] He pointed to how the US experience with judicial review remained unchallenged in spite of its widespread use and extensive scope, and maintained that this could not have

[29] Schjelderup, *Fra Norges kamp for retten: 1940 i Høyesterett* (1945), 220ff. In addition to being cited by Andenæs, this passage is also cited by Melteig as repudiation of a political interpretation of the Waterfall case: Tilfeldighetsprinsippets betydning for uavhengige domstoler (1992), 426.

[30] Ibid. [31] Kierulf and Slagstad, Historikeres fortellinger om juss (2012), 438.

[32] Rt. 1913 s. 449. [33] Citation in Rt. 1918 s. 403, 404.

[34] Morgenstierne, *Lærebog i den norske Statsforfatningsret* (1909), 400ff.

[35] Rt. 1913 s. 449, 449, 459. [36] Ibid., 450.

been the case "had [review] not enjoyed the strongest support in a popular opinion which has regarded it as an indispensable shield for citizen's liberties and established rights."[37] Apart from the US experience, Morgenstierne's arguments for court review may be summed up in three main points: that of *lex superior*, of constitutional review as a protection of the individual and individual rights and that of constitutionalism:

> The courts are not placed above the law, the constitution is; it is placed there above the law and demands respect. And as regards the popular will – it is not limited by the courts, but by the constitution. ... To the extent a sufficient majority of popular will finds the constitutional limits too limiting, they are free to alter them as the constitution prescribes.[38]

Another early opinion dealing with the question of judicial review pertains to an issue even more closely associated with the emerging welfare state: alcohol regulations, as noted by Professor Jon Skeie.[39] The opinion was commissioned as part of the preparations for an amendment to the Alcohol Act of 1904. Alcohol regulations had, since the late 1800s, been a social goal under varying degrees of dispute, with alcohol abuse being seen to have particularly negative effects for the working class, who could not free itself from capitalism without freeing itself from alcohol.[40] The legal amendment opined upon by Skeie aimed to limit the situations in which the state had to compensate trading citizens for regulating what had until then been their right to sell liquor. A. Schjødt, now the lawyer for a group of trading citizens, argued that the new regulations would amount to an unconstitutional retroactive taking of established rights. Skeie rejected this argument. As part of his reasoning for not finding the new regulations unconstitutional, he considered the foundations for – and existence of – judicial review in Norway, and found "absolutely no" basis in the Constitution text for review. He maintained that review powers as argued for are "unknown in Europe."[41] He held that European jurisdictions were the "natural" comparisons for Norway, as opposed to the both contemporary and historically far less similar United States, where he agreed the "special arrangement" of judicial review was indeed practiced. Skeie conceded that both case law and scholarly writings held judicial review as part of

37 Ibid., 453. 38 Ibid., 459.

39 Skeie, *Ang. ot. prp. nr. 43 for 1916: Ændringer i loven av 17de mai 1904 om salg og skjænkning av brændevin m. v. (St. forh. 1917 dok. 1)*, (1917) 5, 4.

40 Furre, *Norsk historie 1905-1990* (1992), 49.

41 As shown by M. Lie (1923; see Section 4.4), an analysis of European countries documented that this assertion was wrong.

Norwegian legal doctrine.[42] Citing the German scholar Friedrich Stein, arguing that academia should not be bound to follow case law they thought wrong,[43] Skeie maintained, however, that the *legislator* should feel even less bound by legal precedent. His reasoning to this end relied on the legal precedent for the question in issue: alcohol regulations. It would be particularly unfortunate for Parliament to feel bound by precedent in a field of law as inconsistent as that produced by the Supreme Court in the question of the constitutionality of alcohol regulations.

Skeie's argument is threefold: First, that of the *countermajoritarian difficulty* – he sees review in general as "court censorship of the legislature." Second, one of *social necessity of regulations*, as review as practiced under the Alcohol Act is one that has hindered "appropriate" control;[44] one "where an unjust claim from a private party disrupts common interests [by] directly frustrating a socially beneficial reform."[45] As a side, Skeie holds that allowing courts to be legal superiors in questions of economic and social principle is not even "good conservatism," as "it would not stop development, only make the battle over it harder and bitterer." For this reason, he thirdly holds that review powers might *undermine the legitimacy of courts*. Even assuming review, Skeie finds courts to be "particularly unsuited" to review in just the area of alcohol regulation.

An interesting element in this story is that the amendment to the Alcohol Act as finally enacted (statute of June 7, 1917) presupposed a right to review. It was formulated in such a way that it entitled licensees to compensation to the extent the law infringed upon their established right. As pointed out by law professor Augdahl, the actual meaning of this formulation is that Parliament wanted the courts, to the extent they were to find the statute to run afoul of § 97, to award compensation rather than explicating that the statute be unconstitutional.[46] In this way, "unconstitutionality" could be monetarily compensated rather than lead to findings of constitutional infringement.

Skeie's opinion is closely tied to the concrete question of alcohol regulation under the Constitution § 97. He does, however, point to how courts' potential rejection of the alcohol license regulations would add to the general case against judicial review as made by review skeptics: Already anticipating the possibility of the Supreme Court finding the waterfall regulations to be

42 Skeie, *Ang. ot. prp. nr. 43 for 1916: Ændringer i loven av 17de mai 1904 om salg og skjænkning av brændevin m.* v. *(St. forh. 1917 dok. 1)*, 5, 4.

43 Stein, *Das private Wissen des Richters* (1893) 42, 43.

44 Skeie, *Ang. ot. prp. nr. 43 for 1916: Ændringer i loven av 17de mai 1904 om salg og skjænkning av brændevin m.* v. *(St. forh. 1917 dok. 1)*, 9.

45 Ibid., 10.

46 Augdahl, *Ingen lov må gis tilbakevirkende kraft* (1938) 402–403.

unconstitutional,[47] Skeie recalled how said skeptics discussed whether to propose judicial review abolished through constitutional amendment. He rounded up his analysis by (sarcastically) asking whether what Schjødt warned could become a "dangerous constitutional conflict" would not be solved with such an amendment – or if it, too, was something the courts were free to neglect following review, to the extent they found it contrary to the "spirit and principles" set out to limit the scope of constitutional amendments?[48] Skeie seems to have held that even though judicial review might exist, Parliament should not feel bound by earlier precedent for its own present understanding and evaluation of the constitution. It is, however, not clear that he meant this proposition to be generalized as one decisive beyond a discussion of § 97 and alcohol regulation.

The close connection between Skeie's view on § 97 and judicial review may be observed following a notable shift in Skeie's arguments concerning review in the subsequent years: In his 1929 treatise on Civil Procedure, following an explanation of review and a recollection of review cases – notable among them a 1922 case which reversed earlier precedent holding § 97 to bar alcohol regulation[49] – he gives his own opinion on the review institute. Now he holds that there is no reason to reject or alter this institute:

> On the one hand one must concede that the legislator, during and after [WWI] has not always treated individual interests with the same caution that distinguishes our earlier legislation. On the other hand, courts' apprehension of the scope for review has changed significantly ... In the long run courts cannot stand in opposition to the legislature. In developing eras, however, with many parties and weak governments, laws conflicting with established legal doctrine may easily be enacted – without any certainty whether these enactments really corresponds to a similar shift in popular opinion ... And the very circumstance that courts have review competence may have the fortunate effect that the question of constitutionality is more thoroughly discussed.

4.4 LEGAL OPINIONS FOLLOWING THE 1918 CASE

As warned by Skeie and others, in the wake of the Waterfall case proposals were put forward to abolish judicial review. The first proposal, jointly

47 At the time of Skeie's report, this question had already been tried by the first instance court, which had found the waterfall regulations constitutional.

48 As mentioned, in the later parliamentary debates and preparations for such an amendment, the § 112 question was taken quite seriously.

49 Rt. 1922 s. 624.

presented by representatives from the Liberal Left and Labor parties, was to alter the Constitution § 81 by adding a second paragraph stating that "A statutory law brought about in the forms prescribed by §§ 76–79 may not be disregarded by courts." It was presented together with proposals to abolish the Constitution §§ 97 and 105 – and one aimed at banning courts from reviewing the constitutionality of constitutional amendments under the amendment provision in § 112.[50]

As a result of the 1920 proposals, the Ministry of Justice commissioned two legal reports analyzing the question of whether § 97, and possibly § 105, could and should be abolished, from professors M. Lie and B. Morgenstierne.[51] The unease with the guarantee against retroactive legislation arose in part because of uncertainty about how (conservative) courts might interpret this guarantee differently than did (more progressive) politicians. Analyzing § 97 brought forth the question of how the guarantee against retroactivity was to be ensured (*quis custodiet ipsos custodes*). The reports thus went on to treat the existence, foundations and reasons for judicial review quite broadly, and parts of their argumentation became formative for the parliamentary discussions on judicial review in the following years.

Lie's opinion has been seen as one critical of judicial review.[52] It does indeed emphasize the arguments against review – both those contradicting its existence and its undesirability. It holds, however, that judicial review is indeed Norwegian constitutional law, established through court practice. To the extent the legislature wanted to rid the legal system of this constitutional customary law institution, it could not be abolished but by constitutional amendment. The opinion concludes by recommending the abolishment of § 97 by constitutional amendment – but not abolishment of judicial review.[53]

Lie provides an extensive assessment of the review situation in twenty-eight foreign jurisdictions,[54] in which the United States takes a prominent place. His ten-page analysis of the US system dwells on literature concerned with effects of review that contribute to "tower up difficulties for social legislation

50 Representatives Fridtjov Hegge and Ludvig Enge, in St. forh. 1920 Dok. nr. 35. no. 17, 77.

51 Lie, *Betenkning angående grunnlovens* §§*97 og 105 og om domstolenes myndighet til å prøve loves indre gyldighet* (1923); Morgenstierne, *Betenkning angående spørsmålet om ophevelse av grunnlovens* § *97 og dermed sammenhengende spørsmål* (1923).

52 See i.a. Seip, Den norske Høyesterett som politisk organ (1965); Seip, Jus og politikk (1965).

53 Lie, *Betenkning angående grunnlovens* §§*97 og 105 og om domstolenes myndighet til å prøve loves indre gyldighet* (1923), 68.

54 Ibid., 8–39 (Anglo-American, US, British Domains, Ireland, France, Belgium, Italy, Romania, Spain, Portugal, Mexico, Brazil, Venezuela, Argentine, Haiti, Cuba, Greece, Switzerland, Holland, Germany, Austria, Czechoslovakia, Poland, Yugoslavia, Sweden, Finland, Denmark and Iceland).

corresponding to modern needs." One such effect is the US Supreme Court's expansion of the "due process" clause of the 14th amendment from a formal to a substantive provision making courts "go so far as to place their own opinion before the legislator's of what standards to hold reasonable and socially justifiable legislation against."[55] Another is an "individualistically biased view of the relation between the individual and the state stemming from natural law ideas of fundamental human rights." Citing *Lochner* and *Truax* as examples of judicial activism,[56] Lie calls to task proponents (hereunder Aschehoug and Morgenstierne) of the "older view" that US review is considered the highest democratic protection of citizens that has not led to any dangerous effects. He maintains that modern doctrine "within wide and influential circles" has come to view the institution quite differently.

Some of the general insights Lie extracted from review in other jurisdictions were that review competencies had nothing to do with the separation of powers. One point in support of this was the fact that France had such separation, but no review. He rejected the view that a constitutional system implies review because courts are the arbiters of law, holding that the question of statutory constitutionality was as much a "particular constitutional" question as a merely legal one: "It is primarily for the political branches of government to practice the constitution."[57] Following this view, it would disrupt the integrated nature of the constitution to have parts of it be subject to judicial, rather than political interpretation. Lie pointed to the effect of precedence to underline that judicial review had consequences outside those actualized in the case at hand: "It is but at the moment a law is adjudicated that it presents itself *as law* – what its real content is, and what effects it produces."[58] Having gone through all jurisdictions, and with what appears as a rather critical focus, Lie still ends up summarizing the reigning modern opinion of Norwegian judicial review as one "decidedly ascribing to courts this [review] competence."[59]

While concluding that judicial review was, and ought to remain, Norwegian constitutional law (provided § 97 was abolished), Lie maintained that such review was no necessity in a constitutional democracy, had no foundation in the constitution, was contradicted by constitutional history, and had little support in early, Norwegian doctrine. He held the legal foundation and scope of courts' review competence to be quite unclear.[60]

[55] Ibid., 14. [56] *Lochner* v. *New York* (1905); *Truax* v. *Corrigan* (1921).

[57] Lie, *Betenkning angående grunnlovens §§97 og 105 og om domstolenes myndighet til å prøve loves indre gyldighet* (1923), 41.

[58] Ibid., 41–42. [59] Ibid., 40.

[60] Ibid., 42–43, 48, distancing himself from the view held by Morgenstierne in his 1909 treatise on constitutional law.

In establishing what he found to be the original, constitutional intent to support his argument that review had no foundation in the Constitution, Lie relied on "the common beliefs of the time." These made the idea that the legislature would disrespect the common law a "foreign thought." Further, the contemporary view that courts had but an "automatic function" could not have supported any idea that judges could opine differently than the legislator. This interpretation is consistent with emphasizing the French influence on the founding fathers. It does, however, stand in some tension with the weight Lie attached to the original thoughts and intent of the constitution in another part of his opinion – that of courts' competencies to review whether a constitutional amendment was contrary to the "spirit and principles" in the amendment provision in § 112: The formulation "spirit and principles" was, in Lie's view, not to be seen as a legal limitation at all, but rather a "political maxim of uncertain value." It was but a result of the "idea of those times" about "certain fundamental and irrevocable rules of law which leads back to the natural law idea of the social contract [Rosseau]. The generation of one time in history has no power to bind future generations like that. A constitution attempting such a thing goes beyond its competence."[61] Why time had ran away from the original motivations for § 112, but not the 1814 "common beliefs" i.a. about the "automatic function" of courts, remains unexplained by Lie.

Lie reads early legal scholarship "clearly" to contradict judicial review.[62] Referring extensively to skeptics such as Stang and Dunker, he cites uncommented (Steenbuch) or marginalizes (Winter Hjelm and Lasson) those opinions he finds to contradict his thesis – and neglects others (Aubert) that argued for judicial review.[63] He presents the opinion of Schweigaard and Motzfeldt from 1841 as one contradicting review, citing a passage where they express "doubt about any legal foundations for appeals over legislative power" to "higher justice" as their "only" comment to the question.[64] This passage in Schweigaard's and Motzfeldt's opinion, however, relates to the question of whether the case at hand ran afoul of the Constitution § 105. In an earlier part of their opinion Schweigaard and Motzfeldt state, on what may plausibly be read as a general basis, that laws taking away rights protected by the

61 Ibid., 51.

62 In a later reading of the positions in the period up until 1870, Slagstad documents how the dominant position within theory seems to have been one acknowledging judicial review. Slagstad, *Rettens ironi* (2011), 380ff.

63 Lie, *Betenkning angående grunnlovens §§97 og 105 og om domstolenes myndighet til å prøve loves indre gyldighet* (1923), 45–48.

64 Ibid., 47.

Constitution § 105 would require compensation to the private party for this taking, "and even though the law clearly denied such compensation, he would still have to be awarded it, as the constitution is stronger than the law."[65] Having established that there was no right to compensation by analogy for rights not amounting to "movable or immovable property" as set out in the wording of § 105, they held that "if there be any occasion where the constitution must be exclusively decisive and one solely has to follow it [the constitution], it must be when the question arises whether a legislative act is in contradiction with the constitution and for that reason must be assumed false and without effect whether to the detriment of the private party or not."[66]

Lie's recommendation to abolish the Constitution § 97 has been seen by sociologist Slagstad as "an indirect strategy to pinion judicial review."[67] It is not clear, however, that a recommendation to abolish this central, constitutional provision would have any higher hopes of realization than would a recommendation to ban the constitutional custom of judicial review. As pointed out (but rebutted) by Lie, several scholars had argued that § 97 was also part of the "spirit" and "principles" of the constitution, not open to alterations. An alternative reading to Slagstad's is that Lie saw just the provision of retroactivity as the one representing the main problem in a constitutional system practicing judicial review: On a textual interpretation, this was the provision with which courts could potentially block most planned or enacted progressive legislation. Such a reading is supported by Lie's emphasis on the particular indeterminacy of § 97.[68] Abolishing § 97 would vacate this threat, clarify the more precise scope of § 105 – and leave in place courts' review competence over the remaining constitutional right-provisions which were important, but did not "present any inordinate occasion for conflict."[69] This one alteration may have presented itself as less interfering still in the body of constitutional law that had gradually developed to be a part of the "common sense of justice." It is the *organic* argument from law's gradual development and the socio-psychological argument for *social legitimacy* of the institution of review that are ultimately decisive for Lie's conclusion:

65 Ibid., 291.

66 Schweigaard and Motzfeldt, *Det juridiske Fakultets Betænkning af 18 Januar 1841 angaaende Ophævelsen af det bergenske Bagerlaugs Privilegier (Rt. 1895 s. 289)* (1841).

67 Slagstad, *Rettens ironi* (2011), 391.

68 Lie, *Betenkning angående grunnlovens §§97 og 105 og om domstolenes myndighet til å prøve loves indre gyldighet* (1923), 53–55: "All agree the scant and definite [text of § 97] cannot be taken literally. But this is also all they agree upon.

69 Ibid., 67.

> If the question were whether to introduce a system of review, the best reasons would be for not doing so. [Judicial review] is, however, an institution embedded as a characteristic and significant part of our constitutional law and thus ingrained in our common sense of justice. There is no reason here to use the knife. The current arrangement affords to the commoner a feeling of safety, which has a substantial social-psychological worth regardless of its foundation in reality.[70]

While Lie ends up concluding against abolishment of review, he certainly provides a number of arguments to be used against it. From a perspective of argumentative scope, the most remarkable omission in Lie's otherwise comprehensive opinion is the lack of any discussion of the liberal argument. This he does not take on even as something to dismiss. He does not cite those passages from earlier scholars where review is discussed as a liberal guarantee. He reiterates Aschehoug's justification for review simply as being of "a principled nature," and maintains that principled reflections cannot, in themselves, justify review.[71]

Agreeing with Lie that the existence of judicial review is manifest in case law and scholarly writings alike, Professor Morgenstierne, in an appendix to Lie's opinion, justifies why, from a theoretical point of view, courts have this competence. His primary argument is one of logical deduction from *mandatory jurisdiction*: Finding how to balance valid legal sources against each other is a legal question. Turning the absence of textual constitutional support for review around, Morgenstierne holds that courts cannot turn away from legal questions in the absence of a clear constitutional provision limiting their competence to interpret the constitution, and consequently have to adjudicate the constitution.[72] On this basis, Morgenstierne rejects Lie's view that constitutional interpretation is something of a particular legislative province, stating that there is no authority supporting this view under Norwegian law.[73]

Morgenstierne's second argument is in line with what Lie presents as the decisive one: he honors the organic nature of law. This argument is one of *tradition* and *public recognition*. If assuming that judicial review is not logically necessary, Morgenstierne argues that it is even more suspect to change customary law created the way judicial review has come to be in Norway: "to interfere into a legal state that has gradually matured abreast of the people's

70 Ibid., 68. 71 Ibid., 48.

72 Morgenstierne, *Betenkning angående spørsmålet om ophevelse av grunnlovens § 97 og dermed sammenhengende spørsmål* (1923), 2.

73 Ibid., 2.

common sense of justice." As to the scope of review competency, he tones down what Lie presents as a disagreement between Morgenstierne and Aschehoug on the significance of interpretational doubt. Rejecting that "doubtful" interpretations present any workable standard for when not to exercise review, he sums up what he finds to be their common ground as follows: Where a judge finds two interpretations equally justifiable, he is likely to give the legislator the benefit of the doubt.

Morgenstierne goes on to a *comparative* argument from European modernity: The abolishment of judicial review would be contrary to the state of affairs in other countries with a written constitution, of which most, as a result of the same legal development, had landed upon the principle of leaving review of the material content of statutes to the judiciary. Morgenstierne maintains there is no example of any country having recognized judicial review that later decides to abolish it. In sum, Morgenstierne seems to highlight and expound what he finds to be the arguments for review in Lie's opinion in a way that creates a sense of scholarly agreement between the opinions on this question.

4.5 PARLIAMENTARY DEBATES ON REVIEW ABOLISHMENT

The constitutional proposals set forth in 1920 were considered by Parliament's Standing Committee on Scrutiny and Constitutional Affairs in 1923, but denounced by a vote of 6–2.[74] They were subsequently rejected by Parliament with a vote of 106–33.[75] Two of the majority representatives in the Committee emphasized that they found courts' exercise of judicial review "as seen in the later years" to be an attempt to "expand their right" wider than what was originally given to them under the Constitution. They still voted against all the proposed amendments due to their form, but stated hope that later proposals would be "better formulated."

As maintained by both Lie and Morgenstierne, the 1923 Committee unanimously held that judicial review, through precedent and customary law, was to be regarded as part of the positive constitutional law of Norway, which could "hardly be altered absent constitutional amendment."[76]

A minority of two Committee representatives, A. Magnussen and E. Stang (both Labor Party; the latter later Communist Party, and, from 1946, Chief

[74] Innst. S. LXXIV 1923, 15 (Holmboe, Brevig, Hambro, Jakhelln Skaar and Øen for [the two latter agreeing in the conclusion mainly due to the form of the proposal]; Magnussen and Stang against).

[75] St. forh. 17.10 1923, 3228. [76] Innst. S. LXXIV 1923, 6.

Justice of the Supreme Court), supported the proposal to abolish judicial review by constitutional amendment. They were also the only ones to support the subsequent proposals to abolish §§ 97 and 105 – both to annul the retroactivity ban altogether and to hold that the state should have an unabridged right to the taking of private property, and that it ought to be the province of Parliament to decide whether to offer any compensation for such takings.[77] Their reasoning was that §§ 97 and 105 represented undesirable private barriers to the necessary development of economic and cultural common interests. Underlining their skepticism regarding review were also "a number of cases" indicating the political nature of courts: They mention a well-known case concerning criminal sanctions for "revolutionary agitation" against radical Labor leader Marcus Thrane in the 1850s, in which there was no sign of the Constitution § 100 in the courts' reasoning. Taken together, review cases in their view indicated the conservative slant of the Supreme Court.

The minority argument for restraining courts' competence to review the acts of parliament can be divided into three:

First, one based on the *legal-historical development* since the enactment of the Constitution: The representatives maintained that judicial review had been "natural" in the early 1800s when separation of powers defined the constitutional order. Nonetheless, the current constitutional order had become "completely changed" to one of "unification of powers" following the endorsement of the parliamentary system in the late 1800s.[78] Any review of parliamentary acts from an institution outside Parliament itself was irreconcilable with such a unified system. Consequently, these representatives saw "no constitutional reason" to uphold judicial review any longer.

Second, the *countermajoritarian difficulty*: "everything contradicts" a system of review which "offends the general sense of justice . . . that a court of seven members should be in the position to ignore a legally enacted and sanctioned law because those seven justices – or four of them – anticipate that the law be unconstitutional."[79]

Third, that the Supreme Court had proven itself "*unsuited*" to have such a power over the "national economic and cultural development." This is an argument about the unwanted consequences of review – one of output legitimacy – the representatives cite several cases in which the Supreme Court had served as a conservative guarantee, both by *not* practicing judicial review under the Constitution § 100 in cases concerning speech critical and challenging the King and the public morale, and by "starting to use the

77 1923, 12–13 ("fra maktfordelingsprinsippet til maktforeningsprinsippet"). 78 Ibid., 7.
79 Ibid., 8.

Constitution §§ 97 and 105 to protecting private interests against necessary societal developments."

This last argument is interesting. It certainly presents quite a valid critique of free speech case law: why not use § 100 to protect what was seen as "radical" writings in the late 1800s? The free speech protection under § 100 – one of the few liberal rights protections outside §§ 97 and 105 – had in fact *never* been found to represent an obstacle to any law or provision, even though legal interferences with free speech happened quite frequently. As an argument for the desirability of review, it does, however, explicate a critique that is clearly ideological: The reason why the courts are "unsuited" is that the outcomes of their decisions run counter to nonconservative interests. What this argument lacks in politically neutral principle, it gains in the inclusion of *nonuse* of judicial review in its evaluation of the institution of review: Courts' nonuse of the constitution in cases involving both the constitution and an ordinary law may be as much of an ideological action – or a political act, as it is often seen – as its *use*.

This "unsuitability" argument remained central to the minority position in the following parliamentary debates.[80] The 1923 Committee majority representatives gave a six-part argument for their position to reject the proposal. Several of these were seconded by the later majority in Parliament: First, one relating to *social legitimacy*: Case law based on the doctrinally accepted principle of judicial review had not produced any widespread public discontent. Addressing the "input-outcome entanglement," the majority distinguished the public view of the *institution* of review from the perspective that many had disagreed with the material *results* in some review cases; this was, in their opinion, a different question.[81]

Second, one of *volume*: As few constitutional provisions gave rise to judicial review, the possible tension created between branches of government was limited.

Third, one of *minority protection* and *levelheadedness*: The oft-used provisions in §§ 97 and 105 were meant to protect individuals against state power. Absent judicial review, those individuals affected would have no other protection than appeals to public opinion or to the legislature. In cases of principle, such conflicts could take on the form of a question of how a minority may find protection against the majority. A sufficiently strong majority may still get its will through constitutional amendment. Through judicial review, however, courts may protect minority individuals against instantaneous acts by any current reigning majority.[82]

80 St. forh. 17.10 1923, 3223–3224. 81 1923, 6, St. forh. 17.10 1923, 3225. 82 1923, 6–7.

Fourth, one of *democracy* and *embedded expertise*: As the Supreme Court had practiced it review powers sensibly and with considerable moderation, the potential downsides of judicial review had been avoided in Norway. This was followed up in the later parliamentary debate: "To the extent courts usurp their competence like in the US, one would have to remedy the situation," but as courts normally use their competence to ensure rule of law, it should instead "be seen as a truly democratic principle."[83]

Fifth, an argument from *sense of security* and *abuse of power*: The existence of such review had contributed to a public sense of security for private interests – particularly important facing the substantial legislative reforms "often passed under conditions leaving little time for thorough preparation and contemplation."[84] Not that Parliament had willfully abused its power but, as in reality it has unlimited power, "history has shown that human nature is such, that those enjoying unlimited power has a tendency, from time to time, to abuse it."[85]

And sixth, the *liberal* argument: "As desirable as it is for branches of government, particularly the legislature, to strive towards best ensuring the common interest as required under developing conditions, one must not forget that one of the basic preconditions for a thriving society is the protection of individual rights."

In support for their view, the majority also pointed to the *poor systemic fit* of barring review: It was "unsatisfactory" to guard constitutional provisions with procedural regulations securing stronger protection for the rule of law if these guarantees were not to be reviewed by the courts, and it was also "unsatisfactory" to consider the Constitution, the supreme law of the land, as a directive to the legislature, while still holding that the courts should prefer the less supreme law to the same higher ranked norm. This argument, in the form of a *lex superior* argument rendering judicial review logically necessary, became a central argument in the following parliamentary debate.[86] It was also emphasized in a Committee debate over a slightly differently formulated version of the proposal to ban review: as a rebuttal to the argument that legislation ought to be respected as a parliamentary expression of popular will, regardless of whether or not it contradicts the Constitution, "it must be remembered that the constitution, too, is such a parliamentary expression of popular will, one even conceived under stricter procedural rules and with greater precautions."[87]

83 St. forh. 17.10 1923, 3225–3226. 84 1923, 6–7. 85 St. forh. 17.10 1923, 3226.
86 Ibid., 3225. 87 Innst. S. nr. 142 1926.

The proposal put forth in 1920 was discussed and rejected in 1923, whereafter different versions of it were re-proposed in 1923, 1926, 1929 and 1932.[88] The "better formulation," as suggested by the review skeptics in the 1923 Committee majority, turned out to be one proposing to ban review not only of statutory laws, but also of constitutional amendment and parliamentary resolutions – their material content as well as their formal legality.[89] None of these proposals were recommended by the Standing Committee on Constitutional Affairs or approved by Parliament.[90] In two of these years – 1926 and 1929 – Parliament simply followed the recommendation of the majority of the Standing Committee without further debate.

The 1926 Standing Committee (6–2) did not recommend the reformulated 1923 proposal partly because the consequences of a more extensive ban were unclear.[91] The Committee majority gave outcome- and input-based arguments for its view: First, that courts had not exercised judicial review in a way where they were "reading wrong meanings into the constitution," thus following up on the "*moderate use*" argument from 1923. Second, one of *constitutionality* and *actual majoritarianism* – that review is not really countermajoritarian, as the constitution too is a product of the common will; one even more formally and procedurally demanding than ordinary laws. The Committee minority simply referred to the 1923 minority reasoning,[92] whereas the countermajoritarian difficulty, as noted by the 1923 Committee – that a one vote majority on the Supreme Court would suffice to overrule a popularly elected majority – was repeated in Parliament, with reference particularly to the 1918 case.[93] In Parliament, conceding that courts' review competence was not always fortunate, "Conservative Representative Andersen" emphasized that review was nevertheless "necessary in an ordered society." Further, courts had practiced review with "sensibility and tact, with precision and judicious impregnability." Having agreed that the reason for the proposals was the 1918 case (in which "even a, well let us call him democratically inclined justice as Chief

88 St. forh. 1923 Dok. nr. 19 no.19; St. forh. 1926 Dok. nr. 20 no. 14; St. forh. 1929 Dok. nr. 14 no. 5; St. forh. 1932 Dok. 12 no. 2.

89 St. forh. 1923 Dok. nr. 19 no.19 The formulation proposed in St. forh. 1926 Dok. nr. 20 no. 14 was approximately the same, but without reference to formal legality.

90 1923 (denounced 6–2); St. forh. 17.10 1923, 3228 (106–33); Innst. S. nr. 142 1926 (denounced 6–2); St. forh. 2.7.1926, 2530 (unanimous); Innst. S. nr. 113 1929 (unanimous); St. forh. 7.6.1929, 1940 (unanimous); Innst. S. nr. 147 1932 (6–2); St. forh. 25.6.1932, 2362 (74–28); Innst. S. nr. 121 1934 (5–4); St. forh. 5.6.1934 (74–67).

91 Innst. S. nr. 142 1926, 317–318 (Hambro, Andersen, Rye Holmboe, Øen, Andersen Rysst og Seip for; Magnussen and Tranmæl against).

92 Ibid., 318.

93 St. forh. 17.10 1923, 3224; St. forh. 2.6.1926, 2530.

Justice Thinn"[94] had explicitly given up his personal opposition against review) over which further discussion was of no use, Parliament unanimously assented to the Committee recommendation to reject the proposals.[95]

The 1929 Committee unanimously recommended that the 1926 proposal be rejected. While it conceded to being split on the issue of judicial review, it did not want to support a proposal banning not only review of formal laws, but also parliamentary resolutions.[96]

In 1932, the Committee minority dissented solely with reference to the opinion of the 1923 minority. The Committee majority gave a three-part reasoning for its position: It recalled the liberal argument from the 1923 majority, citing that even though desirable for the legislature to take necessary societal precautions, it must not forget that one of the "primary premises for the well-being of society is the legal protection of individuals."[97] It pointed to how a city court decision about attempted wage reductions for civil servants had illustrated the situation of individual rightlessness that would have been the result of accepting the 1926 proposal.

Although not a review case, the mentioned wage reduction case is interesting for two reasons: First, the 1932 committee majority viewed it as elucidating the importance of court review as a *liberal guarantee*. Second, it exposes the *input–outcome entanglement*: how Parliament's view of the relation between itself and the courts seems more opportunistic than principled. In 1927, during a period of significant budget deficits, Parliament reduced civil servants' wages by 10 percent. The resolution was adopted pursuant to a wage scale from 1920 opening for such reduction if an "absolute and significant disproportion" between civil and private wages were to develop. Several civil servants filed suit arguing the conditions for reduction were not met. The City Court – in fact an ad hoc substitute version of the City Court comprised of prominent lawyers, as judges were themselves affected civil servants – followed a customary law principle stipulating civil servant wages could not be reduced below what they were at the time of appointment absent clear reservations to the contrary. Finding the legal question to be one of state action rather than ordinary contract law, the court held it was nevertheless clearly competent to review whether the conditions for wage reduction – the "absolute and significant disproportion" – were met. As the state had not fulfilled its burden of proof that the disproportion was "absolute and significant," the court concluded that the 1927 wage reductions were illegal. The question of whether to

94 St. forh. 2.6.1926, 2528. 95 Ibid., 2530. 96 Innst. S. nr. 113 1929 (231).

97 St. forh. 25.6.1932.

appeal the economically very burdensome case was then left to Parliament. Following substantial debate, this was not done. In the debates, the conservatives and nonsocialist parties (who had proposed the reduction) underlined Parliament's sovereign position and expressed principled skepticism against courts' competence to review the question.[98] Labor, on the other hand – the party for labor rights also among civil servants – in this case, very much contrary to the position they adopted on the "conservative" constitutional questions, became defenders of courts' competence to review Parliament's budgetary decisions.[99] They indeed held out how courts were an important guarantee against illegal political action.

The Committee also, importantly, pointed to the Plenary Act of 1926 as a factor mitigating what had formerly been seen as a potential downside of judicial review.[100] Mandating the Supreme Court to decide constitutional questions in plenary sessions, rather than in chamber as it had previously done, this Act safeguarded against decisions made by fewer and potentially unrepresentative members of the Supreme Court.

The Plenary Act had the primary goal of regulating a situation where the Supreme Court considered overturning of legal precedent. It mandated such cases to be decided by the court in plenary. This would subject such cases to a broader and more representative treatment, following up on two of the Supreme Court objectives: clarification and unification of the law.[101] Following a proposal from then Minister of Justice Paal Berg (previously and later a justice and Chief Justice of the Supreme Court – and one of the relative review skeptics in the 1918 case), the Act came to mandate plenary decisions also in constitutional questions.[102] It has been argued that Berg did this not only to ensure clarification and unification of law in these cases too, but also to limit the number of cases in which judicial review was

98 St. forh. 20.3.1929; ibid. 740–770: representatives Witzøe (Conservative), Langeland (Agrarian Party), Minister Lund (Liberal), Lykke (Conservative).

99 Ibid., 740–770: representatives Aarseth and Nilssen (Labor).

100 Supreme Court Act of 1925 [Lov av 25. juni 1926 nr. 2 om forandring i lovgivningen om Høiesterett (Plenumsloven)] § 2, mandating plenary treatment "where a decision is considered to rely on a statutory provision being unconstitutional, when the provision is disregarded due to the Constitution or when the State because of the Constitution is ordered to pay damages not otherwise mandated by the statute, regulation or provisional ordinance."

101 Ot. prp. nr. 28 1926.

102 Following the 1918 case, Justice Berg, who had been taken on as one of the Supreme Court ad hoc justices in 1913 (rather than expanding the number of ordinary justices, the government in this period appointed a group of ad hoc justices ["ekstraordinære assessorer"]), was appointed as regular Justice and became Chief Justice in 1929. From 1919–1920 he served as Minister of Social Affairs in Gunnar Knudsen's second government. He later served as Chief Justice of the Supreme Court from 1929–1940 and 1945–1946.

exercised.[103] Even though a plenary decision to disregard a statute would be powerful, plenary treatment was more cumbersome. A broader-set court also made cases less vulnerable to being decided by only more conservative, more review-friendly justices.

The 1934 minority of the Committee and Parliament reiterated three points from the 1923 minority: first, the *argument against political limits* – that there was no room for limitations outside Parliament in a system of unified powers; second, that the institute of impeachment should suffice as a potential corrective to Parliament and the government; and third, the *countermajoritarian* and *court-skeptic* argument – that it was against all common sense for justice to leave review powers to courts just because of "judges' opinion of unconstitutionality" – that "a court of 6 or 8 or 10 judges is to decide what is right and wrong while this group of 150 representatives is not to be assumed clever enough to reach a reasoned opinion on the same."[104]

Support for abolishing review was maintained. While the ban was rejected by a vote of 106–33 in 1923, it was rejected by 74–28 in 1932 and 74–67 in 1934. An interesting correlation is that the numbers in the same period for proposals to alter or ban the Constitution § 97 were 106–33 in 1923, 101–30 in 1925, 79–31 in 1932 and 75–64 in 1934.[105] All the representatives voting to abolish § 97 in 1932 and 1934 respectively also voted to abolish judicial review – or had lawful absence. It seems plausible to read the overlap in the groups supporting alterations or abolishment of § 97 and judicial review as suggesting that skepticism may have been rooted as much in the perceived tension between popular sovereignty and *constitutionalism* as in that between sovereignty and *courts' judicial review*. After all, limits on the scope of political action are not originally presented by courts' review, but by the existence of a constitution. It was the Constitution itself – or, more precisely, those parts of it that actually functioned as limits on the political powers of Parliament – that represented "undesirable private barriers to the necessary economic and cultural common interests,"[106] not only the additional institutionalization of courts as the final arbiter of it. As one of the arguments for moderating § 97 (to ban retroactivity only of criminal laws) suggested, such moderation will protect the right of individuals "as far as possible, but not to the detriment of societal development, nor changes in the sense of justice, nor changing social and economical needs."[107] Such a reading of the correlation also finds some support in the

103 Eriksen, *Prejudikat og prøvelsesrett* (2000), 37ff.

104 St. forh. 5.6.1934, 1933.

105 St. forh. 17.10 1923, 3228; St. forh. 16.7.1925, 2808; St. forh. 25.6.1932, 2362; St. forh. 5.6.1934, 1935.

106 Representatives Magnussen and Stang (both Labor Party), 1923, 12–13.

107 St. forh. 5.6.1934, 1935.

early proposals which wanted to bar courts from reviewing whether a constitutional amendment was constitutional under the amendment clause of the Constitution. Absent this provision, what were at any given time seen as problematic parts of the constitution could be abolished by reigning (super-) majorities.

Upon looking into the political affiliation of those proposing or supporting – either in Committee or in Parliament – the constitutional amendments, one finds they are members of the Liberal Left and Labor Parties. The historian J. A. Seip has characterized the work toward altering or abolishing judicial review and the Constitution §§ 97 and 105 in this period as "two parallel lines of action" – a "brief Liberal Left-line from 1920–26 and a longer Labor Party-line from 1917 to 1937."[108] Seip describes both lines as motivated by a "desire to put a thumbscrew on the judges": the Liberal Left line choosing to fight against judicial review; the Labor Party against the problematic constitutional provisions directly. This seems an accurate summary of the party affiliation in the voting protocols – every Representative voting to abolish judicial review in 1923, 1932 and 1934 was from the Labor Party. While the 1929 and 1932 proposals were presented by representatives from Labor,[109] however, the 1920 proposal was set forth by representatives F. Hegge and L. Enge, from the Liberal Left and the Labor Party respectively.[110] The 1923 and 1926 proposals were presented by representatives from the Liberal Left[111] in 1926, with support from Representative J. Castberg from the Radical Left ("Arbeiderdemokratene") – a representative who was also a justice at the Supreme Court at the time.[112]

As regards the Liberal Left, the "line of action" seems to be more of a representative and less of a party line: While the 1920, 1923 and 1926 proposals were put forward (partly) by representatives from the Liberal Left, Liberal Left representatives in the subsequent committees did not vote to support these proposals, even though they sometimes expressed sympathy for them. In 1923,

[108] Seip, *Tanke og handling i norsk historie* (1968), 103.

[109] A. Madsen, C. Hornsrud, St. forh. 1929 Dok. nr. 14 no. 5; T. Haavardstad, K. Bergsvik, B. Olsen-Hagen, St. forh. 1932 Dok. 12 no. 2.

[110] St. forh. 1920 Dok. nr. 35. no. 17.

[111] N. Skaar, H. Aarstad, O. Mjelde, G. Eiesland, J. Okkenhaug, St. forh. 1923 Dok. nr. 19 no.19; J. Castberg, H. Aarstad, O. Mjelde, St. forh. 1926 Dok. nr. 20 no. 14.

[112] Holding positions in several governmental branches was not uncommon in the 1800s, but became gradually less so after 1900; see Torgersen, Høyesterett i norsk politikk (1960). From J. Castberg's double position, the division between the executive and the judicial seems to have been more pressing than that between the legislative and the judicial at this time.

only the two Labor-associated members voted in support,[113] whereas all Liberal Left-affiliated members voted against.[114]

This seemingly odd lack of Liberal Left support for Liberal Left proposals is partly explained by unfortunate formulations of the proposals (as in 1923).[115] Other possible factors are the recommendation by the Liberal Left-leaning scholar M. Lie to abolish § 97 rather than judicial review – and the split within the Liberal Left (representatives from the Conservative Left ["Frisinnede Venstre"] being the ones voting against proposals from Liberal Left representatives in 1923 and 1926). The unanimous committee rejection in 1929 may, as also noted by Seip,[116] be ascribed to the increased disagreement between the Liberal Left and the Labor Party following the Labor election victory in 1927 and the brief radical government of Christopher Hornsrud in 1928. The 1932 Committee, however, attributes the unanimous 1929 decision to the preceding case concerning the right of the state to reduce the salary of civil servants, as a case alerting one to the "state of rightlessness which would have been the result of accepting the 1926 proposal [to abolish review]."[117] It claimed (without objection from the minority) that this salary reduction case was indeed the reason why the 1929 Committee had been unanimous in its rejection of the antireview proposal. While elegant, in excluding this liberal aspect Seip's interpretation thus seems insufficient.

The division within Parliament indicates that skepticism toward judicial review remained strong through the 10–15 years the question of abolishing it was being discussed. Apart from the proposing representatives and some of the dissenting minorities in the Committees, however, only representatives from the Labor Party did in fact support abolishment.

4.6 CONSTITUTIONAL CASE ADJOURNED

A view of judicial review as part of Norwegian constitutional law is, in this period, irrefutably confirmed by the 1918 case, the unison opinion of central scholars – and what seems to have been the commonly agreed opinion in political debates. And as the ongoing parliamentary debates assumed judicial review could only be abolished by constitutional amendment, this suggests both a legal and a political attitude that the institution was indeed

113 A. Magnussen, Labor Party Moderates ("Norges Socialdemokratiske Arbeiderparti") and E. Stang (Labor, later Norwegian Communist Party).

114 A. Holmboe, J. Brevig, C. Jakhelln, all Conservative Left ("Frisinnede Venstre").

115 See Skaar's expressed sympathy for the material proposal, Innst. S. LXXIV 1923, 7; and in 1926 equally Andersen Rysst and Seip, Innst. S. nr. 142 1926, 318).

116 Seip, *Tanke og handling i norsk historie* (1968), 103.

117 Innst. S. nr. 147 1932, 362.

constitutional in character as part of customary constitutional law. The institution of review did, in this period, withstand a well-reasoned and persistent opposition, and its legal and political station thus ended up having the unintended consequence of being confirmed and underlined, rather than weakened, by Parliament's five consecutive refusals to abolish it. While relatively frequently employed throughout the 1920s, there are indications that court interpretation of the Constitution gradually shifted in a direction more accepting of the needs for social economic regulation. One example of this is the *Vauvert* case of 1922, holding that the alcohol regulations, as argued by Skeie, did not interfere with the protection of established rights under § 97:[118]

> One must, in my opinion, in questions of legal issues such as the one at hand, the precise scope of which is of substantial importance to the question of what competence the state has to reform an important regulation of commerce to the best of the general public and societal development, be very cautious in judging the acts of the governing authorities in a way tying the free hands of the legislator.[119]

Vauvert set precedent that statutory regulation of ordinary trade conditions is constitutional under the Constitution § 97.

The Plenary Act of 1926 did not codify the institution of judicial review in the form of law. What it did, however, was to build upon the assumption that review existed, and set out procedural rules for its use. It thus positively formalized the view of Lie, Morgenstierne and Parliament: that judicial review with the effect of disregarding or finding statutes unconstitutional was indeed a part of Norwegian law.

To the extent positions with regard to judicial review may be distilled from the underlying constitutional questions discussed during this period, the following may be noted: The two arguments central to uphold review are, first, that of respect for the *organic nature of culture and history* – the customary law of review had gradually matured as a legal and political institution, and had, importantly, even though much contested, not led to any abuse of power from courts. Second, one of *constitutionality*: as lack of review powers would, in reality, leave the constitution to mean what the reigning majorities found it from time to time to mean, one needed something outside politics – courts' review – to ensure constitutional limits had any reality.

Against review, three arguments stand out: first, that of *unwanted outcomes* – the potential outcome of the 4–3 1918 case and disagreements with the

[118] Rt. 1922 s. 624. [119] Ibid., 625.

outcome of other review cases seems clearly motivating for the continued proposals from both Liberal Left and Labor Party representatives. Following this is the argument of *court skepticism*, in both a general and a specific form. Generally, courts consist of fewer members, and leaving constitutional decisions to them might mean that very few people – and perhaps only one person – gets to overrule the entire majority of Parliament. The particular Norwegian legal-historical experience leading up to this period was taken to show that courts are likely to be more conservative than Parliament, thus blocking necessary societal reforms. The third argument is that of *parliamentary development* from a constitutional system of division of powers to one of unification of powers. This may be seen as a version of the argument for *unlimited popular rule*: There really is no democratic room for any limiting institution outside Parliament and the government, not even the institution of restraining constitutional provisions in themselves. At least to the extent that these provisions are taken to mean anything other than what the reigning majority at any given time take them to mean, Parliament is to be the "sovereign interpreter of laws."[120]

Following the 1934 rejection of abolishing judicial review, the Labor Party proposed abolishing § 97 anew, sparking a final, constitutional debate in 1937.[121] No more proposals were put forward to abolish judicial review, so the parliamentary political debate concerning this legal institution ended in 1934. The question of review became less pertinent for other reasons too, a notable one of which was how the judiciary gradually practiced review less intensively after 1930.[122]

Neither rule of law nor liberal arguments appear prevalent in this period. They are notably missing from both Skeie's and Lie's 1917 and 1923 opinions. It may be noted, however, that the liberal argument emerges in Skeie's 1929 discussion of review. Here, Skeie holds out review as a liberal guarantee: a safeguard for representative democracy particularly pertinent in times of political flux, a check on ill-prepared laws and, as exercised in the manner of the Supreme Court (particularly after the Plenary Act), as a furtherance of intragovernmental balance in the way it serves as a tool for institutional dialogue.

120 Innstilling fra Specialkomiteen av 1927 [Special Committee of 1927], 62.

121 St. forh. 1935 Dok. 23 no. 13.

122 Later, Supreme Court Justice Hiorthøy finds courts almost "to bend over backwards to find challenged statutes constitutional" in this period: Nissen, et al., *Den dømmende makt* (1967), 131. For an assessment based on a wider conception of what decisions constitute review cases, see Smith, *Høyesterett og folkestyret* (1993), 217ff.

Morgenstierne emphasizes liberal arguments in his 1912 lecture, but not in his 1923 opinion – the latter instead seems concentrated on expounding the parts of Lie's assessment supporting review existence. And liberal arguments are but peripheral in the parliamentary debates, even from the majorities recommending rejection of the abolishment proposals.

Absent some particular standard for evaluation (good law, liberal rights protection, procedural or deliberative democracy enhancing), assessments of whether the outcomes of review are normatively good or bad are hard to make. And examining single case results in isolation also says little about the general institutional legitimacy of constitutional review. The mere fact that the Supreme Court at times decides cases based on a different interpretation of the Constitution than that of Parliament does not in itself make review outcomes "bad." It does, however, open up for questioning of review case results, and thus their legitimacy. Such questions were raised particularly in the 1920s. The critique against review in this period was clearly motivated by an opinion that *review led to bad results*, unwanted outcomes in a political era driven by a need for regulations that the Supreme Court was reluctant to find constitutional. Underlining this skepticism are also the objections against review by E. Stang and A. Magnussen in 1923, pointing to cases involving sanctions against radical speech that were not found to be contrary to the Constitution § 100 in the 1850s.

The *American argument* remains present both in the time preceding and in the period following the one here discussed. Significant in this period is the fundamental shift in the view of this point of reference. As recalled, the American argument had been one *for* judicial review in the 1800s. Morgenstierne continued and extended this positive view with his focus on review as a liberal guarantee, an individual safeguard. In the early 1900s the American argument, however, turned around. Opposing the traditionally pro-review argument of US practice, the opposite view, portraying the US development as an extensive and detrimental usurpation of power by courts, as seen in Skeie's and expounded in Lie's opinions, becomes the norm. Reference to the US experience continues to be done without much discussion of the jurisdictional and cultural differences between the two systems. In this period, however, it seems to reflect the view of the US Supreme Court that was also prevalent in the US at the time – that it served as a conservative brake on necessary social progressive legislation.[123]

123 See Friedman, The History of the Countermajoritarian Difficulty, Part II: Reconstruction's Political Court (2002).

As a curious sideview, a parallel discussion of Norwegian review practice as seen from the United States took place at about the same time. During a 1923 US Senate discussion about the competencies of the US Supreme Court, review practice was claimed to be an unparalleled example of US exceptionalism. It was argued that the European and Scandinavian countries treated their constitutional provisions as on a par with statutes. The Norwegian–American Senator Knute Nelson (R) rebutted this claim:

> The only other country in the world whose system of government conforms to ours, where the supreme court can declare a law unconstitutional, is the little country of Norway. It is the freest country in Europe. It has a government as free as that of this country; and in that country the supreme court can declare an act of the Parliament unconstitutional.[124]

The shift in the view of the American argument correlates with the decreasing emphasis on liberal arguments in the discussions of review, as indicated earlier in this chapter. Lie rebukes Morgenstierne's view on the "exemplary" US development as being out of tune with that of "wide and influential circles" in the United States. And Lie does indeed seem more up to date on the contemporary US debate at this point. His presentation of the US system mirrors the highly critical scholarly position dominant in the *Lochner*-era commentaries on judicial review. The view of this era as conveyed by Lie remained hegemonic for decades also in the United States, as illustrated by the US legal dictionary entry word "lochnerizing": "to strike down economic legislation under the guise of enforcing the Due Process Clause."[125] Beginning in the 1980s–1990s, this description nonetheless became increasingly criticized for representing a peddling of "winner's history" as told by former reformists in the wake of the progressive turn in US constitutional law in the 1940s. An increasing number of studies nuance the conventional view of the *Lochner* era. They argue that what the US Supreme Court did in this period was neither particularly conservative nor hostile to social regulation as compared to other periods, nor was much "new" law created.[126] This revised view of input and outcome legitimacy is, however, not necessarily indicative of a revised view of its social legitimacy – how judicial review was popularly perceived at the time.[127]

124 64 Cong. Rec. 3861 1923. Passage also cited in Hambro, *Portræter og profiler* (1937), 117.

125 See i.a. Garner, *A Dictionary of Modern Legal Usage* (2001) 536; *Black's Law Dictionary* (1996) 391.

126 A presentation of and expansive list of references to this literature are in fns 5 and 6 in Thomson, *Review Essay: Swimming in the Air: Melville W. Fuller and the Supreme Court 1888-1910* (1996).

127 Friedman, The History of the Countermajoritarian Difficulty Part III: The Lesson of Lochner (2001) 99–100.

The scare of the US example seems to have done little to influence the outcome of the Norwegian political debates in this period. As noted by majority speaker in Parliament, A. Holmboe (Liberal Left), "for the [unlikely] event Norwegian courts, like those in the US, were to assume more and more power, one would have to find means against that."[128] As further expounded in Chapters 5 and 8, following the shift in the perceived legitimacy of US courts, the American argument has remained that of the US judicial review bogeyman.

Viewed against the US development at the time, the 1918 *Waterfall* case has been seen as a judicial formulation of a modern right to property, a "Supreme Court manifestation of the societal abolishment of economic liberalism."[129] As such, it represents an early Norwegian variety of the US *West Coast Hotel* case, in which the US Supreme Court upheld a minimum wage regulation, thus ending the *Lochner* era.[130] Its reasoning, based on the legislative needs to regulate economic questions in particular, points forward to the differentiated view on economic rights versus personal or integrative rights, as explicated in the 1976 *Kløfta* case central to Chapter 5 – a differentiation which again resembles the opening for different levels of scrutiny as set out in the famous footnote four of the 1938 US *Carolene Products* case.[131]

[128] St. forh. 17.10 1923, 3225. [129] Slagstad, *Rettens ironi* (2011), 391

[130] *West Coast Hotel Co.* v. *Parrish*, 300 US 379 (1937)

[131] *United States* v. *Carolene Products Co.* (1938).

5

Post-World War II: Social Democratic Constitutionalism?

5.1 INTRODUCTION: REVIEW REVIVAL

After the Waterfall case and the explicit political discussions of judicial review in the 1920s and 1930s, the first case to spark wide-ranging debate about review appears in 1976: the *Kløfta* case.[1] After a long period in which courts seldom interpreted the Constitution in a way that diverged from that of Parliament, the *Kløfta* case, by a slim majority, found a statute regulating compensations following expropriation (the Expropriation Compensation Act, "ECA") to be unconstitutional under the constitutional takings clause in § 105. The case elaborates on the scope of review, and later became the central point of reference for modern constitutional review discussions and cases.

The long period between the debates following the Waterfall case, which dwindled from the 1930s until 1976, is, however, not void of cases or discussions related to the institution of review. This chapter outlines the questions of review relevant to the occupation and postwar period of 1940–1960 (Section 5.2 and 5.3); the formative debate between historian Jens A. Seip and lawyer Johs. Andenæs in the 1960s (Section 5.4); the arguments leading up to the *Kløfta* decision (Section 5.5); the case itself (Section 5.6) and the review consequences of the case (Section 5.7). What is established with the *Kløfta* case is that, rather than provoke a political antireview reaction such as the Waterfall case did in the 1920s, it instead clarified and entrenched the Norwegian review tradition.

The *Kløfta* case use of review powers in 1976 has been seen as a shift – and one that came as something of a surprise. While recognizing the existence of review powers, law Professor T. Eckhoff did not consider that these powers made the Supreme Court much of a relevant guardian of constitutional law.

[1] Rt. 1976 s. 1.

In a 1975 article on the Supreme Court he stated that: "I doubt these powers will ever be used again in any way worth mentioning."[2] He was wrong. A recollection of the war and postwar political and legal situation and development may provide some background for Eckhoff's statement.

5.2 OCCUPATION AND POSTWAR ADJUDICATION

In the legal domain, powers of judicial review had rarely been used to find laws unconstitutional since the early 1930s. An important instance confirming the persistence of review reasoning did, however, come about just as WWII broke out. Under the lead of Chief Justice Berg – the "true-meaning restraint" justice in the *Waterfall* case and the architect behind the inclusion of review cases in the Plenary Act – the Supreme Court refused to comply with regulations attempting to have the judiciary controlled by the occupying German powers in 1940, on the grounds that they were unconstitutional.

Following German occupation of Norway on April 9, 1940, a civilian occupation regime led by *Reichskommisar* Josef Terboven was set up by Nazi Germany.[3] Terboven governed with what was termed "commissary" ministers – ministers loyal to the occupation regime. Under such a minister, the Ministry of Justice proposed legislation lowering the age limit of Supreme Court justices from seventy to sixty-five years, with the aim of replacing justices with ones true to the regime. Chief Justice Berg found this to alter the station of the Supreme Court in a way incompatible with the constitutional requirement of independence, a position supported by the other justices. Terboven also forbade judicial review of regime regulations, an act further solidifying the Supreme Court opposition. The Court's refusal to comply with these regulations was not accepted by Terboven. This led the Supreme Court justices to sign a letter to Terboven in which they all resigned.[4] The justices maintained it would counter their professional oath not to "review the constitutionality of laws and regulations." In wartime this meant they were obliged to review whether such

[2] Eckhoff, Høyesterett som grunnlovens vokter (1975), 202. Reprinted in *Lov og rett* 1976, 1.

[3] *Reichskommissariat für die besetzten norwegischen Gebiete*. The Reichskommissariat had collaborationist support from the pro-Nazi party "National Unification," led by Vidkun Quisling. In 1942, Adolf Hitler allowed Quisling to form a Norwegian government under German supervision, an institution without any real power, as *Reichskommisar* Josef Terboven governed Norway, and all the military forces stationed in Norway were under German command.

[4] Innstilling fra undersøkelseskommisjonen av 1945, 327ff.

regulations comply also with international law.[5] Notable are both that the court underlined that it was the "duty" of Norwegian courts, under Norwegian constitutional law, to undertake such review, and that the laws of an occupying power could be reviewed also under international law. This review reasoning keeps alive the question of whether liberal and rule-of-law arguments for judicial review may have been unpopular in the 1920s–1930s primarily due to the political debate climate in this period.

Following the collective resignation of Supreme Court justices, a "commissionary" Supreme Court functioned from 1940–1945. As its decisions and precedent have, understandably, not been used as legal reference by either politicians or the Supreme Court since the war, these are not elaborated further here.[6]

Following the speech in which the Supreme Court resigned in 1940, Chief Justice Berg stated in his Supreme Court opening speech in 1945 that

> [i]t is an old legal doctrine in our society that citizens may seek legal protection by courts not only from other citizens' breaches of justice, but also from abuse of power from those ruling the country. As the highest court, the Supreme Court is the primary guardian of law and justice. We have no one above us but the Constitution and binding law. But we are not the masters of the law, we are its servants. And our responsibility is double as our decisions may not be reviewed by any other authority.[7]

Immediately after the war, there were several examples of criminal convictions based on retroactive regulations for war crimes that passed through the judiciary unhindered by the Constitution §§ 96 and 97. Central among these is the plenary *Klinge* case from 1946.[8]

A German Gestapo officer was sentenced to death for his crimes during the war (several instances of torture, one fatal) on the basis of criminal provisions against severe bodily harm. These provisions did not mandate the death penalty, but legal foundation in the form of a provisionary act mandating the death penalty for such crimes had been enacted by the Norwegian government-in-exile in 1945.[9] The officer argued that basing his death penalty on this act was unconstitutional under the ban of retroactivity in § 97 of the Constitution, as his crimes were committed prior to its enactment.

5 Rt. 1945 s. 2, 3–4.

6 A historical analysis of the commissionary Supreme Court to be found in Langeland and Sandmo, *Siste ord* (2005).

7 Speech by Paal Berg, 14.5.1945 (ibid., 5).

8 See i.a. Rt. 1946 s. 198 (Klinge).

9 By "Provisorisk anordning" of May 4, 1945: "provisorisk anordning" is an intermediary form of legislation, a prerogative of the executive under the Constitution § 17.

The Supreme Court upheld the death penalty (9–4), based on a view that the officer had committed war crimes, that such crimes under international law could be punished by death, and that the Norwegian Constitution thus did not apply. The minority found that § 96 of the Constitution (*nulla poena sine lege*) barred using the death penalty absent a valid Norwegian legal foundation, and that the provisionary act did not constitute such a foundation due to its unconstitutional retroactivity under § 97.

The decision resulted in disapproval from several parties in the legal community, notably professors Frede Castberg and Johs. Andenæs, and is central among a series of often-criticized postwar proceedings against Norwegian Nazi collaborators ["landssvikoppgjøret"].[10] It was not reversed before 2010, in a case concerning retroactive penalty increases for war crimes discussed in Section 8.2.3.

In the decades following the war, few Supreme Court cases sat aside or significantly reinterpreted statutory regulations due to conflicting constitutional provisions. Some exceptions to this can be noted. In Rt. 1952 s. 932, a decree suspending police officers who were formerly members of the National Socialist Party without due compensation was set aside as unconstitutional under §§ 22 and 97. In Rt. 1964 s. 1418, a conviction mandating a lenient criminal sanction ("hæfte") under Danish law could not be converted to the stricter Norwegian sanction of a prison sentence because of the protection against retroactivity in § 97 of the Constitution.

5.3 REGULATORY RECONSTRUCTION

In contrast to the skeptical judicial reactions with which the increasing eagerness for political regulation was met by the Supreme Court preceding and following WWI, enactments of an even more expansive regulatory regime following WWII were almost never found unconstitutional. The earliest years after WWII in Norway were characterized by the spirit of solidarity from the war. The dominant parties, formerly divided on central, political issues, all subscribed to a so-called Common Program (*Fellesprogrammet*), stipulating visions for a national reconstruction. It held out goals such as economic growth and bettering and equalizing of life conditions to be reached through collaboration across political and social divides, and aimed at a regulated and planned mixed market economy. Even as a political compromise, this program has been seen to pave the way for what was later been labeled the "Labor Party

10 Andenæs, *Det vanskelige oppgjøret: rettsoppgjøret etter okkupasjonen* (1979). See also Dahl, *Et rettferdig oppgjør?* (2004).

State" ("Arbeiderpartistaten"): the vision of "the Norwegian Enterprise" ("Bedriften Norge"), opening for an idea of the people as a common production apparatus very much in tune with the central ideas of the Labor Party.[11] The Labor Party held the government position from 1945 until 1965 (interrupted by the nonsocialist coalition Lyng government in August–September 1963), and then again from 1971–1981, with one short interruption by the Christian Democrats' coalition in 1971–1972, and it kept a majority of seats in Parliament from 1945–1961.

Two debates central to the understanding of constitutionality in the form of limits on political power occurred in 1947 and 1950, in relation to two different but interrelated sets of regulations: one, a price-rationalizing regime meant to effectivize economic politics in a time of an expanding administrative state; the other, a set of proposed security and defense laws. They had in common the parliamentary use of power delegation to the executive – parliamentary sanctioned bases for substantial executive discretion in two constitutionally central matters: the balancing of state economic regulation against rights of trade and property, and of security measures against individual liberty. And both in ways that challenged the principle of legality.

The defense laws were prompted by the wish to be better prepared than before WWII, now with an eye to the possible threats of the Cold War. Meant to provide a parliamentary sanctioned legal basis for the executive in case of emergency, the proposal opened for the death penalty, internment without trial and press censorship "in the event of war, under the threat of war or when the independence or security of the Kingdom is in danger as a result of aggressive or threatening hostilities between foreign states, *or on other grounds*."[12] The proposal drew broad criticism from the public.[13] In particular, the addition "on other grounds" was seen potentially to encompass almost anything, thus in reality giving the executive carte blanche to curtail central rights when it chose to.[14] The law was enacted in a moderated form in 1950.[15] Debates about the price laws were even more intense. Starting in 1947, and culminating in 1952, the extensive use of delegation laws was criticized as unconstitutional by the opposition Conservative party, with John Lyng as a prominent voice. The architect behind the regulations – Labor Party Finance Secretary, Erik Brofoss – held that such concerns were not

[11] Furre, *Norsk historie 1905–1990* (1992), 208ff. [12] Ot. prp. nr. 78 (1950), emphasis added.

[13] Debates gathered and published in i.a. "Beredskapslovgivningen Ot. prp. nr. 78" (1950); "Front mot frykten" (1950); "Ordskiftet om Beredskapslovene 12 oktober 1950" (1950).

[14] See Sejersted, *Demokrati og rettsstat* (2001), 323ff.

[15] Defense Act of 1950, "Lov om særlige rådgjerder under krig, krigsfare og liknende forhold [beredskapsloven]" 1950-12-15-7.

constructive to an "un-prejudiced debate"; what was central, he maintained, was "the reality . . . the problems of economic organization."[16]

It has been observed that politically, under the Conservative opposition, the constitutional concerns over the price laws were substantially stronger than that over the defense laws.[17] Notably, the central conservative paper *Aftenposten* argued against the price laws, but had little to say against the defense laws. Regarding the price laws, the liberalistic paper *Farmand* argued against "totalitarian concessions," particularly under a Labor government. The communist paper *Friheten*, on the other hand, had no constitutional disagreement with the price laws, but was opposed to the defense laws on constitutional grounds. As has been noted, these media reactions exemplify "[t]wo symbolic examples of constitutional opportunism, one conservative; one communist."[18]

In 1952, a dispute originating in the 1947 debate over increasing delegatory price legislation reached the Supreme Court in plenary. The case before the Court concerned Parliament's right to delegate central parts of its taxation competencies under the Constitution to the executive, in this case, an administrative agency. Even admitting that "the delegation of power to tax the citizens in this case is far more extensive than in any other peace time example," the Supreme Court majority found the delegation constitutional, relying mainly on practical considerations: "I cannot see that courts in this case have any grounds for reviewing the assessment of the legislator as to how far it under the circumstances finds it necessary and constitutionally sound to go." It also stated it was "not for the courts to evaluate price regulation politics, only to assess the legality of the steps taken, hereunder their constitutionality." While not explicitly discussed, the case confirms that judicial review might be merited in other types of cases. It also clarifies that its scope extends to review whether Parliament has exceeded its competencies also in matters concerning the relation between branches of government: here, Parliament and the executive. It maintains, however, that review of the relation between branches of government should be exercised "somewhat more leniently than that under constitutional provisions protecting citizens rights directly, such as §§ 97 and 105," thus underlining the possibility of a differentiated approach to differing constitutional provisions as foreshadowed in the *Waterfall* case.

The various delegation laws were replaced by a permanent Price Act in 1953. While the constitutionality of such delegation, as upheld by the Supreme Court, was defended on principled grounds by professors Torkel Opsahl and

16 Slagstad, *De nasjonale strateger*, 233ff. 17 Ibid. 18 Ibid.

Torstein Eckhoff,[19] professor Johs. Andenæs was skeptical regarding the massive use of such laws, arguing that "[u]ntil the enactment of the permanent Price Act [in 1953] one could say that our entire economic legislative regulation consisted in *in blanco* concessions to the general and particular decisions that the administrative found necessary or practical. The new Price Act represents a shift, a reaction against what I believe one must call a tendency to slippery slope."[20]

The new Price Law was to some extent seen as an answer to reactions against constitutional usurpation, but it sought to abate legislative delegation motivated by a more democratic argument: By delegating power from the popularly elected to the executive, by administrative agencies, decision-making was shifted from open parliamentary debates to less transparent agency decisions, thus reversing the democratic development from the 1800 period of high civil servants' rule.[21]

Generally, in the few review cases that did take place after the period of war-related cases, courts would be very hesitant to overrule Parliament's evaluation where Parliament had assessed the constitutionality of what it saw to be necessary regulations and decided to enact them.[22] This is not to say there were no claims of unconstitutionality brought before the courts: several statutes enacted to implement new regulatory regimes were challenged as unconstitutional and treated in plenary by the Supreme Court.

A central example is a case from 1950 in which two-thirds of the full compensation offered in a case of expropriation was eaten up by taxes, following a steep postwar progressivity of income tax.[23] Holding the question of income taxation to be different from that of a compensation for takings, the Supreme Court did not find this unconstitutional under § 105 of the Constitution. Five justices dissented, pointing to the unreasonable reduction of actual compensation being a result solely of the forced expropriation, and thus representing a taking under § 105.

Another case indicative of the Supreme Court view of review scope is Rt. 1954 s. 478, in which a limited prohibition on Antarctic whaling was claimed to run counter to the "spirit and principles" of § 112 of the Constitution, as it discriminatingly represented a working ban for a small group of whalers. The Supreme Court did not refute the argument that it was competent to

19 See Opsahl, *Delegasjon av Stortingets myndighet* (1965).

20 Andenæs, *Domstolenes stilling til Stortingets delegasjon av myndighet* (1953) in *Avhandlinger og foredrag* (1962), 286.

21 Sejersted, *Høyres historie* (1984), 109 ff.

22 See, i.a. Rt. 1956 s. 952, Rt. 1952 s. 1281.

23 Rt. 1950 s. 831.

review whether a statute was in accordance with the "spirit and principles" of § 112. The statute in question, however, was not set aside.

In 1962, the plenary Supreme Court found a 1923 statute invalidating gold clauses to be constitutional under § 97, even though it affected contracts entered into around the turn of the century.[24] In a 1970 case, the Supreme Court held a temporary construction ban within a 100-meter belt from the sea to be constitutional under § 105, even though this prevented building at all on islets less than 200 meters across.[25] The interpretation of § 105 had by this time come to allow substantial regulation of property in the common interest – a development at the time desirable by political majority standards and judicial review interpretation alike.

In some other cases, judicial review was exercised more cautiously, harmonizing the interpretations of statutes and the Constitution in ways avoiding open conflicts. The overall picture of judicial review in the first decades after WWII is one of a Supreme Court that was extremely hesitant to find statutes unconstitutional.[26] The reasons for this are probably many and complex. It seems fair to assume, however, that the courts were not immune to the widespread consensus-oriented notion by which the reconstruction of Norway was seen as a collective effort, and in which disagreements were downplayed to the benefit of the common goal of national rebuilding and recovery.

Interesting in this regard is an episode noted by Henning Bødtker, Attorney General for Civil Affairs 1945–1962. In his memoirs, in a passage on the ceremonious nature of Supreme Court plenary cases, he recalls one case that "could have ended up in plenary, but was halted *in time*."[27] It concerned the question of a postwar regulation regarding settlement for fishing vessels, modeled on the Nortraship settlement.[28] When the case came before the Supreme Court, it became clear the private party suing the state "could not win unless the regulation was set aside as unconstitutional." The Supreme Court decided to hear it in plenary, but only after some days of initial proceedings. During these proceedings, Bødtker had become "quite aware that a decision in plenary would go against the state":

24 Rt. 1962 s. 369. 25 Rt. 1970 s. 67.

26 Hiorthøy in Nissen, et al., *Den dømmende makt* (1967), 131, 147; Eckhoff, *Høyesterett som grunnlovens vokter* (1975); Smith, Høyesterett og folkestyret (1993).

27 Bødtker, *En advokat forteller* (1970), 156–157, emphasis added. The entry is undated, but Lysø functions as Minister from 1955, so the episode must be from the late 1950s, and before 1962.

28 The shipping company Nortraship, the Norwegian Shipping and Trade Mission, was established in 1940 in London, with the aim of administering the Norwegian merchant fleet during WWII.

> The contact from the Justices' table to the bench was at that point so good, that I could know the lay of the land, and so I calculatingly went to the Minister [of Fishery] Lysø and said: We have to find a solution without further proceedings. He was all ears, and thanks to excellent work from my counterparty's young counsel, we reached a solution acceptable to us both.

Underlining that judicial review was indeed a functioning institution at the time, ready to be used, Bødtker's account also indicates how important at least he, as legal representative for the state, found it that a case of review going against the state was not pronounced.

> Perhaps what the courts do, is to interpret the old and dated constitution in light of the present circumstances, so that the statutes, which are up to date, come to pass . . . when the constitution doesn't lend itself to being changed by ordinary, democratic majorities, it is developed instead through interpretations, interpretations presumed by the legislator with ordinary majority upon enactment of statutes. Courts are inclined to tag along and let the statute pass muster . . . The way judicial review has been practiced, it functions well – as seen from nearly all perspectives.[29]

For a rule of law-oriented constitutional law professor such as Torkel Opsahl to hold the almost nonexistent postwar review practice to be well functioning, as "seen from nearly all perspectives," the public support for main political lines must have been quite broad.

Thematizing the relation between law and politics, in 1964 Johs. Andenæs pointed to how the political is closely tied to law, in that both political and legal cases arise out of *interests*. In politics, questions of colliding interests may lead to compromises; in law, however, they must be answered. When political interests are formulated as assertions of law, this is not hypocritical or intellectually unsound – the more a constitution contains of legal rules binding on political life, the more often conflicting interests must take on the form of dispute over what these rules imply.[30] Andenæs pointed to the United States, where this relation between law and politics is obvious, and to the United Kingdom, where it is not "due to parliamentary sovereignty. . . . And something like this [the UK situation] is the governing principle in Norway today, as constitutional questions relevant to decide the balance between the branches of power have for the most part been solved already."[31]

"On the political arena nothing has been heard about judicial review for almost a generation," F. Hiorthøy wrote in 1964, in a study on the role of courts

29 Opsahl, Plikt og betingelse (1969), 165.

30 Andenæs, Parlamentarisme, jus og statsvitenskap (1964), 64. 31 Ibid.

in the development of law.[32] Hiorthøy pointed to how Parliament and the government, through taxing, monetary and price regulations, had found "efficient means by which to further their socio-economic politics." The reason why judicial review did not hinder this efficacy was that courts, with "support in a legal community more responsible and socially attentive" to "leaving the legislature a wide margin under the constitutional §§ 97 and 105" were less inclined to read the Constitution in a way contrary to what had become a more common view of necessary societal change. For this reason, the Supreme Court had "not found any law unconstitutional in 30 years." And even if such cases were to come in the future, proposals to ban judicial review would hardly be suggested: although used less than before, review powers had been "ingrained in the common sense of justice." Hiorthøy held the review competence to be a valuable societal feature: it had the practical function of forcing Parliament to give serious consideration to constitutional questions, and, more importantly, to safeguard public security by protecting the individual. This notwithstanding – the role of courts as guardians for individual freedom against the state had shifted to a different field of law – that what was now needed was court protection of individuals against decisions by the administrative branch.[33]

Following the observations from the 1920s, the surprise use of review powers in the 1976 *Kløfta* case could be seen possibly to have provoked a debate on the legitimacy of review or attempts at changing the Constitution. As I return to in Section 5.7, however, it seems the debate in the aftermath of the case may instead be an indication that *Kløfta* was not such an unwelcome shift from the lenience of review from 1945–1976. While a central view – descriptively or more or less openly normatively – may have been that of review legitimacy depending on court deference, there were also vocations to the contrary. Two such voices, interestingly from very differently positioned persons, may be mentioned: I. B. Hjort, a then liberal conservative lawyer, held that the "Supreme Court anxiety of reviewing legislative discretion ... is mistaken. The foremost task of courts is to uphold the law, to protect freedom of citizens that state powers attack, in other words to protect minorities, particularly when these are infringed upon by the two other governmental powers."[34] At the same time, political scientist Christian Bay held that "the purpose of any state and any constitution ought to be maximizing the protection of the most

[32] Hiorthøy in Nissen, et al., *Den dømmende makt* (1967), 156, 157. The article was written for the 150th anniversary of the Court Organization in 1964, but left unedited, thus not thematizing the review discussions of 1964–1965. See Section 5.4.

[33] Hiorthøy, Ibid., 159.

[34] Hjort, Grunnloven, et postulat? (1962), 19.

comprehensive human rights possible. . . . One of the main roles of courts should be to interpret legislation and the constitution most favorably to comprehensive human rights."[35]

As noted by F. Castberg in 1952, the way review was practiced after the war left the impression that "one could perhaps have wished for a somewhat stricter constitutional construction in the Supreme Court."[36] The nature of review in this period "approaches that of the Danish principle of clarity": only where the unconstitutionality is entirely clear and unambiguous may courts find a law unconstitutional.[37]

5.4 LAW, POLITICS AND HISTORY

The main discussions about judicial review in the decades after the war gained actuality from a different source than case law – namely, from a seminal academic debate on the historical origins and legitimacy of review in 1964–1965. The impact of this debate, particularly the reconstruction of origins for later discussions of review in Norway is profound. It was instigated not by lawyers, but by a historian. While legal discussions of judicial review in the period following WWII (such as that of i.a. Hiorthøy and Eckhoff) revolved around different understandings of what constitutionalism implied and when customary constitutional practice became constitutional law, the classical historical reconstruction reflected upon the legitimacy of judicial review and focused on courts as *institutions*. As such, it had similarities with another debate concerning the power balance between branches of government: The Kings Bay case from 1963 concerned a mining accident at Svalbard for which the Labor government was held accountable and had to resign. It ascertained the principle of parliamentarism. It also sparked a debate between political scientists and lawyers about the power balance between Parliament and the government, where lawyers were accused of dressing up their political claims as legal ones, thus obscuring their political agenda.[38] The thematizing of law by other disciplines in this period brought forth another perspective on law, courts and judicial review than that which lawyers had primarily focused on, and actualized questions of the relationship between legal and political institutions, between law and politics.

35 Bay, *Politisk forskning og politisk ansvarlighet* (1961), 77.

36 F. Castberg, in *Dommerbladet* 1952, 1117.

37 Nissen, et al., *Den dømmende makt* (1967), 146.

38 Wyller, Kings Bay-saken: jus, politikk og statsvitenskap (1964); Christophersen, Forholdet Storting – Regjering (1964).

The debate was sparked by the prevalent Norwegian historian J. A. Seip, in an article titled "The Norwegian Supreme Court as a Political Institution."[39] In it, he offered a reconstruction of judicial review as a conservative response to the breakthrough of parliamentarism in the 1880s. The 1800s powerful high state officials were the ones, on Seip's account, who had developed judicial review as an instrument to hinder the popular power achieved through the strengthening of Parliament. A historian aiming "not to dress up, but to undress" his historical subject – and subjects – Seip looked for the ulterior and real motives in his historical writings. He asserted that Aschehoug, through "squeezing available precedent hard," had "established" the customary constitutional law of judicial review in his treatise on constitutional law published in 1885,[40] by "concocting, during the impeachment deliberations, this last guarantee" in which the [conservative] Supreme Court could act as an umpire between the executive and Parliament.[41] In his analysis of the work of the Supreme Court, he portrays the Court not as guardian of the Constitution, but rather as an institution acting politically "to an extreme degree" by having "amended" the Constitution with judicial review "by deliberate misrepresentation."[42] The Norwegian judicial review was a "spanner deliberately thrown in the works of democracy, behind the back of Parliament, by the dethroned high state officials."[43] Not only was the institution of judicial review an unwarranted expansion of the Constitution, it was also a competency illegitimately obtained through a willful political act by the Supreme Court. The entrenchment of this antiparliamentary endeavor was, on Seip's account, strengthened by who in his eyes seems a very instrumental legal scientist, T. H. Aschehoug.

One of the studies that Seip relied on was a 1960 article by political scientist Ulf Torgersen on the role of the Supreme Court in Norwegian politics. Torgersen's Master's degree had addressed the development of legal argumentation under the Constitution § 97, the general ban on retroactive legislation.[44] He explained Aschehoug's contribution to the development of judicial review through his view of § 97 as a "new orientation," a "complete reversal of the thesis presented by Stang a generation earlier." He "raised the courts to the position, in theory, of an equal and independent branch of government," and "went on to reinterpret" § 97, conducting

39 Seip, Den norske Høyesterett som politisk organ (1965).

40 Seip, *Høyesterett som politisk organ* (1964) 113, and as published the year after in Seip, Den norske Høyesterett som politisk organ (1965), 7.

41 Seip, Den norske Høyesterett som politisk organ (1965), 7. 42 Ibid. 43 Ibid., 2.

44 Torgersen, *De generelle synspunktene på Grl.* § 97 (1955).

> very much the same theoretical job as was being performed by his American contemporary Thomas M. Cooley in his theory concerning due process of law. In both cases, an old clause aiming at the regulation of *form* was given a new, *substantive* content. Aschehoug thus presented a Norwegian Supreme Court of real power and vigor; and it is significant that he explicitly built his new conception of the role of the Norwegian judiciary after the American model.[45]

Connecting the embedding of judicial review to the courts' role in the period of parliamentary breakthrough had also been done by Eckhoff in 1964.[46] While not claiming that Aschehoug and other scholars were motivated by anything other than what they thought to be scholarly and legally correct, one could not "exclude the possibility that the political situation in the 1880s and 90s may have served as a breeding ground for the idea of judicial review with Aschehoug and other conservative jurists."[47]

Rather than ascribing the relative inactivity in review practice after WWII to the government, and Parliament having found constitutional means by which to accomplish the necessary welfare state regulatory regime, Seip saw this latter period as demonstrating how the political motivation of the Supreme Court shifted with time. According to Seip, the fusion of law and politics had, since 1945, been completed, as had the Supreme Court penance: The justices in this period "struggled to have the law point in the same direction as the political compass"; the Norwegian Supreme Court had become but a "wavering dinghy in the wake of the ship of State."[48]

Particularly offensive to the legal community was Seip's contention that the Supreme Court motivation for acting countermajoritarian was political, not legal.[49] Law professor Johs. Andenæs disputed Seip's analysis. He argued that judicial review had been practiced long before the debates over parliamentarism, and hence did not originate as a politically conservative response, as claimed by Seip.[50] He took issue with Seip's understanding of the Supreme Court as a "political" institution: although courts' practice had political *implications* through norm creation or decisions in politically controversial cases, they were not politically *motivated*. Andenæs did not deny that ideological preferences could indeed be motivating judges, but maintained there was an institutional difference between legal and political practice in their

45 Torgersen in Schubert, *Judicial Decision-making* (1963), 224 (emphasis added).
46 Eckhoff in Lejman, *Festskrift tillägnad professor, juris doktor Karl Olivecrona* (1964), 109, 125.
47 Ibid., 125–126. 48 Seip, *Utsikt over Norges historie* 2 (1981), 106.
49 Seip, Den norske Høyesterett som politisk organ (1965).
50 Andenæs, Høyesterett som politisk organ (1965). Andenæs' assertion was later documented by Slagstad, Prøvingsretten i det norske system (1989) and Smith, *Høyesterett og folkestyret* (1993).

aims and limits: political decisions are primarily motivated by regulative ideas for the society at large. Their choice between alternatives and evaluations of appropriateness and fairness are further free from the bindings inherent in legal doctrine and an existing system of norms, as opposed to legal considerations.[51]

Andenæs did not explicate his arguments for judicial review, but held that the principle of review stood stronger in the political sphere at the time of writing than it did before, the old radical reluctance toward the Supreme Court role as public guardian having quietened down. Acknowledging this might be due to the fact that the Supreme Court had not proven to be any hindrance to social welfare politics, he also pointed to how "the experience from dictator states has heightened [our] awareness of the role of independent courts as guardians for the individual vis-à-vis the state."[52]

These are contentions concerning the social legitimacy of review. It is acknowledged as legitimate for two reasons. One is outcome-based: the Supreme Court's cautious use of review not hindering what is politically considered necessary welfare state development – thus a limited exercise of power, and one not running counter to a fairly widespread belief in what constitutes necessary politics. The other emphasizes both input and outcome perspectives: The institutional view of independent courts as liberal wardens, and the awareness that authoritarian governance is indeed a real possibility against which these courts may serve as guardians.

Underlining that there is no logical necessity to assume that review competences even accept the constitution as *lex superior*, the choice to accept – and not to accept – review is politically motivated, Andenæs contended. The difference between the two choices lies in the institutional consequence: By accepting judicial review, courts are institutionally competent to also consider questions of constitutionality, which in turn have implications for the political.

This is an argument thematizing how normative ideals of legitimacy underlie both the acceptance and nonacceptance, the exercise and nonexercise of review. With review, the liberal perspective is institutionally enforceable by courts, something which clearly may have implications for the political.

51 Andenæs, Jus og politikk (1990), 415–416. This, and the following discussions, however, did not subdue the claims of political motivation, for either the origins or the practice of review. Maintaining the view that legal institutions such as the Supreme Court and constitutional review were indeed politically driven were Seip, *Tanke og handling i norsk historie* (1968), 120; Eckhoff, Høyesterett som grunnlovens vokter (1975); and Seip, *Utsikt over Norges historie 2* (1981), 230.

52 Andenæs, Høyesterett som politisk organ (1965), 33.

Without it, this perspective may (or may not) be protected elsewhere. And, where review exists, both review of and deference to policy choices has political implications: both assessments requires taking stance, in the concrete application, for individual freedom or popular sovereignty as represented by majority will. He could have added that the ideals guiding the discretionary room for such choices are, necessarily, normative or ideological in nature.

Seip's claims of review illegitimacy are clearly based on a view of countermajoritarianism as not only difficult, but normatively untenable. It is also a view which leaves little room for constitutional limits on the political other than those that the political powers at any time might set for itself. In a 1970s reconstruction of the 1800s époque of high state officials, another historian, F. Sejersted, criticized Seip for parenthesizing the role of the constitution as binding and limiting the political by disregarding the role of courts as an independent branch of government.[53] As indicated by Seip's lack of criticism against the toothless postwar Supreme Court, it seems that, in Seip's view, the idea of constitutional limits is indeed more critique-worthy than the notion that the courts act on political motivation. His reconstruction is premised on the lack of legitimacy in courts acting countermajoritarian rather than their exercising political power through the political motivation of "struggling to have the law point in the same direction as the political compass."[54]

5.5 CONQUER AND DIVIDE: PREPARING THE EXPROPRIATION STATUTE

The Expropriation Compensation Act of 1973 (ECA)[55] provided a legislative regulation of a question formerly left to courts: how to assess what amounts to "full compensation" for expropriation under the Constitution § 105. Through case law, guidelines for compensation had become steadily more detailed in the decades leading up to 1973, and property owners could normally choose between being compensated the *utility* value or the *market* value, whichever was higher. The central provision of the ECA held that compensation should be measured by the utility value rather than the market value.[56] One of the explicit motives for enacting the ECA was to have it be one means in the reigning price regulation policy to keep property prices down. Or, as the opposition saw it – to lower compensation costs for the state in a way offering

[53] Sejersted, *Demokrati og rettsstat* (2001), 112, 153 ff. [54] Ibid.

[55] The Expropriation Compensation Act of 1973 (ECA) [Lov av 26. januar 1973 nr. 4 om erstatning ved ekspropriasjon av fast eiendom].

[56] Ibid., § 4 no. 1.

property-owning individuals less than full compensation for their property and even lower property prices, their maximum already being controlled through price regulations.[57]

The main *travaux préparatoires* for the ECA was presented by the Husaas committee in 1969.[58] With the mandate to propose regulation on the details for compensation upon expropriation, it ended up dividing 10–5 on whether to propose such regulation at all. The majority held that regulations ought more or less to codify the principles developed through case law. It emphasized the importance of cautiously formulating regulations for a compensation scheme so that they would not to be disregarded by courts as unconstitutional. Even so, it pointed out that it would be "not irrelevant" to the intensity and scope of courts' review under the Constitution § 105 "that Parliament in the form of statutory law had stated its position" on the issue of the statute. It asserted that § 105 was "primarily directed to Parliament, and the courts must restrain themselves from placing their own assessment above that of the legislator."[59] The minority concluded it would be better not to propose regulations: They would either be obvious, and thus unnecessary, or they would give rise to massive litigation. To the question of what relevance court precedent had on the freedom of Parliament to regulate the issue, the minority underlined that any regulation must be in accordance with the interpretation of full compensation as followed from judicial precedent.[60]

The quite moderate regulation proposal from the Husaas committee ended up being changed significantly in the Ministry of Justice. Central in its proposition was the motivation to counter price increases on real estate, particularly increases "unfairly" awarded to property owners as a consequence of public investments. The proposition went very hastily through the Ministry of Justice. The Bratteli Labor government took office March 17, 1971; its proposition to Odelstinget was presented April 30, 1971,[61] the government being "of the opinion that enacting the legislation was a matter of urgency."[62] According to later commentary on the process by Johs. Andenæs, the expropriation legislation came about following a "particularly deficient legislative preparation." Not only was it "very notably" treated as a matter of urgency in the Ministry of Justice, the Ministry proposal and the parliamentary Committee of Justice report that discussions of the constitutional question were superficial and in part directly misleading. One feels "uncertain whether the legislators were aware of what they enacted."[63]

57 Price regulations for real estate, February 28, 1969.

58 Innstilling fra Husaasutvalget (1969). Committee appointed by royal decree August 6, 1965.

59 Ibid., 140. 60 Innst. O. XXI (1971–1972), 137. 61 Ot. prp. nr. 56 (1970–1971).

62 Berrefjord, *Erstatningsfastsettelse ved ekspropriasjon av fast eiendom* (1974).

63 Andenæs, Grunnlov og ekspropriasjonserstatning (1975), 272–273.

The Parliament Justice Committee was divided between a majority of Labor representatives and a minority of nonsocialist parties, where the Liberal Left formulated its own proposal akin to that of the majority. On a central point, the majority proposal diverged from that of the Ministry of Justice proposal: The word "shall," in a passage mandating additional compensation to be paid where the utility value was significantly lower than the market value, was changed to "may," thus barring property owners from using such significant imbalance as a cause of action. The majority emphasized that, to the extent the legislative branch found that societal considerations and the wish to protect society against a damaging development necessitated legislation, this should significantly influence courts' interpretation of its constitutionality in favor of the statute. As the Constitution assigns the legislative competence to Parliament, "it is not for the courts to review Parliament's assessment as to what laws we should have."[64] This point was agreed on by the minority. While it held Parliament's assessment to be relevant, it rejected, however, that the implication of this was to be that courts pay deference to Parliament: Courts have an independent responsibility, even though § 105 was primarily directed to Parliament. The concern for Parliament was not only how far it might go and still avoid being struck down by courts, but what the constitution directed. Here the proposed legislation, in the minority view, ran counter to the principle of equal treatment in a way contradicting the "common sense of justice."[65]

In Parliament, the central provisions of the statute were enacted by 55–37 votes in the first house (Odelstinget) and 16–11 votes in the second (Lagtinget). The division generally went along party lines, and with the Liberal Left voting with the Socialist parties. From the discussions in the first house of Parliament, Odelstinget, some comments concerning the division of powers between the courts and Parliament may be noted.

A conservative representative, B. Aakre, commented that the often-repeated citation from the Husaas committee – that courts should take care not to overrule the assessment on constitutionality as made by Parliament – was being abused. Rather than to mean that significant weight should be attached to the view of Parliament, it was used as an argument that Parliament, existing precedent notwithstanding, was free to decide the limits of § 105. Also, it was taken to imply that courts were barred from overruling Parliament's decision. She distanced herself from this view.

The view on the legal significance of case law under § 105 that Aakre distanced herself from was the strict textual position advanced by a prevalent

[64] Innst. O. XXI (1971–1972), 9. [65] Ibid., 22.

expropriation and constitutional law professor, C. A. Fleischer. He held that the only constitutional limit of § 105 was to be found in its text.[66] That case law under § 105 did in any way bind the legislature was, in his view, "an elementary jurisprudential misunderstanding."[67] Fleischer held case law under § 105 to be "ordinary Norwegian expropriation law of a lower rank,"[68] derived not from the constitutional text, but from an interpretation of it – the Constitution as an interpretational tool rather than as a barrier for politics.

Aakre saw this general inference from Husaas' position in relation to a particular question as a false induction: "Even though § 105 primarily is for Parliament to assess, this does not change the fact that if legislators do not respect the Constitution, courts are the final guards of the Constitution through their review of the constitutionality of laws . . . There is no reason to believe that a law running counter to longstanding sense of justice and stable precedent about the principle of equal treatment will not be brought before the courts for review."[69]

Representative (and district judge, formerly Minister of Justice) Haugland (Labor) was the chairman of the case in Parliament. Finding § 105 to be primarily directed to Parliament, he underlined he was "entirely aware" that judicial review was an established rule of customary law. He maintained, however, that review was "a dubious principle, and old Fredrik Stang held there were no such right of review." It had been adopted, Stang's position notwithstanding, "by persistent jurists probably of the opinion that when there were no royal power to keep Parliament in check, the courts ought to take on this role." There were, as Haugland saw it, "good reasons" to ask whether "awarding political power to an institution outside the organized *popular will*" was right (emphasis added). Quoting Seip directly, he recalled that "this is really a spanner thrown in the works of democracy." Contending that courts had, for the most part, shown deference to Parliament, he found the conservative attempts to use the Constitution to hinder progress had rarely been successful: "What is socially and politically right, is most often also constitutional. This view has in reality also been that of courts, and I am certain that the majority position today is indeed constitutional."[70] As Norwegian courts

66 Fleischer, *Grunnlovens grenser for lovregulert fastsetting av erstatning ved ekspropriasjon, særlig ved verdistigning som ikke skyldes grunneiers innsats* (1968); Fleischer, Husaas-komitéens forslag til lovbestemmelser om skjønnsordning og erstatningsfastsettelse ved ekspropriasjon (1970).

67 Fleischer, Misvisende om den nye ekspropriasjonserstatningslov (1975). Cf. B. Dunker's shift to this argument in 1869, as described in Chapter 2.

68 Fleischer, Grunnlovens § 105 – foredrag holdt på seminar 4. sept. 1970 (1971), 1.5.

69 Ot. forh. (1972–1973), 79 (Bodil Aakre, Conservative [(Høyre]).

70 Ot. forh. 11.1.1973, 85–86 (Jens Haugland, Labor).

were being substantially more cautious about finding legislation unconstitutional than US ones, Labor representative Totland found it "odd" that the Committee minority distanced itself from Husaas' (normative) position that courts "must be cautious in its exercise of review in the various cases."[71]

Another Labor representative, Aune, underlined that Parliament should be aware of its "extensive authority to interpret the scope of the Constitution," something he found important to emphasize following the objections based on the alleged unconstitutionality of the law. To the extent that the Constitution, against all odds, should end up being a hindrance, "we have to change it . . . It would damage the 'entire rule of law' to keep up constitutional provisions that are this much out of tune with the popular sense of justice."[72]

Conservative representative Endresen took issue with the committee majority view that it was not the province of courts to overrule Parliament's assessments concerning what regulations Norway ought to have: "[This is] a novel constitutional theory. Supreme Court undoubtedly has this competence."[73] Labor representative Treholt maintained, however, that Parliament is entirely free to decide the content of § 105, following an independent assessment of the legal and societal situation: "The opinion of Parliament should obviously direct court decisions."[74]

Conservative representative Willoch rejected the view that courts do not have the right to review Parliament's enactments: "One of the purposes of the constitution is to protect certain minority rights against the majority. As there are regularly more people paying, than receiving compensation for expropriation, it is quite natural that the constitution affords special protection to the minority risking expropriation." This arrangement would "lose its meaning" if Parliament by an ordinary majority could enact laws contrary to this constitutional protection. In any case, judicial review is firmly established through practice.[75]

The desirability and constitutionality of regulating compensation under § 105 was not only a deeply dividing political issue, but one widely debated also in the legal community. There were, both before and after the 1976 decision, several media discussions of the issue, and the legal journal *Lov og rett* dedicated an entire volume to this question in 1975.[76] Supportive of the ECA was C. A. Fleischer, whose views had also been central to Parliament's

[71] Ibid., 90 (Totland, Labor). [72] Ibid., 95 (Aune, Labor).

[73] Ibid., 98 (Endresen, Conservative). [74] Ibid., 106 (Treholt, Labor).

[75] Ibid., 110–111 (Willoch, Conservative).

[76] *Lov og rett* 1975/4. Here, and in other issues, several contributions were made: Sigmond, Lov om erstatning ved ekpropriasjon – forholdet til Grunnlovens § 105 (1975); Andenæs, Grunnlov og ekspropriasjonserstatning (1975); Eckhoff, Høyesterett som grunnlovens vokter (1975),

discussion upon enactment of the Act, as well as for Representative Haugland.[77]

Critical to the ECA was Andenæs, who maintained that contrary to the normal review situation, where Parliament enacts a law which is then challenged under the constitution by a private party and the courts are called upon to settle the constitutional question, the expropriation regulation presents the "opposite situation": This is an area

> where courts, through 160 years, have construed and laid out in detail the implications of full compensation. Then Parliament interferes, neglecting this precedent . . . The question is whether one wishes to respect rule of law principles even when they run counter to widely held convictions or political goals. These are the situations in which the respect for such principles is tested. Courts' reaction to the statute will not only be decisive to the understanding of § 105, but also to the prospect of how courts will function as a guardian for individuals vis-à-vis the state.[78]

He added: "Are courts to be the obedient servants of the parliamentary majority even in questions concerning the constitutional protection of individuals – and even where it entails deviating from precedent? I do not believe this is a desirable position, and neither one having any satisfactory foundation in Norwegian law."[79]

Defending the ECA also in the legal debate was Representative Haugland. Following Andenæs' defense of judicial review powers, Haugland placed him in line with other "prevalent representatives for this legal disruption into politics," such as Aschehoug, Morgenstierne and Hagerup, holding that Andenæs positioned himself in "the wrong century." That courts may exercise judicial review must in principle be accepted as Norwegian law, but the scope of this right had been disputed. As is established, "§ 105 as other constitutional provisions are primarily directives to Parliament. When it has reached the conclusion that a law is constitutional, very much is required before courts may overrule this assessment."[80]

Andenæs rejected this view. He pointed out that the *political* position that courts ought to abstain from review unless the law in question is obviously or undoubtedly unconstitutional (as argued by Haugland with reference to

Haugland, Merknader til ekspropriasjonserstatningsloven (1975); Unneberg, Professor Andenæs og grunnloven (1975); Andenæs, Grunnlov, politikere og domstoler (1975).

77 Haugland, Grunnlov og politikk (1975); Haugland, Merknader til ekspropriasjonserstatningsloven (1975).

78 Andenæs, Grunnlov og ekspropriasjonserstatning (1975), 274.

79 Andenæs, Grunnlov, politikere og domstoler (1975), 386.

80 Haugland, Grunnlov og politikk (1975), 370–374.

Justice Berg) was not the same as a legally valid norm requiring that courts obey this.[81] Andenæs underlined that there existed no case in which a majority had confirmed Berg's formulation of such limits on judicial review.

An editorial in the journal written by Professor Bratholm held the ECA to be problematic under § 105, and thus likely to cause review cases. He warned, on a general basis, against activist use of judicial review: The "existence and survival" of judicial review requires that "courts show considerable deference to the majority will in Parliament, particularly in those cases where the question of constitutionality has been carefully considered."[82] Going on to discuss the various ways in which the Supreme Court could handle the case without "front-colliding" with the majority will of Parliament, Bratholm's stance appears as a normative defense for judicial review legitimacy following a liberal justification, but a defense recognizing the vulnerability of the institution, one linked to arguments of both input and output legitimacy. If used unwisely, the institution of review could well undermine itself; its own legitimacy was rooted in a tradition of cautious use – and also maintained through the relatively moderate exercise of power represented by such use. He thus echoed the concern of Andenæs in the related question of the final interpreter of the "spirit and principles" in § 112 of the Constitution – an attempt from courts to use § 112 "could lead to countermeasures endangering the independence of the judiciary."[83] Whatever comes out of cases brought before the courts under ECA, "one can only regret the dilemma forced upon the Supreme Court, where the loyalty to Parliament must conflict with central rule of law principles."

5.6 THE *KLØFTA* CASE

The 1973 ECA was enacted with a moderate political majority; the *Kløfta* case decided the statute was in conflict with the Constitution § 105 by a slim legal majority. The scope and wording of the statute were ambiguous on several issues but, sitting in plenary, the Supreme Court, by a vote of 9–8, found several parts of it to be unconstitutional. It did so, however, without explicitly stating that the regulation ran counter to the Constitution; instead, parts of the statute were simply not applied.

As to the question of judicial review existence, both the majority and the minority held it to be undisputable. They also agreed that a guiding principle for the scope of review was that the view taken by Parliament of the

81 Andenæs, Grunnlov, politikere og domstoler (1975), 384.
82 Bratholm, Jus og politikk (1975). 83 Andenæs, *Statsforfatningen i Norge* (1948), 238.

constitutionality of the provision at hand represented legal authority of significant weight. For the majority, Justice Blom affirmed courts' review power as "clear constitutional law," and underlined that it was not only the right, but also the duty of courts to examine whether cases did raise constitutional questions, and, where finding that statutes ran counter to the constitution, to follow the Constitution. The scope and intensity of review could not be generally established, but would vary with the constitutional provision in question: "As for provisions to the protection of individual freedom or security, I hold the influence of the constitution to be extensive. On the other hand, as for provisions to the regulation of the competencies of governmental branches, it is my opinion," as it was Justice Bendiksby's in the 1952 *Whaling* case,[84] "that courts should pay significant respect to the opinion of Parliament. Constitutional provisions protecting economical rights place themselves in an intermediary position."[85] Underlining that assessing the political considerations of Parliament is not the province of courts, he held that the only subject for court review was whether the means by which Parliament had sought to realize its intentions were constitutional.

Justice Bølviken for the minority ascribed to the view that review powers were indeed clear constitutional law, but held that weighty reasons were required for courts to use these powers, to place their legal assessment before that of the legislature, particularly where Parliament had considered the constitutionality of a statute. She followed the majority view of differentiation in review intensity, but explained the difference as one between provisions to the protection of personal integrity – citing §§ 96 and 99 – and of economical rights. For the latter group, she cited Justice Berg's argument in the *Waterfall* case, with which she generally agreed. This position was that judicial review is to be employed only to the extent an act is "obviously or undoubtedly" unconstitutional, and not unless the court "with certainty" can establish the right interpretation.[86]

Several important aspects of judicial review became clearer with this case: that the existence of review was beyond discussion; that courts had an independent duty to examine whether cases raise constitutional questions; that courts' exercise of review was both a right (competence) and a duty; and that this right and duty extended to interpreting ambiguous statutes in accordance with the Constitution. Parliament's position on the question of constitutionality is held out as a source of significant weight, particularly where there is reasonable doubt as to whether the statute contradicts the Constitution. The main difference between the majority and the minority is what degree

84 Rt. 1952 s. 1089, 1098. 85 Rt. 1976 s. 1, 5. 86 Rt. 1918 s. 403, 424.

of deference should be shown by courts where Parliament has held a statute to be Constitutional. As later noted by the Attorney General for Civil Affairs, B. Haug: "[t]o be honest, I assumed that the Supreme Court would not set aside the statute when the question of constitutionality had been so thoroughly discussed by Parliament."[87]

Another difference of principled interest is the minority view that judicial interpretation and construction of § 105 in previous case law does not limit the room for later legislative action under § 105. While the majority emphasized that previous case law is not "determinative" for the legislative scope of action, the minority held this scope to be defined by "an interpretation of the constitutional provision itself."[88] Although not clear, it seems reasonable to read the minority position as an answer to the concrete issue at hand – or solely to the question of compensation regulation under § 105 – rather than as a general assertion of constitutional law. As noted in Section 5.5, a central source for this view seems to have been Professor Fleischer's opinion of what should – and what should not – be seen as constitutional limits on Parliament's regulations in the field of expropriation. As a deduction of what had been the effects of case law under § 105, the position that case law did not represent any limits outside the text of § 105 is reasonable. From a principled perspective, however, considering case law as construing constitutional limits that are not authoritative for Parliament as a general norm is in tension with the idea of courts as constitutional guardians: If the limits as drawn up by precedent are not binding on all governmental branches at a constitutional level, the legislature may simply re-enact statutes found unconstitutional, thus vacating the constitutional effect of judicial review – and also the supermajoritarian guarantees of the constitutional amendment clause.

In addition to this, the case developed what had formerly been a distinction between constitutional provisions protecting individuals and those apportioning competences of governmental branches[89] into a tripartite scheme. This

87 Haug, *Mange jern i ilden* (2008), 75. Haug, who did not himself argue the case due to other commitments, added: "I am of the opinion that the Supreme Court was wrong, with as slim a majority as possible, and that I ought to have argued this case myself."

88 In Fleischer, Grunnloven 175 år: utvikling, demokratisering, rettskildebruk og "påvirkningsagenter" i forhold til våre i fredstid viktigste grunnlovsbestemmelser §§ 49, 75, 97 og 105 (1989), 176, it is argued that the majority also supported Fleischer's view that previous precedent does not have authoritative constitutional consequences for Parliament. I read this differently. What Justice Blom holds is that precedent is not determinative for the legislative scope. With the pragmatic approach to precedent prevalent in Norwegian jurisprudence, this is hardly novel. Adjudicative precedent is not binding on any branch of government. This is not the same as it not being authoritative, and sometimes decisive.

89 Rt. 1918 s. 403 on economical rights; Rt. 1952 s. 1089.

scheme has since been cited in a number of later Supreme Court review decisions,[90] and is still considered decisive. In dividing constitutional provisions into three (or two, as the minority), the Supreme Court gives an important clarification of its own view on the balance between the legal and the political. Even though not explicated, the argument seems to be that of review serving in particular as a guarantee for individual integrity rather than the general individual liberty represented by traditional "negative freedoms," such as the right to property. Economic regulations infringing on the individual liberty of property should, according to the majority, be subject to a level of scrutiny somewhere between the strict one applying to individual integrity and the lenient one applying to constitutional provisions regulating the competences of governmental branches.

5.7 *KLØFTA* CASE FOLLOW-UP

Following the *Kløfta* case, the Labor/Socialist parties maintained a majority in Parliament that would last until 1981. However, no constitutional proposal to amend or alter § 105 of the Constitution or to abolish judicial review was put forth following the *Kløfta* decision. There are probably many reasons for this, but it indicates at least that there was no pervasive, political perception of review illegitimacy, even following the surprising review revival.

One of the debates on the relation between Parliament and the courts came after a proposal to alter the 1973 ECA to make it reflect the *Kløfta* case. The proposal, put forth by nonsocialist representatives Korvald (Christian Conservative), Steenberg (Center) and Willoch (Conservative), was debated in Parliament in 1977. The proposal was based on the discrepancy between the law on the books and the law as interpreted by the Supreme Court. The proposal claimed the law had to be altered as the Court had interpreted the statutory provision that full (market value) compensation *may* be awarded, to the extent it is *substantially* higher than that of the utility value, to instead read that the market value *must* be compensated, whether it was substantially higher or not. The core of the 1977 debate thus came to be about whether these two words should be corrected as a matter of urgency.

Aside from reversing the politically disputed use of utility value as the primary compensation for takings, the argument for quickly altering the statutory text to reflect how it was practiced was the *rule of law-argument* of ensuring legal predictability. As the law stood, it was not only unclear, but

90 Rt. 1996 s. 1415; Rt. 2004 s. 1737; Rt. 2006 s. 293; Rt. 2007 s. 1281; Rt. 2010 s. 143; Rt. 2010 s. 1445.

"directly misleading."[91] The main argument against an urgent amendment was that a government committee already worked on reviewing property price regulations and that its conclusions would lead to a full revision of property regulation – possibly with the effect of mandating the use of utility value as a principle for compensation.[92] The proposal of urgent amendment was rejected by a vote of 66–60.

Some remarks in the debate may be illustrative of views on the relationship between Parliament and the Supreme Court. Finding the arguments against amending the law to trivialize the actual conflict between the law and the Supreme Court conclusion, representative Kirste (Conservative) cited professors Opsahl and Andenæs on holding that the *Kløfta* case was a review case that did indeed disregard the ECA due to its unconstitutionality: "When the government or a majority in Parliament does not want to respect the decision of the Supreme Court that a statute is indeed unconstitutional, this shrugs the fundamental principle of division of powers essential to our constitutional system."[93]

Minister of Justice Valle (Labor) conceded that the Supreme Court had indeed interpreted the ECA in a way diverging from its text, and construed it so as to augment the compensation from the utility value. She argued, however, that a committee was already looking into whether a full revision of property price regulations was called for, and that it would be better to await the result of this than to alter the expropriation statute alone. She also argued that, as outlining a compensatory scheme under § 105 in perfect detail would be very difficult, the assessment would in any case have to be undertaken by courts. To the subject of power division, she underlined that an amendment as proposed would be to let a court decision have direct political influence – something that was "not in accordance with the principle of divided powers assigning legislative powers to Parliament, not the courts."[94]

Korvald asked whether the full revision would indeed alter the expropriation regulations so that they came to be in accordance with § 105. He said this presuming that a revision could not legally propose "alterations not in accordance with constitutional provisions as affirmed by the Supreme Court,"[95] thus signaling that he saw the Supreme Court conclusion to be decisive for what limits Parliament must observe following the decision.

Kielland (Socialist, former Labor, who was also in the majority of the Justice Committee recommending the statute in 1972) took a different position, recalling that the intention of the expropriation statute was to compensate

[91] St. forh. 1.6.1977, 4105, B. Unneberg (Center). [92] Ibid., 4107. [93] Ibid., 4107.
[94] Ibid., 4116–4117. [95] Ibid., 4118.

actual use rather than ensure equality of additional compensation. He held that this intention "is something the Supreme Court majority simply has to accept." A continued Supreme Court interpretation of the statute disregarding the word "substantial" was, in his view "untenable" as this word was essential for understanding the intentions of the majority in Parliament.[96] He was followed by Guldbrandsen (Labor) who argued it was "obviously not the province of the Supreme Court, but rather of the legislative branch to interpret the constitution." He maintained the *Kløfta* case to be "an exception, soon to be history, and hopefully a one-off."[97]

Willoch (Conservative), on the other hand, underlined how the Supreme Court had clarified that the Constitution § 105 mandates compensation of market value, and found it enlightening "that Labour does not want to recognize the legal rule affirmed" by the Supreme Court.[98] This interpretation of Labor's position as regards its attitude toward the constitutional clarification by the Supreme Court was not refuted by Valle, who simply declared that full compensation merely meant compensation of the market value as limited through price regulations.[99]

The expropriation compensation statute was not altered until 1984,[100] and then with the *Kløfta* decision as the primary reason for statutory revision:[101] "when a law and the constitution differ substantially, we as legislators have two ways to go; either to change the constitution so that it is in accordance with the statute, or to change the statute so that it is in accordance with the constitution. The Labor representatives have, between these two alternatives, chosen a third: To do nothing."[102] The new statute was enacted against the votes of the Labor representatives,[103] who maintained that the compensation principle in § 105 was already protected; since the *Kløfta* case and other "case law had staked out the most important principles for compensation," there was no need for a revision of the statute.[104]

5.8 JUDICIAL REVIEW CONFIRMED

As summarized by Torkel Opsahl in 1976:

> In the *Kløfta* case, the majority practiced judicial review clearer and more authoritatively than in a long time ... this signal from the third branch

96 Ibid., 4119. 97 Ibid., 4122. 98 Ibid., 4122. 99 Ibid., 4123.

100 Lov av 6. april 1984 nr. 17 om vederlag ved oreigning av fast eigedom (ekspropriasjonserstatningslova).

101 Innst. O. nr. 27 (1983–1984), 2. 102 Ot. forh. 22.3.1984, 322. 103 Ibid., 335.

104 Innst. O. nr. 27 (1983–1984), 8.

> deserves attention, as was the case when Parliament in 1963 proved it could still disperse of the government. As parliamentarism then, judicial review now has defied its assumed death penalty ... this lecture in judicial art is convincing proof of how judicial review may be practiced in a time of political-economic dispute. In this way it may again become a more important institution than what many had envisioned.[105]

With the *Kløfta* case, Representative Haugland's position that "what is socially and politically right is most often also constitutional" was, and was seen to be, challenged. But the way in which the Supreme Court made this point clear did not give rise to any further opposition between it and Parliament. Andenæs saw the cautious formulation of the Supreme Court to be a way to avoid conflict – a "diplomatic obfuscation," giving rise to a number of interpretational challenges, but also sparing the Court from political confrontations that would otherwise have ensued.[106]

With some exceptions, notably the Seip–Andenæs debate, which mainly concerned the political reconstruction of review history, there were few analyses of the general appeal or undesirability of "modern" judicial review, both prior to and following the *Kløfta* case. As a case both at the time and later seen as the start of a Norwegian judicial review "renaissance,"[107] the lack of debate on this issue in this period seems almost curious, particularly following the aversion against review cases going against the state, for different reasons, as furthered by Professor Bratholm and Attorney General of Civil Affairs, Bødtker. Bratholm seems to have worried that review in cases concerning economic questions would threaten the very institution of review – an institution that was in his view necessary for the protection of other rights. The reason why Bødtker did not want to see such a use of review is not clear. Judging from the way he reflects upon the case in his memoirs, however, it seems that avoiding such a loss was more important for him than just the normal avoiding of lost cases. What it signals is at least that the existence of judicial review was a reality, even in the years it was not much in use.

Eckhoff's statement in 1975 – "I doubt these powers will ever be used again in any way worth mentioning"[108] – could possibly be interpreted as an expression of his normative ideal rather than an analysis of the prevalent debates at the time. While judicial review had certainly not been much used in the decades prior to Eckhoff's statement, the preceding years' debate on review as

105 Opsahl, Kløfta-saken, dommerkunsten og dens tolkning (1976), 50.

106 Andenæs, Grunnlovtolking, domstoler og politikk. Randbemerkninger til en høyesterettsdom. (1977).

107 Smith, *Høyesterett og folkestyret* (1993), VII.

108 Eckhoff, Høyesterett som grunnlovens vokter (1975), 202. Reprinted in *Lov og rett* 1976, 1.

concerned both expropriation regulation and petroleum taxation was persistent,[109] as was the presence of scholarly debate assuming review.[110] One way to understand his statement may be as more normative than it appeared, a signal that "these powers" *ought* not to be used again in any way worth mentioning. Support for such a reading may be found in Eckhoff's skepticism toward the Supreme Court's more active use of review powers to strike down economic regulations in the period between 1890 and 1930.[111] The lack of debate following the *Kløfta* case indicates substantial acceptance of constitutional review in a formative period for its revival and clarification.

Attempts have been made to explain the division between the *Kløfta* justices by their political sympathies. One such study finds most of the majority justices to be "conservative," and most of the minority to be "radical."[112] Some justices, Christiansen and Leivestad in the majority and Roll-Matthiesen and Stabel in the minority, do, according to that study not fit into any of these categories, and are placed in an intermediary group. The political findings may be questioned. According to the director of the Supreme Court at the time, Sophie Solheim,[113] Justice Christiansen saw his own vote in the case as decisive for its result. Christiansen did, however, consider himself a (Labor) social democrat.

Two aspects of review were formulated in the *Kløfta* case in a way that would prove formative for later practice of review. First, the follow-up of earlier theory and case law (notably the 1918 *Waterfall* case): that courts ought to pay deference to the views of Parliament in review cases concerning questions which have been the subject of particular parliamentary debate about constitutionality, and have by the majority been found constitutional. This view is sustained under a view of popular participation and deliberative input legitimacy – at least to the extent the majority conscientiously reaches its conclusion. If it instead represents a more or less deliberate circumvention of constitutional limits, it does not.

The second aspect is the *Kløfta* grading of constitutional protection. This represents a development of the difference between provisions concerning the competences and work of the governmental branches, and those to the

[109] See Ot. prp. nr. 26 (1974–1975); Fleischer, Statsrett, oljeskatt og juridiske mistak (1976).

[110] See i.a. Seip, *Høyesterett som politisk organ* (1964); Andenæs, *Høyesterett som politisk organ* (1965); and Nissen, et al., Den dømmende makt (1967), 114–158.

[111] Eckhoff, Høyesterett som grunnlovens vokter (1975).

[112] Østlid, *Dommeratferd i dissenssaker* (1988), 48–51. See also Eckhoff as cited in Andenæs, Grunnlovtolking, domstoler og politikk. Randbemerkninger til en høyesterettsdom (1977).

[113] Conversation between Solheim and Rune Slagstad in November 2013. Solheim was appointed Supreme Court Clerk of the Records by the King in Council on December 17, 1954, and was the Supreme Court Director and Justice Secretary from 1971–1995.

protection of individual rights foreshadowed in the 1952 *Whale Oil* case. Its further grading between rights to the protection of individual freedom or security on the one hand, and those protecting economical rights on the other, was explained simply by reference to how the latter "must" be in an intermediate position. While not cited in the decision, this further distinction echoes some of the critique furthered against review of economic regulations in the early 1900s (see Skeie in Section 4.2, the discussions in Parliament in Section 4.5 and the need for a cautious approach to economic regulations explicated in the *Vauvert* case in Section 4.6). The Supreme Court's lack of explication of reasons for the distinguishing between these types of rights does, however, leave the grading wanting in reflecting several ideals, both input and outcome as well as professional, judicial process legitimacy. The *Kløfta* case grading has since been criticized with regards to its lack of explanation, its unclear categories and its implications.[114]

As mentioned, the 1918 *Waterfall* case may be read as a precursor to the 1937 *West Coast Hotel* case in which the US Supreme Court upheld a minimum wage regulation, thus ending the *Lochner*-era period of business regulatory legislation invalidation.[115] The *Kløfta* case is interesting in this light too, in the way the separation between protection of integrative and economical freedoms resembles the US development as manifested by the *West Coast* case. The *Kløfta* reasoning also brings to memory the famous "footnote four" in the 1938 US *Carolene Products* case, concerning a federal prohibition on interstate shipping of filled milk.[116] In it, the US Supreme Court defined the level of review scrutiny of legislation regulating ordinary economic activities and legislation curtailing important personal liberties: Courts should refrain from questioning the wisdom or policy choices underlying legislation principally aimed at economic affairs, and not overturn them unless they fail to serve a rational or legitimate purpose. Regulations restricting political processes, discriminating against minorities or violating constitutional liberties could, however, be subject to more exacting scrutiny.

Although ostensibly observable in both the *Waterfall* and the *Whaling* cases, in later discussions the formulations in the *Kløfta* grading of constitutional protection have been ascribed to a speech given two years earlier, by law

114 See i.a. Smith, Høyesterett – en trussel mot demokratiet? (1999); Skjerdal, Relativisering av domstolenes grunnlovskontroll – på tide å forlate tredelingslæren? (2013); Tverberg, Det graderte grunnlovsvernet ved tolkning av grunnloven og prøving av lovers grunnlovmessighet (2013).

115 *West Coast Hotel Co.* v. *Parrish*, 300 U.S. 379 (1937)

116 *United States* v. *Carolene Products Co.* (1938).

professor and later Supreme Court Chief Justice Carsten Smith.[117] In a speech with frequent reference to the US role of courts and the 1937 development of the "preferred position principle," he distinguished between provisions for the protection of individual liberties and of economic rights, based on liberal and democratic functional theories. The Supreme Court in the *Kløfta* case, however, does not cite any such reasons for its reasoning, and the causality here is unclear.

117 Smith, Domstolene og rettsutviklingen (1975).

6

Debates of ECHR Review (1950–2000)

6.1 INTRODUCTION

In 1951, Norway ratified the ECHR. The competence of the Commission was accepted in 1955, and that of the ECtHR in 1964. In 1999, the ECHR was incorporated into Norwegian law through the HRA, with a provision of preference for the convention in cases of norm conflict between it and national laws. This chapter attempts to draw up a genealogy of debates informative to views on ECHR review in Norway. The primary focus is on statements in official documents and legal reports prepared to inform the political debate and politicians' statements. Relevant parts of broader legal discussions are referenced for context. The aim is to present a synopsis of arguments concerning Norwegian judicial review under the ECHR. As these arguments are closely connected with those of ECtHR review, these too will be referenced. To the extent that the arguments differ with respect to Norwegian ECHR review and ECtHR review, this is noted.

Arguments about the legitimacy of ECHR review in Norway may be seen as one component in at least four formative debates: Those pertaining to ratification of the ECHR and whether to accept the jurisdiction of the ECHR Commission and the ECtHR in the 1950s–1960s; those concerning what form of incorporation mechanism to choose in the HRA in the 1990s; the HRA discussions in Parliament; and those following the conclusion about ECHR and courts' contribution to "undermine democracy" in the officially commissioned 2003 Power Study.

The so-called "doctrine of clarity" – a requirement that ECHR law be sufficiently clear and unambiguous in order to outweigh Norwegian law – permeates some parts of the work toward the HRA. It, and how it reflects a national legal dualism that gradually turns into legal monism as regard human rights, is thus presented before the HRA discussions.

6.2 "ORIGINAL INTENT"

6.2.1 *Ratification of the ECHR*

The debates between "minimalists" and "broad rights federalists" over the ECHR and its adjudicatory bodies as mentioned in Section 2.4.1 are traceable in Norwegian debates leading up to and following ECHR ratification. The outward- and diplomatic-focused Ministry of Foreign Affairs was more positive toward the ECHR and the elective monitoring bodies, whereas the Ministry of Justice legal department was more cautious.

The first statement from the Ministry of Justice legal department came as a response to the Teitgen report in 1949.[1] Stating that the convention would hardly have any real role in ensuring democracy in practice, and that there were a number of downsides to it, it held that the Constitution barred accession to the convention in its proposed form. Following alterations to the proposed convention, the department still questioned its constitutionality under §§ 1 (national sovereignty), 88 (the final say in legal questions lie with the Supreme Court) and 90 (Supreme Court decisions are inappealable), and stated the principled view that the convention rights should be as exact and defined as possible, thus following the European line favoring a definition rather than enumeration of rights.

Under the Constitution § 26, treaties may be signed by the government, while consent to ratification must be given by Parliament. Norway signed the ECHR on November 4, 1950, and the Ministry of Justice proposed ratification in 1951.[2] The proposal emphasized that the ECHR, contrary to the UNDHR,[3] was a legally binding document. It further added to the work under the UNDHR in uniting European countries the human rights views of which were of a quite similar nature, thus enabling agreement to a greater extent than was possible between the more divergent UN members. Three questions were addressed specifically: The need for Norway to make a reservation to the protection of religious freedom in ECHR art. 9 due to the Constitution § 2.

[1] Memorandum (1949) The following reconstruction is based on available documents as listed from the National Archive and the Ministry of Foreign Affairs Archives (the Ministry of Justice Archives are inaccessible following the July 22, 2011, bombing) as well as the accounts given by Møse in Coward, *Festskrift Lovavdelingen – 100 år* (1986), 148ff., Wold, Den Europeiske menneskerettskonvensjon og Norge (1963), 353ff. and St. prp. nr. 83 (1951).

[2] St. prp. nr. 83 (1951) Norway formally ratified on 21 December 1951.

[3] UN General Assembly, Universal Declaration of Human Rights, 10 December 1948, 217 A (III).

prohibiting Jesuits from entering or residing in the nation;[4] the desirability of establishing a court; and the constitutionality and other challenges posed by article 32 transferring authority to the Committee of Ministers. The ECHR was ratified with a reservation connected to art. 9, and with the agreement that the question of accession to elective monitoring bodies – the Commission and the ECtHR – was to be delayed until one had some experience with how these bodies functioned in practice.

6.2.2 *Recognition of the Commission and the ECtHR*

Law professor Frede Castberg was commissioned to assess the question of acceptance of the Commission. While finding such transferal of power unproblematic under the Constitution § 1 (national sovereignty), he was skeptical of leaving "matters of a purely legal nature" to be decided by the "political-diplomatic" Committee of Ministers which, in addition, was not set up with any procedural guarantees. To the extent the Committee were to have such authority, one should, in Castberg's view, strive to have it regulated with reassuring procedures "more in line with those of a court."[5]

The Ministry of Foreign Affairs shared this view, but found it wise not to insist on it, as the Committee of Ministers had unanimously agreed upon art. 32. As to the desirability of establishing a court, the Ministry of Foreign Affairs was, however, "sincerely in doubt." It agreed with the Ministry of Justice that Norway ought to wait with regard to the question of individual complaints and accession to the Commission and Court until "one has some experience as to how the convention works out in practice."[6]

Following the entry into force of the convention in 1953, the CoE advisory board called upon member states to accept the authority of the Commission. A year thereafter, it repeated this call, expressing regret that the only states to follow up thus far were Denmark, Sweden and Ireland. The Ministry of Justice legal department ended up advising against an individual complaints procedure.[7] As reasons, they cited the possible implications of the open-ended articles of the convention and the way a supernational organ would interpret the provisions.

4 In 1814, the Constitution § 2 prohibited Jesuits and Monastic orders and upheld the existing ban on Jews entering the country. The bans were intended to be exceptions to a main rule of religious freedom, a main rule which, however, was never formulated in the Norwegian Constitution. The prohibition against Jews was abolished in 1851 and that against Monastic orders in 1857. That against Jesuits was however not abolished until 1956. See Sverdrup Thygeson, *Grunnlovens forbud mot jesuitter og munkeordener: Religionsfrihet og grunnlovskonservatisme 1814–1956* (2009).

5 Statement referred in St. prp. nr. 83 (1951), 4. 6 Ibid., 4–5.

7 Møse i Coward, et al., *Festskrift Lovavdelingen – 100 år* (1986), 156.

In a 1955 letter to the Ministry of Foreign Affairs, previous Supreme Court Chief Justice and Norwegian representative to the Commission Paal Berg pointed out that procedural guarantees against abuse were now in place and urged Norway to reconsider its reluctance toward accepting the individual complaints procedure.[8] The Ministry of Foreign Affairs submitted this letter to the Ministry of Justice, expressing its agreement and emphasizing that Norway was now the only ECHR member state not to have recognized the competence of the Commission under art. 25. Conceding that it was unfortunate that Norway remained in this solitary position, and "as the convention is, after all, a fact, and has been ratified by Norway, the arguments for Norway acceding to the individual complaints authority are predominant." It warned, however, that individual complaints might be abused and recommended the accession be time limited to two years. While acknowledging the potential for abuse, the Ministry of Foreign Affairs still held that the prospect of effectuating the aim of the ECHR was a weightier concern. Consent to recognize the Commission for two years was consequently given by Parliament.[9]

In 1958, the Ministry of Foreign Affairs initiated the work toward recognizing the Court of Human Rights. The Ministry of Justice legal department now took the position, contrary to the 1949 one given pursuant to the Teitgen report, that the Norwegian Constitution, following a "renewed assessment" and "in light of recent developments," did not present any legal barrier toward acknowledging the court's competences under art. 46.[10] Still, the Ministry of Justice legal department recommended suspending a Ministry of Foreign Affairs sketch proposal to this effect pending an assessment of what legal steps would be required based upon the potential findings of ECHR breach.[11]

At this point in time, several other countries had accepted ECtHR competencies, and Norway was lagging behind, a development that gradually became a subject of political awareness. In 1962, parliamentary representative Haugan (Agricultural Center Party) put a question to the Minister of Justice Haugland (Labor) during question time in Parliament concerning the delay in recognizing the court. Nils Hønsvald, the Norwegian representative to the Nordic Council, had in a Nordic Council meeting stated that the reason why Norway would not accept the court was that Norway risked having its postwar proceedings against Norwegian Nazi collaborators ("landssvikoppgjøret") tried in Strasbourg.[12]

8 Letter from Paal Berg to the Ministry of Foreign Affairs, May 12, 1955, referenced in St. prp. nr. 104 (1955), 2.

9 Ibid., 2–3. 10 Coward, et al., *Festskrift Lovavdelingen – 100 år* (1986), 157.

11 Letter Ministry of Justice-Ministry of Foreign Affairs, September 1959.

12 For perspectives on these proceedings, see Andenæs, *Det vanskelige oppgjøret: rettsoppgjøret etter okkupasjonen* (1979), Dahl, *Et rettferdig oppgjør?* (2004).

Haugan asked whether this was indeed an official Norwegian reason for delaying court recognition. As Hønsvald had cited the Ministry of Justice opinion as basis for his concern, and as his statement had been broadcast on the radio, Haugan wanted to know whether he represented what was indeed the view of the Ministry of Justice: "although one may have been of the opinion that Norway was right in suspending its recognition of the court, the statement made in the Nordic Council actually made pertinent that we do in fact recognize it."[13]

Recalling that the National Socialist (collaborator) Party did "contain a number of quarrelsome persons" who, even though they had "no case," might well "generate irksome proceedings in Strasbourg," Haugland denied that the question of war traitors was decisive for the Ministry of Justice view of the matter.[14]

While not decisive for the Ministry of Justice, the issue of treason convicts seeking redress under the ECHR seems, however, to have been a real issue. A March 1961 Ministry of Foreign Affairs memo concerns a petition from K. Irgens, who served as Shipping Minister in Quisling's occupational government, that Norway accept the jurisdiction of the court, so that he could appeal to it. The memo also mentions other traitor cases being prepared for complaints under the ECHR. It provides an opinion on the interpretation of the six-month time limit for bringing cases before the Commission in ECHR art. 26.[15] The question of what would happen if the treason convicts were to initiate "irksome proceedings in Strasbourg" persisted. One of several letters to the Ministry of Foreign Affairs from the Ministry of Justice legal department maintaining that the question of accession to the ECtHR ought to be postponed "awaiting further experience with how the convention will work in practice" also asked for information as to how the clause of time limitation in art. 26 had been practiced. This latter part of the letter was annotated in handwriting by a Ministry of Foreign Affairs official as follows:

> Exactly. Norwegian traitors are today lining up to have the post war proceedings [landssvikoppgjøret] tried before the Commission, and if the time limit of six months is not an effective barrier, we risk having the entire proceedings [landssvikoppgjør] brought before CoE organs. But the Ministry of Justice is inconsistent. Why recognize the individual complaints mechanism under the Commission when we cannot recognize the jurisdiction of the Court? The troubles arise by accepting the right to individual complaints.[16]

13 St. forh. 30.5.1962, 3474.

14 Five years earlier, Haugland had been accused by the newspaper Dagbladet of being too soft on war traitors, a statement he, in his diary, says he much disliked. Haugland, *Dagbok frå Kongens råd* (1986), 54.

15 *Memorandum*, Ministry of Foreign Affairs (1961).

16 Annotated letter from the Ministry of Justice to the Ministry of Foreign Affairs (1961).

Haugland's response to this resembles the skepticism toward a "dynamic interpretation" of human rights that has remained a central accusation against ECtHR legitimacy in later years. He emphasized the open-ended texture of the ECHR, and how the understanding of "human rights" varied with group interests and could vary within the different jurisdictions within Europe. While there might, "from an idealistic point of view," be good reasons for international control of national decisions affecting individual rights, the "strong tendencies towards using human rights as arguments in the political and legal debate" ought to perspectivate the desirability of such control. He warned that Norway could be found in breach by the court "because a majority of judges based on *their* legal tradition might find a Norwegian law or Supreme Court decision to be contrary to the convention."[17] This did not allay Haugan, who inquired whether it was not indeed the purpose of the Strasbourg court to censor national decisions on human rights matters to the extent they were in breach of the convention. And was it only when affecting *Norwegian* decisions that this principle was undesirable?[18] Rejecting this, Haugland pointed to how Norway, like Sweden "and many other countries, i.e. Great Britain," was simply observing the situation, awaiting more experience with the court before finally deciding. At this point in time, as mentioned, only one case had been decided by the ECtHR.[19]

In 1963, the question of ECtHR accession was repeated, this time by representative Tande (Liberal Left).[20] Minister Haugland pointed to his answer to the 1962 question, and declared that the government was still awaiting more experience with ECtHR practice before deciding on the issue. He underlined, however, that even though Norway had not yet recognized ECtHR competence, it had "in no way" positioned itself outside the control mechanisms as established by the ECHR: "Norway has accepted the individual complaint mechanism of the Commission" and that of the Committee of Ministers, which "by and large has the same competence as the court. The Commission presently has before it a complaint against Norway concerning whether [the act of compelled civil service for dentists] represents a breach of the Convention."[21]

Representative Edvard Hambro (Conservative), an international lawyer, brought the question before Parliament once more, in 1964, recalling the previous appeals to "await experience," and (under)stating that if all governments were to take such an approach, international cooperation would presumably progress rather slowly. He found Norway's delay in this question

17 St. forh. 30.5.1962, 3475.
18 Ibid., 3475–76.
19 *Case of Lawless* v. *Ireland (No. 3)* (1961).
20 St. forh. 27.2.1963, 2303.
21 Ibid., 2303.

rather peculiar, considering the slim ECtHR case load and the fact that both Iceland and Denmark had already accepted its jurisdiction: "Clearly it is arguable that the court henceforth has had but a symbolic function, but even if this is so, I believe Norway ought to support it. We have always represented the forefront of international rule of law, and should continue to do so. It is by these means we continue to develop international law."[22] The answer from now Minister of Justice Lange (Labor) was that the experience with the court had now been considered, and that a proposition to accept ECtHR jurisdiction was to be presented to Parliament the next day.

Proposition no. 112 (1964) was indeed presented to Parliament the following day. Three arguments were presented as decisive: That the original doubt about the constitutionality of acceding to the court as expressed by the Ministry of Justice legal department in 1949 and 1951 was no longer extant, "following a renewed assessment in light of the present day conditions"; that acceptance of the court in order to strengthen the international rule of law cooperation had been urged by Chief Justice Terje Wold, former Chief Justice Paal Berg and Professor Frede Castberg; and that the Ministry of Foreign Affairs recommended accepting the court "in line with Norwegian tradition in the field of international rule of law."[23] "Certain challenges" notwithstanding, on these grounds the Ministry of Justice proposed acceptance of the ECtHR, for a period of three years and on the condition of reciprocity.[24]

The reluctance in the Ministry of Justice to accept ECtHR jurisdiction was caused by uncertainty about what implications such acceptance would have. As for the Ministry of Justice interpretation of the constitution, however, a shift took place from 1949 to 1958: in 1949, it found ECtHR accession to be unconstitutional, whereas in 1958 it found it to be constitutional "in light of the present day conditions." Whether this shift was a result of a dynamic interpretation by the Ministry of Justice legal department is not thematized in the proposition.

6.3 ON ECHR REVIEW PRIOR TO THE HRA: THE DOCTRINE OF CLARITY

Most of the legal debate relating to the ECHR in the 1960s and 1970s concerned the role of international law in Norway on a *statutory* level, and the scope of the principle of presumption. The question of international law impact on the level of constitutional interpretation presents perhaps an even

22 St. forh. 16.4.1964, 2648.
23 St. prp. no. 112 (1963–64), 3 ("internasjonal rettspleie").
24 Ibid., 3.

more clear-cut version of the meeting between national and international law – and between law as developed by Parliament and law as developed by the courts. A retrospective view of this topic may thus serve as an intake to frame the general debate on the impact of ECHR in this period. One source for such an approach is found in a 1964 article by lawyer and diplomat Edvard Hambro. He pointed to how the Norwegian view of constitutional interpretation was formed by our view of international cooperation:

> Those supporting a dynamic development in international cooperation, will probably hold that the Constitution has to keep up with time and be interpreted in light of modern day conditions, while those favoring more constricted national politics, will demand greater "respect for the Constitution" and greater faith in national values and traditions. . . . In international law, perhaps even more than in national law, it is impossible to draw any clear distinction between adjudication and law creation. This may present an element of uncertainty, but bears hope of progress.[25]

These two positions are traceable in the Norwegian debates on international human rights law in general, and ECHR influence in particular. Following the ratification of the ECHR and the recognition of the Commission, in 1963 Chief Justice Terje Wold held that the ECHR must be applied by Norwegian courts even though it was in contradiction with Norwegian law.[26] Contrary to the established dualist view on all international law, he maintained human rights law had a special position, and that the ECHR in particular was directly applicable in Norwegian law. He acknowledged that the "reigning constitutional doctrine" was that the legislation of Parliament was legal even though in conflict with Norwegian obligations under international law,[27] but maintained that outside the one reservation made to the ECHR, this convention *was* Norwegian law, as it had been ratified based on the assumption that Norwegian law was in accordance with it. This view – that the ECHR was to be considered Norwegian law – gradually gained supporters, and was shared by later Chief Justices Rolv Ryssdal and Carsten Smith.[28] While Wold gave a positive law reason for his view (the ECHR was ratified upon the assumption of unanimity between it and Norwegian law),

25 Hambro, Noen betraktninger om forholdet mellom grunnlov og folkerett (1964), 226.

26 Wold, Den Europeiske menneskerettskonvensjon og Norge (1963), 355.

27 Castberg, *Norges statsforfatning* (1964) II, 230.

28 Smith, Folkerettens stilling ved norske domstoler (1964), Ryssdal, The relationship between the judiciary and the legislative and executive branches of the government in Norway (1981). Ryssdal had early campaigned for a wholly judicial Court to monitor the ECHR. He went on to become a formative figure in the developing years of the ECtHR, as a judge since 1973, as vice president from 1982 and then as its president in 1985, a position he held until 1998.

Smith moored his conclusion in "the power emanating from international human rights."[29]

In Supreme Court practice, there are several cases in which the court used the ECHR in its reasoning in the early years following its ratification, with one of the earliest in 1961.[30] Most early cases were resolved based on a harmonization of international and national rules,[31] but gradually courts came to use the ECHR in ways also explicating its impact on Norwegian law.[32]

Some of the features of the Norwegian legal tradition, as well as the general turn toward rights in Europe, may have contributed to the increasing influence of the ECHR throughout this period. Although the practice of *stare decisis* or binding precedent has not been as stringent in Norway as in Anglo-American law, the use of precedent has been a well-established part of Norwegian legal doctrine since the 1800s, opening for the use of precedent from the ECtHR in legal application. The familiarity with the principle of judicial review, if not all too intensively practiced, is also likely to have paved the way for an understanding of the construction where a higher-ranked norm decides the scope of a lower one in a way transferable to the ECHR: Even though the convention was not incorporated before 1999, it protects fundamental human rights recognizable as comparable to the (few) individual rights protected by the Constitution.

In 1994, the Supreme Court explicitly discussed the question of how to reconcile a conflict between the ECHR and a Norwegian norm.[33] The case was one of criminal procedure, and the Criminal Procedure Act of 1981 contained a rule of "sector deference," stating that the provisions of the Act were valid "within the limits posed by international law."[34] In a competition case against a manufacturer of corrugated cardboard ("bølgepapp"), the question arose whether the duty to give a statement to inquiring price control officials ran counter to the right not to incriminate oneself under ECHR art. 6. The Supreme Court stated that in order for courts to depart from what follows under Norwegian law, the deviant international law provision must appear "sufficiently clear and unanimous." One reading of this formulation is that not only must the solution following from international law be sufficiently

29 Smith, Om internasjonale menneskerettigheter og nasjonale domstoler (1980), 310.

30 Rt. 1961 s. 1350 (Dentist Iversen), Rt. 1966 s. 476 (Dentist Organization), both on the relationship between mandatory service and the ban on forced labor in ECHR art. 4.

31 See Skretting, *The Bøhler Doctrine* (2013), pointing to i.a. Rt. 1974 s. 935, Rt. 1982 s. 24, Rt. 1983 s. 998, Rt. 1983 s. 1004, Rt. 1984 s. 1359, Rt. 1985 s. 22, Rt. 1985 s. 1421, Rt. 1985 s. 1444, Rt. 1987 s. 612, Rt. 1987 s. 1285, Rt. 1988 s. 314, Rt. 1988 s. 476.

32 See i.a. Rt. 1984 s. 1175, Rt. 1984 s. 1359, Rt. 1990 s. 257, Rt. 1991 s. 1096.

33 Rt. 1994 s. 610.

34 Lov av 22. mai 1981 nr. 25 om rettergangsmåten i straffesaker (Straffeprosessloven) § 4.

clear, but also the international rule on which the solution relies. The "doctrine of clarity," as it came to be known, generated debate within the legal community,[35] and was criticized i.a. for being in tension with the principle of presumption and the obligation to ensure and protect human rights in the Constitution § 110 c.[36] Legal scholars theorized as to the reasons for the 1994 formulation: some held it to be a mechanism for Norwegian politicians and courts to avoid undesirable consequences of ECHR dynamic interpretation.[37] The doctrine of clarity was upheld by the majority in a later 1994 case (3–2).[38] In 1997, however, a case finding the Norwegian law mandating direct fines for contempt of court to be in breach of the presumption of innocence under ECHR art. 6 did not mention the doctrine of clarity,[39] thus leaving the impression of a somewhat inconsistent Supreme Court practice in this period. Courts obviously did not consider themselves barred from preferring the ECHR; the doctrine was formulated so that Norwegian law preference was a "starting point." Practice in this period in general has nevertheless been summed up as one reluctant to depart from established Norwegian rules, even in areas where ECHR was incorporated.[40] The work toward greater clarification of what position ECHR should have in Norway may be seen against this backdrop.

6.4 PREPARATIONS FOR THE HUMAN RIGHTS ACT OF 1999

6.4.1 *The Work Toward NOU 1993:18*

As described, the development of ECtHR on the European level surged from the 1970s onward. Following a general European revitalization of the idea of rights in the 1980s,[41] Norway too may have experienced a "liberal revolution,"[42] i.a. as a reaction to the expanding regulatory "Labor Party State."[43] Torkel Opsahl's call to internalize the legal protection of human

[35] Møse, *Menneskerettigheter* (2002); Skoghøy, Forholdet mellom internasjonale menneskerettigheter og norsk rett (1998); Skoghøy, Norske domstolers lovkontroll i forhold til inkorporerte menneskerettskonvensjoner (2002); Uggerud, Den andre bølge? om menneskerettighetenes tilfeldige tilværelse i norsk rett (2006).

[36] Skoghøy, Forholdet mellom internasjonale menneskerettigheter og norsk rett (1998), 2. Section 110c of the Constitution, enacted in 1994, is explained in Chapter 6.4.

[37] Aall, Domstolsadgang og domstolsprøving i menneskerettighetssaker (1998).

[38] Rt. 1994 s. 1244. [39] Rt. 1997 s. 1019.

[40] Skoghøy, Norske domstolers lovkontroll i forhold til inkorporerte menneskerettskonvensjoner (2002).

[41] Judt, *Postwar – a history of Europe since 1945* (2007), 564.

[42] Sejersted, Frihetsrevolusjonen (2007). [43] Sejersted, Den liberale vending (2009), 232.

rights by incorporating international instruments into domestic law gained momentum.

In January 1989, the Labor government stated that international human rights were to be incorporated into Norwegian law. Both the formal and the symbolic implications of incorporation were presented as driving forces.[44] One of the possible consequences of incorporation explicated at the time was that it "could lead to changes in our system of law": "Through the practice of the court in Strasbourg, human rights have been developed continually and there may be gray zones vis-à-vis Norwegian statutory regulations, even though this is not evident from the wording of the convention."[45]

Following the government resolution, the Ministry of Justice appointed a Norwegian Human Rights Committee ("the HR Committee") in the fall of 1989,[46] with the mandate of incorporating central human rights conventions, the ECHR among them, into Norwegian law.[47] The mandate recollected that even in the dualist Norway, international human rights were already observed through the principle of presumption, and seen as a relevant source of law by courts. Their protection, however, seemed somewhat subject to chance and lacking in formal guarantees. The HR Committee was asked to suggest how central international human rights instruments were to be incorporated, and to recommend the necessary constitutional and or statutory amendments for this purpose. In a 1993 "NOU" – a white paper, or official Norwegian report – the Committee presented a recommendation to incorporate the ECHR, the International Covenant on Civil and Political Rights (ICCPR) and the International Covenant on Economic, Social and Cultural Rights (ICESCR) by the enactment of a Human Rights Act.[48] In addition to incorporation, the Committee proposed amending the Constitution with a human rights provision. This Constitution § 110 c should oblige the state to "respect and ensure Human Rights," yet state that the detailed regulation of Human Rights conventions was to be enacted in statutory form.[49] The constitutional amendment aimed at establishing a powerful signal concerning the view and position of human rights in Norwegian law, rather than at creating an actionable basis for individual lawsuits. This is also how it has been used in practice:

44 St. forh. 08.2.1989, 2541 Justice Minister Bøsterud, Question time. 45 Ibid., 2541.

46 September 18, 1989.

47 Ot. prp. nr. 3 (1998–99) Om lov om styrking av menneskerettighetenes stilling i norsk rett (menneskerettsloven), 2.1.

48 NOU 1993:18.

49 The Constitution § 110 c, by Kgl. res. July 15, 1994, "Det paaligger Statens Myndigheder at respektere og sikre Menneskerettighederne./Nærmere Bestemmelser om Gjennomførelsen av Traktater herom fastsættes ved lov." An analysis of the provision is to be found in Vislie, *Høyesterett og menneskerettighetene* (1999).

as a guideline for interpretation, rather than an actionable constitutionalization of international human rights.[50] It has been seen as a constitutionalization of the principle of presumption in the field of human rights,[51] but has otherwise had but a modest legal effect.[52]

In order to ensure the influence in practice of the human rights conventions, the Committee suggested a provision of preference modeled on the Act of the European Economical Agreement (EEA Act) § 2.[53] Following the proposal, convention provisions would have preference before Norwegian statutes in cases of conflict.

The 1993 report extensively explained and discussed the phenomenon of dynamic interpretation.[54] Apart from rendering the development of some legal areas less predictable, the Committee held that this interpretative method would intensify the influence of international law in Norway, and would also lead to a different legal situation in that the amount of relevant legal authority would upsurge and remain in continuous development.[55]

As for the relation between Parliament and the courts, the report noted there was no difference in principle between the suggested law and the judicial review situation thus far: the ECHR had already been used as legal authority in court cases. Based on the *Kløfta* trisection, it assumed human rights would be the subject of high scrutiny review, yet based on Norwegian review tradition there was "little reason to believe that courts would not defer to legislative assessments that laws were in conformity with the conventions." It pointed out that due to the ECtHR, "dynamic interpretation, what was formerly seen as norms in accordance with the ECHR could, following developing societal conditions, become in breach of it." It concluded, however, that there was little reason to believe the HRA would upset the balance between Parliament and the courts to the extent Parliament sought to enact new legislation in a way that was loyal to the ECHR. This would be different "only to the extent laws were to be enacted in willful breach of the convention, a situation which is not one of unwanted shift of power from democratic to judicial institutions, but on the contrary one where courts constitute a bulwark against state abuse of individuals."[56]

50 See i.a. Rt. 1994 s. 1244, Rt. 1997 s. 580.

51 NOU 1993:18, 11.3.3.1, Innst. O. nr. 51 (1998–1999), 8.

52 See i.a. Dokument 16 (2011–2012), 12.2.

53 NOU 1993:18, 12.3.4, Lov av 27. november 1992 nr. 109 om gjennomføring i norsk rett av hoveddelen i avtale om Det europeiske økonomiske samarbeidsområde (EØS) m.v., § 2.

54 NOU 1993:18, pkt. 5.2.2.9, 6.2.4, 6.3.2, Ot. prp. nr.3 (1998–1999), pkt. 5.

55 NOU 1993:18, pkt. 6.3.3, 6.5, 10.4.3.

56 Ibid. pkt. 6.3.2.

6.4.2 1993–1999

While the proposed Constitution § 110 c was endorsed and made effective by Parliament as early as June 15, 1994, the Human Rights Act was not enacted before 1999. Comprehensive legal reforms require comprehensive preparations. While the HRA has had a significant influence on Norwegian law since its enactment, its required preparations do not seem to render it a comprehensive reform: Rather than recommending a thorough administrative examination of all existing legislation with the aim of politically altering laws to ECHR conformity, the HRA in reality left the effectuation of ECHR to the judiciary, through future cases brought before courts. Still, it took five and a half years from when NOU 1993:18 was first presented to the Ministry of Justice before the proposition to enact the HRA was sent to Parliament. This seems a long time for an act containing only six provisions, particularly considering how little the act as proposed by the Ministry of Justice deviated from that of the 1993 report.[57]

Pondering why it took so long from the 1993 report to the proposition, some explanatory factors have been presented: As courts gradually increased their use of the ECHR as basis for review even absent incorporation, some of the internal urgency in enacting the HRA may have been softened. The workload of the Ministry of Justice legal department in this period was also highlighted, by the then director of the Ministry of Justice legal department.[58] The new Ministry of Justice legal department director taking office in 1995 took on two other substantial legal reforms: a new limited liability companies' act, and a reform of forced mental health care.[59] The Lund Commission Report revealing extensive secret surveillance of Communists and Socialists during the Cold War was presented to Parliament in 1996.[60] In the wake of this, it was found that one of the Lund Commission members, historian Berge Furre

[57] To perspectivate, the time between the NOU and the proposition to reform the almost century-old Norwegian civil procedure system was less than three and a half years (from December 20, 2001 to March 4, 2005) The Civil Procedure Act of 2005 contains some 350+ provisions.

[58] Conversation with I. L. Backer, director of the Ministry of Justice legal department (1995–2008), on February 13, 2013. Backer has criticized the methodology of the ECtHR, and the ECHR influence on Norwegian law: see i.a. Backer, *Om Høyesteretts forhold til Den europeiske menneskerettskonvensjon* (2005); Backer, *Den europeiske menneskerettsdomstol* (2009).

[59] The Limited Companies Act 1997 [Lov av 13. juni 1997 nr. 44 om aksjeselskaper (aksjeloven)], NOU 1992:29, NOU 1996:3, Ot. prp. nr. 23 (1996–1997) and The Mental Health Act 1999 [Lov av 2. juli 1999 nr. 62 om etablering og gjennomføring av psykisk helsevern (psykisk helsevernloven)]. [NOU 1988: 8, Ot. prp. nr.11 (1998–1999)].

[60] Dokument nr. 15 (1995–1996) presented to Parliament 28.3.1996.

(Socialist Left Party), had been surveilled by the secret police even during his work for the Lund Commission. Minister of Justice Grete Faremo (Labor) resigned because of this on December 18, 1996. Further, following after Grete Faremo, there were three different Ministers of Justice in the period between 1996 and 1999.[61] Another possible reason for the delay is disagreement between the Ministry of Justice and the Ministry of Foreign Affairs as to the formulation of the provision of preference that became the HRA § 3.[62] I will return to this disagreement shortly.

The hearing following the 1993 report took place very soon after its finalization in May 1993, in July the same year. Most of the consulted bodies were generally positive to the draft HRA, with some notably cautious remarks from the Attorney General of Civil Affairs.[63] On two substantive points, the Attorney General – the administrative body to advise on and litigate cases brought against the state under the ECHR both in national courts and before the ECtHR – expressed skepticism to the proposed Act.

First, as the only consulted body (among 44, whereof twenty-nine had comments), it opposed the incorporation of the ICESCR, as it saw it to represent a judicialization of rights to resources. Removing the allocation of resources from the political sphere would represent a significant alteration of Norwegian legal tradition – particularly with rights as vague as those in the ICESCR. Leaving courts to decide upon these rights could create decisions made on too narrow a basis and ones in which courts could not get a general enough view of what consequences their decisions could produce. It would also inevitably benefit those resourceful enough to undertake court proceedings, thus opposing the very aim of the convention.[64] The Ministry of Justice did not share this view: incorporation of the ICESCR "neither should or will lead to any shift of power to the courts to the detriment of politically elected bodies. To the extent its provisions are vague and teleological; there are reasons to believe courts will be hesitant to set aside decisions made by politically elected bodies because of the convention."[65]

Second, while positive toward a provision of preference from the view of legal predictability, the Attorney General did not trust the report view that judicial review under the Act would be exercised with due respect toward the legislative assessments of the convention obligations as was the tradition of

61 A. Holt (Labor, 1996–1997), G. L. Valle (Labor, 1997–), A.I. Aure (Christian Democrats, 1997–1999).

62 Berg, *Nytt lys over striden mellom JD og UD om utformingen av menneskerettsloven* § 3 (2000).

63 Ot. prp. nr 3 (1998–1999), 2.2, see Section 6.5.1.

64 Ibid., 7.4.2.

65 Ibid., 7.4.3. To date (2013), the ICESCR has been mentioned in three Supreme Court cases (Rt. 2001 s. 603, Rt. 2001 s. 1006 and Rt. 2011 s. 304), but has not been decisive in any of them.

review under the Constitution. The HRA rights were of a character where courts could be expected to review intensively following the trisection set out in the *Kløfta* case. And while the Constitution could be amended, alterations of the ECHR were not possible. Three factors in particular would lead to a strengthening of the judiciary to the detriment of the legislative branch: the extensive rights catalogue of the HRA compared to the relatively sparse limits to legislative power set out in the Constitution; the expansion in practice of these rights through "progressive interpretation" to extending "outside what one may call fundamental values"; and, finally, the discretion left to courts when their foundation for interpretation was as general ("very vague") as those in the conventions.[66]

The Ministry of Justice, however, found the provision of preference to be of less importance, as "Norwegian law will normally be in accordance with our obligations under the conventions," and as it in any event will be presumed to be, and thus be interpreted, accordingly.

In this period of time, the abovementioned 1994 case of *Bølgepapp* and the doctrine of clarity were the subject of debate in the legal community. As outlined, one critique of this doctrine was that it represented a barrier to effective protection of international human rights in Norway, because it heightened the threshold for their direct impact by requiring the international rule to be "clear" in order to outweigh the Norwegian rule in cases of norm conflict. This debate seems to have also influenced the preparations for the HRA. The provision of preference that is of interest is § 3 of the HRA, which states that "*The provisions of the conventions and protocols mentioned in section 2 shall, in cases of conflict, take precedence over other legislative provisions*". This is in accordance with the Ministry of Justice proposal. In the 1993 report, the formulation is that the convention provisions "*shall take precedence over legislative provisions affording less protection of the same rights*".[67] The NOU makes no qualifications of this norm as the one represented by the doctrine of clarity (as it was interpreted).

In the year before the proposal, however, the Ministry of Justice legal department sent a draft proposal out for interministerial comments.[68] In this draft, HRA § 3 was formulated so that international human rights provisions

66 Ot. prp. nr 3 (1998–1999), 8.3. 67 NOU 1993:18, 12.4.

68 I have required access to these documents from both the National and the Ministry of Justice archives, but have been informed they are inaccessible following the July 22, 2011 Oslo bombing. The following reconstruction is consequently based on reference to these documents in Berg, *Nytt lys over striden mellom JD og UD om utformingen av menneskerettsloven § 3* (2000).

were only to be given preference in situations of "clear conflict." This was done because the ECtHR dynamic and teleological interpretation of the ECHR "ran counter to the traditional method of interpretation in international law." ECtHR decisions were marked by the particularities of every case and the composition of the court in these cases, and as

> values and interests that would have been argued from Norway may not have been thematized in [ECtHR case law], one has reason to be careful in authoritatively emphasizing [such case law] unless there has been established as a dominant position in that case law ["utkrystallisert seg en fast praksis"] that is comparable to what the Norwegian court is to assess.[69]

The Ministry of Foreign Affairs did not support requiring the norm conflict to be "clear," as this would lead to the conventions getting "a weaker position in Norwegian law than what was recommended in NOU 1993:18. The Ministry of Foreign Affairs finds this weakening unfortunate." It also commented that the critique of the interpretative focus of ECtHR decisions and the courts' composition created "an unfortunate impression of a general skepticism towards opening for international courts' case law as a source of international law" as well as "a general mistrust of [such] courts."[70]

As outlined, the final Ministry of Justice proposal for the HRA § 3 provision of preference was formulated without any requirement of clarity. In the Ministry of Justice comments on the question of how to formulate the provision of preference, however, it seems still to have held that the preference should be premised on a requirement akin to that following from the *Bølgepapp* decision: From the areas in which provisions of preference already exist, such as on that of criminal procedure, one already has particular experience with this: "the seminal Supreme Court decision pertaining to this question being that of *Bølgepapp* in 1994 s. 996. The Ministry of Justice suggests a similar preference – in a somewhat different formulation – is taken into the HRA. Thus, the system known from the area of criminal procedure – one in which human rights are particularly important – will be made generally valid."[71] As we shall see, the *Bølgepapp* case and its possible implications for the interpretation of the HRA were thematized in Parliament.

69 Draft proposal of March 13, 1997.

70 Letter, Ministry of Foreign Affairs–Ministry of Justice, April 21, 1997.

71 Ibid.

6.4.3 Discussions in Parliament

In Parliament, everyone welcomed the HRA. Some called for incorporating more conventions, such as CEDAW,[72] CERD,[73] UNCRC,[74] and some ILO-conventions, but apart from some disagreements as to what, how and when additional conventions were to be incorporated, both Parliament and the parliamentary Justice Committee was unanimous in recommending enactment of the HRA.[75] To the provision of preference, it stated that the HRA would lead to a "new legal situation based on the overarching goal of strengthening the individual's rights." One of the purposes of the HRA was to "influence Norwegian legal development in the direction of listening to, and opening up for, practice from the ECtHR."[76] It pointed to "courts' freedom to interpret independently [ECtHR case law], and that this freedom naturally would have consequences for the authority of Norwegian case law from before the HRA. ... The Justice Committee wants to underline the predominant purpose that Norwegian law to the greatest possible degree is in accordance with international interpretative practice at all times."[77]

In the parliamentary first chamber Odelstinget, some of the reasons highlighted for the HRA were the fundamentality of human rights to democracy;[78] that it would guarantee against human rights interferences also in Norway; that Norway would be able to criticize human rights breaches in other countries with greater legitimacy; that convention provisions would be positively operative for Norwegian courts;[79] that this would make it easier for the Supreme Court to decide in accordance with the ECHR;[80] that it would reduce potential complaints against Norway to the ECtHR; and that the Supreme Court would get the same review competence as the convention organs.[81]

Minister of Justice Dørum (Liberal Left) was asked whether the provision of preference was more of a signal than a reality, as neither the HRA nor the proposition dealt clearly with the *Bølgepapp* doctrine of clarity. Dørum emphasized Parliament's responsibility for ensuring that its legislation was

72 Convention on the Elimination of All Forms of Discrimination Against Women, December 18, 1979, United Nations, Treaty Series, vol. 1249, 13.

73 International Convention on the Elimination of All Forms of Racial Discrimination, December 21, 1965, United Nations, Treaty Series, vol. 660, 195

74 Convention on the Rights of the Child, November 20, 1989, United Nations, Treaty Series, vol. 1577, 3.

75 Innst.O.nr. 51 (1998–1999), 12, Ot. forh. 13.4.1999, 440.

76 Innst.O.nr. 51 (1998–1999), 8.

77 Ibid., 8.

78 Ot. forh. 13.4.1999, Ågot Valle (Socialist Left).

79 Ibid. Tor Nymo, (Agricultural Center).

80 Ibid. Ane Sofie Tømmerås (Labor).

81 Ibid. Tor Nymo, (Agricultural Center).

in accordance with the conventions, and that the need for a provision of preference would probably not be all too great to the extent Parliament was conscientious when preparing new legislation. His reply to the *Bølgepapp* question was not entirely clear: "The way I have understood [the Bølgepapp decision] it concerns legal norms in the relation between international law sources and national law, and how this may affect the processes."[82] He added: "In any event courts will, with the new Act, be able to strike down statutes in breach of human rights, but I underline that primarily, Parliament ought to be the one to balance the fundamental values inherent in the ECtHR."[83] As we shall see, courts soon came to interpret the HRA without the clarity requirement.

6.5 THE POWER AND DEMOCRACY PROJECT

6.5.1 *Democratic Legitimacy: Two Perspectives*

In 1997, Parliament commissioned a report on power and democracy in Norway.[84] In 2003, the study undertaken in the Power and Democracy Project ("Maktutredningen"; the "Power Study"), led by four political scientists, a sociologist and an art historian, was presented. One of the Power Study conclusions, which generated substantial debate, pointed to the consequences of human rights conventions, particularly in the form of ECHR review, as one factor eroding democracy.[85]

Governmental and parliamentary discussions of the relationships between rights and democracy, and debates among popularly elected majorities on whether popularly elected majorities represent the core of democracy, are interesting perspectives for reflections upon the legitimacy of ECHR review. This chapter recalls the relevant parts of debates over the Power Study as

82 Ibid., 433 Minister of Justice O.E. Dørum: "Slik jeg har forstått den, handler den om rettsregler i forholdet mellom folkerettslige kilder og nasjonal rett, og hvordan dette kan påvirke prosessene."

83 Ibid., 433.

84 December 11, 1997. A scientific group was established by Royal Decree March 13, 1998.

85 See i.a. the dissenting opinion of Study member Hege Skjeie, Petersson, Den sista maktutredningen? (2003); Kinander, *Makt og rett* (2005); Feiring, Demokratiet og rettsliggjøringen av velferdspolitikken (2006); Andenæs, *Om maktens rettsliggjøring og rettsliggjøringens maktpotensial* (2006); Blichner, *Maktutredningens rettsliggjøringsbegrep* (2006); Østerud, Rettsliggjøring og demokrati (2006); Østerud, Makt og urett – kommentar til en rettsteoretisk kritikk av Makt- og demokratiutredningen (2006); Bergo and Kinander, *Politikk, makt og demokrati – tilsvar til Øyvind Østerud* (2007); Kierulf, Rettsstatens overnasjonale vending: den andre prøvingsretten (2009).

traceable in official documents: the Study report, the governmental presentation of it to Parliament and the parliamentary committee report to Parliament. The study conclusion was premised on a conception of democracy as first and foremost procedural: a "formal system of decision-making through majority decisions and popularly elected representatives." With this conception, the Power Study maintained that democracy perceived as *rights*, *deliberation* or *values* amounted but to "supplementary forms of democracy" that might "add to" but never "replace" the procedural "main" democracy.[86] One member of the Study dissented explicitly from this conception of democracy, pointing specifically to the lack of substantial discussion of how international human rights might contribute to democratic responsibility and practice.[87]

Under the heading "Judicial bodies take over politics,"[88] the Study held that the internationalization through courts, and particularly international courts' enforcement of the ECHR, had "augmented power in the judiciary to the detriment of the representatively elected government."[89] This rights focus and rights development through courts had "by and large been an adaption to a US pattern." Through judicial answers to challenges posed by internationalization of economy and society, "individual and group rights become more decisive, while the scope of action for common solutions and democracy becomes more limited."[90] As later expounded,

> [t]he increased power of the judiciary, not least the international courts, originates from the fact that international provisions are unclear and general, leaving much leeway to legal interpretation, and that rights conventions often are contradictory, with the power of making binding priorities left for decisions in court appeals. Judicialization in this sense does thus not indicate a strengthening of the rule of law, but indicates an obliteration of the division between legislation and legal interpretation.[91]

In a consultation letter, the Attorney General for Civil Affairs seconded the conclusion that extensive power had been shifted from elected bodies to courts, asserting that as an institution the Attorney General had "one of the best viewpoints from which to witness the joint influence of international and national rule production and international and national courts' making of law."[92] While agreeing with the dissenting member of the Power Study that

86 NOU 2003:19, 13.1. 87 Ibid., 14.2, H. Skjeie. 88 Ibid., 6. 89 Ibid., 6.3.

90 Ibid., 6.4.

91 Østerud and Selle, Power and democracy in Norway: The transformation of Norwegian politics (2006).

92 Consultation letter, June 24, 2004, III.

democracy was not a question either of popular rule or of fundamental rights and rule of law, and that it had (after all) been right to incorporate the ECHR, the letter expressed grave concern about courts' increasing power. The ECtHR "has interpreted the convention very broadly, far broader than what ordinary people and national practitioners of law would be able to understand is covered by the convention provisions or the term human rights." The interpretative power is not only shifted to international courts, but to national ones – and there are "a number of examples that the interpretation of [the ECHR] takes an entirely different direction than what Parliament foresaw upon ratification and incorporation."[93] While individual fairness is important, the trouble with open-ended norms focusing on individual cases, said the Attorney General, is a lack of foreseeability. Foreseeability must always be balanced against individual fairness, but this balance is now to "a too large extent about to be upset."[94] It also pointed to the lack of democratic legitimacy in court decision-making, how political court decisions would inevitably lead to demands for political nominations of justices and how the interplay between courts and elected bodies on a national level did not apply to the international level, where conventions can hardly be altered.

In its presentation of the report to Parliament, the Christian Democrat/Conservative government was not quite as ECHR-skeptical as its Attorney General. It gave an extensive description of the ECHR legal and practical influence in Norway, hereunder the difference between ECtHR and Norwegian interpretative methods and the extensive Supreme Court case law using the ECHR to review Norwegian law and practice. Signaling better preparations before new incorporations and the main rule in incorporation practice to be incorporation *without* preference provisions akin to the HRA § 3, it underlined that "in a power and democracy perspective, the protection of certain fundamental rights is a central element of democracy." As for the role of courts, the government stated it trusted

> Norwegian courts to be careful not to set aside legislative interpretations of international conventions to the extent the enacted legislation represented a reasonable interpretation of the relevant convention provisions. This is particularly important as pertains to vague provisions, and where the law relies on value prioritization and the relation between the convention provision and the national law has been assessed by the legislator.[95]

[93] Ibid., VI. [94] Ibid. [95] St.meld. nr. 17 (2004–2005), 3.8.

6.5.2 Democracy as Perceived by the Democratically Elected

The Power Study findings were discussed in Parliament by a Particular Parliamentary Committee on the Study of Power and Democracy, comprised of the Standing Committee on Scrutiny and Constitutional Affairs supplemented with MPs from the parties not represented there, so that all parties in Parliament were represented in the Committee.[96] The Committee noted that the Prime Minister's view of judicialization was primarily a worry calling for better and more precise laws:

> There is a risk that judicialization is increasing. The following distinction is, however, important: If Parliament and the Government are able to enact precise laws, individual rights appeals to the courts need not represent a weakening of our democracy; it may instead strengthen it, as our independent judiciary is also a part of our democracy. Should Parliament and the Government instead, to a very great extent, enact laws calling for discretion, that can also be unclear, judicialization may weaken democracy through assigning to others to make decisions perhaps the elected bodies should have made.[97]

The Committee added: "laws regulate the relation between individual citizens and the state, and for a number of them it is both right and necessary that they do allow for judicial discretion. As 'people are different' a number of laws have to allow for a significant amount of discretion in order to satisfy human needs."

Acknowledging that international conventions present particular challenges in that they can hardly be amended, and in that foreseeing all consequences of incorporating them is hard, the Parliament Committee explicitly distanced itself from the view that human rights conventions had contributed to weakening or undermining democracy: "The committee is of the principled view that incorporation of human rights conventions has predominantly *strengthened* democracy and the citizens' rights towards the authorities."[98] It further took issue with the procedural view of democracy, and cited the Prime Minister's statement from the hearing: "The term 'democracy' is in my view meaningful only to the extent it contains both the principle of popular rule and that of individual protection and rule of law . . . The Committee strongly emphasized that individual rights are more than a 'supplementary democracy' as held by the Power Study majority. The Committee relies on a broad conception of democracy including both popular majority rule and the protection of fundamental rights and freedoms. Recognizing there are certain tensions in such

96 Innst. S. nr. 252 (2004–2005), 1.1. 97 Ibid., 3.7. 98 Ibid., 3.7, emphasis added.

a conception, the Committee pointed to how a strengthening of individual rights and opportunities by and large had contributed to strengthening democracy."[99]

6.6 POSTNATIONAL CONSTITUTIONALISM?

The way in which Norwegian courts have employed rights review under the Constitution in many respects resembles the way they engage the ECHR as a constitutional minimum standard or rights guarantee. In very few cases has the Supreme Court disregarded a Norwegian provision because it conflicts with the ECHR; the usual way of resolving conflicts in meetings between a ECHR norm and a national norm is through interpreting the Norwegian provision in light of the ECHR, and harmonizing it so as to avoid conflict.

Norwegian ECHR review is strong in the sense that there is little Parliament can do to alter the Supreme Court interpretation of a convention right. And the efficiency of the power exercised by the Supreme Court under ECHR review is stronger than that of the ECtHR. The amount of rights is obviously greater under the ECHR than under the Constitution. While the effects of the ECtHR are based on its authority, Norwegian courts' ECHR review has the same execution effects as does its constitutional review.

The lack of majority competence to overrule decisions adds to the liberal legitimacy of such review, but weakens its procedural democratic legitimacy. Other conceptions of democracy – notably, those stressing individual rights as an essential feature for democracy, as Parliament did in its Power Study debate – may view this strength of review as a legitimating factor. Through review, courts contribute to a reaffirmation of those individual rights required for establishing the ruling state majority. Thus, the people regain some of the power that is dwindling from them through the system of procedural democracy. In these respects, Norwegian ECHR review resembles ECtHR review. From a deliberative, democratic perspective, Norwegian ECHR review may be seen as more legitimate than ECtHR review, in that the Supreme Court is closer to the Norwegian public debate, and is not immune to it though its mandate is to rule by law. This may potentially add to two ideals: First, the general ideal of democratic deliberation: ignited by review cases, societal issues could become the subject of a broader and more well-informed debate. Second, it could render the Supreme Court more perceptive than the ECtHR with respect to how the public receives and reacts to review cases. The arguments furthered in such debates could influence later Supreme

99 Ibid.

Court ECHR review decisions, thus contributing to more of a dialogue between the rulers and the ruled.

As is the case for constitutional review and ECtHR review, the fact of pluralism bars a clear conclusion regarding the outcome legitimacy of Norwegian ECHR review. Of the fields in which ECHR has influenced Norwegian law through national ECHR review, aspects of criminal and civil procedure are particularly pertinent.[100] While posing several methodological challenges, and also sometimes being inconsistent with what follows from ECtHR review, none of these developments have been generally held out as undesirable with regards to national ECHR review. From a liberal-outcome perspective, it may also be noted that the influence of Norwegian ECHR review seems to have revitalized the awareness of the need for state–citizen rule-of-law balance that is also present in constitutional review. Further, and of relevance to the process legitimacy not only of constitutional and ECHR review, but to all court adjudication, is the stricter and more detailed criteria used to decide judges' legal disqualification.[101]

What is clear from the recollection of arguments concerning Norwegian ECHR review is that the tension between those emphasizing liberal legitimacy and those emphasizing representative legitimacy has been steadily present since the very development of the ECHR. And the arguments for the different positions have, with some variations, remained fairly stable.

An ideal of *liberal legitimacy* carries the arguments for incorporation, for recognition of international adjudicating bodies and for giving preference to the ECHR in cases of conflict throughout the ratification documentation. Apart from the obvious liberal legitimacy inherent in the idea of protecting human rights, also at the international or regional levels this ideal carries the two other arguments for ratifying the ECHR. First, the prospect of constitutional binding – it was a *legally binding document* between countries with similar (liberal) views of human rights. Second, as a legal document it would constitute a protection of such legal rights *nationally* as well as *internationally*. What I call the Opsahl line – that human rights needed to be incorporated to

[100] See Section 7.2.4. On the ECHR influence on Norwegian criminal procedure generally, see Johnsen, Menneskerettsvernet i straffeprosessen. Er det behov for en mer aktiv lovgiver? (2002); on the right of the accused to be present at first detention meeting and of the right to contradiction in criminal cases, see Matningsdal, Kontradiksjon i sivile saker og straffesaker (2013); Matningsdal, Siktedes tilstedeværelse i fengslingsmøtet ved første gangs fengsling (2013); on *ne bis in idem*, see Rui, Forbudet mot gjentatt straffeforfølgning (ne bis in idem) i Den europeiske menneskerettighets-konvensjon protokoll 7 artikkel 4 – på ny (2009); on civil procedure see Skoghøy, *Betydningen av Den europeiske menneskerettighetskonvensjon på sivilrettens og sivilprosessens område* (2009).

[101] Skoghøy, Dommerrollen gjennom de siste 50 år – noen utviklingstrekk (2011), 4.3.

be efficient[102] – together with the principle of subsidiarity, the recognition of increasing ECtHR case load and the wish to give Norwegian courts an efficient human rights tool, are arguments for national courts' review. The 1962 question concerning the war collaborator cases in Parliament may be seen as one example of awareness that even Norwegian courts could indeed have blind spots in some human rights cases, thus necessitating and making desirable international review. The repeated call to recognize the signal effect of Norwegian acceptance of the ECtHR may be seen as one of solidarity – how could Norway (continue to) be a driving force for rule of law in other countries?

Central arguments against accepting the ECtHR are the lack of experience and predictability. These may be seen as lines of argument addressing the inadequate *professional or judicial legitimacy* – the uneasiness of leaving decisions in the hands of organs the insight and professionalism of which was yet unclear. The opt-out options retained by accepting ECtHR competencies with time limits may be seen as a way of appeasing this legitimacy deficit.

It may be noted how the prospect of deliberative *democratic input* legitimacy was originally, by Professor Castberg and the Ministry of Foreign Affairs, considered an argument *against* ratifying the convention as presented; the idea of having "matters of a purely legal nature" be decided by the "political-diplomatic" Committee of Ministers created serious doubts. This is an argument for *judicial independence* and *legal procedural guarantees* as more important sources for legitimacy than that of democratic input.

In the debates over the individual complaints procedure and the ECtHR acceptance, the tension between the democratic input (popular sovereignty on the national level) and liberal outcome (efficient rights protection) legitimation strategies that remain formative become clear. In particular, Haugland's skepticism toward accepting the ECtHR explicates arguments that have remained central. To varying degrees, some legitimacy challenges posed by ECtHR review are expressed from the 1950s through 2005 by the Ministry of Justice, the Attorney General and the Power Study: Their open-ended texture leaving too much discretion to courts, the strong tendency "towards using human rights as arguments in the political and legal debate" and the foreign legal culture of those

102 See Section 2.4.2. Opsahl outlined four criteria for international legal protection of human rights: 1) that human rights need to be legally protected both *for* and *within* the states; 2) that this protection gives rise to individual complaints to international organs; 3) that such organs are competent to decide with binding effect; and 4) that their decisions may be backed by sanctions. See Opsahl, Internasjonale tiltak til fremme av menneskerettighetene (1969), 111.

interpreting it, endangering the proper sensitivity toward national, Norwegian particularities.

Among central liberal/constitutional EC(t)HR activists in this period is a notable contingent of Supreme Court Justices and Chief Justices. Their eye for the necessity of courts and human rights instruments may be understood in light of their position. And, as mentioned in Chapter 5, the decades preceding the ECtHR and the HRA were hardly marked by much court activism on the human rights field, whereas the increase in legislative and regulatory rules had been substantive. While justices are much respected societal figures, their support for what some saw as an aggregation of court power may not have appeared entirely disinterested. What additional effect this may have had on court and ECHR skeptics, however, evades evaluation.

ECtHR review only started to pick up toward 1980 (see Section 6.4), a feature that arguably weakened the basis for the original procedurally democratic legitimacy: Precisely how the ECHR was to be developed through ECtHR review and what the implications of such review would be, particularly within well-established and functioning democracies, could not be foreseen in 1959. Whether the original consent to review hinged on such foreseeability, or whether it was indeed relying on an efficient human rights protection presupposing ECHR development in a way by nature unpredictable, is subject to debate.[103]

It has been suggested that Nordic skeptics of supernationally influenced judicial review are fueled primarily by national/supernational tension, rather than by a tension between the judicial and legislative powers.[104] While Euroscepticism certainly contributes to this position, there seems also to be a significant overlap, at least in Norway, between the arguments against various types of European integration and those against judicial review in general. As recounted, the Power Study conclusion of human rights undermining democracy was part of a general argument that juridification and judicialization contribute to shift power away from the legislature and to the judiciary.

[103] See i.a. Backer, *Om Høyesteretts forhold til Den europeiske menneskerettskonvensjon* (2005); Backer, *Den europeiske menneskerettsdomstol* (2009); Hoffman, *The universality of human rights* (2009); Lord Sumption, *The limits of law (the 27th Sultan Azlan Shah Lecture)* (2013). For an attempt to seek out what the member states intended in preparing the ECHR, Nicol, Original intent and the European convention on human rights (2005) concludes these questions were the subject of debate throughout the ECHR *travaux préparatoires*, so there is no *one* "original intent" to be established: see Section 2.4.1.1.

[104] As for the EU, see Jakobsen, The conception of "Nordic democracy" and European judicial integration (2009).

Two paradoxes concerning the actors in the debates may be noted: In the discussions on both the HRA and the Power Study, the actors with the highest degree of *political* and thus *procedurally democratic legitimacy* – the Government and Parliament – are explicit that their view of legitimate rule, indeed of democracy itself, is one where the protection of human rights by courts, even supernational courts, plays a central role. These actors continue to emphasize the importance of rights and review even while aware of the effects of dynamic interpretation as described in the 1993 Human Rights Committee Report. This tendency persists following the enactment of and some formative practice under the HRA – effects which are indeed highlighted and explained both in the Study and, in more detail, in the Government report to Parliament. Confronted directly with the question of what democracy is – and how rights and judicialization also contribute to erode the influence of popular power – the Government and Parliament explicitly distance themselves from holding out popular rule as the sole idea of democracy. Instead, they point to democracy as a *combination* of popular rule, individual rights and rule of law.

Conversely, and equally interesting, among those emphasizing *popular representation* as the primary source of legitimate rule are actors with the highest technocratic or *knowledge-based* legitimacy: the professional advisors to the government (the Ministry of Justice legal department and the Attorney General for Civil Affairs) and the academics behind the Power Study. On their reasoning, procedural democracy in the form of the elected bodies should normatively be the prime decision-making organ even as concerns questions of human rights – clearly not necessarily because they are always *right*, but because they are *popularly elected*. Taking this normative legitimacy ideal seriously, what these elected bodies say – about what democracy is, what rights are and how rights should be protected – ought to be something that these actors, on their own reasoning, should defer to. Their critique of the judicialization of rights needs at least to address why it is not affected by the fact that the Government and Parliament not only do not share their view of what democracy entails, but expressly reject it. It is hard to see from what Archimedean point decisions and views of popularly elected bodies can be criticized at all, for i.e. being naïve, party strategic or a politically correct bow to "human rights": What, on their own account, provides the normative basis for the legitimacy, the soundness even, of such critique?

7

Dual Review Expressed (2000–2010)

7.1 BASIS AND CASE SELECTION

The question posed by then Norwegian Minister of Culture, Trond Giske – whether seven judges from Strasbourg know better about free speech than does the Norwegian Parliament majority – came in the wake of a 2008 decision from the ECtHR finding Norway in breach of the ECHR.[1] Parliament had legislatively enacted a total ban on the use of the TV medium for political advertising. It saw such a regulation to be but a question of how to ensure a well-functioning democratic process.[2] The Norwegian Supreme Court enforced the ban for the same reason. The ECtHR, however, held political TV advertising to be a form of expression protected as a fundamental right. A total ban on such expression needed a principled justification, which the ECtHR did not find in the Norwegian ban as applied.

This chapter looks into two cases concerning the right to free speech. This right enjoys the dual protection of the Constitution § 100 and ECHR art. 10. It has also been substantially developed in Norway following courts' review.

The field of free speech is certainly not the only area in which ECHR influence through court practice has been substantial. Particularly in the field of criminal procedure, ECHR rights have been elaborated primarily through judicial application.[3] In this field, the legislator has been criticized

[1] *TV Vest AS & Rogaland Pensjonistparti* v. *Norway* (2008).

[2] The Broadcasting Act of 1992 [Lov av 4. desember 1992 nr. 127 om kringkasting og audiovisuelle bestillingstjenester] § 3.

[3] On the ECHR influence on Norwegian criminal procedure generally, see Johnsen, Menneskerettsvernet i straffeprosessen. Er det behov for en mer aktiv lovgiver? (2002); on the right of the accused to be present at first detention meeting and of the right to contradiction in criminal cases, see Matningsdal, *Kontradiksjon i sivile saker og straffesaker* (2013), Matningsdal, Siktedes tilstedeværelse i fengslingsmøtet ved første gangs fengsling (2013); on *ne bis in idem*, see Rui, Forbudet mot gjentatt straffeforfølgning (ne bis in idem) i Den europeiske menneskerettighets-

for being too passive in following up with regulation, leaving too much to the courts.[4] Another area of substantial ECHR influence is its contribution to stricter and more detailed criteria used to decide judges' legal disqualification.[5]

The reason why free speech provides an interesting example is that it brings out some other perspectives on the review questions around which this book revolves. The traditional narrative of the countermajoritarian difficulty in Norway is that the Supreme Court has protected some constitutional rights – in civil cases, primarily those protecting some kind of property – to the detriment of politically desirable societal progress. This history has manifested judicial review as an institution primarily settling claims of *individual* rights for those citizens already in the advantageous position of ownership, either of positions or estates, against the *collective* interests of economic, nature or welfare regulations. Free speech, on the other hand, requires a balancing where the individual–collective dichotomy is less clear, thus bringing out some different perspectives on review legitimacy. Free speech case law is illustrative both of how the influence of ECHR law contributes to change fundamental Norwegian law, and also of how judicial review may in fact contribute to the opposite of the traditionally democracy-challenging narrative: through *strengthening* one foundation for most conceptions of "democracy" – a principled approach to free speech.

As I return to in concluding this chapter, two lines of reasoning are often used to explain why free speech needs fundamental protection. One is a *liberal*, or individual reason, holding free speech to be an essential feature of a just political society, as all its members must be treated as responsible moral agents free to hear others' opinions and speak their own mind.[6] The other is a *collective consequential* reason: free speech is a necessary feature for society as a whole, its protection is in our collective interest because it enables our common search for *truth* and the possibility of *democracy*.[7] Of these two lines, the collective or consequentialist justifications are the primary ones in legal practice to carry free speech protection. This is

konvensjon protokoll 7 artikkel 4 – på ny (2009); on civil procedure, see Skoghøy, *Betydningen av Den europeiske menneskerettighetskonvensjon på sivilrettens og sivilprosessens område* (2009).

4 Johnsen, Menneskerettsvernet i straffeprosessen. Er det behov for en mer aktiv lovgiver? (2002).

5 Skoghøy, Dommerrollen gjennom de siste 50 år – noen utviklingstrekk (2011), 4.3, Skoghøy, Praktiseringen av krav til dommerhabilitet i Norges Høyesterett (2009).

6 Scanlon, A theory of freedom of expression (1972); Dworkin, *Taking rights seriously* (1977), 191; Strauss, Persuasion, autonomy, and freedom of expression (1991).

7 Mill, *On liberty* (1989), ch. II, Meiklejohn, *Free speech and its relation to self-government* (1948).

the case under both the Constitution and the ECHR.[8] Efficient free speech protection may be seen as desirable not only from an individual but also from a collective point of view; it is a *sine qua non* for both rule of law and democracy. Prior to tracing review debates in Norway, I had observed free speech as adjudicated here, both under the Constitution and the ECHR, and noted the different ways in which courts approached this right under the two instruments.[9] Perhaps surprisingly, of the substantive (as opposed to procedural) rights giving rise to cases against Norway before the ECtHR, free speech cases – as such, or in cases balancing free speech against the right to privacy or reputation – dominates. While traditionally a right not giving rise to many review cases under the Constitution § 100,[10] this relatively recent development makes free speech law an area of some interest to a study of judicial review under both the Constitution and the ECHR in Norway. The ECtHR free speech case law against Norway also provides a basis for comparison between ECHR review as undertaken by Norwegian courts and by the ECtHR.[11] Such comparisons may serve to clarify differences between the two levels of review. Another facet of this area of Norwegian law is that its development throughout the last 20 years seems to draw on related, but diverse legal processes. In addition to the contributions following from ECHR review that are central to this thesis, and for which effectuation was promoted by the Human Rights Act of 1999, the Norwegian Constitutional protection of free speech was amended through a process lasting from 1996–2004. This parallel material opens for perspectivation of Constitution and ECHR review legitimacy.

As a concept and as a right, free speech is quite abstract. Hoping to encompass all forms of speech in need of protection, regulations of speech must take on a very general form allowing for contextualized interpretation of the speech in question and concrete assessments of each case. This, in turn, necessarily leaves the elaboration of the more precise content of the right to courts, through application in concrete cases.

While free speech was an important issue to the founding fathers, and has been constitutionally protected in Norway since 1814, substantial changes in its actual effect have come about following the Norwegian incorporation of the ECHR, as developed by the ECtHR and the Supreme Court. It is thus a right clearly developed by courts. One way to discuss the legitimacy of Norwegian

8 See Section7.4.

9 As a media lawyer working with cases of defamation and privacy (2001–2009) and as a judge in Ringerike City Court (2004–2006).

10 See Section 7.2.4.2. For an early comparative study of other courts' protection of free speech in the West, see Castberg, *Freedom of speech in the West* (1960), 414ff.

11 Ibid.

review under international human rights instruments is to view it against the perspective of "ordinary" judicial review under the Constitution and review as undertaken by the international treaty bodies. This approach allows for reflection upon what ideals of legitimacy guide the various forms of review, and how differing aspects of these review forms call for legitimation of disparate kinds. The approach attempted here is to use elements from Norwegian case law along with ECHR elements as a basis for discussing various aspects of legitimacy that arise in the nexus of national and international judicial review in Norway. This may also fuse the dual perspective of analytical and historical-sociological approaches to the question of judicial review legitimacy.

Within the body of free speech case law, several cases could be used to highlight legitimacy issues arising in many judicial review situations. Two cases giving rise to discussions of quite different ideals are singled out to serve as bases for further analysis. One deals with a Norwegian free speech tradition classic: that of balancing between the right of free speech and the right of personal honor. This is the protected personality right most adjudicated in Norwegian legal practice. The other concerns an issue never previously adjudicated in Norway: that of how to balance free speech against procedures to ensure democracy. This case is perhaps the most explicit example of a conflict between the fundamental individual right of free speech and the collective interest in regulating such speech. The cases both invoke the right of free speech in a way actualizing its constitutional function, and the further thought behind the case selection is fourfold.

First, the two cases have been adjudicated nationally, and then by the ECtHR, in ways leading the two courts to *different conclusions*. They may consequently divulge dissimilarities of approach at the national and supernational levels. This may serve to underline different emphases of legitimacy ideals at the two court levels. Additionally, it gives rise to explorations of what constitutes legitimate public authority on the two levels: are there issues that may legitimately be decided by courts on the national, but not on the supernational level, and vice versa?

Second, the cases are cases of *dissent on the national level*. As such, they help to illuminate the difference of legitimating strategies between the majority and the minority positions, strategies that both function within the existing "legal" room for legal consideration.

Third, the cases present free speech adjudication of *two different kinds*: one balancing the individual right of free speech against a policy or collective interest, the other balancing it against another individual right. Both cases, however, balance issues that are conceivable as all being central to conceptions of democracy. What institution is in a better position to conduct this balancing?

Finally, the cases do in principle concern *both ECHR and Constitution review*. The Constitution aspect is represented by the free speech protection of § 100. Though not decisive, and even little discussed in some of the cases, this constitutional protection is obviously a relevant and possibly influential legal source in the adjudication. The international aspect is represented by the presence of one or more convention provisions supplementing, guiding or contradicting the assessment of free speech protection through § 100 interpretation or otherwise.

Viewed against these four perspectives, the cases presented provoke a number of questions, not only concerning what free speech is and how it is legally protected, but also about how judicial review affects or ensures various ideals of individual rights, popular sovereignty and constitutional democracy.

7.2 SPEECH VERSUS PERSONALITY RIGHTS: REPUTATION

7.2.1 *Background*

In 2000, two men were convicted of raping and murdering two girls aged eight and ten in an area in the city of Kristiansand called Baneheia. The crimes were committed under particularly aggravated circumstances and the investigation and trial were the subject of considerable media coverage. During the police investigation, a former murder convict ("A") from the crime scene neighborhood was called in for questioning by the police. His status was as that of a witness, but the police's interest in him attracted considerable media attention from national as well as local media. He talked to the media, but never agreed to have his identity published. The largest local newspaper, *Fædrelandsvennen*, carried the following on its front page on May 24, 2000:

> Convicted Murderer: I am completely innocent. At 7.10 this morning, a 42-year-old convicted murderer from Kristiansand toddled off to the bus to return to work. Last night, he had been driven home by the police, after having been interrogated for approximately 10 hours about his movements on Friday, the day when C and D were killed. Alibi: – I am completely innocent, said the 42-year-old to Fædrelandsvennen in the early hours of today. The man says he has an alibi for Friday night. The 42-year-old, who was seen by several witnesses in Baneheia on Friday, is probably the most interesting of several criminally convicted persons whose movements are now being checked by the police. Sentenced to security measures: In 1988, the 42-

> year-old was sentenced to 11 years imprisonment and five years of security measures [*sikring*] for one murder by knife, one attempted murder and several other acts of knife violence. The term of the security measures imposed on him expired on 20 September last year, but as late as in March this year, he was sentenced to another three years of security measures. The judgment has been appealed.[12]

Inside the paper were several pages of coverage, including a large picture of A being accompanied by two police officers with his eyes blurred out. Although emphasizing that he was only being interrogated as a witness, the paper held its focus on him in the following days, citing the police as "searching for a locally known murderer." Details of where A lived and worked were disclosed. Based on these publications, A sued *Fædrelandsvennen* for defamation and breach of his right to be presumed innocent.

7.2.2 *Summary of Decisions*

7.2.2.1 Supreme Court Review

In the defamation proceedings, the Supreme Court acquitted *Fædrelandsvennen* in a 3–2 decision.[13] Justice Stang Lund for the majority found the newspaper coverage, taken as a whole, to leave the impression that A was possibly being investigated not only as a witness, but also as a suspect. It thus fulfilled the objective constitutive elements in the defamation provision, § 247 of the Penal Code. Relying on the criteria explicated in case law under ECHR articles 8 and 10 of the ECtHR and the Supreme Court, he held the speech to be protected under ECHR art 10.

While conducting such a balancing, the majority rejected an argument from A that the actual balancing of personality rights against free speech had changed as a consequence of several ECtHR cases explicating that the right of reputation was protected under ECHR art. 8.[14] Rather than shifting the relevant balancing criteria, the Supreme Court held that the legal approach to assessing whether media coverage was or was not protected by art. 10 remained the same, but such that they required that the values protected under both articles were duly considered.

In general, there is no ECtHR requirement that national authorities explicitly link their assessments under the ECHR to ECHR articles, as long as they consider the relevant legal criteria as explicated through ECtHR case law.[15]

[12] *Fædrelandsvennen*, May 24, 2000. [13] Rt. 2005 s. 1677. [14] Ibid., para. 70.
[15] *Axel Springer AG* v. *Germany* (2012), 88.

Indeed, in its own balancing of speech rights against reputation, the ECtHR has not always referred to ECHR art. 8 in defamatory cases where someone's reputation is affected.[16] In two Grand Chamber cases from 2012, the ECtHR emphasized the importance of recognizing this balancing more explicitly.[17] In these cases it outlined a model followed thereafter, at least in cases concerning *privacy invasions*.[18] For such cases it explicated five criteria that go into the balancing of the two rights: (i) contribution to a debate of general interest; (ii) how well known the person exposed is, and what the subject of the report is; (iii) prior conduct of the person concerned; (iv) the journalistic method of obtaining the information and its veracity/ circumstances in which the photographs were taken; and (v) content, form and consequences of the publication.[19]

The first element emphasized under the concrete balancing of the Supreme Court in the case of A was that the coverage of the investigation was of momentous public interest. So was the information that A was, in fact, a convicted murderer and that he was being interrogated by the police as a witness. This public interest had to be balanced against A's rights to protection for his personal life under ECHR art. 8. There was not at the time any right of information for the public under ECHR art. 10 to gain access to detailed information about the police work during early stages of an investigation. Still, the public interest in knowing that a former murder convict was present was seen to be particularly high at the time in the region where *Fædrelandsvennen* was published.[20] Justice Stang Lund emphasized that A had contributed to the media coverage himself; that the information conveyed was of a true, factual nature; that the police had confirmed that A was, in fact, "the most interesting of several criminally convicted persons whose movements are now being checked by the police"; that it was clearly conveyed that the police said there were no suspects, only witnesses being interrogated; and that the paper had not acted negligently: the published articles did, on the whole, give a balanced impression.

Justice Coward for the dissent agreed that the articles amounted to a defamatory innuendo under § 247, that A was a suspect, not a witness. She held that the requirement of factual basis for factual statements both under

[16] See i.a. *Lindon, Otchakovsky-Laurens and July* v. *France* (2007); *Ruokanen and Others* v. *Finland* (2010); *Otegi Mondragon* v. *Spain* (2011); *EON* v. *France* (2013). For criticism of ECtHR practice on this point, see concurring opinion of Judge Luocaides in *Lindon, Otchakovsky-Laurens and July* v. *France* (2007).

[17] *Axel Springer AG* v. *Germany* (2012), *Von Hannover* v. *Germany (no. 2)*, (2012).

[18] See i.a. *Lillo-Stenberg and Sæther* v. *Norway* (2014).

[19] *Axel Springer AG* v. *Germany* (2012), §§ 89–95.

[20] Rt. 2005 s. 1677, paras. 76, 77.

national defamation law and under ECHR arts. 8 and 10 were not satisfied, and that the publications thus amounted to an unjustified interference with art. 8 read in conjunction with the right to be presumed innocent under ECHR art. 6 § 2. Conceding that there was indeed a substantial public interest in the case, she still questioned what public interest could justify presenting A as the most likely suspect in the case at such an early stage of the investigation. Considering this, she found that even though such an interest could exist, it was not sufficient to justify the paper's detailed identification of A, particularly its disclosure of where he worked and lived. Seen in light of how careful the press normally is not to identify individuals during early stages of investigations, the detailed information underlined the impression that A was, in fact, a suspect.

7.2.2.2 ECtHR Review

A brought Norway before the ECtHR, arguing that the media coverage represented a breach of ECHR art. 6 § 2 protecting his right to be presumed innocent, and art. 8 protecting his privacy, including his reputation.[21] Norway disputed his claim under art 6 § 2, disputing its horizontal effect (*drittwirkung*), maintaining art. 6 § 2 provides but a vertical protection of individuals vis-à-vis national authorities. Between private parties, accusations of criminal guilt could raise a legal issue of defamation, but not a legal issue under art. 6 § 2. The ECtHR agreed, and found the complaint under art. 6 § 2 inadmissible. It underlined, however, that this did not prevent it from taking into account the interest protected under art 6 § 2 in its balancing of articles 8 and 10.[22]

The ECtHR interpreted the newspaper coverage like the Supreme Court had, to convey not only that A was an interesting witness, but that he was in effect a likely suspect.[23] It held that the "attack on personal honor and reputation must attain a certain level of gravity and in a manner causing prejudice to personal enjoyment of the right to respect for private life" for ECHR art. 8 to come into play – a level indeed met by A being portrayed as a suspect. In combination with the identification of A through the publication of his picture and details of his work and residence, the coverage thus directly affected A's rights under art. 8. The question was whether Norway had struck a fair balance between the newspaper's freedom of expression under art. 10 and the applicant's right to respect for his private life under art. 8.

Relying on its case law, and the difference in member states' positive obligations to protect articles 8 and 10, it underlined that states should be

[21] A. v. *Norway* (2009). [22] Ibid., paras. 44, 45, 47. [23] Ibid., 68.

accorded a wide margin of appreciation in assessing the need to protect the applicant's private life under Article 8 as opposed to that of safeguarding the newspaper's freedom of expression under Article 10.[24] It also was "mindful of the careful and thorough review carried out by the national courts of the various factors that are relevant under the Convention." This observation and the scope of the margin accorded to Norway under art. 8 notwithstanding, the ECtHR disagreed with the concrete balancing of the Supreme Court: it was not satisfied that the Supreme Court had duly protected A's art. 8 rights, and thus was not satisfied that it had struck a fair balance. It consequently found that Norwegian courts' handling of the A case represented a violation of ECHR art. 8.

7.2.3 *Current Legal Situation*

The question of balancing free speech against the personality right of honor has a long tradition in Norway. Most cases on this issue concern media speech. The balancing has seen a shift during the last 20 years, due to the Supreme Court's use of the ECHR and ECtHR case law. Particularly in the aftermath of three cases in 1999–2000,[25] in which the Supreme Court first found for the allegedly defamed party and against media free speech – cases that were all overturned in the ECtHR – the shift in Supreme Court practice in defamation cases became apparent.

The traditional doctrinal approach to defamation in Norwegian law started with an assessment of whether an alleged defamatory statement represented a breach of the detailed criteria outlined in the defamation provisions of the Norwegian Penal Code (NPC) 1902. Only in very hard cases was this followed up by an evaluation of the free speech protection in § 100 of the Constitution. With the increasing influence of the ECHR, defamation assessments instead became more rights-based, looking to the ECHR protection of free speech and/or the personality rights set out in ECHR art. 8, the interference into (and balancing between) which had to be justified in the concrete situation at hand.[26]

Starting gradually in the 1990s, and finding its form around 2002, the approach of the Supreme Court has followed the balancing method of the

24 Ibid., 66. 25 See Section 7.2.4.

26 Before 2004, it was unclear whether the protection against defamatory statements was to be found in the exceptions from free speech protection in ECHR art. 10 § 2, or followed from the protection of privacy in art. 8. After 2004 it was clear that art. 8 protected also against illegal defamation: cf. *Radio France and others* v. *France* (2004); *Chauvy and others* v. *France* (2004); *Cumpănă and Mazăre* v. *Romania [GC]* (2004); see also *White* v. *Sweden* (2006).

ECtHR and the relevant criteria for balancing speech against personality rights as set out in ECtHR case law. It has done so, interestingly, via a two-tiered approach: like the ECtHR, it reiterates relevant ECtHR case law in order to find the criteria by which to balance the case at hand. Additionally, it cites its own recent case law as precedent for this method. Two Supreme Court cases later oft cited are 2002 s. 764 (on 773)[27] and 2003 s. 928 (para. 44).[28] The procedure stipulated in the latter case, which is now the main guideline for assessment of this type of free speech cases in Norway, translates as follows:

> The decision in Rt. 2002 s. 764 and ECtHR case law shows that the concrete balancing must amount to an assessment along several criteria. Of these I highlight the degree of public interest, the type of accusation at hand, hereunder whether it is to be seen as a "value judgment" or a "factual statement," whether it is directed against a public or private person, the degree of carefulness with which it is advanced, included if, and to what extent media at the time of publication had some factual basis for assuming the accusation to be true. Generally, speech enjoys strong protection if it concerns issues of public interest, value judgments, reporting of others' statements, public persons and there is a factual basis for assuming the accusation to be true. Conversely: If the issue at hand is of little public interest, is a statement of fact, concerns an original rather than reported accusation, private person and there are little factual basis for its truthfulness, the impugned speech enjoys less protection.

While nuanced and explicated through later ECtHR case law, this remains the core of the present Norwegian free speech doctrine in media defamation cases.

7.2.4 *Background: Defamation Law Development and the Role of Courts*

7.2.4.1 Briefly on "Traditional" Norwegian Free Speech Protection

While protected since 1814, Norwegian free speech protection has for a long time deviated from the text of the Constitution § 100 – in some instances to the detriment of free speech protection. Aside from prohibition against incitement to illegal action and threats, the main challenge to the protection of free speech as set out in the Constitution has, in practice, been rules to the protection of personality rights, primarily personal honor. Until 2014 there

27 Cited in Rt. 2002 s. 764, Rt. 2003 s. 914, Rt. 2003 s. 1190, Rt. 2004 s. 1483, Rt. 2005 s. 1677 and a number of lower-level court decisions.

28 Rt. 2004 s. 1483, Rt. 2005 s. 1677 and a number of lower-level court decisions.

was no constitutional protection of such personality rights:[29] rules to this effect were codified in the Criminal Act of 1842, and continued in the NPC 1902.[30]

Given the hierarchical relationship between these two forms of rights protection, one would perhaps assume that constitutionally protected free speech regularly trumped the protection of honor as regulated by ordinary statute. This has, however, not been the case: the protection of honor has in many respects been stronger than that of free speech. The criminally sanctioned defamation rules contradicted even the constitutional text in several respects "for generations":[31] While § 100 as set out in the 1814 constitutional version mandated regulation of defamation, it required that such provisions be to the protection of "honor"; that the defaming statements regulated took the form of accusations ("Beskyldninger"); that they were false; and that the infringing of someone's honor was intentional ("forsettelig"). All of these limits have been neglected either directly in the statutory text or through interpretation: NPC 1902 § 247 textually expanded "honor" with the "loss of necessary professional trust"; § 249 nr. 2 sanctioned some true defamatory accusations; § 247 was interpreted so that there was no requirement that accusations were *intentionally* false, and that the requirement of accusations did not only encompass false statement of fact, but also value judgments.

Further, and importantly, as the defamation rules were criminal provisions, the extent to which something could be seen as defamatory at one particular moment of time became essential to the assessment of whether a crime of defamation was committed. Modifying statements uttered at another moment in time, even though immediately related to or later following up on speech which in isolation could be seen as defamatory, was irrelevant, thus barring courts from viewing speech and intention as conveyed as a connected whole.[32]

[29] One side of privacy was protected in the Constitution § 102, prohibiting unwarranted house searches. A general constitutional right to privacy was evaluated, and proposed Innst. S. nr. 270 (2003–2004), but not amended at the time: see kapittel 4.2.1., NOU 2009: 1. The considerations were used as a basis for Dokument 16 (2011–2012), 30, which led to amending of the provision in the constitutional reform of 2014.

[30] Lov angaaende Forbrydelser af 20 August 1842 kap. 17 §§ 5–7, Almindelig borgerlig Straffelov av 22. mai 1902 nr. 10 §§ 246, 247. It may be noted that these regulations protect both against written and oral infringements of honor, as opposed to the distinction in some other legal systems between defamation and slander.

[31] Mæland, *Ærekrenkelser* (1986), 65.

[32] That the conveyed message assessed as possibly defaming or invading privacy should be seen "in light of the case as a whole" is longstanding ECtHR practice: see i.a. *The Case of the Sunday Times* v. *The United Kingdom* (1979). Norwegian courts gradually adopted this view around 2000: see i.a. Rt. 2002 s. 764 and Rt. 2003 s. 593, but an example where Norway was found in breach of ECHR art. 10 on this point did occur as late as in 2007 – the case of *Tønsberg Blad AS and Marit Haukom* v. *Norway* (2007).

Complications related to the accessibility and predictability of Norwegian defamation regulations gave rise to a number of calls for reform,[33] with scant result. The shortcomings of Norwegian law in this field were increasingly thematized through the 1990s; as mentioned earlier, Norwegian law seemed increasingly out of tune with the ECHR.[34] As late as 1996, however, the central criminal law and constitutional scholar Johs. Andenæs held that "An analysis of [ECtHR] case law shows that the principles [there] employed on the whole is the same as those recognized by Norwegian courts. There is therefore no reason to believe that ECHR considerations will necessitate any significant adjustment in Norwegian defamation assessments."[35] As discussed in Section 7.3.3, this proved wrong.

The relatively weak position of § 100 as a constitutional limit cannot be explained by the general deference of Norwegian courts' review practice alone: other constitutional provisions have, as we have seen, given rise to a number of review cases. A relaxed attitude toward legal, even constitutional text is, however, not something distinguishing practice under § 100 from a general Norwegian legal approach, as outlined in Section 2.3.2. Nevertheless, the embeddedness of such general pragmatism may contribute to explaining why such an attitude was, within much of the legal community, seen to be unproblematic – and that this view persisted even following the awareness of the differing ECtHR free speech case law.

Some of the shortcomings of Norwegian free speech protection as represented by the understanding of the defamation rules were problematized along the way. One prominent voice in this respect was that of law professor C. A. Fleischer. In law review articles of 1984 and 1985,[36] he took to task the two most prominent professors in criminal law and defamation law, Johs. Andenæs and Anders Bratholm, holding their defamation theories unwarrantedly to curb free speech as protected by the Constitution § 100. Fleischer was particularly critical about the lack of differentiation between statements of facts and value judgments – and about how focus on the likely reading of statements suppressed the inclusion of a more contextual approach in which the intentions behind the speech was also a central element.

[33] See NOU 1995:10.

[34] Eggen, Ærekrenkende ytringer (1994); Wolland, *Norsk ytringsfrihet i et menneskerettslig perspektiv*; Eggen, Journalistisk formidling av ærekrenkende ytringer (1999), NOU 1999:27.

[35] Andenæs, Ytringsfriheten og ærens rettsvern etter grunnlovens § 100 og Europakonvensjonens art. 10 (1996).

[36] Fleischer, Om anmelderansvaret – og om retten til fri vurdering, kritikk og karakteristikk (1984); Bratholm, Fleischers ytringsfrihet og bruken av den (1984); Fleischer, Gjeldende injuriebestemmelser og strafferettsteoriens faglige svikt (1985).

Professor Andenæs was a central, even hegemonic figure in the field of constitutional and criminal law.[37] For a period of two decades, his and Bratholm's works were standards within the field of criminal law. His theories were regularly cited by the Supreme Court, including in the field of defamation law. Fleischer's critique gained little foothold against the positions of Andenæs and Bratholm, both in case law and in the legislative initiatives toward defamation law reform. This left ample room for means of change other than those of the legislative or national legal community, when such means became authoritatively relevant. Following the influence of the ECHR, Fleischer's main points of critique have now become central tenets of Norwegian defamation law.

Andenæs' assertion, in 1996, that the free speech doctrines of the ECtHR and the Supreme Court were more or less the same directly concerns defamation law. It is clear, however, that what made the ECtHR find Norwegian practice in defamation cases to be in breach of the ECHR in no less than three defamation cases just a few years later, was the lack of principled justifications for interventions into the right of free speech.[38] The Norwegian understanding of free speech as a constitutional right the interference into which requires principled and coherent justifications had, if ever there, faded through centuries of pragmatic compromise. This approach had long since been accepted by courts, the legislature and much of the legal community.

7.2.4.2 A Right First Underdeveloped, then Substantially Developed by Courts

Several studies have been published on the relationship between free speech and personality rights in Norway.[39] This section outlines only one strand of its development, that of defamation law, in order to show how courts and judicial review have been essential to its progress. The judicial contribution has taken place alongside other drivers for free speech fortification initiated by the legislature. It may thus serve as one example illustrating the contingency of judicial review impact.

37 See Flaatten, *Høyesterett, straffen og tyveriene: straffeutmålingsbegrunnelser i etterkrigstiden* (2017).

38 See i.a. Eggen, Ytringsfrihet, personvern og ærekrenkelser – tre norske saker for EMD (2000); Kierulf, Rettsstatens overnasjonale vending: den andre prøvingsretten (2009).

39 See i.a. Skeie, *Om ærekrænkelser efter norsk ret* (1910); Andenæs, *Spesiell strafferett* (1990); Fleischer, Gjeldende injuriebestemmelser og strafferettsteoriens faglige svikt (1985); Mæland, *Ærekrenkelser* (1986); Wolland, Norsk ytringsfrihet i et menneskerettslig perspektiv (1994); Eggen, *Ytringsfrihet* (2002); Borvik, *Personvern og ytringsfridom* (2011).

The parts of Norwegian defamation law substantially changed by ECHR influence were the media's possibility to criticize the exercise of power and public figures, and to legally refer from official documents. While the shift was certainly implemented with the help of courts, the possibility of free speech judicial review under the Constitution was not enough: § 100 has never led to any speech-limiting statute being set aside.

Prior to ECHR influence, Norwegian free speech law was characterized by a sometimes unprincipled and incoherent approach. While other constitutional provisions from time to time gave rise to review cases, § 100 did not. It was mentioned, but not used in a case finding, that a general prohibition against exports and imports could not be used against communist propaganda to and from Russia.[40] As pointed out in the *Waterfall* chapter, the absolute lack of § 100 bite was central to a review discussion in the 1920s, there as proof of the true conservative slant of the Supreme Court. In a seminal 1952 Supreme Court case establishing the court-made personality right to protection against movie portrayal, the movie-makers' constitutional right to free speech was not even mentioned by the majority.[41] In 1979, a newspaper was convicted for having used the word "torture" in an investigative series on inhuman treatment of mentally disabled persons, and in 1985 another newspaper was found to have defamed Greenpeace by characterizing their actions as "nature conserving terror" in an editorial[42] – both because the Supreme Court found such value judgments to be "unnecessary."[43] And even where no "unnecessary" words were used, or accusations made that could not be proven, in 1987 yet another newspaper was convicted for "having created the general impression" that a public servant had received substantial extra pay for job-related tasks. It had not explicitly said so, but this was how the Supreme Court found "an average newspaper reader" would be likely to read the story. Rather than conducting a literal interpretation reading the story as a whole, the Supreme Court found this assumed impression determinative, the Constitution § 100 notwithstanding.[44]

As an aside, having free speech "on the books" without much using it as a legal protection is no unique Norwegian experience. One pendent, *mutatis mutandis*, is the US First Amendment history. Today the First Amendment represents one of the most protective free speech provisions in the world, but it has only done so for some 60–70 years of its more than 200 year history.[45] Throughout the 1800s, the old common law doctrine holding free speech to be

[40] Rt. 1922 s. 41. [41] Rt. 1952 s. 1217 [42] Rt. 1985 s. 1421. [43] Rt. 1979 s. 727.

[44] Rt. 1987 s. 1058.

[45] See Lewis, *Make no law: the Sullivan case and the First Amendment* (1991).

a right only against "previous restraint" remained the dominant view also of the First Amendment.[46] Through a series of cases starting with prosecutions under the 1917 Espionage Act, this view was gradually changed,[47] and with seminal cases from the 1940s to 1960s it was completely abandoned.[48] Through review cases and a shift in popular views of what free speech *ought* to protect, not only the consequences but also the justification for protecting free speech under the First Amendment came to be fundamentally altered.

Following the increasing awareness of ECtHR practice and effects in courts as well as elected bodies throughout the 1980s and 1990s, the view of Norwegian speech protection changed – not in a way effectuating any more direct use of Constitution § 100, but by a greater understanding of and respect for other sides of free speech protection as represented both by the Constitution § 100 and the ECHR art. 10, but primarily as expounded by the ECtHR. In the last 15–20 years, the embedded, but little used constitutional free speech protection in Norway has seen a revival. It seems plausible to ascribe this to the influence of the ECHR. Contrary to what the Constitution § 100 did, the ECHR art. 10 has led the Supreme Court to new interpretations of defamation rules.[49]

At least three different, but interrelated phenomena contributed to this shift: 1) the enactment of the Human Rights Act in 1999: 2) the work toward an amendment of the Constitution § 100, initiated in 1996, finished in 2004; and 3) judicial review under ECHR art. 10 – first by the ECtHR, and gradually also by the Supreme Court.

As mentioned, both the scope of ECHR art. 10 and the dynamic interpretation of the ECtHR as established in *Tyrer*,[50] and followed since, were considered in the work toward the Human Rights Act of 1999.[51] In the decade after enactment of the HRA in 1999, the Supreme Court based its assessment of defamation cases on the approach to such cases as taken by the ECtHR. It did so by reference first to ECtHR case law, and then also to its own precedent using this case law – pointing out that this precedent represented a "mark that it is the convention and the practice under it by the ECtHR which today is the primary legal authority when Norwegian courts assess defaming statements."[52]

46 Blackstone, *Commentaries on the laws of England Book the fourth* (1770), 151.

47 See i.a. *Abrams* v. *United States* 250 *U.S.* 616 (1919) and *Whitney* v. *California* 274 *U.S.* 357 (1927).

48 See i.a. *Chaplinsky* v. *New Hampshire* 315 *U.S.* 568 (1942) and *New York Times* v. *Sullivan* 376 *U.S.* 254 (1964).

49 Rt. 2002 s. 764 (value judgments), Rt. 2003 s. 1190 (public interest, good faith journalism), Rt. 2004 s. 1483 and HR-2014-445-A (more integrated interpretation of alleged accusations).

50 *Tyrer* v. *the United Kingdom* (1978).

51 NOU 1993:18, 4.2.3, 5.3.1.

52 Rt. 2003 s. 928, para. 38, referring to Rt. 2002 s. 764.

A central reason for the work toward an amended constitutional § 100 was a recognition that the provision had not represented much of a constitutional limit, that the defamation regulation presented particular challenges and that the Norwegian constitutional free speech protection needed to be seen in light of international speech protection[53] – in practice, ECtHR case law. The preparations were undertaken by the Freedom of Expression Commission working from 1996–1999, led by historian and chairman of the Nobel Peace Prize Committee, Francis Sejersted. The Constitution § 100 as amended deviated some from the proposal made by the Commission in NOU 1999:27. The proposal for a new § 100 was presented as one text by the Commission, but the Government[54] split it into several partial proposals, to "ensure broader freedom of action" for the representatives of the next Parliament, which was to vote on them.[55] Only after the election, however, did the Ministry of Justice legal department present its own view as to how these parts were to be put together as a whole.[56] This proposal was criticized for "hardly ensuring the minimum standard required by ECHR art. 10."[57] Parliament split almost in half regarding the two main proposals, but ended up, after some amount of lobbying, with a compromise closer to that of the Freedom of Expression Commission.[58]

The ECHR had been mentioned by, and had influence on, the Supreme Court in some cases prior to the late 1990s development,[59] but the main ECtHR contribution to the review-ignited portion of the shift came in 1999 and 2000. Then, the relative scarcity of Norwegian cases in the ECtHR was supplemented with three cases finding Norway in breach of the ECHR in defamation cases. *Bladet Tromsø* made clear that the media should to be able to report from official documents without having to verify them if it were to fulfill its role as a public watchdog. Contrary to Norwegian courts, the ECtHR held the Norwegian practice of convicting a newspaper that had reported on an issue of significant public interest – in this case, seal hunting – in a way compromising the reputation of a private individual to be a hindrance of its role as a public watchdog.[60] *Bladet Tromsø* had relied on the contents of an official report, and such reports, in ECtHR's view, are normally something newspapers can report from without having to undertake independent

53 Kgl. Res. August 23, 1996. 54 As prepared by the Ministry of Justice legal department.

55 St. meld. nr. 42 (1999–2000). 56 St.meld. nr. 26 (2003–2004).

57 Lorentzen, *Ytringsfrihet på norsk* (2004).

58 Seminar held by representatives of Fremskrittspartiet (right-wing Progress Party) on September 23, 2004, with contributions from Commission members Sejersted and Lorentzen and the Association of Norwegian Editors. See Innst. S. nr. 270 (2003–2004).

59 See i.a. Rt. 1990 s. 257. 60 *Bladet Tromsø and Stensaaas* v. *Norway* (1999) para. 68.

research, and still be seen to act in good faith and in accordance with the ethics of journalism.[61]

The case of *Nilsen and Johnsen* v. *Norway* clarified a distinction significant to ECtHR case law, but not to Norwegian doctrine, between statements of fact and value judgments.[62] The latter enjoy a far wider protection than the former, presuming it has some factual basis.[63] Law professor Bratholm had written critically about police violence in Bergen. The Chairmen of the Norwegian Police Association and of the Bergen Police Association questioned the motives of Bratholm's conclusions, characterized as "pure misinformation intended to harm the police." Bratholm sued for defamation and won in the Norwegian courts. The ECtHR, however, found Norway to be in breach of ECHR art 10. Contrary to the Supreme Court, the ECtHR held that contentions about a person's motives could indeed be protected by ECHR art. 10 to the extent they were seen as value judgments, not statements of fact, as they were in this case.

In *Bergens Tidende* v. *Norway*, the ECtHR clarified that consumer protection was a matter of "public interest," that there are limits to what illegal speech can be read into articles containing no untrue statements, and that newspaper coverage based on facts presented in good faith and in accordance with the ethics of journalism is usually protected. The case concerned critical coverage of a cosmetic surgeon, which included interviews with some of his discontented patients. The Supreme Court had found the newspaper series on the whole to imply that the surgeon was incompetent, based on the newspaper coverage as assumedly read by an "average newspaper reader." The ECtHR, however, underlined that defamatory statements could not be read into the articles:

> This meaning was one derived by the Supreme Court, not from the express terms but from the general tenor of the articles, whose common sting, however, lay in the true allegation that Dr. R. had failed in his duties as a cosmetic surgeon in not providing proper or adequate post-surgical treatment to remedy the results of unsuccessful operations. Reading the articles as a whole, the Court cannot find that the statements were excessive or misleading.[64]

While some ECtHR criteria still posed challenges for traditional Norwegian defamation doctrines, most of the relevant ECtHR factors have

[61] A. v. *Norway* (2009) 65. [62] *Nilsen and Johnsen* v. *Norway* (1999).

[63] See *Nilsen and Johnsen* v. *Norway* (1999), *Cumpănă and Mazăre* v. *Romania [GC]* (2004).

[64] *Bergens Tidende* v. *Norway* (2000), para 56.

become quite embedded in Supreme Court defamation practice since 2002. One exception is the case of *Tønsberg Blad* from 2003. It concerned a local newspaper that had published what was seen as defamatory statements when connecting a business leader to a list of persons possibly in breach of permanent residence requirements. A follow-up article published when new facts came to light about a month later, which clarified that this business leader was wrongly put onto the list, was disregarded as irrelevant by the Supreme Court.[65] It found the *Tønsberg Blad* coverage fell short of the free speech protection in ECHR art. 10, but the ECtHR viewed the case differently.[66] One central deviation in the ECtHR assessment was that the follow-up article was indeed considered relevant to assess the newspaper coverage seen as a whole. It seems plausible to understand the Supreme Court position on this point as remains of the traditional Penal Code approach to defamation assessments holding the moment of the committed crime to be decisive.

While both the HRA enactment and the Freedom of Expression Commission and amendment of the Constitution § 100 contributed to the shift in Norwegian defamation law, the primary driving force underlying this development is that of judicial review. The HRA enactment was a general, political mandate for Norwegian courts to contribute to such a shift, but one that left to them the otherwise legislative burden of undertaking the necessary adjustments of traditional doctrine. The amendment of § 100 contributed to raise awareness of *why* free speech should be protected. It has also served, through the Commission report and subsequent preparatory work, as a national anchoring of principles otherwise found only in ECtHR practice. It should be noted, however, that § 100 as amended in itself is hardly notable as a source of authority in free speech cases following its enactment: in the period 2004–2011 the Supreme Court ruled on twenty-four free speech cases. Only five of these relied on the Constitution § 100, and then only as one authority alongside that of ECHR art. 10. The remaining nineteen cases were decided without reference to the Constitution § 100.[67] While the Constitution itself was not much referred to, a source sometimes used was the Constitution § 100 *travaux préparatoires*. These were used not to contradict or modify factors relevant under ECtHR case law, but to make many of the same points that were also used there. In this somewhat surprising way, the Supreme Court's

65 Rt. 2003 s. 928, para. 34. The Supreme Court was criticized on this point by Kierulf and Strømme, Tolkning og injurier (2004). The authors at this time worked in the same firm as counsel for Tønsberg Blad in the Norwegian proceedings.

66 *Tønsberg Blad AS and Marit Haukom* v. *Norway* (2007).

67 Kierulf, Hvilken rolle spiller Grunnloven § 100 i Høyesteretts ytringsfrihetspraksis? (2012). For a continuation of this tendency, see HR-2014-445-A.

traditional Norwegian use of *travaux* has in fact served as a tool for the integration of ECHR law into Norwegian law – one that out of legal tradition was familiar and possibly thus more acceptable to Norwegian jurists. The confluence of drivers for a strengthened free speech protection notwithstanding, this underlines the contribution of judicial review – first in the form of case law from the ECtHR; then as adopted, refined, accommodated and embedded through Supreme Court review.

Some commentators have taken issue with the assertion that the free speech development around 2000 was primarily a consequence of Supreme Court adjudication, holding it instead to be a result of recent developments in ECtHR case law,[68] or to be but a natural development following what had always been Norwegian doctrine.[69] The first position is at odds with the predictions of what parts of Norwegian defamation law were in tension with ECHR art. 10 as presented in the time prior to the new case law against Norway in 1999–2000.[70] The latter position is contradicted by the persistent critique of Norwegian defamation law,[71] the discouraging Norwegian record in ECtHR in defamation cases and also by how the Supreme Court itself viewed the shift, maintaining it in 2002 to be a result of "a substantial development" in the field. The Supreme Court indeed found the development so substantial that it, contrary to the main rule of litigation costs being the burden of the losing party, split the costs between the parties because "it must have been difficult for the parties [due to the shift] to predict their legal position."[72]

While the altered scope for political regulations of defamation was made clear through the case law of the Supreme Court from the years around 2000, and while alterations of the defamation provisions had been discussed and called for at least since 1995,[73] no *legislative* proposal to the effect of bringing the defamation legislation more up to date was furthered until 2008. The process for this initiative deviated somewhat from the ordinary procedure of legislative preparations. Rather than being analyzed and explained by the Ministry of Justice legal department or some compound expert group, the department tasked it to one associate professor, Bjørnar Borvik. While not a unique solution, it seemed a less than obvious procedure in a field with such

68 Bratholm, Injurieretten og personvernet (2002).

69 Danielsen, Injurier verre enn knyttneveslag (2002).

70 Eggen, Ærekrenkende ytringer (1994), NOU 1999:27 app. 2; Eggen, Journalistisk formidling av ærekrenkende ytringer – med særlig vekt på betydningen av Menneskerettighetsdomstolens avgjørelse i Tromsøsaken (1999).

71 Fleischer, Om anmelderansvaret – og om retten til fri vurdering, kritikk og karakteristikk (1984); Fleischer, Gjeldende injuriebestemmelser og strafferettsteoriens faglige svikt (1985), NOU 1995:10, NOU 1999:27.

72 Rt. 2002 s. 764 (777). 73 NOU 1995:10.

an extensive history of legal discussion, disagreement and legislative reform proposals.[74] Contrary to the normal three-month hearing period, the proposal was sent out in July 2008, with the time limit for comments set as August 20 – in the middle of the Norwegian summer holiday period.[75] Following comments and recommendations from a number of parties, including the Director General of Public Prosecution, the proposal was significantly altered, i.a. by abolishing the writ of "mortifikasjon" (to have a statement declared null and void) and having defamation decriminalized.[76] One reason for the decriminalization was the fact that assertions of defamation hardly ever led to criminal proceedings; parties were instead referred to instigate ordinary, civil proceedings. The remaining principled justifications did, however, rely extensively on court-made development of the field.[77] As called for earlier,[78] defamation in 2009 ended up being decriminalized, contrary to the reform proposal of the Ministry of Justice Legal Department. It was, upon the enactment of the new NPC 2005 in 2015, moved from the Penal Code to the Civil Damages Act, to a provision giving cause of civil action for damages based on the factors relevant under ECHR art. 10 case law.[79] This legal reform may be seen as a legislative endorsement of the legal development of free speech law originating in the courts.

The free speech development up until and after 2000 indicates two things: that judicial review was a necessary driver for free speech development, but also that it alone was not sufficient. Rather, courts have been a driving force because the legislative branch has supported and encouraged judicial development of a legal field in which the shortcomings of national doctrine and detailed regulation became increasingly clear. Free speech is among those rights the scope and limitations of which are subject to substantial reasonable disagreement, even within relatively homogenous societies such as Norway. Such disagreement may, however, be an inadequate source for legal change in smaller societies where certain positions become hegemonic. The influx from

74 Ibid., NOU 1999:27, NOU 2002:4.

75 Hearing letter June 2, 2008 from then Head of the Ministry of Justice legal department, I.L. Backer.

76 Ot. prp. nr. 22 (2008–2009), 5.14, Innst. O. nr. 73 (2008–2009), 5.2. I was part of a group assisting the Association of Norwegian Editors at the time in working out an alternative legislative proposal. This proposal was later, with some alterations, adopted by Parliament, see ibid., 5.2.

77 Meling, *"Privatlivsvern og æresvern": Hva er gjeldende rett og hvilke problemstillinger reiser seg i møte med de endringer som vil finne sted ved ikrafttredelsen av ny straffelov?* (2013).

78 See i.a.Schiøtz and Strømme, Paradigmeskifte i injurieretten (2002).

79 Lov av 13. juni 1969 nr. 26 om skadeserstatning (skadeserstatningsloven) § 6a. Due to "computer challenges," the NPC 2005 has been delayed several times. It entered into force in September 2015.

other legal cultures has the potential of revitalizing lost attentiveness to dissenting approaches to questions the answers to which are given more out of habit than of attentive reasoning and consideration. Rights contingent upon enduring disagreement of this kind challenge the ideals of legislative law-making characterized by a general, forward-looking perspective. At the same time, they open for a case-to-case assessment, based on predetermined criteria, but in the concrete – such as in the case of free speech and personality rights balancing, through judicial review.

7.2.5 *Perspectives*

The right to personal honor, reputation and privacy was protected under Norwegian law, and defamation and invasion of privacy was criminalized in the NPC 1902 §§ 246, 247 and 390.[80] The right to free speech was, and is still protected by the Constitution § 100.[81] These provisions were and are supplemented by ECHR arts. 8 and 10. In the case of A, it may be noted that A complained only under ECHR for the Supreme Court, not under the Norwegian Constitution or Penal Code 1902. The Supreme Court is, however, not precluded from taking into account legal provisions other than those relied on by the parties, and found the alleged defamatory statement in *Fædrelandsvennen* to be covered by NPC 1902 § 247. Having concluded thus, however, the Supreme Court relied wholly on case law under ECHR, either from the ECtHR (nine cases[82]) or its own precedent (five cases where ECHR was the decisive authority;[83] one relying on NPC § 247[84]) to decide that a conviction under § 247 represented an unjustified interference in ECHR art 10. Also interesting is that the Constitution § 100, amended only a year earlier i.a. with the aim of bringing free speech protection "home," was not mentioned, either in *Fædrelandsvennen*'s arguments or in the reasoning of the Supreme Court.

The case of A thus illustrates what has been an increasing tendency in Norwegian free speech proceedings for the last 15–20 years – that of courts looking to the ECHR and ECtHR case law not only for guidance, but also as

80 Parliament decided to decriminalize defamation in 2009, a change effective upon the entering into force of the Penal Code of 2005 in 2015., see Ot. prp. nr. 22 (2008–2009) 5.14.3, 165–168.

81 In 2014, also the right to privacy was added to the Constitution, in an amendment to § 102.

82 *Jersild* v. *Denmark* (1994), *Nilsen and Johnsen* v. *Norway* (1999), *Janowski* v. *Poland* (1999), *Cumpănă and Mazăre* v. *Romania [GC]* (2004), *Pedersen and Baadsgaard* v. *Denmark [GC]* (2004), *Selistö* v. *Finland* (2004), *Radio France and others* v. *France* (2004); *Von Hannover* v. *Germany* (2004), *Chauvy and others* v. *France* (2004).

83 Rt. 2002 s. 764, Rt. 2003 s. 914, Rt. 2003 s. 928, Rt. 2003 s. 1190, Rt. 2004 s. 1483.

84 Rt. 1999 s. 1742.

the primary authority for solving the cases at hand;[85] and, if looking to the Constitution at all, then only to pay its § 100 what the then Chief Justice Schei in 2002 called a "courtesy visit" before moving on to the analytic criteria following from ECtHR case law.[86] Several factors may explain this tendency, an obvious one being the amount of cases decided under the various ECHR provisions, representing a broad and detailed basis for authoritative citations. In the absence of explicated judicial reasons this tendency does, however, give rise to the following questions: What is the legal significance of relying on the ECHR rather than a national constitution? What is the relationship between overlapping national and international constitutional rights?

By representing a review case in which two fundamental rights are balanced against each other, and where this balancing is one with a long national tradition, the Supreme Court decision in A v. *Norway* raises some other interesting questions. What ideals are furthered or challenged by the Supreme Court use of the ECHR instead of the Constitution? And by its use of Supreme Court precedent as legal authority rather than "only" ECtHR case law? At the outset, holding the Constitution to be the highest expression of national, popular will, it seems to challenge national sovereignty not to use the Constitution where relevant and applicable. Even though the ECHR has a substantial amount of input legitimacy from a procedural democratic perspective, being incorporated and given preference by a unanimous Parliament through the HRA, disregarding the Constitution as legal authority seems at odds with the position of constitutions in a doctrine of norm hierarchy. It may still be understandable, as free speech doctrine is far more developed under the ECHR art. 10 than under the Constitution § 100. By not providing such a possible explanation for disregarding § 100, however, the reasoning of the Supreme Court in cases where both rights instruments are authoritative challenges the process ideals requiring Supreme Court reasoning to be transparent and standardizing for other legal practitioners. The Supreme Court abandonment of (or lip service to) even as fundamental parts of national law as constitutionally protected rights may also be interpreted to signal that human rights are better protected by the ECHR than by national law. While somewhat explained as an unintended consequence of ECHR law being more practicable on this point, this challenge reveals one of the shortcomings of the pragmatic Norwegian approach to the Constitution: it leaves courts with little

[85] See i.a. Rt. 2002 s. 764, Rt. 2003 s. 914, Rt. 2003 s. 928, Rt. 2003 s. 1190, Rt. 2004 s. 1483; and Schiøtz and Strømme, Paradigmeskifte i injurieretten (2002); Kierulf, Hvilken rolle spiller Grunnloven § 100 i Høyesteretts ytringsfrihetspraksis? (2012).

[86] Referred in Dahl, *Norsk presses historie* (2010), 476.

theoretical and principled guidance in the still rather new dual review situation.

When choosing to use the ECHR rather than the Constitution, the Supreme Court use of its own precedent under the convention rather than that of the ECtHR may be in tension with the Supreme Court mandate to itself in cases under the ECHR: to use the method of the ECtHR. Absent a transparent justification, this too challenges ideals of judicial legitimacy. This method in approaching cases of dual rights protection does, however, serve to further another legitimacy ideal – that of history and tradition. "Anchoring" its reasoning in its own precedent rather than "only" in ECtHR case law serves the dual function of making its methodological approach familiar to those schooled in traditional Norwegian legal reasoning, while at the same time underlining the relevance of Supreme Court case law. In addition to this, it may be seen to further an ideal of popular input legitimacy: through the HRA, Parliament asked the Supreme Court to ensure the effective incorporation of the ECHR into Norwegian law. Reliance on Supreme Court precedent in cases concerning the ECHR is a loyal answer to this question: it very clearly exposes how ECHR law has become an integrated part of Norwegian law.

With the dual approach illustrated by the Supreme Court, citing both the ECtHR and its own precedent in media defamation cases, the Supreme Court has contributed to enforce the authority represented by the ECHR itself as well as the legislative nationalization of this authority through the HRA, with the authority of its own precedent. The ECHR is thus, through the approach of the Supreme Court in such review cases, being institutionally sanctioned by several different means of legal authority.

Moving on to the ECtHR review of the A case, it can be noted that this court explicitly accepted the understanding of the newspaper coverage as interpreted by the Supreme Court. It saw "no reason to disagree with the national courts' finding that, for an ordinary reader, this must have been perceived as if the applicant could be a suspect in the case and their finding that the coverage was defamatory of him."[87] In addition to underlining the well-established position that the ECtHR regards itself competent to review national courts' interpretation of impugned speech, this expression also exposes that such interpretation is not restricted to the express meaning of the terms employed. Whether the aim of speech interpretation is to divulge the intent with which the *speaker* spoke, or what impression the speech has left its *audience* with, it opens for a substantial amount of contextualization. Is it legal rules, then –

[87] A. v. *Norway* (2009), 69.

either under the ECHR or national law – that should guide courts' interpretation of impugned, but nonlegal speech in free speech cases? What place do legal rules have alongside rules of general language interpretation?

From the perspective of international review, two interesting features possibly explain why the ECtHR reached the opposite conclusion of the Supreme Court. First, it seems the criteria otherwise determinative of protected speech under ECHR art. 10 –namely, degree of public interest, factual basis and publication according to the ethics of journalism – are little emphasized. This could make the case an example of a feature of the Court's case law sometimes thematized: When weighing ECHR rights against each other, it has sometimes appeared to make a difference under what article the individual victim is complaining.[88] Until properly thematized, such as in the aforementioned *Axel Springer* case from 2012,[89] this "framing-effect" blurred otherwise operational balancing criteria in ways obscuring the scope of each individual right, the proper balancing of rights against each other and the adjudicative method looked to by national courts.

Second, rather than taking issue with particular mistakes or omissions in the Supreme Court decision, the ECtHR without further explanation conducted a different balancing between ECHR arts. 8 and 10 than did the Supreme Court.[90] This was done notwithstanding the wide margin of appreciation granted to Norway in the case at hand, and even though the ECtHR is explicit that it considered the Supreme Court reasoning a "careful and thorough review" of "the various factors that are relevant under the Convention."

Overruling national courts balancing without further justification appears in tension with the principle of subsidiarity under which it is primarily for the nation states to ensure to its citizens the protection set forth in the ECHR. Further, it contradicts the "fourth instance" doctrine, under which the ECtHR is not to function as a court of appeal above the national courts. It also seems to disagree with an increasing body of ECtHR case law emphasizing the principle of subsidiarity, holding that the court will respect decisions made by national courts where those courts have taken into account the relevant criteria established in the ECtHR case law without any manifest error or omission of any important

88 See generally De Schutter, *Rights in conflict: The European Court of human rights as a pragmatic institution* (2006); explaining this phenomenon in cases concerning free speech and the right of reputation is Smet, Freedom of expression and the right to reputation: Human rights in conflict (2011).

89 *Axel Springer AG v. Germany* (2012), § 87.

90 A. v. *Norway* (2009) 74.

factor.[91] A v. *Norway* consequently highlights three possible limits to legitimate ECtHR review.

A very different approach to this may be found in the 2014 ECtHR decision *Lillo-Stenberg and Sæther* v. *Norway*.[92] Here, the ECtHR defers to the Supreme Court decisions because it – both the majority and minority votes – "carefully balanced the right of freedom of expression with the right to respect for private life, and explicitly took into account the criteria set out in the Court's case law which existed at the relevant time,"[93] underlining that under such circumstances "the Court would require strong reasons to substitute its view for that of the domestic courts." This approach seems more in line with the principle of subsidiarity and the fourth-instance doctrine, thus furthering both rule of law and judicial legitimacy ideals. It may be noted that in the *Lillo-Stenberg* case, the ECtHR not only commends the Supreme Court on weighing the ECtHR criteria relevant at the time of Supreme Court assessment; it also adds that "de facto, the Supreme Court assessed all the criteria identified and developed in the subsequent case-law" too – namely, that of the abovementioned *Springer* case from 2012, four years after the Supreme Court case was decided. The *Lillo-Stenberg* case consequently illustrates how both the Supreme Court and the ECtHR may make decisions heeding the complex combination of legitimacy ideals expected from them – the Supreme Court by following the HRA mandate from Parliament to adopt the ECtHR way of reasoning about the ECHR (even before the ECtHR does so itself in a way it later finds satisfactory), and the ECtHR by explicating (gradually) relevant criteria for balancing, and recognizing when these criteria have been carefully employed and assessed by domestic courts.

To the extent that one reason for the ECtHR finding of a violation was that it was brought in as an art. 8 complaint rather than an art. 10 complaint, this case may be one example of the aforementioned "framing" effect that challenges

[91] See Brems, *Procedural Review in European Fundamental Rights Cases* (2017), Spano, Universality or Diversity of Human Rights: Strasbourg in the Age of Subsidiarity (2014), Rui, The Interlaken, Izmir and Brighton Declarations: Towards a Paradigm Shift in the Strasbourg Court's Interpretation of the European Convention of Human Rights? (2013). Underlying this tendency also in free speech cases against Norway are two three-judge panel decisions from 2018: *Dagbladet* v. *Norway* (2018) and *Avisa Nordland AS* v. *Norway* (2018). Both cases were found inadmissible with similar references to the national balancing of relevant ECHR criteria, see paras 34 and 49 respectively: "the Court finds that the Supreme Court carried out the exercise of balancing the interests protected by Articles 10 and 8 of the Convention in conformity with the criteria laid down in the Court's case-law and that, while opinions on the outcome may differ, there are not 'strong reasons' for the Court to substitute the Supreme Court's assessment with one of its own."

[92] *Lillo-Stenberg and Sæther* v. *Norway* (2014). [93] Ibid., § 44.

other ideals: liberal and judicial legitimacy require equality before the law. Such equality is not ensured, either for the individuals or the member states, if the result of ECtHR balancing depends on who brings a complaint before it.

From the perspective of liberal legitimacy, cases balancing two rights should preferably provide new, general elaborations of the rights protected, or clarify what criteria for balancing should be observed when applying it to later cases. Neither the Supreme Court nor ECtHR reasoning in the A case does this – and neither one better ensures liberal legitimacy, the national one siding with free speech, the supernational with personality rights. Considering the subsidiary role of the ECtHR, however, as well as its role as something other than a fourth-instance court, it is the overturning by that court which begs a better justification. Absent a clarification as to why the ECtHR weighs the relevant balancing factors of articles 8 and 10 differently than does the Supreme Court, such an overturning challenges both the process legitimacy of judicial justification and the institutional legitimacy of its nonappeals court role. Additionally, the judicial legitimacy remains wanting also on the outcome level, by leaving unclear what makes the ECtHR reach a different conclusion than the Supreme Court.

7.3 SPEECH VERSUS POLICY: POLITICAL ADVERTISING

7.3.1 *Background*

The case of *TV Vest*[94] raised the question of whether the prohibition against political advertising on TV as set out in § 3 of the Norwegian Broadcasting Act represented a permissible restriction on free speech.[95] The case represents a good example of a fundamental right – free speech – and the balancing of it against a desirable, societal policy.

Political advertising in other than broadcast media is allowed, but the Broadcasting Act § 3 sets out a total ban of such ads on TV, stating that "Broadcasters shall not transmit advertisements for ... political opinions on television." The main reason for the ban is that political TV advertising could result in financially powerful groups having a greater opportunity than others to disseminate their views to the detriment of parties and special-interest organizations with fewer resources, thereby impairing pluralism and democratic equality. It is also based on a fear that the commercialization of political opinions leads to sloganized and manipulative communication and

94 *TV Vest AS & Rogaland Pensjonistparti* v. *Norway* (2008).

95 Lov av 4. desember 1992 nr 127 om kringkasting og audiovisuelle bestillingstjenester.

democratically unfavorable forms of debate. The reason for banning only TV ads is that TV is presumed to be a particularly effective advertising medium, and hence to have a greater ability to influence the public.[96]

Norway has no regulation of party political broadcasts outside the scope of § 3; the choice whether to give political parties the possibility of presenting themselves to the electorate is left to the editorial discretion of broadcasters. Consequently, there are no guarantees that small parties get equal or proportional representation, or indeed any representation at all in the general political TV coverage or in TV debates arranged in election periods.

The plaintiffs in the case of *TV Vest* were a small local broadcasting company, TV Vest, and a regional variety of the marginal Pensioners' Party (with a national vote of 1.3 percent in the 2003 local elections), "Rogaland Pensjonistparti." The party was not financially powerful, and had hardly had any editorial TV coverage by the national broadcaster NRK or its major commercial competitor TV2, or by the regional TV station TV Vest in the election campaign period. None of the coverage that it had received concerned the party's politics.[97] TV Vest broadcast three ads for the party during the campaign period, arguing that such ads should be protected, political speech, the total ban notwithstanding, because of the scant interest of editorial coverage of the party.

7.3.2 *Summary of Decisions*

7.3.2.1 Supreme Court Review

TV Vest and Rogaland Pensjonistparti were fined for violating the Broadcasting Act § 3, and challenged the fine in court. Having lost in the city court, TV Vest was granted direct appeal to the Supreme Court.[98] The Supreme Court split 4–1, finding the total ban on political advertising to be justified under the free speech protection in both the Constitution § 100 and in ECHR art. 10.

Justice Oftedal Broch for the majority first assessed how the ban related to § 100. Having reiterated the differentiated protection offered by constitutional provisions – where those guaranteeing individual freedom or security are

96 Ot. prp. nr. 58 (1998–1999), 12.

97 A substantial part of the coverage concerned the fine imposed on the party for having politically advertised.

98 By the Supreme Court; a (seldom used) possibility for cases of principled significance to other cases under Lov av 13. august 1915 nr 6 om rettergangsmåten for tvistemål (tvistemålsloven), § 6 [now Lov av 17. juni 2005 nr 90 om mekling og rettergang i sivile tvister (tvisteloven) § 30–32].

subject to strict scrutiny – he nevertheless took the position that even though "political," the speech in question was not of a character at the core of the § 100 protection. Rather than representing a content-based restriction on political speech, the ban represented a regulation of the *framework for democratic processes*, one for which it could "forcefully be argued that the political authorities are in a better position than the courts to evaluate what measures are more conducive for heightening the quality of political discourse."[99] To the extent Parliament had considered the constitutionality of a legislative provision, and its interpretation did not "appear unfounded or in other ways biased," courts should defer to the will of Parliament. Justice Oftedal Broch did not find any "unfounded" bias in the preparatory works and the deliberations in Parliament that emphasized i.a. the potentially lowered quality of political debate resulting from commercialized speech and the importance of avoiding financially powerful groups having a greater opportunity than others to disseminate their views to the detriment of parties with fewer resources. Nor did he find the ban to be otherwise unconstitutional, noting that it was but a regulation of *form*, not of content, prohibiting political advertising on TV, leaving the Pensioners' Party access to other media through which to convey its message.[100]

To assess whether there had been any change in the view of the relation between § 100 and the ban since the enactment of the statute, Justice Oftedal Broch looked to debates from Parliament undertaken in connection with the 2004 amendment of § 100. Here, the majority of the parliamentary committee had argued to lift the total ban on political advertising. Nothing in the debates suggested that they had considered the ban to be automatically voided upon the amendment of § 100, however – only that both the government and Parliament opened up for more nuanced regulations than the total ban.

Having found the ban to be justified under § 100, Justice Oftedal Broch turned to question whether the ban could be seen as a necessary and proportional interference with ECHR art. 10,[101] not in general, but as applied.[102] Considering two ECtHR cases – *VgT Verein Tierfabriken* v. *Switzerland* (where a total ban on TV advertising as applied to ads for protecting animal welfare was held to be in violation of ECHR art. 10), and *Murphy* v. *Ireland* (where a total ban on religious advertising in Ireland was found compatible with art. 10 due to the margin awarded to balancing of religious freedoms with particular reference to the place of religion in Ireland) cases[103] – he found neither of them to be fully comparable with the case at hand, but held *Murphy*

[99] Rt. 2004 s. 1737, 39. [100] Ibid., 43. [101] Ibid., 55. [102] Ibid., 58.
[103] *VgT Verein Tierfabriken* v. *Switzerland* (2001) and *Murphy* v. *Ireland* (2003).

to be rather parallel. Rather than embarking on an analysis of the necessity and proportionality of the ban, his further assessment under ECHR art. 10, however, concentrated on the margin of appreciation. He found the margin to be quite wide due to the lack of European consensus and the type of interference the ban represented. Explaining the latter, he relied on his finding under the § 100 evaluation that the ban was "less a question of the individual's freedom of expression and far more a question of how best to promote political debate and ensure good frameworks for the democratic electoral process."[104] This view was one promoted in the preparatory works preceding the amendment of the Constitution § 100 and by the Ministry of Justice, and now furthered by Justice Oftedal Broch both in relation to his construction of the amended § 100, and in his assessment as to what type of interference in ECHR art. 10 the ban could be seen to represent.

Evaluating the margin of appreciation, Justice Oftedal Broch pointed to one implication of the changed view of the ban on political advertising as exposed in the debates on the amendment of § 100: that the argument from the legislative will and the democratic foundation for the ban supporting a wide margin no longer had the same force. Nonetheless, following his interpretation regarding the lack of European consensus on regulation of political advertising, he rejected that the altered majority will concerning the issue had the effect of narrowing the margin.[105]

Considering the ban as applied, he noted the fact that the Pensioners Party had a weak financial position and claimed to need TV advertising in order not to be disadvantaged compared to the stronger parties. He dismissed this as irrelevant for the ban lawfulness under ECHR art. 10, as it would be impossible to differentiate between the various political parties in a democratic manner – at least just before an election.[106] He repeated that the ban primarily established limits for political debate, and that such limits ought to be decided by a country's democratic institutions. As a result, democratic institutions must be given considerable freedom of action in relation to art. 10 in determining such limits. For this reason, Justice Oftedal Broch held that the ban represented no violation of the ECHR.

The dissenting Justice Skoghøy interpreted the total ban in light of ECHR art. 10, without discussing § 100. He emphasized how the central democratic role of free speech gave rise to strong objections against attaching too much importance to the opinion of the political majority when determining the scope of political freedom of expression.[107] Even though he found the reasons supporting the ban to be legitimate, he did not find a total ban proportionate to

104 Rt. 2004 s. 1737, 62. 105 Ibid., 64. 106 Ibid., 63. 107 Ibid., 75.

these legitimate aims.[108] Taking issue with the majority interpretation of the ECtHR *VgT* case as one concerning idealistic, not commercial advertising, Justice Skoghøy held *VgT* to concern political advertising in general. Contrary to the majority, he also found *Murphy* to underline the undesirability of total advertising bans, as the ECtHR acceptance of such a ban in *Murphy* relied explicitly on the extreme sensitivity of the question of broadcasting of religious advertising in Ireland.[109] Justice Skoghøy did not look to the Constitution § 100 for guidance. In his assessment of ECHR art. 10, however, he argued that the debates in Parliament preceding the amendment of § 100 showed that the majority was in favor of abolishing the ban and instead wanted to introduce restrictions, and that this indicated there was no pressing social need for the ban – the change in opinion was not caused by changes in society, but by the realization that there was no need for the ban as currently formed.[110] The requirement that an interference in ECHR art. 10 must correspond to a pressing social need was thus not met, and the total ban as applied was, in his view, invalid.

7.3.2.2 ECtHR Review

When the case of *TV Vest and Rogaland Pensjonistparti* v. *Norway* was brought before the ECtHR as an ECHR art. 10 violation, the Norwegian state argued that the case did not primarily concern the protection of freedom of expression, but rather the integrity of the democratic process and specifically the right of the public – the electorate – to fair democratic elections.[111] The ECtHR, however, approached the case from the perspective of free speech. Considering the ban on political advertising an interference into art. 10, it set about assessing "whether it was supported by relevant and sufficient reasons and was proportionate to the legitimate aim pursued, regard being had to the balance to be struck between the applicants' freedom of expression, on the one hand, and the reasons adduced by the Norwegian authorities for the prohibition of political advertising, on the other."[112]

The ECtHR accepted the view that the TV medium had a special impact, and found both the aim of limiting election campaign costs to ensure pluralism and quality of the democratic debate and that of supporting the integrity of the democratic process to be legitimate reasons for the ban. It did not, however, find them sufficient to justify the total ban as applied.

[108] Ibid., 79. [109] Ibid., 81. [110] Ibid., 83, 84.
[111] *TV Vest As & Rogaland Pensjonistparti* v. *Norway* (2008), 41. [112] Ibid., 69.

First, it pointed to the fact that the Pensioners' Party was not in a financial position to gain any particular advantages from political advertising on TV, and could thus not be considered part of the group primarily targeted by the disputed ban.[113] Second, it noted that the party not only was not in the target group, illustrating that the ban did not further the aims pursued, the ban in fact affected the party *adversely* as regards the legitimate aims pursued: as a marginal party that received no editorial coverage, and which only had the chance to get its message across to the public by the impactful TV medium through paid air time, it was in fact at a disadvantage compared to the larger and financially stronger parties because of the ban.[114] Third, the ads run by the party were not of a kind likely to lower the quality of democratic debate.[115] Finally, the ECtHR rejected the view that there was no viable alternative to a blanket ban. Distinguishing this from *Murphy*, a case relied on in the government's argumentation, the Court pointed to the lack of comparable reasons for not relaxing or modifying the ban in the present case.

The particular sensitivity stemming from the Irish history and culture in matters of religion that could justify a blanket ban on religious advertising rather than a case-by-case filtering or other more targeted regulation in Ireland, was absent in the *TV Vest and Rogaland Pensjonistparti* v. *Norway*.

In a concurring opinion, the Norwegian Judge Jebens underlined that a central reason for finding the blanket ban lacking in proportionality was the failure of Norway to regulate party political broadcasts, thus leaving it entirely to a broadcaster's editorial discretion which political groups received – and did not receive – coverage during election campaign periods.

7.3.3 *Current Legal Situation*

7.3.3.1 Norway

The ECtHR decision is one of the few judgments against Norway that has created substantial public debate in media other than legal journals.[116] Its conclusion was, obviously, applauded by opponents of the total ban.[117] Supporters of the ban, however, not only criticized the outcome, but also questioned the review competencies of the ECtHR – namely, that a European

113 Ibid., 72. This is an argument of overbreadth similar, but not equal, to that of the Supreme Court dissent.

114 Ibid., 73. 115 Ibid., 74. 116 Iversen, *Overtramp eller valgkamp?* (2012).

117 Conservatives, Liberal Left and right-wing Progress Parties; see Fjelldal, SPLITTES – etter ny EU-dom [sic.] Nå blir det lov med politisk TV-reklame (2008). See also NTB, *Frp mener regjeringen tøver* (2009).

court should have the competence to overrule decisions made by Parliament.[118] (ECtHR competency to overrule the Supreme Court was not criticized.)

There was little governmental rejoicing. The Minister of Culture questioned the scope of the decision, and indeed the legitimacy of the ECtHR.[119] No alteration to the Broadcasting Act or other acts regulating political advertisement financing was proposed. A basis for alternatives to the blanket ban, such as making room for discretionary assessments or deciding a limit on amounts used for political advertising in one or more media, already existed in previous legislative reports thematizing political financing.[120] Instead of following up on the proposals these set forth, several other measures were employed. An unsuccessful attempt was made to alter the charter of the Norwegian Broadcasting Company (NRK) with the aim of forcing it to reserve certain slots in its editorial election campaign period coverage, by demanding that "all lists and parties representing a certain percentage are normally covered by the ordinary editorial election campaign period coverage."[121] In addition to being criticized for leaving out the very small parties ostensibly most in need of coverage, this alteration was claimed to be an illegal interference with the editorial freedom of NRK. NRK stated that it refused to be instructed on how to make editorial decisions, and would continue its coverage based on free editorial discretion.

Another move made was to grant a new, unedited "free" TV channel ("Frikanalen") subsidies of NOK 10 million provided it granted all lists and parties equal coverage, particularly during the three weeks preceding elections.[122] This drew different critiques: first, for in fact representing political TV advertising prepaid by the government; second, for amounting to an unfair preference of one channel over the others; and third, for being in conflict with EU regulations of state subsidies.[123] In any event, few people had access to Frikanalen, and even fewer actually watched it. No further measures to comply with the judgment were made. Based on a report from the Government reflecting none of the abovementioned criticism, the Council

[118] Sejersted, Misvisende om rett og politikk (2009); Sejersted, Misvisende om rettsstaten (2009); Graver, Avvik tåles ikke (2009); Wessel-Aas, *Giske og politisk reklame: Hadde ett problem – "løser" det ved å lage flere* (2009); Andresen, *Gledelig demokratiforakt* (2010).

[119] "It is certainly a good question, on principle, whether seven judges from Strasbourg – from Azerbaijan and six other countries – know better about free speech, than does the Norwegian majority in 'Stortinget' (the Norwegian parliament)." Minister of Culture, Trond Giske, on the TV newshour "RedaksjonEN" (National Broadcasting station "NRK"), April 15, 2009.

[120] St.meld. nr. 26 (2003–2004), 8.4, NOU 2004: 25, 8.7.

[121] Innst.S.nr 237 (2008–2009), 1.5.

[122] Ibid., 1.6.

[123] Wessel-Aas, *Giske og politisk reklame: Hadde ett problem – "løser" det ved å lage flere* (2009).

of Europe Committee of Ministers in 2011 found the measures taken by Norway to be appropriate.[124]

The Broadcasting Act remained unaltered, and there were no other *legislative* measures taken to make Norwegian law reflect the *TV Vest* judgment. The administrative authority responsible for overseeing TV advertising, the Media Surveillance Authority, however, adjusted its practice to comply with the ECHR as explicated. Of the (few) cases decided by the Media Surveillance Authority following the ECtHR decision, two may serve to illustrate this: The Conservative party (established in 1884, holding some 15–30 percent of the electorate since 2000) challenged the total ban by screening a modest and informative ad with several local TV broadcasters. A small action group ("Save Hardanger!") screened ads with the national broadcaster TV2, protesting against a proposed high voltage power line through the environmentally vulnerable region of Hardanger. While Conservative Party ads were struck down and fined as a breach of § 3 of the Broadcasting Act, the ads by Save Hardanger were not. The Media Surveillance Authority held that while none of the ads reduced the quality of democratic debate, the Conservative Party was seen to have both the financial strength and the impact to gain airtime on TV without advertising. Save Hardanger, on the other hand, was not.

On the national level, to the extent these cases are representative not only for the Media Surveillance Authority, but for the general present legal status, they still leave the legal situation unclear for a potentially large group of political actors. Is political TV advertising allowed for those groups who represent messages of significant interest to the democratic debate and are financially resourceful, but are still marginalized in public debate, if left editorially uncovered by the major TV channels?

7.3.3.2 Europe

On the European level, an interesting sequel to *TV Vest* v. *Norway* was decided in 2013. The case of *Animal Defenders International* v. *UK*[125] concerned a group defending animal welfare which was found in breach of the English total ban on political advertising. The application to the ECtHR was lodged with the court prior to the decision in *TV Vest*.[126] The Chamber to which the case had been allocated relinquished jurisdiction in favor of the Grand Chamber,[127] where the case was heard on March 7, 2012. Apart from

[124] Resolution CM/ResDH(2011)234.

[125] *Animal Defenders International* v. *the United Kingdom* (2013).

[126] September 11, 2008.

[127] Decision of November 29, 2011.

Rogaland Pensjonistparti being a political party and ADI an interest group, the main difference between the two cases seems to be that the UK, contrary to Norway, had some regulation of TV political coverage, including "Party election broadcasts" (PEBs), as well as a requirement of impartiality on the part of broadcasters.

The Grand Chamber decided in favor of the UK by a 9–8 majority.[128] Rather than initially placing the case in the context of the *VgT*, *Murphy* or *TV Vest* decisions, the Grand Chamber labeled the advertising ban as a "general measure." Contrary to prior restraints, such measures "apply to pre-defined situations regardless of the individual facts of each case even if this might result in individual hard cases"[129] and give rise to a different tripartite test of proportionality assessing the "quality" of the parliamentary and judicial review of the necessity of the measure, the legislative choices underlying the general measure and any risk of abuse if a general measure is relaxed. Such a categorization represented an approach not previously employed in cases of advertising bans, and allowed the ECtHR to apply a more deferential standard of review.

The grounds on which *Animal Defenders* is distinguished from the case of *TV Vest* remains largely unexplained in the decision. As its principled distinctions are somewhat difficult to discern, both in fact and in law, the relative silence with which the majority treats this difference is understandable. It is, however, no less problematic from a precedent point of view. As the ECtHR has stated, it is not formally bound by precedent, yet "it is in the interest of legal certaintly, foreseeability and equality before the law that it should not depart, without cogent reason, from precedents laid down in previous cases."[130] Why the relation between the two cases is not much explained by the dissenting judges is harder to understand. Not only would it seem to provide them with a solid argument for dissent, but their lack of doing so also leaves uncertain whether this argument was even one the two factions disagreed about. Had *Animal Defenders* explained there was a distinction between it and its previous case law, member states and the public would have some basis for discerning whether their case fell into one or the other category. Had it even held there was no distinction, *Animal Defenders* could be considered legal authority following a *lex posterior* principle. The lack of thematizing what distinguishes *Animal Defenders* from *TV Vest* leaves the legal status of blanket bans on TV advertising unclear.

128 *Animal Defenders International* v. *the United Kingdom* (2013).
129 Ibid., para. 106.
130 See e.g. *Chapman* v. *UK* [GC] (2001) § 70.

7.3.4 *Perspectives*

The two main ideals guiding the Supreme Court decision are the majority will of the people and the individual right to free speech. The Constitution clearly states that there shall be freedom of speech. Which ideals support the Supreme Court embracing the bureaucratic assessment made by the Ministry of Justice that political advertising is not *really* about free speech, but rather about the organization of democratic processes to the detriment of the constitutional text? The *TV Vest* case first raises a question central to most review cases – indeed, to much adjudication in general – namely, what constitutes the "popular will"? This "will" is a construction based on procedural requirements for legitimate popular decision-making through representative majorities. And it may be more or less realistic – the greater the majority, the closer to an actual representation of popular will. In the *TV Vest* case, the popular will referred to by the Supreme Court majority seems quite a stretched concept, at least as concerns what became the foundation for the majority conclusion – that the question of advertising was not really a question of free speech, but one about the processes for democracy. That a majority in Parliament embraced this view is at best an inferred assumption; the only clear basis for this view is that it is the opinion of the Ministry of Justice legal department. As such, it has little democratic input legitimacy.

The case is illustrative of Norwegian courts' reliance on preparatory material (*travaux préparatoires*). While the text of the Constitution § 100 ("There shall be freedom of expression") contradicted interpreting the total ban as *prima facie* valid, the Supreme Court majority relied on a preparatory opinion from the Ministry of Justice about the constitutionality of the ban to define the constitutional question. This method of adjudication may be seen both to preserve and to challenge the ideal of the majority will. Substantially, it aims to further the actual will of the people (to the extent such a will may be credibly established), yet procedurally it contradicts it, as it is not the majority will as represented by the constitutional text that is regarded as the higher authority.

Even if a majority of Parliament explicitly had endorsed the Ministry of Justice view, and said so in the statutory text, this part of the Supreme Court reasoning is lacking in outcome legitimacy from a liberal perspective. Can a majority of the people circumvent constitutional limits by defining legislation as something other than interference into a constitutional right? With the effect that courts cannot review such actions? The Supreme Court seems to hold this, as it can "forcefully be argued that the political authorities are in a better position than the courts to evaluate what measures are more conductive for heightening the quality of political discourse."[131] While the institutional difference between legislatures and courts will often support leaving detailed regulations to the former, this position seems fundamentally flawed from a free speech perspective. It is hardly difficult to conceive of ways in which almost any troublesome minority opposition could be silenced if this were to be used as a guiding principle of free speech law.[132]

Looking to the quality of the Supreme Court majority reasoning, one could also question to what extent it reflects relevant legal authority under the Constitution and the ECHR, whether ECtHR case law is coherently construed and whether it is applied in a consistent manner making transparent the adjudicative methodology applied.

From a process-focused judicial legitimacy perspective, a weakness of the Supreme Court reasoning is clarified by the ECtHR review: its lack of thematizing how the legitimate aims sought ensured by the total advertising ban were not threatened in the present case. The general reasons given by Parliament for a ban – namely, to avoid financial dominance of the political discourse and prevent undue use of as strong a medium as TV – were legitimate. In the concrete case, however, upholding the ban not only did not contribute to meet these ends, it instead contradicted them, as the Pensioners' Party was financially weak and too insignificant to enjoy the effects of the TV media that the other parties were given through editorial coverage. While the ban represented an interference with free speech "necessary in a democratic society," it did not do so in the concrete application. These are precisely the types of individual considerations under general regulations that are, and must be, left to courts' reviewing legislation. Not doing so leaves the Supreme Court reasoning wanting in judicial legitimacy.[133]

It may be noted how neither the majority nor the dissent questions the *quality of the reasoning* produced or endorsed by Parliament. The Supreme Court could in fact have pointed to how the justifications motivating the ban are actually being *undermined* by the ban as applied: Not only does it not further the aims it is set out to promote, it in fact contradicts them in the case at hand.

[131] Rt. 2004 s. 1737, 39.

[132] Kierulf, Rettsstatens overnasjonale vending: den andre prøvingsretten (2009),270.

[133] An example of a contrary approach, ensuring both judicial, democratic input and rule of law outcome legitimacy through a conscientious use of ECtHR interpretative method, is the Supreme Court decision in Rt. 2008 s. 1089. Not only did the Supreme Court read the Norwegian provision on review in light of the relevant ECtHR provision at the time, its consideration of the ECtHR criteria also satisfied what the ECtHR itself only listed as the exemplary list of such criteria four years later, in *Axel Springer* AG v. *Germany* (2012); see *Lillo-Stenberg and Sæther* v. *Norway* (2014) para. 44.

The dissent, however, invokes an argument of overbreadth from the ECHR requirement of proportionality. Because the norm of the Broadcasting Act § 3 applies in all situations, it makes no difference that the ads sanctioned appeared in the period of political campaign where narrowly tailored regulation could otherwise be permissible. The role of questioning or providing a second opinion on the soundness of legislative reasoning may be seen as a legitimating factor of judicial review.[134] The way this reasoning is treated by the Supreme Court in the *TV Vest* case may serve as a basis for reflection on this legitimating factor.

Looking to the ECtHR decision in the case, the primary legitimation concern is connected to the judicial legitimacy, both in process and in outcome, as regards the relationship between *TV Vest* and the later *Animal Defenders*. It seems unclear both why the ECtHR came to a different conclusion in the two cases, and how the law now is to be understood – an ambiguity also at odds with the ECtHR doctrine of precedent, emphasizing the interests of legal certainty, foreseeability and equality before the law.[135] While a shift in favor of national sovereignty through dynamic interpretation could have been justifiable if explained, it appears wanting in judicial legitimacy not only for not being given a good reason, but also for wanting any other reason on this point. Whether to the benefit of an individual right or a member state's sovereignty, deviances from previous precedents need explaining to be judicially legitimate. As a possible overruling of *TV Vest* is not made explicit, it is not clear that the *Animal Defenders* view should prevail under a *lex posterior* rationale.

It seems fair to read the pursuant *Animal Defenders* decision as inspired by the increasing emphasis on the *margin of appreciation* awarded the member states following the Brighton Declaration and the proposed Protocol 15, adding this doctrine to the ECHR preamble,[136] and thus making it more of an ingrained part of the convention. There are many good reasons for the reconsiderations of ECtHR practice as treated in these declarations and other reform processes. When such potentially direction-altering guidelines are not made into explicit parts of the court's reasoning, the effect of seemingly comparable cases with opposing conclusions do, however, threaten another aspect of judicial and liberal legitimacy: ECtHR independence. By not providing a better justified distinction between the cases, an impression may be left that the court is guided by political signals not open to the scrutiny and

[134] Bickel, *The least dangerous branch* (1986),26; Kumm, The idea of Socratic contestation and the right to justification: The point of rights-based proportionality review (2010).

[135] *Christine Goodwin* v. *the United Kingdom* (2002), para. 74.

[136] ECHR Protocol No. 15 amending the Convention for the Protection of Human Rights and Fundamental Freedoms, CM(2012)166 rev, adopted May 16, 2013.

professional criticism necessary for it to be judicially legitimate. Such legitimacy could have been ensured by opening up the court reasoning. This could also entail a potential benefit for its normative input legitimacy as well as its problem-solving and legally clarifying outcome legitimacy by contributing to establish a more consistent, predictable and thus practicable margin of appreciation doctrine as represented by later cases.

Moving away from the reasoning of the courts, some of the political and public reactions to the *TV Vest* case – among them Minister Giske's initial reaction not only criticizing the case conclusion, but also arguing against the ECtHR competency to review the issue (and for revoking the ECHR) – makes the *TV Vest* case an example of the input–outcome entanglement, the mixing up of assessing the general legitimacy of an institution and the particular results it produces.

7.4 FREE SPEECH REVIEW: A SYNTHESIS OF IDEALS?

A number of philosophical, historical and legal theories may be employed to explore why a right to free speech exists or if such a right ought to be protected in some form. One is the argument from personal freedom to develop a self. It is hard to conceive of any personal growth and development absent the freedom to form and formulate thoughts. Another is the recognition of the importance of the search for truth, either autonomously justified as a universal good or as a means to societal progress. Free speech is widely considered an essential prerequisite for democracy: through enabling citizens to educate themselves and directly partake in democracy, through voicing their opinions, engaging in debates and casting their votes and also by making possible continuous critique of government and public and private power.

A central distinction among free speech justifications goes between those emphasizing *collective consequentialist* arguments and those focusing on *individuals as moral agents*. Into the first category fall arguments pointing to the good societal effects that may follow from free speech, such as Mill's continuous search for truth,[137] the probability that better societies and politics result from free trade in the marketplace of ideas and the possibility for self-government and democracy. *Individuals as moral agents* justifications hold that free speech needs to be protected because people have an intrinsic moral right to think and say what they want. Instrumental and moral justifications are not mutually exclusive, as set out i.a. in the Constitution § 100 – both are listed among the foundations carrying free speech protection. Depending on what

[137] Mill, *On liberty* (1989).

justification is emphasized, protecting free speech consequently may further both of the two societal ideals inherent in a constitutional democracy: the liberal, protecting individual rights, and the republican, enabling the people collectively to form a society based on free, popular will. Free speech cases thus hold the potential of furthering collective ideals even where legislation is affected or reinterpreted on review, even where the individual interest seems to prevail over the collective.

In any liberal democracy based on some idea of a social contract, individuals' free speech seems a necessary prerequisite. How would such a form of government be possible, not to say legitimate, if the individuals entering into the contract were not able freely to express their (hypothetical) consent? While social contract theories are idealized illustrations of bases for state formation, they are theories by which state sovereignty may be understood as normatively desirable. So even though the entire people are not there to agree upon the contract, the justificatory strengths of these theories stem from common – and free – consent being part of its idealized theoretical background. And there cannot be consent, uninformed or not, without someone voicing it through some form of speech: free speech.

All accounts of democracy presuppose free speech, either in the form of actual participation, enfranchisement, informed votes, deliberation or otherwise. Viewed from the perspective of free speech, it is fair to assume that the constitutionalization of societies depends on at least some individual rights. Going beyond the traditional justifications for free speech – the argument from autonomy and personal liberty, from the possibility to form a democracy and from search for truth – another central argument holds that free speech is required by individual autonomy: if the state prevents certain speech from becoming part of public debate, it also takes away the possibility of individuals to decide how to react or respond to it.[138]

Elaborating further on the liberal justification for free speech – that of personal autonomy and freedom – this freedom may be seen as a necessary requirement for legitimate government in that a just political society requires that a government treats all its adult members as responsible moral agents.[139] A government banning speech that might persuade citizens to do dangerous things bars citizens' independent reactions and represents an insult that denies their moral responsibility. Further, it hinders their opportunity to assume the inherent moral responsibility of expressing to others what they themselves believe to be important or good. On this account, there can be no right to

138 Scanlon, A theory of freedom of expression (1972).

139 Dworkin, *Freedom's law* (1996), 200.

rule – for the popularly elected or for other governmental branches – absent a substantial protection of free speech, both as a principle and as basis for the critique of power.

Whether the ECHR-induced contribution to a shift in Norwegian free speech doctrine is seen as an improvement or not could seem to depend on whether one does or doesn't value the personality protection of honor and reputation over that of free speech. Nevertheless, absent clear indications that the shift has led to a corresponding impairment of protection for personality rights, this need not be determinative. While fewer statements are now found defamatory by the Supreme Court than they were under traditional Norwegian doctrine the protection of personality rights has also been strengthened through ECHR influence.[140] Personality rights are protected not only due to individuals' interest in privacy or honor, but also due to the collective interest in ensuring for all the private space required for dignity and human development. The potential provided by the ECHR necessitates that a concrete balancing between the two rights challenged in defamation cases – free speech under ECHR art. 10 and the protection of reputation in ECHR art. 8 – is in fact undertaken.[141]

On the whole, the strengthening of free speech protection, as compared to traditional doctrine, seems normatively desirable, for four reasons: First, it recognizes that both free speech and personality rights are fundamental values the relation between which must be found through case-by-case application, by a concrete balancing process. Second, it makes clearer what criteria are relevant for this balancing, and for assessing free speech questions in a way more transparent, predictable and practicable than the situation was under the many quirks of the traditional Norwegian free-speech doctrine – the foundations of, and legal authoritative justifications for which were quite vague. Third, through this more principled balancing approach, the potential for a broader and more widespread understanding of free speech in particular, and the interaction between fundamental rights and between rights and policy in general, is enhanced – both within the legal community and also more generally. And fourth: while a more principled and predictable protection of free speech certainly benefits the individuals that would have had their speech sanctioned by traditional doctrine, the main benefactor of such a protection is society at large – it

140 Borvik, Ytringsfridom på norsk – ein kritikk (2004).

141 Which means that what is, under current ECtHR case law, relevant criteria under the two provisions must be balanced, not necessarily that the criteria are explicitly connected to the respective articles.

is by the democratic, not the individual justification of free speech that this right is now explained.[142]

Norwegian dual constitutional and ECHR review in the field of free speech seems to further liberal, professional judicial and democratic outcome legitimacy ideals. Not only has it led to a better and more consistent protection of this essential right against regulative interests, it has also clarified and made more practicable how and why free speech should be balanced against other rights. And, moreover, through a better and more practicable protection of free speech, this outcome contributes to further ideals of deliberative democratic legitimacy. The outcome has also been supplied by substantial procedural, democratic input legitimacy: first, from the enactment of the HRA in 1999, codifying the preference for ECHR at the same time as Norwegian free speech cases were overturned in the ECtHR, thus setting new standards for Norwegian ECHR review; second through the revitalization of the Constitution § 100 in 2004, constitutionalizing central elements of the ECHR free speech influence; and third, through the following up of Norwegian courts' ECHR review through the decriminalization of defamation in 2009.

142 See i.a. Dijk, *Theory and practice of the European Convention on Human Rights* (2006), 14.4.3. In Supreme Court practice, it is also clear from i.a. Rt. 2002 s. 764, Rt. 2003 s. 914, and Rt. 2005 s. 1677 that the predominant free speech justification found decisive is the collective consequentialist democratic argument. One exception is Rt. 2001 s. 1720, where statements from a rape victim naming her alleged rapist to friends, even though it could not be proven he was the rapist, were not found defamatory. In this case, it was the significance to her personal autonomy of her being able to confide in someone which led the Supreme Court to find the statements to be protected speech under ECHR art. 10, by a 3–2 vote.

8

A Triple Constitutional Review Revival: 2010

8.1 PRELUDE

The year 2010 sparked a renewed interest in judicial review, in the general public, as well as in political and legal circles – and this time under the Constitution. The Supreme Court decided three cases in plenary in three very different areas of law. All cases concerned relatively recent parliamentary or governmental regulations, and in all cases these regulations were found to be unconstitutional. This chapter outlines and discusses the review issues in these three cases, as well as the political statements preceding and following the cases, both as presented to the wider public through media, and as argued in Parliament. The development in constitutional interpretation of the relevant constitutional provisions is not the object of analysis, but will be discussed where interpretations are central to questions of review.

The *Kløfta* case was seen to represent a judicial review revival.[1] Compared to the thirty-year postwar period of highly deferential review, the period following *Kløfta* shows a gradual increase in review cases.[2] However, the revival did not lead to substantially more constitutional claims being furthered or treated before the 2000s. The yearly average of Supreme Court cases *mentioning* the Constitution in the 1970s was 8.8; in the 1980s it was 6.8 cases. In the 1990s, the total caseload of the Supreme Court increased significantly,[3] yet the average of cases mentioning the Constitution was only 8.7 per year. Following docket-reducing reforms in the 1980s and 1990s, in the period 2000–2009 the total number of cases almost halved.[4] In this period, however, the yearly average of cases in which the Constitution was mentioned increased to 11.8.

[1] Smith, *Høyesterett og folkestyret* (1993), 278 ff. [2] Ibid.

[3] From 5,136 cases in total in 1980–1989, to 7,900 in 1990–1999. [4] From 7,900 to 4,833 cases.

In the period between *Kløfta* and 2010, two official studies on power and democracy were produced: the first during 1972–1978; the second (as discussed in Section 6.5) during 1998–2003. The first Power Study pointed to the shift of power from Parliament to the executive: to administrative agencies, through widespread delegation by the use of enabling acts. Necessitated by an increasingly complex society, this shift made the expert public officials and technocrats more powerful. Another trend observed was the increasing power of organizations and mass media. Judicial power was hardly mentioned.[5] In the 1980s, legitimacy and power-balance were thematized from the perspective of administrative challenges to popular political power. Identifying the "new high state officials" – the bureaucratic "technocrats" – former Justice Minister Inger Louise Valle (Labor) warned against the lack of checks and balances in a system where a professional central administration – through both preparing legislation and deciding administrative cases – in practice took on both the legislative and the adjudicating role, the latter at times based on interpretations of the very same laws the administration had itself prepared.[6] Like the First Power Study, the Second Power Study, as we have seen, was also concerned with the declining power of Parliament. Concerned about the international-rights influence on the judicialization of politics, it thematized the undermining of procedural democratic ideals and the suppression of parliamentary power as represented by courts' decision-making, particularly international courts basing their decisions on international rights instruments.

In 2010 it was instead national courts and the national Constitution that gave rise to the three review cases. One reason for the increasing number of review cases in the 1990s and 2000s may have been the influence that the legal turn towards international rights had had on Norwegian courts. As the practical use and actual incorporation particularly of the ECHR was mainly left to courts, review under the ECHR increased gradually throughout the 1990s, and particularly following the Human Rights Act of 1999. This use of the ECHR and of ECtHR case law ostensibly contributed to revitalizing the inherent, but traditionally subdued potential of Norwegian courts' rights review under the Constitution.

In this chapter, the three cases of review under the Constitution are presented with the aim of clarifying their subject and the review elements relevant to further analysis. The presentations focus on the cases, the political

5 Judicial power and constitutionalism was, however, thematized in another field critical of the First Power Study, the philosophical, political science and legal project "Democracy and Social Steering," led by Jon Elster, with contributions from i.a. Francis Sejersted and Rune Slagstad; see Elster, et al., *Constitutionalism and democracy* (1988).

6 Valle, Demokratiet og menneskerettighetene (1983).

debates in Parliament preceding and following them, and politicians' media comments. After this, some perspectives on three doctrinal review issues are discussed in light of legitimacy ideals.

8.2 2010 CASES

8.2.1 *Rt. 2010 s. 143*: Shipping Tax

The shipping industry is of a nature enabling incorporation into any harbor jurisdiction. Shipping companies often aim for jurisdictions with the most favorable tax terms. With the objective of ensuring the competitiveness of Norwegian shipowners and preventing them from registering abroad,[7] in 1996 Parliament enacted a new tonnage tax system. Under this system, shipowners paid a set tax on the tonnage of their ships each year, rather than paying tax on turnover. It implied a conditional tax exemption or latent tax burden: Shipowners could defer paying tax on profits as long as they did not pay out in dividends. When the system was adjusted in 2007, i.a. to reflect the standard European models of tonnage tax, the government demanded companies pay all the deferred tax – a sum of approximately NOK 21 billion. Several shipping companies faced large back-tax bills, and claimed that these bills would prevent companies from reinvesting, thereby damaging the Norwegian maritime sector. Some companies sued the Norwegian state, claiming the retroactive effect of the 2007 regulations was unconstitutional under § 97.

The 2007 amendment had been thoroughly prepared and extensively debated in Parliament. In addition to the legal opinion of the Ministry of Justice and the Ministry of Finance, the Norwegian Shipowner's Association procured three independent legal opinions. The parliamentary Committee on Finance held an open hearing where, in addition to the Minister of Finance and her advisors, two professors of law and one retired Supreme Court justice took part. As later noted by the minority in the Supreme Court review case, this assessment is probably the most extensive ever undertaken by a parliamentary committee in preparing a constitutional question.[8]

The plenary Supreme Court split 6–5 on the question of constitutionality. Indeed, the two factions split on all central questions leading to their respective conclusions. They viewed the facts, i.e. what type of tax regime the 1996 regulations really represented differently; they disagreed on whether the assessment of constitutionality should be concrete or general, and on which of the constitutional tests as developed under the Constitution § 97 case law to

[7] Innst.O.nr.81 (1995–1996) 1.2.1. [8] Rt. 2010 s. 143, para. 247, Matningsdal J., diss.

apply. The majority found the 1996 regulations to levy a tax burden that was realized if, and only if, the shipowners decided to pay dividends – and thus that there was no tax burden absent such a decision on the part of the shipowners.[9] It opened up for looking to the general effects of the regulations, but held that the concrete assessment – or what it saw to be a reasonably representative case – must be as applied.[10] And it held the proper § 97 test to be one considering whether the regulations corresponded to "pressing societal needs,"[11] requiring a "proportionality assessment"[12] – something it did not find the regulations to do.

The minority, conversely, viewed the 1996 regulations as levying a latent tax burden all along, and the 2007 amendment to change only the point in time for when the latent burden came to be realized. It held that the constitutionality must be assessed generally,[13] and found the 2007 tax regime to be a regulation of "quasi-retroactivity," calling for a test of whether this retroactivity was "clearly imbalanced and unfair."[14]

In line with the norm set out in *Kløfta* and later upheld,[15] finding the 2007 amendment to be "clearly" unconstitutional, the majority saw no reason to look to what the majority in Parliament had opined on the question of constitutionality. In an *obiter dictum* on the relevance of Parliament's view, the majority held that where Parliament bases its assessment of constitutionality on a norm other than the one the Supreme Court finds to be the correct one, the balancing of interests in Parliament cannot be a weighty argument to the Supreme Court assessment. Some aspects of this argument are analyzed in Section 8.4.3.

From the *travaux préparatoires*, one aspect to note is how all its chronological elements, from the governmental proposition and on,[16] take the limits of § 97 *as clarified by the Supreme Court review case law* as the obvious starting

9 Ibid., para. 125. 10 Ibid., para. 155.

11 Ibid., para. 150 and 154 ("sterke samfunnsmessige hensyn").

12 Ibid., para. 150 ("samhøvevurdering"). Proportionality analyses have not traditionally been used in § 97 adjudication (Høgberg, *Forbud mot tilbakevirkende lover* (2010), 304), but are central to ECHR P1-1 assessments. The formulation has been read as one signaling the influence of ECtHR law in constitutional adjudication; see Andenæs, Norske verdier og EMK (2010); Kierulf, Er internasjonale menneskerettigheter en relevant rettskilde ved grunnlovstolking? (2011). Support for these readings can be found in Rt. 2013 s. 1345 (Strukturkvote) *Plenary*, 9–8. Here, the majority asserts a concrete proportionality assessment is a "natural" part of considering whether the retroactive effect of a law is unreasonable (para. 55), and the minority underlines that proportionality assessments are "central" to deciding the lawfulness of retroactive regulations – with reference to the *Shipping Tax* case para. 150 (para. 190).

13 Rt. 2010 s. 143 para. 222.

14 Ibid. paras. 191–200, 209 ("uegentlig tilbakevirkning"; "klart urimelig eller urettferdig").

15 In variations, see i.a. Rt. 2007 s. 1308. 16 Ot. prp. nr. 1 (2007–2008), 3.4.7.9.

point for assessing the scope for political action. And these limits are also the ones central to the legal opinions procured.

The Ministry of Justice legal department opinion relied on the "clearly imbalanced and unfair" test for its evaluation of the shipping tax amendment, and also emphasized the latent tax burden aspect of the obligations levied on the shipowners under the 1996 arrangement. The legal opinions from the law firms all concluded differently on these questions, and the nongovernmental "experts" called in for the Committee hearing all expressed doubt about the constitutionality of the proposed amendment.[17] These differing views on two of the central questions for assessing constitutionality were consequently adopted by the government and opposition party parliamentary representatives respectively. The degree of correspondence between the majority reasoning in Parliament and the minority reasoning in the Supreme Court – as between the Parliament minority and Supreme Court majority reasoning – is striking.

In the Parliament Committee on Finance, the majority stated it had subjected the question of constitutionality to a "thorough, independent assessment."[18] The majority did indeed give a thorough presentation of the various questions arising under § 97 in the shipping tax case, albeit one primarily relying on the legal opinions of the Ministry of Justice and the Ministry of Finance. On the matter of what legal positions were affected by the proposed regulations and the potential consequences of them, however, the majority refers and refutes several of the arguments presented in the alternative legal opinions. On the remaining issues, the primary reasoning given for refusing the "expert" counterarguments consists in referrals to the Ministry of Justice and Ministry of Finance legal opinions.

8.2.2 *Rt.* 2010 s. 535: *Church Endowment Foundation*

In 2010, the Constitution § 106 stated that "[t]he purchase money, as well as the revenues of the landed property constituting ecclesiastical benefices, shall be applied solely to the benefit of the clergy and to the promotion of

17 Innst. O. nr.1 (2007–2008), 3.2.

18 Ibid., 3.2. Such preparation may be contrasted with that of a review case concerning ground and building lease regulations, the Property Lease Act, from 2007, in Rt. 2007 s. 1308. In it, a provision on minimum redemption sums to lessees had in Parliament been altered significantly from the government proposal. The Supreme Court found the provision as enacted to be "lacking entirely in reasoning" in the *travaux*. As the Supreme Court found the constitutional provision to be unconstitutional without doubt, Parliament's assessment had little general weight. The Supreme Court added, however, that it "could not see that the consequences of the provision have been anticipated or had its constitutionality assessed."

education." The estate and assets of the Church of Norway date back to the middle ages. With some shifts in the early and late middle ages, the collective estates were considered a form of self-owned endowment ("det beneficerede gods"). In 1814, most of this estate consisted of property connected to local rectories around the country, sustaining the church officials located therein. In addition, property lease, forestry, watercourses, leased properties and office premises generated revenues used as a form of wage for the clergy, and also to finance local schools. Following debate prior to the enactment of the Constitution § 106 in 1814, where some argued this estate and its revenues should be considered state property, it was decided the estate should remain committed to its original purposes. The estate was later organized in an endowment called "Opplysningsvesenets fond" (OVF), the ownership of which remained unclear. This undecided issue notwithstanding, the use of OVF revenue continued to follow its original purposes. The OVF Act of 1996 consequently refers to § 106 as decisive for the administration of the OVF estate and revenue.[19]

As part of its reregulation of the Property Lease Act – a reform aimed at bettering conditions for long-term property lessees – the Labor government, with support from the Socialist Left and (more reluctantly) Agrarian Center parties, in 2005 decided to instruct state-affiliated foundations to redeem their property lessees at favorable rates. Central among these foundations was the OVF. Following an extensive and heated debate in Parliament, the initiative was sanctioned against the votes of all opposition Representatives, through the Property Lease Instruction ("PLI") in 2007 and an amendment of § 5 in the OVF Act in 2008.[20] One of the consequences of the PLI was that OVF was instructed to sell off its thitherto leased out property at set, low prices, thus siphoning the endowment assets by approximately NOK 1 billion – to the benefit of the lessees. The constitutionality of this move was much debated. The Ministry of Justice legal department gave an opinion concluding the § 106 limits on disposing OVF revenue did not necessarily bar instructions such as those of the PLI. It conceded, however, that the issue was disputed, and recommended that Parliament be given the "best possible information for a concrete evaluation" of the question.[21]

19 Church Endowment Fund Act of 1996 [Lov av 7. juni 1996 nr. 33 om Opplysningsvesenets fond], § 2.

20 Ibid. amended by Lov av 28. november 2008 nr. 81 om endring i lov 7. juni 1996 nr. 33 om Opplysningsvesenets fond.

21 Ministry of Justice legal department letter, January 12, 2006, appendix to Innst. S. nr. 254 (2007–2008).

This led the opposition party Representatives in the Standing Committee on Constitutional Affairs to the unusual step of proposing that Parliament consider requesting an opinion on the constitutionality from the Supreme Court.[22] Such opinions may be requested following the Constitution § 83, but this happens very rarely, the last opinion having been given in 1945.[23] The central arguments *against* such requests and against the proposal were two: That a prejudicial opinion from the Supreme Court disrupted the balance of competences between the branches of government, and that it weakened the independence of the Supreme Court in relation to its later assessment of the issue. There was also little reason to believe an opinion would be so clear that it would stop the affected parties from trying their case before the courts.

All statements in the discussion of § 83 do, however, presuppose that Parliament's decisions are subject to court proceedings and hold this to be but a normal part of the constitutional system: "Almost all decisions made by Parliament may end up in court. We are fully aware of this, and it is the right of every citizen or others to seek out the courts to the extent they disagree with anything. It may happen, it happens all the time, and it will surely happen in this case."[24] Parliament ended up voting against requesting a Supreme Court § 83 opinion 59–44.

While the government representatives in Parliament held the PLI to be constitutional with reference to the Ministry of Justice legal opinion, the opposition argued it was not, based on opinions from a private law firm and a law professor, both of whom concluded that the PLI was "clearly" unconstitutional. There were hearings of all "experts" in the parliamentary Committee on Church, Education and Science. The ensuing debates were extensive, but ended with enactment of the PLI by the votes of the representatives from the governing parties. Following the effectuation of the PLI, the question of constitutionality soon reached the courts. About a year after the PLI enactment, Oslo City Court found that it was "without doubt" unconstitutional.[25]

Before the Supreme Court, as before the City Court and in Parliament, the main argument for constitutionality was that a reading of § 106 strictly to limit the disposal of OVF revenue to the original purposes was outdated, as the financing of churches and the educational system is now largely carried by the state. The main argument against constitutionality was that such a reading was incompatible with the wording, purpose and continuous understanding of the

[22] Ibid. [23] Dokument nr. 10 (1945). [24] Ø. Djupedal, Socialist Left.
[25] TOSLO-2008-182790.

limits set out in § 106. Whether time had run away from § 106 was for Parliament, following correct constitutional amendment procedure, and not the courts to decide.

The Supreme Court in plenary held the PLI to be unconstitutional by 9–4. As for the use and scope of review, the majority referred to the tripartite test of the *Kløfta* case and found, with reference to the longstanding political practice of treating OVF as self-owned endowment, that § 106 was a provision for the protection of its economical rights. For this group of rights, where courts are in doubt about the constitutional question at hand, Parliament's view on the constitutionality of regulations is important. As Justice Støle for the majority was not in any such doubt, but instead found the PLI to cause effects "clearly contrary to § 106," even the explicit view to the contrary in Parliament could not be decisive: "If judicial review is to have any real effect, courts must, in such a situation, exercise it."[26]

A minority of three justices agreed § 106 was a provision to the protection of economical rights, but that the similarity between the purposes that § 106 sought to protect and the budgetary competences of Parliament left it resembling the lenient scrutiny applied to provisions regulating the work and competence of other governmental branches. This led the minority to underline that Parliament's view should be even more influential on the assessment of constitutionality. Seeing as the subject of § 106 protection was to a large extent taken care of by the state and that the purposes sought protected by the PLI were permissible also under § 106, this minority thus found Parliament's view to be decisive for the question of PLI constitutionality.

A quite different view on judicial review was presented in an *obiter dictum* by dissenting Justice Endresen, who held § 106 to be a different kind of constitutional provision than an economical one, as held by the majority. He does not clearly state whether he finds § 106 to belong in one of the three *Kløfta* categories or fall outside them altogether. He questions, however, whether provisions in the *Kløfta* case lenient scrutiny group – provisions regulating the work and competence of government branches – may even be the subject of judicial review. He holds out the *Kløfta* statement about subjecting this group of provisions to lenient review intensity to be an "understatement," and points out that no case has ever found unconstitutional legislation regulating in the area of such constitutional provisions.[27] He further asserts that the tripartite division in *Kløfta* does not cover all constitutional provisions, and that there are clearly provisions in the Constitution that are not subject to judicial review. In discussing where to draw the line for provisions

[26] Rt. 2010 s. 535, 146–148. [27] Ibid., 184.

subject to review, he presents the 1800s development of judicial review as "the natural starting point." The argument he extracts from this period is that Supreme Court review cases concerned disputes between citizens and the state. He also asserts it was "entirely characteristic" in this period that the liberal theme – "the necessity of protecting citizens against the state" – was "what is emphasized as the foundation for review." He does not cite any cases to support this thesis. Theoretical support for this assertion he finds in L. M. B. Aubert's lecture from 1864 (discussed in Section 3.4), which he reads to state that cases concerning provisions regulating governmental branches are subject to impeachment proceedings, rather than ordinary judicial review. No other theoretical work from the period is referenced.

Both of the two minority votes, in their assessment of constitutionality, point to the importance of Parliament's view of the PLI constitutionality. Although not finding it relevant in the case at hand, as the unconstitutionality was "clear," the majority too points to how Parliament had "clearly" found the PLI constitutional, and that this would have been determinative had the court itself found the question of constitutionality unclear.

Both the "clarity" with which Parliament held the PLI to be constitutional and the significance of this view are thematized in Parliament. Some elements from four parts of the preparatory work, an interpellation to the Church minister and the debates in the Committee and two chambers of Parliament, respectively, may thus be of interest.

In November 2007, the constitutional question came up before the legislative debates in Parliament through an interpellation by Conservative Representative Eriksen Søreide about the constitutionality of the plans to interfere with the OVF management. Asked how the PLI related to the Constitution § 106, Minister Giske conceded that the question of constitutionality was "an interesting legal discussion," but maintained Parliament "is first and foremost a political forum. We are here to discuss political questions. And even questions about the OVF and the Church economy are indeed political questions."[28] Pressed on the constitutional aspect of the PLI, Minister Giske stated that the Government was of the opinion that what it did was indeed constitutional:

> Then there is the possibility to review whether what we do is in accordance with the constitution ... and this review is up to the Supreme Court. Representative Eriksen Søreide has in my view offered good reasons for presenting her points as part of her first oral argument before the Supreme

[28] St. forh. 22.11.2007, 609 ff., 611.

> Court.[29] But this is, for others to decide, we, of course, trust [our position] to be in accordance with § 106.[30]

The opposition pointed to the "substantial legal uncertainty" concerning the constitutionality of the PLI – and rejected the view that this was but a question of politics: "The Constitution concerns more than questions of politics. It also concerns questions of law."[31] Representative Lønning (Conservative), citing legal expertise holding the PLI to be unconstitutional, maintained that the constitutional question was to be taken seriously, even in Parliament, and offered to make a wager with the minister as to the result of a review case.[32] Representative Dørum (Liberal Left), skeptical about the government view that OVF was but a part of ordinary state finances, cited a previous official statement from Minister Giske: "this fund [OVF] really is not that important, as it is only to be considered a hot dog in a large hot-dog stand managed by the state." Dørum pointed out that as opposed to most national hot dogs, "this hot dog is constitutionally protected."[33]

In the proposal from the standing Committee on Church, Education and Science, the constitutionality of the PLI was specifically addressed.[34] One difference in the argumentation from the committee majority (the government representatives) and the minority is notable: The majority cited parts of the Ministry of Justice opinion supporting the constitutionality of the PLI and stated its agreement with the cited passages. It also referred to the conclusion from the law firm Hjort, from which it distanced itself. However, it did not provide any independent reasoning for *why* it agreed and disagreed with the cited arguments or conclusions. The minority, on the other hand, listed all the opinions they had obtained for the committee assessment and underlined that both of the non-Ministry of Justice opinions concluded the PLI was beyond doubt unconstitutional. It also gave its independent reasons for why it disputed parts of the Ministry of Justice opinion, taking issue on three points: it disagreed with the argument that as Parliament had previously agreed to heighten OVF revenue requirements, it would be competent to lower it as well. Second, it rejected that the lowering of revenue was really the issue in question, holding the PLI instead to require that the OVF *distribute* fund assets. Finally, the minority rejected the Ministry of Justice view that defining the limits for who may benefit from the OVF revenue was a political question, arguing that the

29 A reference made to one of the two cases Norwegian lawyers have to argue before the Supreme Court to be admitted to the Supreme Court bar. Eriksen Søreide is a lawyer.

30 St. forh. 22.11.2007, 612. 31 Ibid., Anundsen (right-wing Progress Party), 613.

32 Ibid., 614. 33 Ibid., 616. 34 Standing Committee on Church, 2.7.

constitutional limits could not be altered by political decisions through a simple majority in Parliament.

In the first chamber of Parliament, Odelstinget, the right-wing Progress Party, raised doubts about the integrity of the Ministry of Justice legal opinion, pointing out it was the only one among the legal opinions holding the PLI to be constitutional. Representative Anundsen (right-wing Progress Party) questioned the traditional assumption that the Ministry of Justice legal department was beyond political motivations. The legal department, in his view, should probably be seen more as what it was – namely, a tool for interpreting law in connection with the political work of the government. It was, in his view, impossible to see how giving away more than a billion NOK failed to represent such a "systematic redisposition" of ÖVF means that was held out as unconstitutional even by the Ministry of Justice. The government, in his view, abused majority power to trample on constitutional provisions, only to leave the cleaning up to the courts.[35]

Another right-wing Progress Party representative, Hagen, pointed out that the Ministry of Justice legal opinion call for serious constitutional debate in Parliament had an impact beyond generating actual debate – namely, in following judicial proceedings, to serve as an argument of constitutionality in itself. According to traditional doctrine, and clarified in *Kløfta* and later cases, parliamentary debate and conclusions on questions of constitutionality may have authoritative influence on courts' constitutional review. Hagen noted that as the government held the majority in Parliament, whatever the debate content, its conclusion would be one of PLI constitutionality. If Parliament, with a qualified majority of at least two-thirds, claimed the PLI was constitutional, courts would, in Hagen's view, be right to look to its conclusion; in such a situation the courts could know that Parliament had been in a position to amend the Constitution following its supermajority amendment procedures, even though this had not been formally done. Nevertheless, the PLI constitutionality was held by but a small majority: only the government Representatives. As these Representatives also had significant control over what reached Parliament from the Ministry of Justice legal department, the Supreme Court should independently conclude on the constitutional question without looking to what the small majority in Parliament argued. To the extent the majority presented arguments for the PLI constitutionality, these largely coincided with those from the Ministry of Justice opinion.

Traditionally, under the two-chamber parliamentary system, legislation was primarily debated only in Odelstinget. The second chamber, Lagtinget, was at

35 Ot. forh. 23.10.2008, 6–7.

the time of PLI preparations about to be abolished by a constitutional reform.[36] The decision to abolish Lagtinget had been made the year before, but it was still formally in function. The PLI was still a subject of serious debate also in Lagtinget, over nine pages; something Representative Langeland (Socialist Left) called an attempt at "revitalization" of Lagtinget resembling flogging a dead horse.[37] The Minister of Justice repeated that the question of PLI effectuation was primarily one of politics, not of law.[38] The arguments for and against PLI constitutionality remained similar to those forwarded in the earlier debates.

In sum, the majority in Parliament provided few independent assessments of the PLI constitutionality. Its evaluations and conclusions were mainly those of the Ministry of Justice legal department, and little was done to refute in a reasoned way any of the counterarguments presented by the other legal opinions or by the opposition. When the two factions in the Supreme Court held Parliament to have "thoroughly" assessed and concluded on the question of constitutionality,[39] this was based on the majority having perused one of three available legal opinions and subscribed to it.

8.2.3 *Rt. 2010 s. 1445: War Crimes*

The new NPC was enacted in 2005.[40] One novelty compared to the NPC of 1902 was chapter 16 regulating genocide, war crimes and crimes against humanity. This chapter came into effect in 2008.[41] As opposed to the general rule of nonretroactive effect as set out in NPC 2005 § 1, chapter 16 is, following § 3, effective retroactively, on two conditions: its provisions may be applied to acts committed before NPC 2005 to the extent they were punishable following other Norwegian criminal provisions in effect at the time of action; and if they were considered as genocide, crimes against humanity or war crimes under international law. The punishment for such crimes could not, however, supersede the punishment the person would have been sentenced to under the Norwegian criminal provisions in effect at the time of the crime.

The dualist principle in the area of criminal sanctions has been understood to bar international law from serving as the sole legislative foundation for

36 As the two chambers were composed by the same apportionment of party candidates, and rarely disagreed, the two-chamber system became increasingly superfluous. It was abolished by constitutional amendment of 20.02.2007, effective from 01.10.2009.

37 Lt. forh. 3.11.2008, 7. 38 Ibid., 11. 39 Rt. 2010 s. 535, paras. 148, 169.

40 Norwegian Penal Code 2005, Lov av 20. mai 2005 nr. 28 om straff (straffeloven).

41 Lov av 7. mars 2008 nr. 4.

criminally sanctioning anyone in Norway. This understanding of the *nulla poena sine lege* principle set out in the Constitution § 96, para 1 ("No one may be convicted except according to law, or be punished except following a court decision"), read in conjunction with the ban on retroactivity in § 97, seems from the outset to bar criminally sanctioning acts punishable by international but not Norwegian law at the time of action. It has also been seen to bar retroactively increasing the severity of criminal sanctions. Case law has held the ban on retroactive criminal legislation disadvantageous for the accused to be absolute,[42] thus rendering the standard of review scrutiny in cases concerning criminal retroactivity very strict. The question discussed prior to the NPC 2005 chapter 16 and § 3 was whether retroactive application of the new rules could pass muster under the Constitution § 97 and relevant case law. The Ministry of Justice legal department concluded this was doubtful. It held to be constitutional, however, retroactive application of the new provisions to actions encompassing the same subjective and objective criminal criteria punishable by already effective criminal provisions. Conceding the increased stigma in being convicted under the new chapter 16, it argued such retroactivity would be permissible under the conditions set out in § 3.[43] A unanimous parliamentary Committee on Justice "was pleased that the new regulations were to be used also on acts committed prior to their entry into force." It cited and accepted the Ministry of Justice assessment of constitutionality without making any independent arguments about constitutionality.[44] There were no more discussions of constitutionality in Odelstinget and Lagtinget, and the regulations were enacted with the support of a unanimous Parliament.[45]

A Bosnian charged with depriving the liberty of civilians in Herzegovina in a period from May to November 1992 was in 2008 also charged under NPC 2005 chapter 16, §§ 102 (crime against humanity) and 103 (war crime). The plenary Supreme Court split 11–6 in finding the application of the new rules unconstitutional. The case came before the Supreme Court as a pure case of constitutionality, the original charge being postponed. The later assessment of the original charge led to conviction for "ordinary" deprivation of liberty, first to five years and four-and-a-half years by the City and Appellate courts, respectively, but in the end increased to eight years by the Supreme Court.[46]

42 Rt. 2006 s. 293. 43 Ot. prp. nr. 8 (2007–2008), 5.5.4.3.2–5.5.4.3.4.

44 Innst. O. nr. 29 (2007–2008), 5.2.

45 Besl. O. nr. 43 (2007–2008), Lt. forh. February 28, 2008, 12.

46 TOSLO-2008-18985, LB-2009-24039, Rt. 2010 s. 1445.

Justice Møse, for the majority, found that applying the new legislation was unconstitutional under the Constitution § 97. Even though application would not lead to any stricter punishment in terms of prison sentence length, he found the characterization of the criminal acts as genocide, crimes against humanity or war crimes – "serious violations of international humanitarian law," in international law vocabulary – to be "undoubtedly" more legally burdensome and stigmatizing for the perpetrator.[47] He found support for differentiating between these new and the "ordinary" crimes in international law, as well as in the Ministry of Justice legal opinion preceding the legislation in question.[48] He concluded that the stricter punishment awaiting perpetrators in other countries or before international tribunals notwithstanding, "in our country the Constitution § 97 constitutes an absolute barrier in the area of criminal law, and this barrier must apply to all."[49]

Citing the graded standards of review as set out in *Kløfta* and repeated in later cases, Møse adopted the most intense scrutiny under which there is little, if any room for looking to the view of Parliament in assessing the constitutionality of disputed legislation when it concerns individual freedom and integrity. Having concluded that NPC 2005 §§ 102 and 103 were unconstitutional if applied retroactively, he thus maintained that Parliament's opposite constitutional interpretation had little weight.[50]

Justice Skoghøy for the minority did not find that the Constitution § 97 barred the retroactive effect of NPC §§ 102 and 103, because the crimes regulated therein were punishable as crimes against humanity both under international law and also under the law of Bosnia-Hercegovina at the time of crime. He conceded that § 96 of the Constitution (*nulla crimen sine lege*) together with Norwegian dualism barred the use of international law directly as basis for criminal sanctions. Pointing to the majority reasoning in the 1946 *Klinge* case, the minority found it relevant, however, to assess not only how someone charged with what amounted to a crime under international law at the time of the crime would be sanctioned under national law, but also under international law. Even if Norway would not, or could not, have prosecuted under such rules at the time of the crime, an international tribunal could have done so. The minority did not find that a national conviction under the same characteristics as would have been used at an international tribunal amounted to any retroactive reaction contrary to the Constitution § 97. The burden of being convicted for crimes against humanity or war crimes in Norway now would not, in the eyes of the

47 Rt. 2010 s. 1445, para. 106. 48 Ibid., paras. 111–113. 49 Ibid., para. 119.
50 Ibid., paras. 89–91, 120.

minority, be any greater than being convicted for the same crimes under an international tribunal.

8.3 2010 CASES DEBATE AND FOLLOW-UP

In May 2010, following the decisions in the *Shipping Tax* and *OVF* cases, opposition Representative Syversen (Christian Conservative) asked, during parliamentary question time, what the Prime Minister or Justice Minister thought about twice having had legislation proposed by the government found unconstitutional by the Supreme Court. Minister of Justice Storberget (Labor) stated he was "delighted" to be able to discuss "this kind of question in Parliament, for these are important questions of balances, checks and democracy." He maintained it was the privilege of the government to work within what presented itself, following a conscientious assessment of constitutional limits, as its political scope of action. That courts sometimes interpreted the constitution differently was to be expected, and "judicial review of legislation is part of our constitutional system ... Democracy must endure separation of powers and constitutional control of power. Additionally, democracy and its institutions must endure that politicians – sometimes me – express disagreement with the [Supreme Court] majority view and agreement with the [Supreme Court] minority."[51]

The immediate response from government members indicates the undoubtedness with which the existence and scope of judicial review is accepted as part of the Norwegian constitutional system. It is also worth noting, as opposed to the reform delay after the *Kløfta* case, that the 2010 Supreme Court decisions caused immediate preparations for changing policy and regulations so that they conform with the courts' conclusions. Minister of Finance Johnsen (Labor) stated on the day of the pronunciation of the *Shipping Tax* case that

> I take into account that the Supreme Court has concluded that latent tax from the old shipping tax scheme can not be collected according to the transitional regulations from 2007 ... The Government must assess the situation and the alternative courses of action, before we can conclude in the matter. We will continue to ensure competitive conditions for the Norwegian shipping industry.[52]

The very same day as the Supreme Court decision in the *OVF* case, Minister of Church Rigmor Aaserud (Labor) stated that ongoing purchases of leased

[51] St. forh. May 26, 2010, 3453–3454.

[52] www.regjeringen.no/en/dep/fin/press-center/press-releases/2010/Finance-minister-Johnsenss-comment-on-the-supreme-court-verdict-.html?id=593369.

properties from OVF would be stopped following the Supreme Court decision, and that the questions concerning properties already sold would be assessed by the Attorney General for Civil Affairs.[53] The day that the *War Crime* decision came down, the Ministry of Justice issued a press release announcing the conclusion of unconstitutionality. In it, Justice Minister Storberget clarified that the decision "does not mean Norway becomes a free haven for war criminals."[54]

Based i.a. on the *Shipping Tax* and *OVF* cases, Representative and member of the Standing Committee on Constitution and Control Foss (Conservative) criticized the Government for being "arrogant" in its use of majority power.[55] In a reply, two government members of the same Committee conceded that the two cases were indeed serious, but maintained they "illuminate a core value in our constitutional democracy: control of power, balance between the branches of government ... The Government, Parliament and the Supreme Court have a joint responsibility to follow the Constitution and obey by the rules. And that is just what is happening."[56]

As for the *Shipping Tax* case, Minister of Finance Johnsen (Labor) highlighted that he found it to be "an interesting decision."[57] Not all party representatives of the government parties were as diplomatic. The leader of the Socialist Left secretariat in Parliament, Braadland, implied the Supreme Court split in deciding the *Shipping Tax case* indicated that had been a party political decision,[58] and leader of the Radical Left Party, Dahle, saw the case as "confirm[ing] that Norway is a class state."[59] These statements aside, few politicians expressed any lack of confidence in Supreme Court professionalism, or suspicions of political activism or other illegitimacy concerning the institution of review. Parliamentary leader for the Socialist Left, Holmås, was "surprised and disappointed"; Socialist Left Andersen was "resigned and disillusioned" (...) "This is no gracious landing," Andersen conceded, "but rule of law must, after all, protect even shipowners."[60] The Socialist Left party group in Parliament was reportedly muzzled shortly after the decision.[61] The former State Secretary, lawyer Ørbeck Sørheim (Labor), criticized the Supreme Court disregard for Parliament's view. He was also skeptical about

53 May 12, 2010, www.regjeringen.no/nb/dep/fad/aktuelt/nyheter/2010/Tomtefesteinstruksen-grunnlovsstridig.html?id=604819.

54 www.regjeringen.no/nb/dep/jd/pressesenter/pressemeldinger/2010/hoyesteretts-dom-i-krigsfor brytersaken.html?id=627209.

55 Foss, Regjeringens arroganse (2010). 56 Kolberg, Demokrati, ikke arroganse! Ibid.

57 www.dn.no/forsiden/naringsliv/article1837961.ece.

58 http://thoregil.blogspot.no/2010/02/pa-baten.html.

59 www.hegnar.no/bors/article410086.ece.

60 Johansen, Får i pose og sekk etter SV-selvmål (2010). 61 Ibid.

how random the result seemed, as it was produced with a number of justices having recused themselves, thereby leaving only eleven to decide a plenary case. Socialist Left Representative Chaudhry maintained, however, that

> Parliament simply has to take note of the Supreme Court decision and continue working according to it. I am not concerned about the relation between the legislature and the courts. The Supreme Court was split on this issue, but courts are free to interpret the legality of legislation under the Constitution. This is something we have to respect and work according to.[62]

Parliamentary Vice Chair of the Agrarian Center Party, Ola Borten Moe, stated he was "happy to be put in place." Not a particularly eager supporter of the shipping tax he had voted for, Borten Moe held that the Supreme Court adherence to the constitution was "what makes the constitution meaningful and weighty. Some hold the decision to be challenging democracy. I, however, see the decision as important for democracy – as Parliament by a simple majority should not be able to abolish people's constitutional rights. This is what marks the difference between the tyranny of the majority and a constitutional democracy."[63]

Less than a month after the Supreme Court decision, a press release from the Ministry of Finance outlined the main elements of alterations to be proposed following the review case,[64] and a proposal to Parliament stating that the new regulations had to conform to the Supreme Court's interpretation of § 97.[65] Though the opposition disagreed with certain elements of the new regulations, it did not dispute that they were within the limits clarified by the Supreme Court.[66] The loyal attention to the decision proceeded in the parliamentary debates, although one of the government representatives emphasized that the court decision had come by a "slim majority – I underline a slim majority."[67] This, in turn, was countered by a Representative noting that while the Supreme Court majority constituted 54.5 percent, the majority in Parliament had only been 51.4 percent.[68] The new shipping tax regulations were enacted and effectuated from July 1, 2010.

Between the City Court and the Supreme Court decisions in the *OVF* case, representative Lønning (Conservative) stated that if the Supreme Court were to uphold the City Court conclusion, he would support impeachment proceedings against the Government for deliberately neglecting the Constitution.[69] Following the Supreme Court finding of unconstitutionality, Lønning

[62] *På tynn is* (2010). [63] Hanssen, Glad for å bli satt på plass (2010). [64] March 26, 2010.
[65] Prop. 126 LS (2009–2010), 4.1. [66] Innst. 351 L (2009–2010), 2.2.
[67] I. M. Thorkildsen, (Socialist Left) St. forh. 14.6.2010, 4049.
[68] A. Kambe, Conservative, Ibid., 4052. [69] Lønning, Når grunnloven setter grenser (2010).

maintained the handling of the OVF was "no ordinary working blunder" by the Government, but rather a conscious attempt at circumventing constitutional limits. Instead of proposing an alteration of the Constitution § 106, the Government had, in Lønning's view, willfully challenged the Constitution. "Not only has the Government weakened its position towards its constituents, it has also added to a fading popular trust in a functioning, legislative system. A Government opposing the Constitution only to have its opposition be struck down does not look good. It makes people skeptical."[70]

Approximately one month after the *OVF* case, all opposition parties proposed to Parliament an abolishment of the troublesome OVF Act.[71] The government replied it was working on the legal questions raised by the case, and that there was no immediate hurry to alter the OVF Act, as the PLI had become void as a direct consequence of the Supreme Court decision,[72] and hence would not be used. For this reason the proposal was rejected.[73] A written question about what the government had done following the Supreme Court decision was posed in October 2010, and the Church Minister was informed about the ongoing compensation proceedings with the OVF and the assessment of the OVF Act.[74] In April 2011, the government itself proposed to abolish § 5 section 2 of the OVF Act as part of a proposal on other church issues,[75] and the Act was thus amended.[76] In 2012, Labor proposed constitutional amendment of § 106 to alter the provision so that it reflected the Supreme Court minority view.[77]

The *War Crime* case seems, from the Parliament web archives, to have been immediately followed up only by a question from Representative Asmyhr (right-wing Progress Party) directed to the Minister of Justice, on what would be done to ensure that this and other war criminals were punished. Both its formulation and its answer indicate the Supreme Court review conclusions were considered fully decisive for the constitutional question of retroactivity by both the government and the Parliament representatives. The Minister of Justice in fact answered all of Asmyhr's questions by referring him to the relevant parts of the Supreme Court decision.[78]

Asmyhr repeated his parliamentary question time call-out for new legislation in the media.[79] He was answered there too by the Minister of

[70] Vårt Land, 14.5.2010, 4.
[71] Dokument 8:164 S (2009–2010), proposal to abolish § 5, para. 2.
[72] St. forh. 17.6.2010, 4339–4340. [73] Ibid., 4352 (57–48).
[74] Dokument nr. 15:1 (2010–2011), nr. 58. [75] Prop. 81 L (2010–2011), ch. 6.
[76] August 26, 2011 no. 40 (effective 1.1.2012, following res. 26.8.2011 no. 866).
[77] Dokument 12:12 (2011–2012). [78] Dokument nr. 15:3 (2012–2013), nr. 449.
[79] Similar inserts in *Altaposten* December 9, 2010, *Telemarksavisa* December 9, 2010, *Dagsavisen* December 10, 2010, *Romerikes Blad* December 10, 2010, *Nationen* December 11, 2010, *Stavanger Aftenblad* December 27, 2010.

Justice,[80] who disputed that "Norway would become a free haven" for war criminals as a consequence of the Supreme Court decision, a decision he "took into consideration." In his inserts, Asmyhr maintained that the Supreme Court clarification that the Constitution § 96 would be a barrier for using the existing laws retroactively was "OK" ("i og for seg greit"). This, however, should not prevent Norway from promptly enacting new legislation to ensure the punishment of war criminals. Asmyhr did not propose any constitutional amendment. On how he envisioned the desired ordinary legislation to reach war criminals while respecting § 96 and the *War Criminal* decision, he did not elaborate.

From 2011, a parliamentary Human Rights Committee (chaired by Conservative PM Lønning; see Section 9.1) prepared a report on possible constitutional amendment by a bill of Human Rights, aimed to be enacted for the Constitution's 200-year anniversary in 2014.[81] The Committee did not propose any alteration of § 97. Following the *War Criminal* case, however, it did discuss whether to alter § 96 to open up for criminally sanctioning acts not only prohibited by "Norwegian law," but also by "international law." It dismissed this possibility, arguing that such an alteration would not only radically change the traditional understanding of § 96, it also had the potential to substantially weaken the individual protection against retroactive penal sanctions. As the Committee mandate was to *strengthen* the protection of human rights, it concluded unanimously against any alteration of § 96. The part of the Committee proposal containing these views on §§ 96 and 97 was formally presented by a group of representatives from all parties.[82]

At the same time, however, six of the same representatives formally presented an alternative proposal to amend § 97 with a second paragraph, making the exception to the ban on retroactivity for crimes "clearly criminal according to human rights law and directly punishable under international law at the time of criminal action."[83]

Another discussion of interest to the political view of courts and review powers is an initiative originating prior to the 2010 cases, but gaining attention following their conclusions. Representative Ola Borten Moe (Agrarian Center), then Vice Chairman of Parliament's Standing Committee on

80 *Dagsavisen* December 21, 2010. 81 Dokument 16 (2011–2012), 24.2.4.

82 Dokument 12:30 (2011–2012) Per-Kristian Foss (Conservative), Martin Kolberg (Labor), Marit Nybakk (Labor), Jette F. Christensen (Labor), Anders Anundsen (right-wing Progress), Hallgeir H. Langeland (Socialist Left), Per-Olaf Lundteigen (Center), Geir Jørgen Bekkevold (Christian Democrat), Trine Skei Grande (Liberal).

83 Dokument 12:36 (2011–2012) Per-Kristian Foss, Martin Kolberg, Marit Nybakk, Jette F. Christensen, Hallgeir H. Langeland og Per Olaf Lundteigen.

Constitutional questions, argued that Parliament had lost too much power, not to the courts, but to the executive, and proposed constitutional reforms.[84] One of these was to have Supreme Court justices be appointed by Parliament rather than by the Government, to "ensure independence" and provide for "a more courageous Supreme Court." As the Supreme Court is not beyond politics, but rather "an important, political institution," Borten Moe envisioned a system "much like the US, where there is considerable public debate on Supreme Court nominees,"[85] "and no one questions the independence of the US Supreme Court."[86] "It would substantially enhance the legitimacy of the system,"[87] and "is only a constitutional amendment away."[88] Of the other parties, only a Representative from the right-wing Progress Party supported Borten Moe's position.[89] Representatives from the Conservative, Labor and Socialist Left Parties held that the proposal would lead to an undesirable politicization of the Supreme Court, and pointed out that the role of Parliament would in any case be but rubber-stamping, lacking the capacity to conduct any independent evaluation of nominees.[90]

Borten Moe's initiative was premised on a 2010 article by political scientists Grendstad, Shaffer and Waltenburg, titled "Revealed Preferences of the Norwegian Supreme Court Justices."[91] Going through a select number of dissent decisions from the Supreme Court, they found a correlation between "socialist" government appointees and later "socialist" voting on the Supreme Court, implying Justices voted "with" the government that appointed them. The contention that Justices were in part motivated by party politics generated controversy within the legal community. This part of the argument by Grendstad et al. was also explicitly rejected by representatives from the judiciary.[92] Chief Justice Schei refuted the idea of a causal explanation for Justices voting with "their" appointing government as "meaningless."[93]

84 Borten Moe, *Regjeringen må vise respekt* (2009).

85 Haugli, *Vil la Stortinget utnevne Høyesterett* (2010).

86 Borten Moe, *Stortinget inn i Høyesterett – igjen* (2010).

87 Haugli, *Vil la Stortinget utnevne Høyesterett* (2010).

88 Borten Moe, *Stortinget inn i Høyesterett* (2010).

89 Bjørgum, *Nei til dommerforslag* (2010).

90 Haugli, *Vil la Stortinget utnevne Høyesterett* (2010), Bjørgum, *Nei til dommerforslag* (Representatives Dørum, Foss, Kolberg, Solhjell).

91 Grendstad, et al., Revealed preferences of Norwegian supreme court justices (2010).

92 I.a.Skoghøy, Dommeratferd og dommerbakgrunn (2010). For further critique, see i.a. Sunde, Andre premiss og anna resultat (2012); Nadim, Er Høyesterettsdommere politisk farget? – En undersøkelse av 17 dommeres votum i dissenssaker (2013); and Kierulf and Slagstad, Høyesteretts dommere (2015).

93 Schei, *God sammensetning* (2009), Lecture 31.3.2011, later printed as Schei, Har Høyesterett en politisk funksjon? (2011).

Conceding that the Supreme Court did indeed function politically and that the judicial ideology of justices was naturally shaped by their value preferences, he pointed to how the party political affiliation of justices is neither visible nor in focus in any part of appointment proceedings, and how the Minister of Justice has never disregarded the recommendations of the independent appointment board. While publicly debated by Representatives, commentators and others in 2010, Borten Moe's initiative led to no formal reform proposal.

8.4 CONSTITUTIONAL REVIEW REFLECTIONS

8.4.1 *Customary Law: Review Reconfirmed*

From the perspective of political and general conceptions of judicial review, the 2010 cases highlight at least three perspectives relevant to the question of review legitimacy. First, their contribution to clarify the embeddedness of judicial review. Second and third, to thematize two aspects of its scope – its possible limits and how review relates to Parliament's view on the constitutional interpretation in question.

The cases make clear the established position of constitutional review. The *Kløfta* case may have represented the start of a review renaissance, and was formative in elucidating the Constitution and judicial review still being a reality. This insight gained a foothold within the political and legal communities following that decision. The 2010 cases are dependent on this embedding and the development following it. In the political preparations for the three legislative issues reviewed, not only the Constitution, but also case law under the Constitution is seen as decisive for the scope of legal (legitimate) political action. The way case law is taken to be the natural starting point for assessing constitutional limits is not something new in 2010, but is illustrative of one central difference between the 2010 and 1960s–1970s attitudes to constitutional limits. Contrary to the legal and political discussions preceding the *Kløfta* case, there are no legal or political discussions disputing the relevance of constitutional case law for later political action in the 2010 cases.

The cases also underline the embedding of judicial review as a functioning part of an integrated constitutional democracy: To the extent the Supreme Court decides the constitutional limits are narrower than what is politically desirable, politicians act to alter or amend the Constitution following constitutional amendment procedures. Both the *OVF* and the *War Crime* cases led to proposals to alter §§ 106 and 97 respectively. Through this follow-up, these cases serve as an illustration of judicial review as a generator of the institutional dialogue between Parliament and the government and the Supreme Court.

The *War Crime* case was one rejecting the legislative decision of a unanimous Parliament. The *Shipping Tax* and *OVF* cases, contrarily, are based on regulations voted through by rather slim parliamentary majorities. The *War Crime* case concerned an individual charged with very grave acts, whereas the other two cases concerned "only" economical goods. One might think that the *War Crime* case would be more controversial due to the complete difference between political and legal constitutional interpretations of a question concerning such a central individual right, but this was not the case. Instead, the two other cases generated the most debate and are the ones primarily discussed in later reflections on 2010 and judicial review. There may be several reasons for this: The *War Crime* case is one in which judicial review is used to ensure a rights guarantee very fundamental to rule of law – that of nonretroactive criminal sanctions. It is pronounced in the area that under the *Kløfta* tripartite test is subject to very strict review, with little room for looking to the view of Parliament on the constitutional question. Although perhaps misunderstood by some readers, it is also a ruling deciding only the quite narrow constitutional question. Had the new provisions been applied, this would not have led to any manifestly stricter penalty than what the defendant could be sentenced to under other applicable criminal provisions. It also left open the question of whether the defendant could be punished under these other provisions – which he later was.

While the *Shipping Tax* and *OVF* decisions ended up protecting "only" economical goods, they also protected such goods for groups/entities traditionally politically contentious either for historical, class or other reasons. Both shipowners and the Church serve as markers for popular stereotypes also held by political factions ("elites," "already rich," "state in the state," "outdated/irrelevant"). Alluding to such a stereotype was a statement by then Minister of Finance Halvorsen (Socialist Left) in 2007, "calming down" the public by assuring them that the government would not waive the shipowners' tax credit.[94] The view of § 106 as outdated, and of the OVF as but a hot dog in a state-owned hot-dog stand, also conform well with the stereotype of particularly Labor party views on the role of the Church in the state. Having the Supreme Court decide these traditionally contentious matters affects the perceived or social legitimacy of the decisions.

The debates on the regulations disputed in the *Shipping Tax* and *OVF* cases were deeply divided along political lines. The division into two political blocks

94 VG Nett blog, 27.8.2007, referred as a central premise also in Rt. 2010 s. 143 para. 37.

in Parliament was mirrored by a division into two legal blocks in the Supreme Court. And the real consideration arguments from the two opposing sides in Parliament were also, to a substantial extent, adopted in reverse order by the Supreme Court majorities and dissents respectively. This latter element – the correspondence in argumentation – may easily be taken to imply there is a political, and not only a legal, motivation for the court's decision. In contrast to the unanimous War Crime legislation decision in Parliament, a "political decision" impression may also be strengthened where the Supreme Court is perceived as "taking sides." The War Crime question is possibly more easily perceived as one in which Parliament decides based on a political assessment and the Supreme Court on a legal one. This would leave the impression of the Supreme Court operating within the scope of its professional legitimacy, rather than as an arbiter of political debate.

The existence of *dissent* may be seen to challenge the legitimacy of review, from a social perspective – courts are more easily perceived as political actors – and from a normative one – the particular professionalism of courts, that there is *one right answer* in law, seems less convincing when justices disagree. As we have seen, such dissent is, however, more the norm than the exception in cases of Norwegian constitutional review,[95] which in and of itself is no challenge to review legitimacy. An interesting factor to note about recent dissents, however, is that not only do the Supreme Court factions disagree about the *law*, they also disagree about how to interpret the *facts*. In the *Shipping Tax* case, one central reason for the differing norms applied by the majority and the minority is their differing interpretations of what kind of tax they were dealing with. The majority saw the tax burden as one arising only upon the shipowners' decision to pay dividends, whereas the minority viewed the 1996 regulations as levying a tax burden that had been there, latently, all along. While certainly interconnected, judicial assessments of law and fact depend on different approaches. And the more complex the subject of regulation becomes, the more is required from courts in establishing what fact is the relevant one for judicial assessment. Such factual assessment raises the question of what judicial professionalism really consists in. It is possibly more dependent on

95 Provoked by a later 2013 § 97 review case on fishing quotas (Rt. 2013 s. 1345), in which the Supreme Court split 9–8 in favor of the State, a suggestion was made to amend § 97 to make adjudication under it easier: see Sejersted, *Grunnlovsendring må til* (2013). Given the multitude of different questions that may arise under a provision to the protection against retroactive civil laws, the chances of altering § 97 in a way barring judicial disagreement over its application seem slim. As was also pointed out (Banoun, *Må la Grunnloven ligge* (2013)), with reference to Parliament *willfully* challenging § 97 in the *OVF* and *Shipping Tax* cases, rather than trying to solve the judicial challenges under § 97 through constitutional amendment, why not instead urge Parliament to take § 97 more seriously?

the professional experience that judges have obtained out of law school than on the legal interpretation. This underlines the significance of ensuring lawyers of different backgrounds are represented in the Supreme Court. The quality of factual assessment is also more dependent on counsels' ability to present complex facts to the court in an understandable manner. While difficult without guidance from counsel, the court has an independent obligation to know the law, whereas it must rely on the parties to present the facts. To the extent review cases coming before the Supreme Court are increasingly factually complex, this may cause a continuance of divisions in the court, not only over law, but also over facts.

If review decisions are seen as "taking sides" politically, this imperils their social legitimacy. Whether they are in fact politically or ideologically motivated may not be decisive; the challenge arises to the extent they are perceived as political. Such perceptions are perhaps more apparent in two-party systems, such as in the United States. As questions of constitutionality come in a dual form – legislation is either constitutional or it is not – political systems in which the political is polarized to two fronts mirror this duality. As such, in the "double duality" of two-party systems, positions of constitutional interpretation will most often correspond with one of the two parties, and may thus easily be identified with a political rather than a legal position. They may also arise in multiparty systems, as political parties in such systems often form blocks for ideological or other reasons when presented with substantial, societal questions. Examples of this in Norway can be found in all the periods studied. They became particularly prevalent in the two 2010 cases, where the political parties divided between those in position or in government and those in opposition. These were the two cases to generate most debate, whereas the War Crimes case, in which a unanimous Parliament was overruled, did not.

Even though the economic cases generated more debate than the War Crime case, the 2010 cases did, in all, generate surprisingly little discussion on the legitimacy of judicial review. Considering the very heated political debates preceding the disputed legislation, it is really the lack of court critique that comes out as the notable aspect of the 2010 cases. One possible explanation for this is that potentially stronger critique against courts may have yielded to concerns about an even more pressing challenge to Parliament's actual power: that of several years of majority government leaving Parliament to rubber stamp rather than be an actual check on government politics. In this light, it is interesting to note the comment by opposition Representative Lønning (Conservative) on how the 2010 cases illustrate a challenge not to judicial legitimacy, but to *political* legitimacy: To the extent the majority representatives in Parliament abuse their power through neglecting or willfully challenging the Constitution, this leads to a declining legitimacy of representative politics. As judicial decisions may be criticized for illegitimately judicializing politics, political decisions can be seen as equally critique-worthy to the extent they illegitimately politicize law. It is only through actual deliberations by the popularly elected that their reasoning takes on the additional legitimacy of having been carried out by the popularly elected.

Legal discussions about the 2010 cases' contributions to the proper interpretation particularly of § 97 have been and will probably continue to be held. On the question of judicial review, however, the main impression left by the general debates over the 2010 cases is one of relatively high political and social acceptance of judicial review: Even though politicians may disagree with the result, they accept and even acknowledge the necessity of this institution.

8.4.2 *Judicial Review Exceptions?*

Justice Endresen's single-vote *obiter dictum* on the possible exception of § 106 from judicial review does not make law, but does raise some questions about the scope of judicial review that merit a closer look. One of these is whether some constitutional provisions are exempt from review, and, if so, which and why. Some constitutional provisions fall outside the tripartite division in the *Kløfta* case, and are less suitable or indeed unsuitable for judicial review. One obvious exception is the constitutional responsibility of Representatives, government ministers and Supreme Court Justices. This is, under the Constitution § 86, subject to impeachment proceedings, not to review in ordinary courts. What was until 2014 the Constitution § 94 mandating a new civil and penal code to be enacted by the second Parliament following 1814 seems by nature unreviewable, as does the King's obligation to confess to Lutheranism under § 4, particularly as he is immune against charges under § 5. The nonreview character of §§ 2 and 4 are also held in the 1983 case mentioned by Justice Endresen.[96]

Distinguishing between reviewable and nonreviewable provisions is not only theoretically interesting. The Human Rights Committee preparing the bill of human rights amendments to the Constitution in 2014 did indeed systematize its proposal around a distinction between directly actionable and nonactionable provisions: between provisions stating human rights were meant to be legally enforceable causes of action, and provisions meant to serve as expressions of value, that were to be of a guiding and weighty, but not

[96] Rt. 1983 s. 1004.

binding character. The interesting question is *why* some provisions are, or ought to be, nonreviewable. The human rights examples fall into this category for being more of a political guideline nature.[97] The Human Rights Committee distinction is made in recognition of the dual function of the Constitution as a legal and political instrument: at the same time, a real and functional limit on legal political action and also a reflection of fundamental societal values.

In the *OVF* case, however, Justice Endresen seems to argue that the Constitution § 106 is not subject to review because it is a provision regulating the competence and work of the governmental branches. This prompts the question of how he justifies his theory holding that only provisions regulating affairs between the state and the individual place actual limits on the legislator. He sees the *Kløfta* case call for "lenient review" under inter-/intra-branch constitutional questions as being "an understatement," and claims such review has never occurred. He does not, however, discuss the implied understanding in the *Whaling* case that such review is indeed within courts' competence.[98] A banal example illustrating that courts cannot defer to Parliament's view in *all* questions concerning governmental branch work and competences is one pointed out since Fredrik Stang: Any legislation disregarding central *formal* requirements for enacting legislation in the Constitution §§ 75ff. cannot be respected by courts even though it were to be conducted following a willful, majority decision in Parliament.

The further argument for excluding inter-/intra-branch provisions from review is an assertion that the predominant justification for review in the 1800s was the liberal argument, and that the *conditions under which judicial review developed* then are decisive for its scope today. As for the first assertion, one may question whether case law or theoretical analyses from the 1800s supports Justice Endresen's thesis. As recalled in Section 3.3, disputes between citizens, primarily high state officials, and the state were certainly the predominant subject of the review cases of the 1800s. But that the liberal constellation was central in those cases does not necessarily imply that the institution of judicial review was justified solely or primarily by the liberal argument. Case law certainly does not support such a thesis: most commentary seems to agree that the only case openly reasoning about the existence and scope of review is the 1866 case. Although concerning the relation between an individual and the state, the justifications for exercising review power in that case are the *lex superior* and *courts as legal arbiters* arguments.

97 Dokument 16 (2011–2012), see i.a. §§ 93, 102, 104, 108, 109.

98 Rt. 1952 s. 1089.

While the liberal argument can be traced as one of several justifications for review with some scholars,[99] legal theory from the 1800s seems to rely primarily on *validity, constitutional* and *lex superior* justifications.[100] Justice Endresen, however, reads Aubert (1864) to reserve judicial review for cases between individuals and the state – inter-/intra-branch constitutional questions are, in Endresen's reading of Aubert, subject to impeachment proceedings. As pointed out in Section 3.4, I take Aubert to prescribe impeachment for unconstitutional ministerial acts and resembling actions, not constitutional cases concerning the relationship between governmental branches per se. Read as a whole, the paragraph in which Aubert sets out the different types of unconstitutional government acts seems to list three types of constitutional issues: the state–citizen disputes, inter-/intra-branch constitutional questions and suits for damages against ministers having acted unconstitutionally. Aubert seems to mean that impeachment is the solution only for the latter group. Support for this view is found in the Constitution § 86 on impeachment, which explicitly mandates impeachment for unconstitutional ministerial actions. This mandate has later been held to bar such cases from courts' ordinary jurisdiction.[101] The six impeachment proceedings in the period before Aubert's writing (1814–1845) were all against ministers. Further, in Aubert's listed examples of questions concerning nonstate-citizen questions is one making reference to an ordinary Supreme Court decision, not an impeachment proceeding (Supreme Court decision 27.4.1841). There appears, on the whole, to be little support in the 1800s for any general theory excluding inter-/intra-branch constitutional questions from judicial review.

8.4.3 *On the Role and Significance of Parliament's Assessments*

The Supreme Court majority decision not to look to "the view of Parliament" in its assessment of shipping tax constitutionality has been criticized. The critique is based on the doctrinal development on what place the view of Parliament should be awarded in review cases. As held in all the four review periods in Chapters 3 to 8, the view of Parliament is a relevant and sometimes decisive legal argument when assessing constitutionality. Parliament's view is found *relevant* where courts are *seriously in doubt* as to whether a disputed regulation is constitutional, and the *weight* of

99 Lasson, Supplement og Ord- eller Realregister til det i 1868 trykte Skrift om "Straffeprocessen i dens nyeste Skikkelse m. v." (1869); see Section 3.3.

100 Steenbuch 1824, Gaarder 1845, Winter Hjelm 1863, Aubert 1864.

101 Rt. 1910 s. 100.

this view varies with the review intensity stipulated by the three categories set out in the *Kløfta* case.[102]

The *Shipping Tax* and *OVF* cases underline that when reviewing questions concerning constitutional protection for economical goods and finding the question doubtful, Parliament's assessment is emphasized only when it meets a certain quality requirement. This doctrinal situation raises several questions: How is the question of doubtfulness to be decided? What legitimacy ideals are upheld and challenged through the doubtfulness/doubtlessness divide? What ideals are furthered and challenged by requiring that Parliament's assessment meets a certain quality, and how is this standard to be defined? The quality requirement has three different elements: It requires that "Parliament" has "clearly evaluated and concluded the law is constitutional"; that its "primary consequences, that clearly present themselves as problematic in relation to the Constitution are observed and constitutionally assessed during the preparations for the law";[103] and that Parliament's position "must be the result of a deliberate view"; where "potential misunderstandings may influence on the weight to attach to the view of Parliament."[104] Following the *Shipping Tax* case, Parliament must also have assessed the *right norm*.

In its pure form, the *right norm* part of the quality requirement is quite uncontroversial: If Parliament debates an entirely different question – say, a different constitutional provision than the one Supreme Court finds to be guiding the legal question at hand – its debate is of little interest as a source for legal assessment of the question that the parties and/or the Supreme Court finds problematic. Closer links of relevance between the different norms assessed may, however, easily be envisioned, such as in the *Shipping Tax* case. In that case, Parliament's view was held to be less important, following the doctrinal divide between situations of doubt and situations without doubt, a divide following decades (centuries) of developing and sometimes inconsistent court practice and legal commentary.[105] In a situation where there is doubt, however, it seems inconsistent to hold that misunderstood debates in Parliament are entirely *irrelevant* to courts' assessments. Under the Norwegian pragmatic legal doctrine, where almost any legal or political sources that in any way serve to enlighten the legal question at hand are permissible and relevant, excluding Parliament's view on constitutional questions entirely seems quite strange. To the extent Parliament's assessments contain

102 For a recent analysis of the significance of Parliament's view, see Tverberg, Det graderte grunnlovsvernet ved tolkning av grunnloven og prøving av lovers grunnlovmessighet (2013).

103 Rt. 2007 s. 1308, para. 42.

104 Rt. 2007 s. 1281, para. 76.

105 Høgberg, *Forbud mot tilbakevirkende lover* (2010).

discussions of themes relevant to the assessment under the "correct" norm, it must on principle surely be possible to take them into consideration, even though the proper *weight* to attach to them will vary. Such an approach seems to fit also with the what the *Shipping Tax* majority actually says: Although its formulation leaves somewhat unclear whether its *obiter* is formed as a general statement, or only pertaining to the case at hand, it seems to be a statement of what *weight* to attach to debates over the wrong norm, not one of the *relevance* of such debates in general.[106]

The remaining aspects of the quality requirement follow the same reasoning, it is only where Parliament has actually made up its mind about the right constitutional question that it has in fact struggled with the same question that later comes before the courts. The two main legitimacy ideals furthered by looking to the view of Parliament, where it has, in fact, evaluated a norm relevant to the potentially problematic consequences, is one of *justification* and one of *representative popular input*. During legislative preparations deliberating on constitutional questions, popular input is provided to two processes: how to interpret the coming law in relation to the constitution, and what the law is meant to regulate; and why it is politically desirable. Under Norwegian legal doctrine, with its focus on preparatory work, the latter is always of interest to courts' interpretation of the intention of a disputed law. But of these two processes, only the popular input on constitutional interpretation and application is relevant to courts' assessment of the constitutional question – if the point is to look to what Parliament meant about the law's constitutionality.

This leads to the question of what the quality requirement that Parliament must "clearly [have] evaluated and concluded the law is constitutional" implies. It would seem both the majority and the minority in the *OVF* case found this standard to be satisfied in that case. As discussed earlier, however, Parliament's view in the PLI deliberations is but one of a scarce majority consisting in the government party Representatives. It is also a view exposing very limited, if any, actual deliberation on the constitutional question from this majority. One may question whether the legitimacy ideal of *justification* takes on a particular authority simply by being ascribed to by Parliament, or whether Parliament must actually consider it to merit this enhanced authority. Is it the rubber-stamping of less than a supermajority of Parliament that heightens the view of the Ministry of Justice legal opinion to a level relevant to constitutional interpretation, or is the legitimacy of the majority stance

106 Rt. 2010 s. 143, para. 172: "vanskeleg å leggje vekt på." Høgberg reads this differently, to be a statement of *relevance*: see Høgberg, Grunnloven § 97 etter plenumsdommen i Rt. 2010 s. 143 (2010), 731.

weakened with the lack of independent justification? Legal doctrine seems to rely on the former: as long as Parliament has approved, or not actively disapproved, of a governmentally prepared reasoning for legislation, this is taken to imply that this view becomes Parliament's view for the purpose of legislative (and constitutional) interpretation.

From the perspective of *justification* as a factor of *process* or *input legitimacy*, this may be different. Here, it is the *quality* of argument for constitutionality from the ones in fact representatively elected rather than the adherence to others' arguments that makes their stance more normatively legitimate. The parliamentary process of interpreting the constitution may be separate from what the party representatives find to be politically desirable, as all political representatives in Parliament are independently responsible under the Constitution. Both proponents and opponents of potentially unconstitutional legislation then take on a burden of proving their constitutional credibility as long as their constitutional interpretations coincide with what they see as politically desirable. The minority representatives in the PLI debates, to some degree, lift this burden by pointing to weaknesses in the Ministry of Justice legal opinion and by reasoning independently about how § 106 is to be understood. The majority, conversely, does little to argue against any counterarguments, referring instead to parts of the Ministry of Justice opinion.

To signal that their stance is one of principled justification rather than merely political opportunity, it seems that at least some degree of independent MP reasoning about constitutionality is required. Absent such reasoning, it is unconvincing that one's stance is one of independent parliamentary and constitutional responsibility rather than "only" politics. This becomes apparent in the PLI debates, where the Agrarian Center representatives, who were not very enthusiastic about the PLI and are also traditionally conservative in constitutional questions, point to the Ministry of Justice opinion supporting the government agreement as their only justification for finding the PLI constitutional. It is by learning *why* elected representatives subscribe to one opinion, and *why* they do not find the others persuasive, that the electorate is given any real justification by the representatives for why legislation should be considered constitutional, and consequently legitimate. Absent such independent justification, representatives may challenge both the legitimacy ideals of liberal democracy and those of division of power: What they do is to contribute to the opposite of legalization of politics – namely, the *politicization of law*.

Also from the legitimacy perspective of *procedural democratic input*, the lack of independent and sincere assessment of constitutionality surpassing the level of rubber-stamping seen in the PLI debates is problematic. As pointed out by Representative Hagen,[107] the potential of abusing majority power is otherwise obvious: If the Supreme Court legal requirement of "thorough evaluation" by Parliament can be achieved by "discussing" constitutionality through leaving opposition from the minority un-answered by the majority, the majority can easily "safeguard" toward court review by generating such "debate." In this way, the qualified majority and intermediate election procedures required for constitutional amendment to enable desirable regulations is circumvented, *pro forma*. If the "quality requirement" can be met by the majority acting in this way, this undermines the legitimating factors of democratic and constitutional procedure. And it is difficult to see what ideals of legitimacy such "justification" furthers.

The question of looking to Parliament's view arises only where the Supreme Court is in *doubt* about the constitutional question. How to decide when such doubt exists? Law professors Graver and Høgberg, among others, have been critical of how the majority in the *Shipping Tax* case holds the unconstitutionality to be "doubtless." They argue that the dissent makes this holding implausible. When five justices, following a meticulous assessment, conclude opposite of the majority, surely there exists reasonable doubt about the constitutionality.[108] This argument seems persuasive, but raises one question: In relation to what is the potential doubtfulness of a constitutional review to be assessed? Three alternatives stand out: the question of doubt may be assessed in relation to some *objective* norm of reasonable doubt, where all legal opinions and evaluations are relevant; it may be assessed in relation to *a court internal* norm looking to what the court as an institution finds to be doubtful/doubtless; or it may be assessed in relation to what the reasoning justice her-/himself finds to be the right answer *independently*. This relates to the self-understanding of colloquial courts in general, and that of the Supreme Court in particular, and to the personal, professional and constitutional responsibility of every justice. Assessing the question *objectively* seems vulnerable to rendering most questions of constitutionality doubtful. Of the cases reaching the Supreme Court, very few will present constitutional questions on which everyone agrees. A *court internal* norm would establish its very own norm for the assessment of constitutional questions. Internal disagreements on reasonable doubt of facts and law in ordinary civil and criminal cases, which are not solved through deliberations, lead to dissents, not to any general

107 See Section 8.2.

108 Graver, *Refleksjoner om rederibeskatningsdommen* (2010); Høgberg, Grunnloven § 97 etter plenumsdommen i Rt. 2010 s. 143 (2010).

acceptance of the existence of reasonable doubt whenever other members of court conclude differently than oneself. Following this reasoning, it would seem the question of legal doubtfulness/doubtlessness must in principle be a personal assessment made independently by each justice. In this personal assessment, however, many impulses and impressions contribute, among them surely also those of general and colloquial arguments and conclusions.

One may question what ideals are heeded by the doctrinal element of doubtfulness/doubtlessness. From the outset, some seem obvious – that of legal legitimacy, of the separation of law and politics and of respect for the popularly elected parliament. If a question is legally clear and doubtlessly unconstitutional, what the court does is simply to apply the right rule, as opposed to a wrong one. And a clearly unconstitutional law also indicates that it has been enacted following only political, rather than actual constitutional considerations, thus leaving courts to uphold the law rather than interfere in politics. Upon adjudication of legislation presenting both constitutional and unconstitutional possible interpretations, however, respect for popularly elected representatives' views on the question calls for emphasizing the view of Parliament in the overall assessment.

But is it practical, or even plausible, that a constitutional question reaching the Supreme Court is doubtlessly unconstitutional? Particularly looking to the complex mix of fact and law to be considered under the constitution in the two civil 2010 cases, the answer to this is likely negative.[109] This impression is strengthened when considering the often seemingly inconsistent practice under the most used constitutional provisions, §§ 97 and 105.[110] If most constitutional cases reaching the Supreme Court, or even courts in general, present questions the legal answers to which contain some reasonable element of doubt, how viable is the doubtfulness/doubtlessness doctrine for review? Advancing it would seem to cement the constitutional view of Parliament as a weighty factor to be considered in almost all review cases. This could be furthering the ideal of procedural democracy legitimacy. Nevertheless, it only does so to the extent the conception of this input legitimacy ideal is satisfied by the immediate simple majority view. This, again, would be a procedural democracy view seriously challenging the legitimacy ideal of constitutionalism, even in its procedural form, as constitutional amendments require a supermajority (and an intermediary election). Should the view of a simple

109 For a detailed presentation of the differing experts views prior to the *Shipping Tax* case, see Tverberg, Det graderte grunnlovsvernet ved tolkning av grunnloven og prøving av lovers grunnlovmessighet (2013), 301.

110 See, i.a. Høgberg, *Forbud mot tilbakevirkende lover* (2010).

majority be determinative for most review cases, this is, at least over time, likely to gradually widen the constitutional limits presented by the various constitutional provisions. And this, in turn, means that the Constitution is altered without following the procedure set out in § 112/121. The procedural requirement for constitutional amendment is premised on the input legitimacy ideal of popular participation. Thus, while seemingly furthering ideals of procedural democratic input through listening to what the parliamentary majority says, from time to time, this approach in fact threatens such ideals, by undermining the election input and popular supermajority constitutionally required by § 112/121.

It is not clear that the doubtfulness/doubtlessness dichotomy is very helpful to courts pondering what weight to attach to Parliament's view in review cases. This seemingly categorical "either/or" solution to the complex set of problems arising in review cases also seems a strange bird in an otherwise pragmatic Norwegian approach to legal theory and practice. Legal questions are generally solved through an open approach to most all available legal sources and societal policy considerations, the closer balancing of which rarely follows more of a hierarchy than (usually) ranking the legal text rather high. Holding Parliament's view to be very weighty in doubtful cases – or, as the case was, irrelevant even to consider in the assessment of "doubtless" constitutional questions – seems to beg some additional justification, particularly when these debates contain parliamentary views on the balancing of interests that are otherwise relevant to the adjudication, such as in the *Shipping Tax* case.

The role and significance of Parliament's view will probably continue to be debated. In sum, however, the 2010 cases in some ways represent a synthesis of the 1866 emphasis on the role of courts as constitutional guardians and the 1920s debates about the role of the Supreme Court in a modern democracy: The 2010 cases, the preparation for and debates following them, bring forth and clarify the principled constitutional questions and the tension inherent in constitutional democracies with the institution of review. The two economical 2010 cases illustrate the bite of the Constitution and the Supreme Court as functioning protection and guardians against abuse of majority power, and the *War Crime* case as the actual protection of individual integrity rights ensured through these institutions.

9

2014–2015: Rights Reform and Judicial Review Constitutionalization

9.1 THE 2014 CONSTITUTIONAL REFORM

In 2014 the Constitution was amended, with several new rights provisions added. As part of the 200-year anniversary of the Constitution, many of the classic civil and political rights of the ECHR and the ICCPR were amended in the Constitution, as were some of the economic, social and cultural rights of the ICESCR as well as the rights of the child as protected by the UNCRC.

All the new 2014 rights already existed in Norway, either through customary law or through binding human rights treaties as incorporated by the 1999 Human Rights Act, which also gave them preference before other Norwegian law in cases of conflict. As such, they already enjoyed what was for practical, if not strictly formal purposes, a constitutional form of protection.

A constitutional human rights reform had been discussed in the legal community for decades,[1] without much progress. The idea only gained political momentum during preparations for the 2014 bicentennial constitutional anniversary. In June 2009 Parliament decided to set down a Human Rights Committee to prepare a constitutional human rights reform. In 1814 the constitution had established Norway as a "rettsstat" (state based on rule of law); now it was time to upgrade and constitutionalize Norway also as a "menneskerettsstat" (state based on rule of law and human rights).[2]

The mandate from Parliament was to have a proposal prepared to amend the Constitution in order to "strengthen the position that human rights have in Norwegian law by ensuring central human rights are protected at the constitutional level."[3] The mandate was given "as part of the preparation for the Constitution's 200-year anniversary in 2014," and the constitutional reform

[1] See i.a. Helgesen . Bør vi – anno 2002 – modernisere individets grunnlovsvern in *Lødrup, Rettsteori og Rettsliv* (2002).

[2] Smith, C. Bør menneskerettigheten styrkes i vår grunnlov? (2006). [3] Ibid., 11.

thus originated neither in a crisis,[4] nor as a continuation of the ordinary political process.[5] The reform initiative was presented to Parliament by then parliamentary president Thorbjørn Jagland of the Labor Party as one of the last things he did before being elected Secretary General of the Council of Europe in 2009. There was some internal resistance to this proposal in Labor, notably from then Prime Minster Jens Stoltenberg (since 2014 the Secretary General of NATO), but a Human Rights Committee was established nevertheless. It was labeled the Lønning committee (hereinafter "the Committee"), after its leader MP Lønning, of the Conservative Party, and had members from most political parties, as well as one law professor and one Supreme Court justice. The Committee members presented their thoughts and answered questions, primarily at some legal community seminars, but there was no broad engagement of or interaction with the general public or the legal or political community. In December 2012, the Committee delivered a thorough proposal that seventeen central human rights were to be added to the Constitution: the right to free and secret elections; protection of liberty; the right to a fair trial by free and independent courts; the presumption of innocence; equality before the law; freedom of assembly; the right to privacy; freedom of movement; the principle of legality; the right of the child; the right to life; the right to marry and protection of family; the right to education; the right to work; the right to a healthy environment; the rights of the Sami people; the right to participate in cultural activities and the right to health. Of these, the right to work, the right to a healthy environment and the rights of the Sami people were already protected, but it was proposed that they be reformulated.

In addition to the enumerated rights, the Committee proposed a reformulation of the already existing general human rights provision in § 110 c,[6] with the aim of continuing it, but possibly underlining its importance to the interpretation of human rights. The Committee discussed whether to add to the formulation to "respect and ensure human rights" the words "as enshrined in this Constitution and in human right treaties to which Norway is a party." It ended up not proceeding with this, however, as it could "make uncertain whether also the material content of the provision is changed, even though this Committee report makes clear that the alteration is meant but as an underlining of existing legal doctrine."[7] When Parliament proposed the new § 110 c, it did so by endorsing the Committee's recommended formulation – but alongside four other formulations, one of which contained the addition

[4] Elster, *Forces and mechanisms in the constitution-making process* (1995).
[5] Ginsburg, et al., *Does the process of constitution-making matter?* (2009). [6] See 6
[7] Dokument 16 (2011–2012), 66.

rejected by the Committee. The proposal, furthered by representatives from almost all the political parties, did not give any reason for the alternative formulations proposed.[8]

As pointed out earlier, the Committee made a central distinction between rights directly actionable, and rights meant to function more as guidelines for legal interpretations in ways heeding the right in question, but without making them directly actionable. While actions could be brought also under the latter category, they were meant to function in a way the realization of which left more discretion to the legislator: These rights had "a core substance that may be subject to judicial review, even though the main function of the provision is as a value and a political guideline."[9] Courts were expected to "grant the legislature a wide margin of discretion in deciding what structures should be established to ensure the[se] rights."[10]

This distinction was explicated by formulating the rights provisions differently. The typical formulation signaling directly actionable rights was directed toward the citizen ("Everyone has the right to . . ."; "No one may be subject to . . . "),[11] whereas the other category was formulated as a state responsibility ("The authorities of the state shall ensure/create conditions . . ."). One Committee member dissented regarding some of the rights not directly actionable, holding only the civil and political rights suitable for constitutionalization.[12] Another member dissented over part of the proposed protection of family life, disagreeing with a formulation that the family is a fundamental societal institution.[13]

In line with the Norwegian tradition of formulating constitutional provisions in a way tending to be quite succinct, the Committee chose to propose the rights as rights, and to single out the requirements for interfering into the rights as a separate provision, rather than as a second paragraph in all the rights provisions themselves.[14] There were two main reasons for this: to have the requirements for interference be explicit for the people to read in the Constitution, and to avoid burdening the text with many repetitions.[15] The proposed provision required that interferences into the constitutional rights must be founded in law, respect the core of the rights in question, and be proportionate and necessary to ensure common interests or others' human rights.[16] In addition to this, the Committee proposed a provision constitutionalizing the requirements

[8] Dokument 12:30 (2011–2012) [9] Dokument 16 (2011–2012), 62 [10] Ibid., 60.

[11] See i.a. §§ 108, 109, paras 2, 110, 112, para. 3.

[12] Committee member Hagen (right-wing Progress Party), Dokument 16 (2011–2012), 11.4.2.

[13] Committee member Nordheim-Larsen (Labor) Dokument 16 (2011–2012), 31.5.6

[14] Such as i.a. in the second paragraphs of the ECHR art. 8–11.

[15] Dokument 16 (2011–2012), 72ff. [16] Ibid.

for derogation from the Constitution inspired by the derogation provisions in ECHR art. 15 and ICCPR art. 4: That in cases of a war or other public emergency threatening the life of the nation, the derogation may take place by measures strictly required by the exigencies of the situation that are also in compliance with the state's obligations under international law.[17]

Finally, the Committee proposed constitutionalizing the customary law of judicial review. It cites three reasons for this. First, as the central motive for the reform is to strengthen the constitutional protection of human rights, and as judicial review is central to actual effectuation of the rights proposed, this spoke for constitutionalization of review. Second, that other customary law traditions formerly existing only outside the text of the constitution had recently been amended, notably parliamentarism (established in the 1880s, constitutionalized in 2007). And third, that writing judicial review into the Constitution would expose the existence of this institution in a way accessible and foreseeable to the public.[18]

Fundamental rights were, until the reform, protected and adjudicated under conventions through the 1999 Human Rights Act. One purpose of the 2014 reform was to "bring rights back home" – to strengthen the position of human rights in the Norwegian system, and to expose what was already seen to be a central basis for Norwegian democracy and rule of law by placing it in the written constitution. This served the second main reform goal: to have as much of what was the actual, Norwegian legal and political fundamentals be written in the Constitution.[19] The customary law-based parliamentarism from the 1880s had, for the same reason, been amended to the written Constitution in 2007. The third goal, one increasingly emphasized during the later part of the reform process, was a pedagogical one: to make constitutional law as popularly accessible as possibly. To this end, the rights reform was supplied with a general language reform of the entire constitution, upgrading the increasingly complicated attempts at keeping its original archaic Norwegian to the modern variety spoken and understood today.

Formally, constitutional amendment proposals must be presented by members of Parliament. As the text of proposed constitutional amendments cannot be altered following the intermediary election mandated by the Constitution § 112/121, the proposals were presented in many different formulations. The proposed amendments were hardly central in the 2013 election. They

[17] Ibid., ch. 16. [18] Ibid., 14.4.2.

[19] As was noted, Norway protected about the same amount of constitutional rights as did most modern, Western countries. Formally, however, the Norwegian Constitution lagged far behind modern constitutional protection standards. See i.a. Ginsburg, The virtues of evolution in an age of revolution: Norway's enduring constitution in comparative perspective (2014).

were not mentioned in the various party programs, and the media showed little interest in them. Gearing up to the May 2014 constitutional anniversary, however, political and public awareness of the proposed reform awakened, and discussion began, both formally in the Parliament preparatory committee and, gradually, in the media. But it was only during spring 2014 that these debates gained any force. The reform commission proposal was endorsed by most political parties before the 2013 election. Due to the predicted possible disagreement on whether all economic, social and cultural rights were "true" human rights on a par with the civil and political ones, the rights were split into two proposals, furthering the different types of rights respectively.[20]

Both proposals were, however, supported by representatives for almost all parties. While furthering the spirit of consensus, this procedure blurred the possibility for real popular input in the election (not that the constitutional amendments were what motivated most people's votes, but still – which parties really supported what rights?). To those interested, which parties supported what rights could possibly be inferred by looking to traditional party positions. Historically, as we have seen, these positions have roughly been that the Conservative Party has believed in courts and the rule of law against majority regulations; the Agrarian Center Party value conservatism, including reluctance to change the Constitution; and the Labor Party, the belief in a political majority regulation state unhindered by the Constitution and courts. During the reform process, in the period after the 2013 election, however, these parties took rather unpredictable stances on certain issues: The traditionally constitution-conserving Agrarian Center Party wanted to soften up the most fundamental judicial safeguard from 1814, the ban on retroactive criminal laws, in order to facilitate prosecuting war criminals retroactively following the *War Crime* case. The traditional rule-of-law Conservative Party, surprisingly, in 2014 was skeptical not only of the noncivil and political rights amendments, but also reluctant to constitutionalize judicial review. And Labor, a party historically little impressed with constitutional limits to majority rule – and particularly when such limits were enforced by courts – stood out as the primary constitutional driving force as regarded both the totality of the proposed rights reform and the constiutionalization of review.

The parties reached agreements on almost all the proposed civil and political rights provisions (minus the right to marriage and family life), and simplified two of the six economic, social and cultural rights ones. The right-wing Progress Party voted against all the latter, whereas the otherwise skeptical Conservative Party ended up supporting the right to education.

[20] Dokument 12:30 (2011–2012), Dokument 12:31 (2011–2012).

Socioeconomic rights were subject to substantial debate in Parliament. What ended up being amended to the Constitution were the rights to education (§ 109), to work (§ 110), to a healthy environment (§ 112) and of the Sami people (§ 108), whereas the right to participate in cultural activities (§ 107) and the right to health (§ 111) were not.

The civil and political rights unanimously accepted in May 2014 were the right to free and secret elections (§ 49), protection of liberty (§ 94), the right to a fair trial by free and independent courts (§ 95), the presumption of innocence (§ 96, 2), equality before the law (§ 98), freedom of assembly (§ 101), the right to privacy (§ 102), freedom of movement (§ 106) and the principle of legality (§ 113). Most of § 104, protecting the right of the child, was also confirmed. Due to the question of abortion, the right to life (§ 93) was subject to further debate, but was confirmed in a modified version from that which the Lønning committee had proposed. The right to marry and protection of family (§ 103), however, was not confirmed, as the Conservative and Liberal parties opposed a formulation that the family was a fundamental societal structure, and as the Conservatives were opposed to "mixing symbolic goals and concrete rules" in the same provision.[21]

In the parliamentary Constitution Committee, the new § 110 c (which ended up as a new § 92) was subject to substantial debate. The majority in the parliamentary Constitution Committee preferred the formulation with the addition that the Lønning Committee had warned against. The whole committee stated it wanted § 92 to be "a continuation of § 110 c." The majority, who wanted the addition, said that the addition – the reference to the international conventions binding on Norway – "would not alter today's legal situation."[22] A minority (Conservatives and the Green Party) objected to this. They found the reference to "incorporated human rights conventions binding on Norway" unfortunate, as it might "lead to the question of whether new conventions … immediately will obtain constitutional rank from the moment they become binding on Norway" and pointed out that any addition to the Constitution should follow the amendment procedures of § 112 (§ 121).[23] The minority consequently voted for the alternative without this reference, as it was the one which signaled that "the only human rights norms with constitutional rank are those expressed in the Constitution itself."[24] In line with the majority vote, § 92 came to be amended thus: "The authorities of the State shall respect and ensure human rights as they are expressed in this Constitution and in the treaties concerning human rights that are binding for Norway."

[21] Innst.183 S (2013–2014), 4. [22] Innst. 186 S (2013–2014), 22. [23] Ibid. [24] Ibid.

Some of the proposed provisions were postponed for later debate. One was the provision containing the requirements for lawful interference into the rights about to be constitutionalized. The other was the proposal to codify judicial review. Both postponements were done out of the parliamentary Constitutional Committee's "respect for the conflicting opinions furthered in the public debate" on what the implications of constitutionalization would be.[25]

9.2 JUDICIAL REVIEW CONSTITUTIONALIZATION

The "conflicting opinions" upon which Parliament decided to postpone the proposed review amendment refers to what became a rather intense public debate particularly among legal academics and practitioners. It was about the reform in general, about the differences between the two groups of rights and also about the more precise formulation of the interference and review provisions. In the months leading up to the May 17 "birthday" of the Constitution, before which the reform was to be voted over, debate intensified. It peaked in April 2014, with some forty articles, letters and op-eds about the otherwise little debated Constitution.

The incoming Attorney General for civil affairs, Fredrik Sejersted, argued that Parliament should write into the preparatory works precisely how it wanted the courts to exercise judicial review and to understand the interference provision,[26] a view supported by editor Bjørgulv Braanen in the radical newspaper *Klassekampen* ("Class struggle") the following day, and then repeated by Sejersted a week thereafter.[27] Law professor Eivind Smith was interviewed by the same paper some days later, and said that with the proposed formulation – "a technical blunder" – constitutionalizing review would potentially leave Parliament to abdicate its decisive power over the Constitution to the ECtHR.[28]

Political science professor Hege Skjeie (the dissenting voice in the 2003 Power Study) asserted that personal disagreement between two central MPs in the Parliamentary constitution committee, Martin Kolberg (Labor) and Michael Tetzschner (Conservative), was the real reason why there was now chaos in the run-up to the reform.[29]

25 Innst. 186 S (2013–2014), 2.1.13., Innst. 187 S (2013–2014), 2.10.

26 *Klassekampen*, April 1, 2014. I argued against this, pointing to the democratic aim of the amendment provision barring any changes in the proposals from before to after the election, *Klassekampen*, April 5, 2014.

27 *Klassekampen*, April 8, 2014.

28 *Klassekampen*, April 4, 2014.

29 *Dagens Næringsliv*, April 26, 2014.

Arne Fliflet, the Parliamentary Ombudsman from 1990 to 2014, surprised many by arguing against the entire parliamentary reform; it should, in his view, be further elaborated and not effectuated only because of the bicentennial. Among his many critical arguments, he also cautioned that the proposed review amendment was imprecise and should be reformulated.[30]

Professor Inge Lorange Backer, former head of the Ministry of Justice legal department (1995–2008), warned against the reform in its entirety and pointed to several interpretational queries that could arise from it, among them some concerning the proposed interference provision. He held that the belief that constitutionalization of human rights was necessary for their protection signaled a fundamental lack of confidence in Parliament.[31] Paal W. Lorentzen, lawyer and member of the Lønning Committee, expressed astonishment that the parliamentary Ombudsman was arguing against a parliamentary reform ensuring constitutional protection for human rights.[32]

Following the lack of support of the Conservative and Agrarian Centre Party, discussions about this provision were taken up again in late fall of 2014. Some media comments discussed the question of constitutionalizing review during spring and fall of 2014, and the Constitution Committee also held a hearing concerning this question. The issues debated were for and against a codification, and whether it would mainly lead to a continuation of the already existing review doctrines (as was the explicit purpose of the Lønning committee) or change them in any way. The coming Attorney General for Civil Affairs, Fredrik Sejersted, argued in the media and the parliamentary hearing that if the provisions were to be voted in, Parliament should clarify how it wished review doctrines to be practiced in the preparatory works. Representative for the Bar Association, Frode Elgsem, underlined that such a procedure would only serve to give the Attorney General legal litigation arguments for coming review cases against the state. Parliament was also warned by legal commentators that preparatory work clarifications going beyond a normal understanding of the proposed amendment text could also represent a circumvention of the amendment procedures in Constitution § 112/121. Following it, the text of proposed amendments cannot be altered by the Parliament after the intermediate election. "Changes" made through the preparatory works would have even less procedural democratic input legitimacy.[33]

The parliamentary Constitution Committee worked on this and other constitutional questions during spring 2015. The Conservatives shifted position and ended up supporting the review provision, in spite of earlier

30 *Aftenposten*, April 28, 2014 31 *Klassekampen*, April 29, 2014 32 *Dagbladet*, May 3, 2014
33 *Klassekampen*, April 25, 2014

resistance, whereas the Agrarian Center Party remained opposed to it. Parliament ended up voting for the constiutionalization of review in June 2015, just in time for that year's Supreme Court bicentennial. With the 2015 constitutionalization of review, based on a vote of 150 to 17, the Norwegian parliament confirmed broad political support for human rights as made effective by judicial review. It also gave its highest formal approval to this central tenet of the constitutional nature of Norwegian democracy.

9.3 CONSTITUTIONAL REVITALIZATION

Measured by the way the Supreme Court uses the Constitution, the reform has already led to a strengthening of the constitutional rights protection in line with the reform mandate. As with the increased *mentioning* of the Constitution as recalled in Section 8.1, the *use* of constitutional provisions in the Supreme Court's reasoning has steadily risen.[34] The average number of such cases per year was 4.4 in the 1990s (0.6 percent of the total caseload) and 5.9 in the 2000s (1.2 percent of the total). In 2010–2016, the average was 8.6 cases using the Constitution per year, with the years 2015 and 2016 as top years, at 13 and 20 cases respectively.

Even with this marked increase in the *mentioning* and *use* of the Constitution, cases disregarding or substantially reinterpreting legislative acts so far seem to have remained much the same. With an exception for 2014, which saw two cases of constitutional reinterpretative influence, 2015 and 2016 are back to the average number of such cases in the period 2000–2017, of one to two per year. While this kind of review case so far seems little fueled by the reform, the Supreme Court has decided several cases of interest when it comes to reflecting upon the inherent constitutional tension between the political and judicial branches. An interesting tendency is how the Court's reasoning has gone from using solely or primarily international bases for its human rights references even in cases where such bases had relevant Constitutional counterparts (such as in § 100), to greater use of constitutional provisions. This, and some other changes in methodological approach, merit interest. They clarify questions previously unanswered or undertheorized – and they prompt discussion of constitutional law questions in the political and legal community.

The first case with a clear discussion of a reform amendment was decided in November 2014. The case marked a tendency that seems to be the start of

34 Search in database "Lovdata," Supreme Court civil and criminal cases, reasoned decisions from chamber and appeals committee for all years, and "grunnlov*" in the free term search. "Substantial reinterpretation" refers to cases where the influence of a constitutional provision visibly leads the court to interpret a statute differently.

a gradual "reconstitutionalizing" shift in legal–methodological strategy under the dual review of the Constitution and the ECHR. It also clarifies the legal relevance of practice under overlapping ECHR provisions in constitutional interpretation, and it answers the question of what to do with absolute constitutional rights in the absence of the nonamended provision on rights interference. The case concerned a 2013 amendment to the Criminal Procedure Act (1981) directing that additional information (surplus material) from otherwise legal police wire-tapping should be admissible as evidence. The surplus material in the case at hand should, under the rules of that time, have been deleted in 2011, when the indictment was filed. The evidence sought used thus was inadmissible, and the police storing of the surplus data in contradiction to the right to privacy under ECHR art. 8. The continued use of the material following May 2014 constituted a breach also of the Constitution §§ 102 and 113 (the principle of legality).[35] The case is notable in several respects.

First, the way justice Bårdsen for the majority makes use of the Constitution is methodologically opposite to that used in traditional, Norwegian constitutional cases. Before the 2014 reform, even cases concerning constitutional questions were normally treated as constitutionally "upside-down": Assessments of relevant Constutional provisions would usually be undertaken only *after* interpretation of the statutory regulation in question (if at all), to establish whether some additional norm (the *lex superior* Constitution) would lead to a differing interpretative result than what followed from the regulation, its preparatory work and legal precedence. In this case, however, the Supreme Court reasoning very much starts in the Constitution: not only in the protection of privacy as ensured by § 102 – it opens instead by pointing to the § 113 constitutional demand for a legal basis. Reciting the requirement that interferences into peoples' integrity require a foundation in law, the reasoning points to how the significance of such a basis as a requirement for the exercise of popular majority power was emphasized as a central rule-of-law precondition in the 2014 reform preparations. It goes on to reiterate that this requirement ensures equal treatment under the law in § 98 and that the formal procedure for enacting laws in § 75 supports the "democratic idea behind placing the formal enactment competence in a popularly elected parliament, namely that the executive branch may not exercise its public authority to a greater extent than what the legislative has authorized through its legal acts."[36]

Second, when deciding on the question of the defendant's protected right to privacy, the Court starts its dual review in the Constitution § 102 before

[35] Rt. 2014 s. 1105. [36] Ibid., para. 26.

moving on to the interpretation of the ECHR art. 8 and the ICCPR art. 17. The reference to § 102 is not just a "courtesy visit," like then Chief Justice Schei called the use of the Constitution in dual review cases before the reform;[37] instead, it first cites the entire text of the provision, then reiterates how the Lønning Committee proposed it as a more extensive formulation covering also the "systematic collection, retention and use of personal data" and how the Parliamentary Constitution Committee chose a briefer formulation, but still stressed just this point in its preparatory work as a directive guideline for "how § 102 shall be read," before underlining that such interferences into peoples' privacy must also be prescribed by law. The Court states that this is how it, too, interprets § 102, adding that "whether a law prescribing the interference into someones' privacy, family life, home, communication or personal integrity is constitutional under § 102 also depends on it pursuing a legitimate aim and is proportionate."[38] Having thus effectively read into the Constitution the nonamended interference provision, and solved the question of what to with the seeming absolute 2014 rights, he finds support for this interpretation in how such requirements for interference also follow from ECHR art. 8 and ICCPR art. 17.

Only after this does he discuss whether data storage in and of itself constitutes an interference. This is established by citing three ECtHR cases stipulating that the mere storing of such data amounts to an interference, and how the preparatory works for the amendment in question to the Criminal Procedure Act also mention such storing as an interference.

Establishing what the prescribed-by-law requirement of the Constitution and the ECHR more precisely entails – that it must be accessible; as precise as possible; contain guarantees as pertain to the form of storage and use of the material; that the person whose data is stored must have possible access to or information about the material – he cites central ECtHR case law under ECHR art. 8.[39] The majority concludes that read in light of these constitutional requirements, the wire-tapped data in question should have been eradicated, and was not admissible evidence. The minority did not explicitly discuss § 102 of the Constitution, and did not find the legality requirement to be as strict as the majority. It would have allowed the evidence.

A few months later, in January 2015, the Court decided a case in which the new rights of the child provision led to invalidation of an administrative deportation decision.[40] The immigration authorities decided that a Kenyan woman illegally living in Norway should be deported. It denied her application to stay on the basis of family reunification with her five-year-old daughter,

[37] See Section 7.2.5. [38] Rt. 2014 s. 1105, para. 28. [39] Ibid., para. 30. [40] Rt. 2015 s. 93

a Norwegian citizen, for whom she was a lone parent. Deporting the woman would mean that the daughter would be barred from the safe childhood and upbringing in Norway that she, as a Norwegian citizen, had rights to under the Norwegian Childrens Act, under the Convention on the Rights of the Child and under the new § 104 on children's rights in the Constitution.

The Supreme Court unanimously concluded that deportation of the woman would be a disproportionate interference into her and her daughter's family life as protected by the Constitution § 102, as it had to be read considering § 104 and art. 3 of the Convention on the Rights of the Child ensuring decisions emphasizing what is in the best interest of the child.

In its assessment of the Constitution §§ 102 and 104, the Court explicitly stated that they are to be interpreted in light of ECHR art. 8 and the Convention on the Rights of the Child article 3, and convention practice under these provisions.[41] While solidifying the 2014 decision on this point, the case went on to explain that it is "the Supreme Court – not the international convention organs – that have the responsibility to interpret, clarify and develop the human rights enshrined in the Constitution." In addition to hedging the Constitution from development in the international convention organs alone, this formula entrenches the position of the Supreme Court: while not formally a "constitutional court," it is indeed a court functioning constitutionally with the effect of ultimately deciding upon questions of constitutional interpretation, even when such interpretation runs counter to that of the other branches.[42]

Three 2016 cases are also worth mentioning, although the first is not directly connected to the 2014 reform. It deals with the dual review of the Constitution § 105, which is not new, and the ECHR Protocol 1, article 1 – a double protection that has led to a number of court cases following a particular, Norwegian property regulation. Since around 2000, a reregulation of the Norwegian *ground lease* arrangement has created numerous controversies: politically, in Norwegian courts and in the ECtHR.[43] In the post-WWII era, limited resources made ground lease arrangements attractive. Property owners could expediently obtain a steady income from their land without making investments or selling it, and nonproperty owners could lease land at affordable prices. There exist some 300,000 ground lease contracts, most which are for private homes.[44] Prior to 1976, such agreements were governed by

[41] Ibid. para. 57. This view has later been underlined by the Court in plenary, HR-2016-2554-P.
[42] See Bårdsen, *The Nordic Supreme Courts as constitutional courts*, (2015).
[43] Case *of Lindheim and others* v. *Norway*, 13221/08.
[44] Proposal No. 41 to the *Odelsting* (2003–2004), p. 11.

contracts, often concluded for a period of 99 years and with clauses giving the lessee a right to extension upon expiry. A new Ground Lease Act granted all lessees the right to claim extension of their lease on the same conditions as previously and without limitation in time. With real estate prices soaring in the 1980s, many lessors used the opportunity to demand redemption under the law, which resulted in lessees being put in a difficult financial position. Because of the dramatic increase in pressure on real estate prices, the legislator thought it necessary to intervene to protect lessees' interests. The level of possible rent increases was regulated so that they could only reflect general inflation, not the rising cost of land, and by allowing the lessee a right to extension upon expiry under unaltered conditions.[45] The Supreme Court in Plenary upheld this right of extension in a decision from 2007,[46] while in *Lindheim* v. *Norway* the ECtHR found it to interfere unduly with the right of property under Protocol 1 no. 1 in 2012.[47] Parliament altered the Act in 2015.[48]

The first 2016 Grand Chamber case of interest dealt with a concrete estimation of redemption price.[49] What sets it out is how it is based on a reasoning that differs substantially from that of the 2007 Supreme Court decision: Where the ECtHR found the reasoning in the 2007 case to fall short of demonstrating that the Supreme Court had properly understood and balanced the conflicting interest consistent with ECtHR case law criteria, this 2016 case is reasoned in a way both properly discussing the redemption regulation under the constitution and the ECtHR criteria, and explaining how Parliament has reasoned before striking the balance as regulated.

The second case of interest, *Holship*, is the only plenary case of 2016. In it the Supreme Court clarified how the new § 110 c of the Constitution, § 92, was to be understood. It concerned the Norwegian Transport Workers Union aiming to boycott the Danish-owned company Holship Norge AS, to prevent Holship from using its own stevedores to load ships in a Norwegian port.[50] The Union wanted to force Holship into signing a Norwegian collective agreement assuring registered stevedores preferential rights. The Supreme Court concluded on dissent (10–7) that the boycott ran counter to the right of establishment under the EEA Agreement Article 31, emphasizing also an interpretation obtained from the EFTA Court on the matter. It further held that the primary object of the boycott was to prevent Holship from establishing itself in the loading and unloading business at the Port of Drammen. In balancing the right to boycott under the Norwegian Boycott Act, as seen

45 The Ground Lease Act (1996) § 33. 46 HR-2007-1594-P
47 Case of *Lindheim and others* v. *Norway*, 13221/08. 48 Act 2015-06-19-63.
49 HR-2016-304-S 50 HR-2016-2554-P

in light of the unincorporated rights following from The International Labour Organization (ILO) Conventions nos. 87, 98 and 137, the revised European Social Charter[51] and the EEA right to establishment, the latter prevailed.

While divided on the material question of the case, the Court held *en banc* that § 92 was a continuation of § 110 c, and did not entail either an incorporation of nonincorporated conventions, or an "upgrading" of the protection under such conventions to the legal hierarchical constitutional level. The Court stated the formulation of the actual provision was "unclear," and that the contradictory statements from the parliamentary Constitution Committee added to the confusion. It held, however, that the interpretative alternative of reading § 92 as incorporating nonconstitutionalized human rights was entirely inconsistent with the collective view of the constitution committee that § 92 was not meant to alter the existing legal situation. It would also obviate the need both for the Human Rights Act of 1999 and the freshly amended 2014 rights provisions in the Constitution. Consequently, it concluded that regardless of the wording and the confusion created by the *travaux preparatiores*, rights not constitutionalized remained of the same hierarchical (nonconstitutional) status as before, but that § 92 mandated courts and other public authorities to enforce human rights at the level on which they have been taken into Norwegian law.[52]

The principle thus established was one central basis in the third case decided four days later,[53] on what influence the Convention on the Rights of Persons with Disabilities (CRPD) – a convention binding on Norway, but not incorporated into Norwegian law – should have in a case concerning the legal capacity of a mentally disabled patient. Under the Guardianship Act (2010) § 22 (2),[54] the legal capacity of mentally disabled patients may be lifted in economic matters. Under CRPD article 12, however, persons with disabilities retain their legal capacity in all areas. Upon the ratification of the CRPD, Norway reserved the right to lift the legal capacity of patients where such a measure is "necessary as a last resort and subject to control mechanisms."[55] The CRPD Committee does, however, interpret the CRPD art. 12 in a stricter way, potentially barring provisions such as the Guardianship Act § 22.[56] Citing

[51] Convention concerning Freedom of Association and Protection of the Right to Organise (Entry into force: July 4, 1950); Convention concerning the Application of the Principles of the Right to Organise and to Bargain Collectively (Entry into force July 18, 1951); Convention concerning the Social Repercussions of New Methods of Cargo Handling in Docks (Entry into force July24, 1975), ETS No.163.

[52] HR-2016-2554-P, 70.

[53] HR-2016-2591-A.

[54] LOV-2010-03-26-9, "the Guardianship Act (2010)."

[55] Prop.106 S (2011–2012), 15.

[56] General Comment No. 1 (2014) [GC-2014-1-CRPD] part III, "Obligations of States Parties," section 28.

Holship as having decided § 92 was not a provision leading to the incorporation of nonincorporated convention rights, and the doctrine of restraint where Parliament has enacted a Norwegian rule even after assessing a potentially conflicting treaty provision, the Supreme Court held that the Guardianship Act § 22 would prevail even though it might be in conflict with CRPD article 12.

9.4 DUAL REVIEW CONSTITUTIONALIZED

A number of questions arise over the constitutional human rights reform of 2014, and of what reflections upon judicial review and constitutionalism it contributes to.

First, the way in which the constitutional amendments came about signals scant interest in the reality behind the ideals of the democratic input into constitutional questions that judicial review may be seen to threaten. It also seems to reflect how, to the popularly elected, the Constitution still has more of a symbolic than an actual political importance.

Second, to the substance of the amendments, questions arise as to how the reform may, has and will affect Norwegian judicial review of those rights that overlap, and hence may be dually protected, under international conventions and the Constitution. What ideals of institutional dialogue and adherence to democratic signals and what ideals of professional judicial legitimacy are in play here?

Finally, is there any judicial review legitimacy left to debate when a broad majority of Parliament has voted to codify it as a written part of the Constitution?

With regard to the question of legitimacy ideals furthered and challenged by the reform, contrary to the countermajoritarian difficulty represented by judicial review, the reform represents a majoritarian path to rights protection – indeed, a supermajoritarian one. As such, it may be a reform furthering many of the ideals sought promoted by a constitutional democracy. It seems to advance at least procedural, democratic input by following the amendment procedure in § 112/121, opening for electorate participation in the constitutionalization of rights. Additionally, the September 2012 deadline for a proposal based on a mandate given by Parliament in 2009, seen together with the intermediary election in 2013, provided ample time and opportunity for popular deliberation over the proposed amendments. The actual enactment of the reform ensured popular procedural majoritarianism by requiring two-thirds of the vote in Parliament.

But did reform heed these ideals in practice? When considering the input to the constitutional reform, while formally correct, there was little debate over, or mention of, the proposed constitutional amendments in the time leading up to the 2013 parliamentary election. Little was done from representatives in Parliament and by the political parties to have the constitutional questions discussed. Satisfying ideals of deliberative, democratic input requires actual debate and deliberation, not merely the possibility for deliberation. While the procedure for constitutional amendment as set out in § 112/121 was followed (the proposal presented before an election for possible adoption by the next Parliament), the ideals sought ensured by this procedure – to give the people the chance to vote based on what alterations the parties do or do not support – was not. The proposals of substantial alterations – the one containing civil and political rights,[57] as well as the one containing social, economic and cultural rights[58]– were put forth by a coalition of parties across the political spectrum, making it seem as if both proposals had broad political support. There were, however, no substantial explications of the party position toward the constitutional proposals in *any* of the political programs outlining the political goals of the various parties in the 2013 election. Not even the parties behind the proposed alterations mentioned the alternative amendments in their programs. As it turned out, however, as late as March 2014, less than two months before the reform enactment, the major parties disagreed on several of the central proposed amendments – even those proposed by the very same parties in 2013.[59]

It is fair to assume that few constituents cast their vote based solely on what constitutional amendment a party supports or not. From a *procedural democratic* perspective, however, this lack of information is troubling. It makes impossible any procedural popular input to the proposed amendments in a way following the purpose and objective of § 112/121. It is also unsatisfactory from a *deliberative* perspective in that the parties and the media do not invite and initiate debate on these questions, and the people get little chance to do so too, based on the lack of information about what the various party positions on them are. Considering that arguments of deficient procedural and democratic input are precisely central to discussions of judicial review legitimacy, the failure to respect these ideals before a constitutional amendment – the potentially democratic way to ensure rights protection – seems unfortunate.

57 Dokument 12:30 (2011–2012).

58 Dokument 12:31 (2011–2012). As was the one concerning § 97, Dokument 12:36 (2011–2012).

59 Based on impressions at the Official Hearing in the Committee on Constitutional affairs on February 28, a Civita Breakfast meeting on March 5 and a PluriCourts seminar at Litteraturhuset on March 10, the position signalled is that the major party representatives (Labor and Conservative) were divided on many of the central proposals, hereunder with which human rights to amend the Constitution.

With regard to the second question of substantial adjudication, three scenarios could be envisioned as to how courts could potentially approach the question of dual review. They could choose to use only the Constitution, now that all or most rights already protected by the ECHR or other international instruments are also in the Constitution. Or they could disregard the Constitution entirely, continuing to use only the international bases for review, almost as they did under the dual protection of the "new" constitutional § 100 and the ECHR art. 10. Or they could seek to use the two legal norm bases in combination. The first scenario was not viable. As Norway is bound also by agreements to ensure rights "the international way," disregarding i.a. the ECHR would be disloyal and impractical because it could easily lead to breaches of these rights, as interpreted by the ECtHR. The second scenario is also implausible. While possibly upholding some legal *status quo* ideals by allowing legal interpretation and constitutional adjudication to continue as it did prior to the 2014 reform, disregarding freshly amended constitutional provisions supported by two-thirds of Parliament fundamentally challenges ideals of democratic input. This leaves the third approach: to find some way to combine the two. And this is just what the Supreme Court has done.

Combining the two sets of norms could be done by interpreting the two bases separately and finding some way to choose which of the conclusions should prevail. This could lead to two parallel, potentially different systems of rights protection, possibly in conflict with one another. Such a development would pose no challenge where the Constitution better protected individual rights than did the ECHR – it follows from ECHR art. 53 that the ECHR shall not be construed to limit rights already protected by member states. If the ECHR provided better rights protection, however, this way of combining the two would potentially actualize the challenges of either scenario one or scenario two above: If relying on the Constitution, even if it were to provide less rights protection than the ECHR, one would likely at some point reach a legal conclusion in breach of the ECHR. If instead relying on the ECHR, one would implicitly acknowledge that the ECHR provided better protection than the Constitution. That again, would imply that the 2014 rights reform had failed its mandate of strengthening human rights protection in Norway by constitutionalizing them.[60]

Another way of combining the two would be to interpret them jointly, so that the constitutional provisions were understood in light of the ECHR provisions. This is the solution suggested by the Committee report,[61] but

60 Dokument 16 (2011–2012), 11. 61 Dok 16 (2011–2012), 48.

one that was debated in legal theory prior to the reform.[62] No constitutional provision regulating this question existed before the reform, nor is it proposed in the reform. Nor was there any clear Supreme Court precedent: case law in this field indicated that international sources could be relevant, but not mandatory for constitutional interpretation.[63]

In practice, this interpretational question was one of the first to be solved by the Supreme Court.

Loyally adhering to the comments of the Human Rights Committee and the parliamentary Constitution Committee preparing the human rights amendments, in the two first cases it decided after the reform enactment, [64] held that Norwegian lawyers and courts are to interpret the constitution *in light of* its international convention counterparts.[65]

Two modifications to this rule important to the balance between the legislative and the national and international judiciary have also been stated: When assessing international precedent, the weight attached to it may vary according to whether the precedent existed prior to the 2014 reform, or came about after its enactment.[66] The Court also underlined that "According to our Constitution it is the Supreme Court, not international adjudicators that are responsible for interpreting, clarifying and developing the human rights provisions in the Norwegian constitution,"[67] thus hedging against the development of constitutional development by international organs, and reaffirming the decisive position of the Supreme Court in constitutional matters.

This shows how the 2014 reform leads the Court to a significantly different approach than the path taken in the comparable "dual review" situation of § 100, as discussed in Chapter 7, where a modernized constitutional amendment of a human right overlaps with a right protected by the ECHR. In the unclear waters of dual review prior to the 2014 reform, Supreme Court case law varied between all three scenarios listed.[68] Considering the factors

[62] Based on somewhat differing reasoning i.a. Smith, *Konstitusjonelt demokrati* (2012), 381, Stub, Om forbudet mot husinkvisisjoner i Grunnloven § 102 (2009), 100, and Boe, *Rettskildelære under debatt* (2012), 400ff. argue that the rights provisions of the Constitution should be interpreted autonomously, whereas Eggen, Ytringsfrihet (2002), 102, Stavang, *Parlamentarisme og folkestyre* (2002), 18, Fauchald, Forfatning og miljøvern – en analyse av Grunnloven § 110 B (2007), Strand, Forholdet mellom den norske Grunnlovens menneskerettigheter, de internasjonale menneskerettighetskonvensjonene og ordinær lovgivning (2007), Kierulf, Er internasjonale menneskerettigheter en relevant rettskilde ved grunnlovstolking? (2011), and Dokument 16 (2011–2012), 15.4 argue they should be interpreted in light of corresponding international rights, to the extent case law under the latter is comparable and relevant to the case at hand.

[63] Kierulf, Innenfra og utenfra – Grunnloven og menneskerettighetene (2013).

[64] Rt. 2014 s. 1105, Rt. 2015 s. 93. [65] See Rt. 2014 s. 1045, Rt. 2014 s. 1105, Rt. 2014 s. 1292.

[66] Rt. 2015 s. 93 [67] Ibid.

[68] Kierulf, Hvilken rolle spiller Grunnloven § 100 i Høyesteretts ytringsfrihetspraksis? (2012).

relevant for legal assessment, the situation as concerns the 2014 amendments is different from that of the 2004 § 100 amendment only by the explicit mandate in the *travaux préparatoires* that the new rights be interpreted in light of their international counterparts. Another explanatory factor for the shift is the substantial *informal* focus on the Constitution in the period leading up to 2014. Numerous events and increased awareness about both the Constitution and the possibility of having it amended with a bill of rights due to the Constitution's 200-year anniversary. Together with the scope, volume and political debates over the possible 2014 reform, this may have served to bring about if not a constitutional moment,[69] then at least greater public awareness about the existence, function and relevance of the Constitution transcending debates of ordinary politics. This awareness in the broader public, legal and political professional spheres alike seems substantially more in focus as regards the renewed bill of rights than it was under previous rights-additions to the constitution. A central example of an opposite effect is the lack of public awareness towards the 2004 new § 100. This heightened awareness would make it seem more normatively and socially legitimate to use the new constitutional provisions, thereby effectuating the purpose of the constitutional reform.

Looking to the solution to the dual review question as presented by the Human Rights Committee and adopted by the Supreme Court, a process and outcome perspective may make attractive the fusion of the two bases too. The common origins of human rights, regardless of what positive legal source expresses them, as well as their common anchoring in the European "deep culture," may contradict drawing any clear distinction between convention and constitution human rights. An additional motive for viewing the ECHR as a relevant source of interpretation also on the constitutional level is ponderings over potential consequences of *not* doing so. Might not a strict dualism render the Constitution quite obsolete as a practical tool for legal decision-making? And, absent some conscious shift in the way courts use the Constitution, will this not be the case even for modernized amendments to the Constitution? Considering the substantial Constitution review legitimacy as suggested, reducing the legal constitutional role of the Norwegian Constitution in questions of rights review seems a paradoxical effect of amending it with a bill of human rights. A joint interpretation thus seems the only feasible way to restore the role of the Constitution as an actual, constitutional rights protection – to bring human rights home.

69 Ackerman, *We the people. 1, Foundations* (1993).

As mentioned in Sections 9.1 and 9.3, the Supreme Court approach to the Constitution has proven quite different in practice following the 2014 reform: both the mentioning of and the actual use of the Constitution in Supreme Court practice in the years following 2014 have surged. These surges have been criticized by commentators claiming it shows that the reform has led the Court to become more political and to exercise judicial activism.[70] If this increased use of the Constitution had led the Court to a corresponding increase in the Supreme Court setting statutes aside, in the classical, counter-majoritarian difficult way, this critique would have more bite. Looking into the 2014–2016 constitutional cases reveals, however, that it does not. While the numbers for this way of using the constitution in 2010–2013 are 4, 2, 3 and 0, in 2014 it is 3,[71] and in 2015 and 2016 it is 1 case per year.[72] It may also be noted that in all these cases review was conducted under the Constitution and the international human rights pendent to the relevant constitutional provision jointly. This suggests the "activist" consequence of using the Constitution may as well be ascribed to the international rights provisions in question. This critique does not explain why it holds the increased use of the Constitution to be more "political" than the nonuse of the new 2014 provisions would be.[73] While formally and legally not very different from the § 100 amendment, the 2014 reform has manifested itself quite differently in Norwegian constitutional culture: as an actual revitalization of national, constitutional rights, and as a statement of how the dual review situation may be considered in the time to come.

With regard to the third – and, to this study, central – question of judicial review legitimacy, formally, the democratic input legitimacy of review is increased, as there really is no stronger formal-democratic way to state that review has popular backing than through a constitutional amendment. While the formal requirements are satisfied, the actual popular input suffers from the same lack of substance for this amendment as for the rest of the reform. There really weren't any actual, popular discussions of this provision either before or during the 2013 election. What adds to the deliberative legitimacy perspective, however, is the fact that the review provision was more thoroughly discussed in the parliamentary Constitution Committee; it was even delayed by a year for this purpose.

70 See i.a. Robberstad, Mener Høyesterett undergraver demokratiet (2016); Robberstad, Viljen til å skape lov og Grunnlov (2016); Kinander, Fra tilbakeholdenhet til aktivisme – Nyere utviklingslinjer i forholdet mellom rett og politikk i Høyesterett (2016).

71 Rt. 2014 s. 1292, Rt. 2014 s. 1105, Rt. 2014 s. 238.

72 Rt. 2015 s. 39, HR-2016-2171-A

73 A point noted i.a. by Schei, Uten dekning (2016); Elgesem, Ikke dramatisk (2016); Kierulf, Lite teori om grunnlovstolking (2016); Kierulf, Grunnloven som irrelevant rettskilde (2016).

Parliament refused to take a stance on the more precise content of review: how it ought to be practiced, what should be its intensity and so on. The committee explicitly stated in the *travaux préparatoires* from spring 2015 that rather than doing this, what the amendment is meant to do is to codify review as it has been developed in practice up until then – including the 2010 review cases. This conforms with the view of the Human Rights Committee, and is as such a weighty expression of "the popular will" as regards review. Reinforcing this view is that the committee also explicitly acknowledges that the way the Supreme Court practiced review in the otherwise legally and politically debated 2010 cases is the kind of review they voted to constitutionalize.

This position has since been expressed also via a less formal channel. In a 2015 seminar on the institutional distinctiveness of the Supreme Court,[74] one of the issues discussed was the scope and intensity of judicial review. The 2010 review cases were central to the debate. When asked whether these did not show that review indeed had democratically troublesome sides too, Martin Kolberg, former party secretary in the Labor Party and leader of the parliamentary Constitutional Committee, had a surprising answer. The Labor Party's central role in the preparation of the shipping tax regulations that were later set aside on review notwithstanding, Kolberg underlined that what the Supreme Court had done in 2010 was both right and legitimate – and, in retrospect, far more legitimate than the political decision to drive the constitutionally suspicious regulations through, in spite of the majority knowledge of all possible troubles this implied. This political process was undignified, Kolberg now stated, and the Supreme Court review had been practiced just the way review legitimately should be carried out. While other aspects of review legitimacy have remained much the same in the years since 2010, its democratic input legitimacy is clearly strengthened by having review constitutionalized, both formally and deliberatively.

74 "Høyesteretts institusjonelle egenart," Oslo 12.10.2015.

10

Looking Back – and Forward

10.1 LEGITIMACY IDEALS DISENTANGLED

The constitutionalization of review in 2015 provides a solid procedural and deliberative democratic fundament for the legitimacy of review under both the Constitution and the ECHR. Discussions of review legitimacy are, however, likely to persist; disagreements over how review is practiced from case to case will continue to spark debate.

One challenge for such debates is the *input–outcome entanglement*: that what is formed as critique or praise of the institution of review is instead critique or praise of certain outcomes of review. Looking back at Minister Giske's question of what the seven foreign judges could possibly know better than the Norwegian Parliament, due to the way it was posed, the question may be understood as a critique of the very institution of review for lack of national, democratic input. Seen in light of Giske's view of political TV-advertising, however, an interpretation equally as likely is that the question was prompted by disagreement with the outcome of the particular case.[1]

While this is an understandable reaction from disappointed politicians having their politics reviewed, the input–outcome entanglement becomes problematic as a basis for institutional critique of review. Yet, the entanglement has been a formative feature in Norwegian review legitimacy debates: from voices critical of the high state official constitutional protection in the 1800s, via Skeie's 1916 legal opinion based on unfortunate outcomes in

[1] Giske was Member of Parliament when Parliament unanimously enacted the HRA in 1999. While he opened for abolishing the ECHR preference provision in HRA § 3 following his disagreement with the *TV Vest* decision (NTB, *Giske anker trolig dom om politisk TV-reklame* (2008)), he never followed up on this. His ministerial colleague, then Foreign Minister Støre, characterized Giske's saber-rattling on this point as a position from which "he departed rather quickly," see Lien, *Kaffegildet på Bislet* (2009).

Supreme Court review cases of alcohol regulation, through Eckhoff's and Seip's skepticism in the 1960s toward the political effects of review in the late 1800s, and the Attorney General's worry that review under human rights would stretch "outside what one may call fundamental values" in 1998, to some of the reactions following the *Shipping Tax* case in 2010 and the case of Maria and her Kenyan mother in 2015. What the entanglement does is to blur what ideal is at stake: Is it the lack of democratic, professional or other legitimizing input that is critique-worthy, or the outcome of it? Or a combination? If it is the outcome, is it just the result in a particular case, or all outcomes of review cases, whether they serve the property interests of 2010 shipowners, 1920s civil servants' salaries, or the radical 1850s dissenters' right to free speech?

If one finds the outcomes of review *generally* to be less desirable than those of other public decision-makers, critique of judicial review based on undesirable outcomes is relevant. If so, an outcome-focused critique may also be supported by input and process legitimacy objections. As the outcome legitimacy of review also entails judicial problem-solving in the concrete, such critiques would benefit from being part of a more comprehensive normative theory outlining how alternatives to review would better ensure both general outcome ideals and problem-solving in the concrete. If judicial review is instead criticized only when it produces outcomes in particular cases that one finds disagreeable, such outcomes are a dissatisfactory foundation on which to base critique of the institution of review. While an outcome perspective is certainly a potentially valid basis for criticizing the particular outcome in question, it is not a much more convincing argument against the institutional legitimacy of review than discontent with a parliamentary decision is a convincing argument against the institution of constitutional democracy.

An interesting illustration of the entanglement is the attempts of review abolishment from Labor and related parties in the 1920s. Opposition to judicial review was based on the reasoning that courts had no place interfering with political decisions. The attempts at abolishment of the institution of review do appear in a different light when perspectivated with Labor trust in courts when it came to the liberal government decision of reducing civil servants' wages in 1927: The countermajoritarian nature of courts suddenly was no problem; certainly, courts were competent to review the budget decisions of the popularly elected. Some of the debates following review cases obviously only take issue with the results, without aspiring to opine on the institution of judicial review, such as the right-wing Progress Party reaction to the 2010 *War Crimes* case. But, more often, they seem directed toward the very institutional legitimacy of review, such as the above-discussed question in relation to the *TV Vest* case.

One way to understand the input–outcome confusion may be to look at what *interests* are protected in those cases where judicial review leads to some interference with statutory provisions. In the earlier periods of review, the outcomes of these cases generally protected the particular constitutional privileges of high state officials, a group increasingly seen to represent a *conservative* delay to progressive, democratic societal forces. The review cases leading up to the antireview discussions before and after the 1918 *Waterfall* case, as well as the 1976 *Kløfta* case, also preserved the politically conservative (at least nonsocialist) interests of some forms of private property against more collective interests – a feature also notable in the 2010 *Shipping Tax* case. As §§ 97 and 105 have been the dominant review provisions, and with a lack of actively enforced provisions protecting weaker societal groups, this may have accentuated an interpretation of review as a politically conservative force. Combined with the inherent conservative nature of review, this may have served to strengthen the impression of review as a political rather than a legal exercise of public authority.

Interestingly, of the cases from 2010, the ones to generate debate of review legitimacy were not the most *countermajoritarian*. The review case most lacking in procedural, democratic input legitimacy was the *War Crimes* case, as the statute reviewed and rejected in it had a unanimous Parliament behind it. Yet it created relatively little popular and legal debate. The cases creating debate were the ones in which Parliament had split: the *Shipping Tax* and *OVF* cases. In these cases, review conclusions had a large minority in Parliament behind them. Underlining the input–outcome inconsistency, these cases also illustrate another connection between legitimacy ideals, namely between the normative and social ideals. That these less countermajoritarian review cases are perceived as more problematic may be seen as a consequence of their perceived lack of *professional input and procedural legitimacy*: Rather than being seen as politically undesirable but legally motivated decisions of what were initially political questions, they were seen as *politically* motivated "legal" exercise of political authority. An impression of court cases as "political" is strengthened by the correspondence between political majority/minority and judicial minority/majority. In this, the two 2010 cases resemble the *Kløfta* case, and actualize the legitimacy challenge of "US double duality" as mentioned in Section 8.4.1: the dual-natured constitutional questions corresponding to a duality in political disagreement, making judicial decisions of constitutional questions appear like playoffs over the same question that was politically decided.

A notable feature of historical Norwegian debates on judicial review is that the critics against review rarely concern themselves with review cases *not* finding statutes unconstitutional or reinterpreting them. Only where statutes are found unconstitutional is the question of review legitimacy actualized. Thus, while the particular outcomes may be subject to debate, there is little critique of the institution of review when it results in the upholding of a contested law, such as in the *Hvalolje* case in 1952, certain welfare rights cases from the 1990s,[2] or the *Lindheim* case in 2007. Correspondingly, there is little Norwegian critique of ECtHR review legitimacy in cases where the ECtHR finds *for* the Norwegian state rather than for the applicant. And if review does disregard a statute, it is criticized by those in favor of the statute, not the ones in opposition to it, as shown i.a. by Labor reactions to the ECtHR *TV Vest* decision contrasted with the positive response from the Liberal Left and the Conservative and right-wing Progress Parties. An obvious answer to this phenomenon is that as long as courts agree with the legislative majority, the case does not raise any countermajoritarian difficulty. As we have seen, however, the countermajoritarian nature of review is not the only cause of difficulty. This answer also confuses the existence of an institution of judicial review with the concrete outcomes of the practice of such review in concrete cases, while one feature central to institutional legitimacy is that legitimacy persists, even though one does not agree with all of the outcomes produced.

10.2 POLITICAL REVIEW CHALLENGES

Moving from the disentanglement of legitimacy ideals in review debates, the institutional conditions for review in the political branches could be improved. One issue pertains to government and Parliament alike – namely, the necessity of using a constitutional approach when preparing legislation that affects human rights as protected in the Constitution and in the ECHR or other human rights instruments. By constitutional approach, I mean to consider what constitutional or other rights provisions are potentially affected by the planned legislation, and to observe the requirements necessary for interfering into these rights, and adjust and justify the desired legislative provisions accordingly. Such an approach requires familiarity with both Supreme Court and ECtHR reasoning, and necessitates the explication in the *travaux préparatoires* (either in the Ministry of Justice or in the Parliamentary committees) of the legitimate aims sought to be regulated, the necessity of interfering into the right in question, and the proportionality between the legitimate aim sought to be ensured and the rights interference.

2 See Kjønstad, Er Høyesterett statsvennlig? (1999).

As is evident from some of the Norwegian ECtHR cases (and many other such cases from other member states), there seems to be an unused potential for dialogue also between the executive/legislative and the ECtHR of particular actuality in Norway. Being a country with a tradition for extensive – and judicially relevant – *travaux préparatoires*, Norwegian political branches have a legally embedded medium for such dialogue: If both the administrative preparations and the legislative debates took the constitutional approach to rights-questions seriously, they could easily argue the case for legislation toward the ECtHR in a legal language familiar to the ECtHR. In addition to strengthening deliberative ideals, this would also have the potential for enhancing liberal legitimacy, in providing a more structured approach to justifications for exercise of power.

The executive branch is reasonably well equipped to take on these challenges, with its administrative expertise that also includes extensive legal and constitutional skills. Parliament, however, while set up with a competent fact-finding and advisory section,[3] has no institutionalized readiness for independently assessing the ever more complex constitutional questions arising under various rights instruments. While ideally Parliament could be equipped with dedicated professional advisors within all fields affected by its legislation, constitutional questions take on a particular importance for a legislature.

The lack of politically independent and highly qualified advisors of constitutional law in the broad sense seems particularly unfortunate for a legislative branch. It needs, after all, to be aware of the constitutional implications of legislative alternatives to know the scope and maneuvering room for its own legislative power. Playing the main role as adversary to court authority in the dichotomous narrative of judicial review legitimacy, having no independent constitutional law competence seems to unbalance the potential for equal footing of governmental powers and checks: the institutional equality of arms. Furthermore, it encumbers Parliament's role as an institutional dialogue partner to the Supreme Court and the ECtHR alike by diminishing the role that Parliament itself has as a *forum of principle*.[4] While certainly open to political disagreement, proportionality approaches to constitutional rights-balancing presuppose that political battles are fought through principled discussion. In this light, to the extent that dialogue and equality of government branch arms are to be realistic, Parliament may benefit from having its constitutional expertise reinforced.[5]

[3] Parliament's Research Section ("Utredningsseksjonen"). [4] See Section 1.1.

[5] This is no new thought: 203 years ago, the founding fathers Adler and Falsen had the idea to place the Procurator General in "Lagmannstinget" as a permanent legal professional representative, to ensure good laws. In addition, all laws with "a legal content" were to be assessed by

Strengthening the popularly elected representatives by institutionalizing parliamentary constitutional proficiency would be an asset for Parliament in general, and for making real and efficient the plurality of party voices of which Parliament consists. This seems especially acute in periods of majority government: With the disagreements over fundamental legal questions arising in preparation for what became the 2010 review cases, arguments are wanting as to why Parliament should not have some independent and more permanent counterweight to that of the very competent administrative expertise represented by the Ministry of Justice, the Attorney General of Civil Affairs and other government departmental legal advisors.

A proposal to have the Presidency of Parliament consider whether to establish such a department was presented in June 2013 by the right-wing Progress Party.[6] Part of the reasoning behind the proposal was the discussions preceding the three 2010 review cases, in which the neutrality of the Ministry of Justice legal department was questioned. Also, it asked the Presidency to establish a commission for assessing how Parliament may best strengthen its capacity autonomously to monitor legislative work and ensure an independent and competent assessment of legislative proposals, hereunder whether they may be at odds with constitutional limits such as those mandated by the Constitution, rule of law, civil liberties and human rights.[7]

Acknowledging that none of the other Nordic countries has an institutionalized parliamentary legal department (and not looking outside these countries, i.e. to the UK Joint Committee on Human Rights), the proposal referred to the Swedish "Lagråd," in which members of the Swedish Supreme Court and Supreme Administrative Court constitute an independent advisory board that assesses important legal proposals before they are discussed in parliament.

> In cases of significance, Parliament seems ill-equipped to establish a counterbalance to the Ministry of Justice legal department in legal questions. To the extent there is disagreement in Parliament over the consequences of a legislative proposal, its constitutionality or effects on other legislation, one needs to be able to consult an authoritative legal body for advice. . . . The aim would be to improve the balance of powers between the executive and legislative branch.[8]

While discouraged by the Conservative representative for the majority in the Presidency,[9] the substance of the right-wing Progress Party initiative received

the Supreme Court. *Adler and Falsen* § 90, as interpreted in Holmøyvik, *Maktfordeling og 1814* (2012), 340.

6 Innst. 491 S (2012–2013).

7 Dokument 8:120 S (2012–2013), Innst. 491 S (2012–2013).

8 Innst. 491 S (2012–2013).

9 Ibid., and St. forh. 20.6.2013, Reps. P. K. Foss.

support from an unexpected ally: the Socialist Left Presidency representative.[10] The initial proposal was voted down 67–33, against the votes of the right-wing Progress Party, the Socialist Left and the Liberal Left Party. The equality of arms argument carrying the initial proposal was expounded by the Socialist Left representative, who also pointed to how the expense of commissioning ad hoc legal opinions would preclude small parties from obtaining the desired constitutional expertise.

The arguments against the proposal were mainly based on the capacity problems that would arise if parties were to further many independent legislative proposals. Moreover, it relied on constitutional tradition – the executive, at least since the establishment of the Ministry of Justice legal department in 1885, has had the responsibility of undertaking the professional preparations of laws. Additionally, "it has been assumed that this department provides its advice on professional grounds independently of the political Ministry of Justice leadership."[11]

These are reasonable objections, as concerns both the capacity and the integrity of the Ministry of Justice legal department. Having a fully staffed office to attend to all reasonable (and less so) legislative proposals would indeed tie up resources, and there is no reason to believe the Ministry of Justice legal department provides anything but legally defensible advice. As regards the latter, however, both the mandate for and sometimes the selective use of advice from this department remains politically administered by the government. And, as has been observed, the legal department "knows where it sits."[12] Further, the Attorney General for Civil Affairs, which acts not as an independent advisor but as the government attorney, has in recent years had both its structural and its financial position strengthened.

Parliament has two main constitutional roles: as the legislative and the budgetary authority. Assistance in budgetary and auditory questions is provided by the Office of the Auditor General, who ensures that assets are used and administered in keeping with Parliament's decisions. Following auditing logic, this assistance is mainly carried out as a monitoring or an ex-post control. For Parliament in its role as legislator, however, potential constitutional questions arise prior to the enactment of laws. A constitutional advisory board should consequently be ready on request to offer advice on constitutional implications of legislative proposals before their enactment, thus to

[10] Innst. 491 S (2012–2013), Reps. A. Chaudhry.

[11] St. forh. 20.6.2013, Reps. Foss. Foss' view of the Ministry of Justice legal department on this point seems to differ from that taken by his party colleague, I. Lønning, in 2010, see Section 8.3.

[12] Taube, Lagrådet imorgon: Kan eller bör Lagrådet och lagrådsgranskningen förändras? (2009).

enable any party to propose and justify its desired legal regulations – or question the ones it may be skeptical of. This would address the current imbalance between small and financially weak parties and strong parties who can afford privately commissioned legal opinions. It would also enhance the potential for *travaux préparatoires* justifications that would not only have a better chance of holding up against constitutional and ECtHR review, but also facilitate the institutional dialogue between the legislature and the courts.

What the best institutional design would be for ensuring the party-independent expertise Parliament needs is unclear. But weighty arguments as to why Parliament should not be institutionally equipped to independently and professionally evaluate the legal boundaries of its own limitations remain unexpressed.

An interesting development that could address some of the constitutional expertise shortcomings of Parliament took place almost in parallel with the 2014–2015 constitutional reform. In May 2015, the Norwegian National Human Rights Institution was established.[13] National Human Rights Institutions (NHRIs) are a type of institution present in a number of countries under the UN Paris Principles.[14] This Norwegian Institution is independent, and formally functions as the Parliamentary ombudsman ensuring that all state officials, hereunder Parliament itself, abide by human rights as set out in the Constitution and binding international human rights documents. Having been operative only since around 2016, it has yet to function as a constitutional rights advisor to Parliament. Such an advisory function is, however, in its legally enacted mandate. Section 3 b of the National Human Rights Institution Act states the institution shall "advise ... Parliament ... about the effectuation of human rights."

10.3 JUDICIAL REVIEW CHALLENGES

To the extent that a constitutional democracy of divided powers remains the ideal fundament for national decision-making, the ideals one seeks to ensure by judicial review are not only a judicial, but also a joint yet differentiated institutional responsibility. For the courts, this implies that they need to be as open in their professional, judicial assessments as possible – to facilitate institutional dialogue vertically and horizontally, but also to provide sufficient reasoning for their judicial legitimacy to be preserved.

13 Lov av 2015-05-22-33

14 Principles relating to the Status of National Institutions, adopted by General Assembly resolution 48/134 of December 20, 1993.

The main review challenge for Norwegian courts in a dual review situation is explicitness about what ideals are emphasized in their adjudication, and why. The need for such explicitness is nothing new from a perspective of justification and judicial legitimacy. It takes on a new dimension, however, as the primary judicial tool for institutional dialogue both with Parliament and with the ECtHR. And the challenge has been intensified by the parliamentary mandate to and Supreme Court's increasing use of constitutional rights provisions in a legal culture where questions of constitutional interpretation have been little discussed and are academically undertheorized.

From an outcome perspective, the political implications of review decisions require clearer discussions of judicial review doctrine, and of what ideals are emphasized and why in the various cases. While legally defensible, it is less instructive to insist that the "other norm" doctrine of the *Shipping Tax* case follows seamlessly from *Kløfta* than to clarify why a *Kløfta* principle not explicated in the same way at the time that case was decided requires the Court to conclude the way it does in the *Shipping Tax* case. Both ideals of judicial professionalism and of rule of law, such as equal treatment and predictability, would benefit from review cases explaining and rejustifying – or questioning – the *Kløfta* tripartite review intensity. This could be done under various constitutional provisions, and in principled differentiations between state–citizen and citizen–citizen dilemmas.

A central challenge is that of review under constitutional limits in the dual form it presents itself in Norway. Norwegian courts have, all in all, met the challenges posed by this dualism quite convincingly in the form it has had until now, with a few rights of double protection, such as the Constitution §§ 100 and 97/105 corresponding to ECHR arts. 10 and P1-1. The interpretational inconsistencies exposed by the Constitution-avoiding practice in free speech cases, and the lacking ECHR approach i.e. in the 2007 *Lindheim* case, could possibly see some improvements as a consequence of the 2014 constitutional reform: As we have seen, the Supreme Court seems to strive to use the Constitution as a basis for deciding cases of dual review following the reform, even though ECHR or other international provisions will end up having a greater practical impact on the cases. Under the 1999 Human Rights Act and now the Constitution § 92, it falls on courts and the general legal community to establish an interpretative strategy implying a coherent, jurisprudential approach to dual rights protection. Central tasks here include what the relationship between the differing constitutional instruments ought to be; what role the text of the two (or more) instruments should be relative to other interpretational sources, such as case law; and how to pave the way for a consistent approach to these questions accessible to legal practitioners in a way attending to rule of law ideals of predictability.

Adjudicative openness as to what democratic or rule of law ideals are at stake, and why some of them are emphasized to the detriment of others in concrete assessments, does not make legally reasoned decisions political; instead, it opens them up to understanding and critique. Judicial exercise of authority could address the different aspects of epistocratic, liberal and democratic strategies for justifying the relevance of various sources of law. Judicial process and rule of law outcome legitimacy ideals would benefit from judicial avoidance of blanket references to "the popular will" when assessing Parliament's justifications. If the premises for this will are but preparatory works the actual parliamentary acceptance of which remains unclear, neither procedural or deliberative democratic input ideals will suffer.

The Supreme Court's increasing use of constitutional rights provisions serves to further ideals of democracy, in that courts adhere to the political signal that the Constitution be used more. To the extent these provisions lead to significantly different interpretations of statutes, however, such use may challenge the democratic ideals underlying those statutes. Emphasizing one over the other merely by reference to "democratic ideals" thus seems an unsatisfactory justification strategy if the aim is to clarify what ideals guide interpretation. Rather, the Court should explicate why the one form of democratic will is preferred over the other in the concrete case at hand. One example of such explanation is the *Holship* case from 2016. "Democratic ideals" could certainly support following the reasonable intention of the Parliamentary majority in interpreting § 92 of the Constitution, thereby opening up for the ILO convention having been incorporated and protected on a constitutional level. Other democratic ideals, such as the general aim of the entire 2014 reform, supported the opposite conclusion: namely, that § 92 did not incorporate formerly unincorporated binding human rights conventions. Rather than justifying the interpretative result by reference to "democratic ideals" or "legislative will," the Court instead explained it by reference to the lack of logic in the constitutional amendment process and the poor legal systemic fit of the opposite conclusion: It would effectively have voided the point of all the recently amended constitutional rights provisions. This justification opens up what ideals are at play, and why the Court chose to emphasize one of them.

The same applies to questions of ECHR interpretation. While preferring the statutory provision of the Ground Lease Act and its *travaux préparatoires* such as in the 2007 *Lindheim* case can certainly be said to safeguard democratic ideals, it is not clear why the democratic ideals underlying that Act are more democratic than the legislative will underlying the 1999 Human Rights Act mandating courts to ensure i.a. ECHR rights.

To further the ideals of strengthening human rights and democracy, as underlying the Human Rights Act and the new rights provisions in the Constitution, Norwegian courts may contribute to judicial dialogue by continuing to follow and improve the mandate to use the ECtHR method when assessing ECHR rights. A good way to do this is by combining the national and international legal terminology as concerns criteria weighed and tests used, such as illustrated by the *Lillo-Stenberg* case,[15] and such as in the *Lindheim* follow-up case in 2016.[16] Upon acceptance that the potential readership of judicial decisions is wider than the case parties and national legal audience, particularly when explaining national deviations from international norms, decision reasoning may be less prone to misunderstandings.

10.4 A BICENTENNIAL DEBATE

The Norwegian story of constitutional democracy presents a curious correspondence between the informal and formal emergence and embedding of perhaps the two foremost institutions of constitutionalism and democracy, respectively. First, in the 1800s, as represented by the gradual development of judicial review and then parliamentarism; and then in the 2000s, in which first the institution of parliamentarism and then judicial review were written into the Constitution. Seen in light of the 2014 constitutional reform, the start of the twenty-first century indicates a form of constitutional revival. Seen in light of the history of review, the 2015 review constitutionalization also suggests that the countermajoritarian difficulty inherent in review is less pressing in Norway than what normative theories on this difficulty generally suggest.

Some factors seem particularly relevant when reflecting on what has contributed to this Norwegian story. One such factor is the way the Supreme Court has been working as a brake on, rather than a block for, politics in its exercise of review in those periods review has been practiced at all. The Court has been attentive – some times too attentive – to the societal needs underlying political regulatory eagerness. While underprotecting central rights during some periods, in retrospect the interplay between the political and judicial branches looks less like a power struggle than a slowly working institutional dialogue. The informal popular participation perspective that may be read out of this interplay could be seen also to heed deliberative democratic ideals. The degree of interplay causality is

[15] Rt. 2008 s. 1089, *Lillo-Stenberg and Sæther* v. *Norway* (2014). [16] HR-2016-304-S

difficult to measure, and any shift of review scope or intensity directly following popular outrage or demand would seriously threaten ideals emphasizing court independence. Shifting intensity and gradual responsiveness to popular reactions over time, however, may be seen as a form of institutional dialogue between the courts and the people. The decline in review cases following the political attempts to abolish it in the 1920s, and the increasing demands of the welfare state in the same period, may attest to this. Much contested by parts of the political and popular constituents in periods of time, the Supreme Court's review seems to have responded to criticism in a way resembling such institutional dialogue. Characteristically, a conservative and lagging force in times of reform – such as attempts to modify privileges of high state officials in the 1800s, to regulate growing industrialization and lay the basis for an emerging welfare state in the early 1900s, and modernizing and effectuating it in the postwar period – constitutional review has rarely barred what has later been seen as necessary societal progresses. Rather, while sometimes contemporarily cumbersome, in the way review has been practiced, it has never represented any unsurpassable hindrance to politics. In some periods, it may even be seen to have served as an institutionalized mechanism for Socratic contestation – forcing or bringing about better democratic justifications for the rights-infringements necessary for this progress. Exemplary in this Socratic and dialogical respect are the legislative attempts at regulating alcohol licenses in the early 1900s and justifying the balance between collective and individual rights to property following the *Kløfta* decision, and the 2010 review cases leading to proposals to amend the Constitution §§ 97 and 106. To the extent Parliament is, in fact, unhappy with the judicial interpretation of the Constitution, the way to handle it is through the procedures set out for such disagreements: constitutional amendments.

Legitimacy of review under the ECHR may have been enhanced by the long period of adaption leading up to the enactment of the HRA. In 1999, the dynamic and evolutive interpretation of the ECHR was well known, had been extensively debated, and was thematized throughout the preparations for the incorporation of the ECHR into Norwegian law. Arguments for and against codifying the institution and scope of Norwegian ECHR review were central in the preparatory work leading up to the HRA. And Parliament explicitly and unanimously endorsed the strengthening of review competence and scope. From a procedural and a deliberative democratic perspective, the long-lasting debate (1989–1999) and the unanimity of Parliament's endorsement are factors enhancing the input legitimacy of Norwegian ECHR review. From this perspective, however, the lack of means to amend or alter the ECHR is, as with the ECtHR review, a delegitimizing factor, both as concern input and as outcome legitimacy.

One empirical study on the social or perceived legitimacy of ECtHR review interviewing domestic politicians, apex court judges, and lawyers litigating cases before domestic courts and the ECtHR from the UK, Ireland, Germany, Turkey and Bulgaria,[17] concludes that ECtHR review enjoys a high level of social and professional legitimacy, and that there is strong constitutive support for a human rights court above and beyond the state in actively intervening in states' domestic decisions in rights protections.[18] In a 2012 survey of popular perceptions of supranational courts, a substantial majority of the population in Norway, UK, Poland, Bulgaria and Ukraine said they found that the existence of the ECtHR was "a good thing" – and, except for the UK, an overwhelming majority held that the ECtHR ought to have the final say over the national parliaments in deciding the content of a contested parliamentary law.[19]

Social attitudes toward the institution of judicial review in Norway –under either the Constitution or the ECHR – have not been measured. Surveys do, however, show a steady – indeed, increasing – tendency in the level of popular confidence in *courts*. In the period from 1996–2005, the percentages of people with "high" or "very high" confidence in courts lay between 60+ and 70+.[20] In 2010, 84 percent said they had "very high" or "high" confidence in the judiciary; in 2017, 86 percent did.[21] Interestingly, public confidence in courts increased in the very same period that debates about judicialization of politics intensified. The time from the mid-nineties until 2010 is marked not only by a significant rise in rights-thinking, rights-adjudication and the influence of supernational legal regulations on the scope of politics, but also by the professional and public debates over these phenomena brought forth i.a. by the Power and Democracy Project. Further, public confidence was not negatively

[17] Bruch, et al., *The legitimacy of the ECHR: The view from the ground* (2011). [18] Ibid., 35.

[19] Grødeland, *Perceptions of European supranational courts: The legal insiders' and outsiders' perspective* (2012). In Norway, the numbers were 72–28 percent in favor of the ECtHR; see table 5 in ibid.

[20] See www.domstol.no/en/Domstoladministrasjonenno/News/News/Rekordhoy-tiltro-til-domstolene/.

[21] Synovate for the Norwegian Court Administration www.domstol.no/no/Aktuelt/Nyheter/stor-tiltro-til-domstolene/. The year 2012 was the first in which courts surpass the police in these statistics. One reason for this may be the nationally observed Breivik case, following which the police were heavily criticized for systemic weaknesses (NOU 2012:14, 6, 7, 19.9), while the Oslo City Court was seen to handle the case very well. A tendency of increasing faith in courts from around 2000, and then a stable, high confidence from 2010, continues in 2011: see Arnstad, Høy tiltro til domstolene, *Rett på sak* 2013. The corresponding numbers for the government and Parliament, respectively, are 59 percent and 69 percent in 2010; 62 percent and 72 percent in 2012; and 74 percent and 85 percent in 2017.

affected by discussions of judicial power following the 2010 cases, nor by the potential augmented power of courts following the 2014 constitutional reform. In fact, confidence continued to increase in those years.

Norwegian constitutional review functions within a unitary system of law. This system represents a possible institutional advantage to preserving democratic and judicial ideals: Contrary to constitutional courts, Norwegian review is carried out in a nonconstitution-specific court system of general jurisdiction. From an institutional design perspective, this may safeguard courts' broader focus on judicial problem-solving within the system as a whole, rather than "only" on rights protection – the weighing of individual rights against each other or against some state policy. It is plausible to see this as one explanatory element for the traditionally lenient review intensity under the Constitution. The unitary court system, as well as the legal and cultural embeddedness of courts' judicial review in Norway, contributes to the historical legitimacy of this functioning of courts. While ECHR review differs from constitutional review in both scope and intensity, the constitutional review history may have enhanced two ideals: that of expertise – courts know how to exercise review; and that of social acceptance – the people and the branches of government are familiar with the concept of constitutional limits being pronounced by courts in cases raising questions of fundamental rights.

Taking a step back from the contemporary discursive and institutional review challenges, I conclude with this: The case of Norwegian review represents a particular example in discussions of judicial decision-making and review legitimacy. The Norwegian combination of an early, yet provident and durable constitution, a long-lasting and embedded practice of judicial review and a solid, parliamentary democracy tells a different story than do some of the national and international experiences that provide the bases for theoretical discussions of review legitimacy. While historically at times quite polarized, debates on Norwegian review legitimacy have been gradually defused. Looking back, questioning review legitimacy seems a less distinctive feature of Norwegian legal history than does the pragmatic interaction of law and politics, between the academic, legal and political institutions within which review has developed. While today constitutionalized and long embedded as an integral part of the Norwegian system, discussions are likely to continue over the scope and intensity of review, particularly under the 2014 amended rights provisions – and in a way contingent, in part, on how ECtHR review of corresponding rights is undertaken and perceived.

Bibliography

Aall, Jørgen, Domstolsadgang og domstolsprøving i menneskerettighetssaker, *Tidsskrift for rettsvitenskap* 1998, 1–181.

Aasland, Gunnar, Argumentasjonsmønsteret i nyere høyesterettspraksis, *Lov og rett* 2006, 387–396.

Ackerman, Bruce A., *We the people. 1, Foundations* (Belknap Press of Harvard University Press 1993).

Alexander, George S., Comparing the two legal realisms – American and Scandinavian, 50 *American journal of comparative law* 2002, 131.

Andenæs, Johs. *Domstolenes stilling til Stortingets delegasjon av myndighet (1953) trykt i Avhandlinger og foredrag* (Universitetsforlaget, 1962).

Andenæs, Johs., *Statsforfatningen i Norge* (Tanum 2nd edn., 1948).

Andenæs, Johs., Parlamentarisme, jus og statsvitenskap, *Lov og rett* 1964, 56–65.

Andenæs, Johs., Høyesterett som politisk organ, *Lov og rett* 1965, 22–43.

Andenæs, Johs., Jus og politikk, *Lov og rett* 1965, 456–464.

Andenæs, Johs., Grunnlov og ekspropriasjonserstatning, *Lov og rett* 1975, 243–274.

Andenæs, Johs., Grunnlov, politikere og domstoler, *Lov og rett* 1975, 380–386.

Andenæs, Johs., Grunnlovtolking, domstoler og politikk. Randbemerkninger til en høyesterettsdom, in *Rett og humanisme Festskrift til Kristen Andersen* (ed. H. Jakhelln; Tanum-Norli 1977).

Andenæs, Johs., *Det vanskelige oppgjøret: rettsoppgjøret etter okkupasjonen* (Tanum-Norli 1979).

Andenæs, Johs., Jus og politikk, *Lov og rett* 1990, 414–425.

Andenæs, Johs., *Statsforfatningen i Norge* (TANO, 7th edn., 1990).

Andenæs, Johs., *Ytringsfriheten og ærens rettsvern etter grunnlovens § 100 og Europakonvensjonens art. 10*, *Lov og rett* 1996, 3–21.

Andenæs, Johs. and Bratholm, Anders, *Spesiell strafferett* (Universitetsforlaget 2nd edn. 1990).

Andenæs, Kristian, *Om maktens rettsliggjøring og rettsliggjøringens maktpotensial*, Tidsskrift for samfunnsforskning 2006, 587–600.

Andenæs, Mads T. and Kravik, Andreas, Norske verdier og EMK, *Lov og rett* 2010, 579–599.

Andresen, Nils August, *Gledelig demokratiforakt*, www.minervanett.no/gledelig-demokratiforakt/ Minervanett, February 22, 2010 [retrieved March 26, 2014].

Arnstad, Iwar Høy tiltro til domstolene, *Rett på sak* 3/4 2013, 6–7.

Arnstad, Iwar, Høyesterett konsentrerer seg om det prinsipielle, *Rett på sak* 3/4 2013, 10–11.

Aschehoug, T. H., *Norges nuværende Statsforfatning* (Malling 1875–1885).

Aschehoug, T. H., *Norges nuværende Statsforfatning III* (Malling 2nd edn. 1893).

Ashenden, Samantha and Thornhill, C. J., *Legality and legitimacy: Normative and sociological approaches* (Nomos 2010).

Aubert, L. M. B., *Om den dømmende Magts Virksomhed som Kilde til Udviklingen af vor Ret ved Siden af Lovgivningsvirksomheden*, Ugeblad for lovkyndighed 1865, 65–82.

Aubert, Vilhelm, *Løsning av konflikter i par og trekant*, Tidsskrift for samfunnsforskning 1961, 89–102.

Augdahl, Per, *Ingen lov må gis tilbakevirkende kraft*, Tidsskrift for rettsvitenskap, 1938, 379–407.

Augdahl, Per, *Rettskilder* (Aschehoug 2nd edn. 1961).

Backer, Inge Lorange, *Om Høyesteretts forhold til Den europeiske menneskerettskonvensjon*, Nordisk Tidsskrift for Menneskerettigheter 2005, 425–432.

Backer, Inge Lorange, *Den europeiske menneskerettsdomstol*, Nytt norsk tidsskrift 2009, 278–285.

Backer, Inge Lorange, *Loven – hvordan blir den til?* (Universitetsforlaget 2013).

Balkin, J. M., *Living originalism* (Belknap Press of Harvard University Press 2011).

Banoun, Bettina, *Må la Grunnloven ligge*, *Dagens Næringsliv*, November 30, 2013.

Bårdsen, Arnfinn, The Nordic Supreme Courts as Constitutional Courts, speech at Joint seminar between the Constitutional Court of Austria and the Supreme Court of Norway Vienna the 29–30th of October 2015.

Bay, Christian, *Politisk forskning og politisk ansvarlighet*, Tidsskrift for Samfunnsvitenskap 1961, 71–88.

"Beredskapslovgivningen Ot. prp. nr. 78" (H. Aschehoug & Co. 1950).

Berg, Jens Petter, *Nytt lys over striden mellom JD og UD om utformingen av menneskerettsloven* § 3, Kritisk juss 2000, 343–350.

Bergo, Knut, *Høyesteretts forarbeidsbruk* (Cappelen akademisk 2000).

Bergo, Knut and Kinander, Morten, *Politikk, makt og demokrati – tilsvar til Øyvind Østerud*, *Lov og rett* 2007, 89–106.

Bernhardt, Peter L., *Politisk svada om Høyesterett*, *Dagens Næringsliv*, March 22, 2010.

Bernt, Jan Fridthjof, Mæhle, Synne Sæther and Jacobsen, Jørn R. T., *Rett, samfunn og demokrati* (Gyldendal akademisk 2007).

Berrefjord, Oddvar, *Erstatningsfastsettelse ved ekspropriasjon av fast eiendom*, Jussens venner 1974, 177–198.

Bickel, Alexander M., *The least dangerous branch: The Supreme Court at the bar of politics* (Yale University Press 2nd edn. 1986).

Bjørge, Eirik, The status of the ECHR in Norway: Should Norwegian courts interpret the convention dynamically?, 16 *European Public Law* 2010, 45.

Bjørgum, Lars Henrik, *Nei til dommerforslag*, *Dagens Næringsliv*, March 29, 2010.

Blackstone, William, *Commentaries on the laws of England book the fourth* (printed for John Exshaw, Henry Saunders, Boulter Grierson, Elizabeth Lynch 1770).

Blandhol, Sverre, *Juridisk ideologi* (Jurist- og Økonomforbundets Forlag Universitetsforlaget 1999).

Blandhol, Sverre, *Pragmatismens aktualitet i rettsvitenskap og rettsanvendelse*, Tidsskrift for rettsvitenskap 2004, 365–391.

Blichner, Lars and Molander, Anders, *Maktutredningens rettsliggjøringsbegrep*, Tidsskrift for samfunnsforskning 2006, 601–611.

Bodansky, Daniel, Legitimacy in international law and international relations, in *Interdisciplinary perspectives on international law and international relation: The state of the art* (eds. J. L. Dunoff and M. A. Pollack; Cambridge University Press 2013).

Boe, Erik, *Rettskildelære under debatt* (Universitetsforlaget 2012).

Bohman, James and Rehg, William, *Deliberative democracy: Essays on reason and politics* (MIT Press 1997).

Borten Moe, Ola, *Regjeringen må vise respekt*, *Dagens Næringsliv*, December 30, 2009.

Borten Moe, Ola, *Stortinget inn i Høyesterett*, *Dagens Næringsliv*, March 18, 2010.

Borten Moe, Ola, *Stortinget inn i Høyesterett – igjen*, *Dagens Næringsliv*, March 29, 2010.

Borvik, Bjørnar, Ytringsfridom på norsk – ein kritikk, *Lov og rett* 2004, 72–98.

Borvik, Bjørnar, Nasjonal skjønnsmargin etter EMK, *Lov og rett* 2011, 575–595.

Borvik, Bjørnar, *Personvern og ytringsfridom* (Universitetsforlaget 2011).

Brandt, Frederik Peter, *Repertorium for praktisk Lovkyndighed* (Abelsted 1855).

Bratholm, Anders, Fleischers ytringsfrihet og bruken av den, *Lov og rett* 1984, 56–62.

Bratholm, Anders, Jus og politikk, *Lov og rett* 1975, 97–117.

Bratholm, Anders, Injurieretten og personvernet, *Lov og rett* 2002, 629–631.

Brems, Eva, *Procedural Review in European Fundamental Rights Cases* (Cambridge 2017).

Bruch, Nicola, Çalı, Başak and Kock, Anne, *The legitimacy of the ECHR: The view from the ground*, http://ecthrproject.files.wordpress.com/2011/04/ecthrlegitimacyreport.pdf University College London (2011).

Bryce, James Bryce, *Constitutions* (Scientia Verlag 1980).

Bødtker, Henning, *En advokat forteller* (Aschehoug 1970).

Cappelletti, Mauro, Judicial review of legislation: European antecedents and adaptations, 79 *Harvard Law Review* 1207 (1966).

Castberg, Frede, *Grunnlovens forbud mot å gi lover tilbakevirkende kraft* (Cappelen 1920).

Castberg, Frede, *Dommerbladet* (Medlemsblad for den norske dommerforening 1952).

Castberg, Frede, *Norway and the western powers* (University Press 1957).

Castberg, Frede, *Freedom of speech in the West* (University Press 1960).

Castberg, Frede, *Norges statsforfatning* (Universitetsforlaget 3rd edn. 1964).

Christophersen, Jens A., Forholdet Storting – Regjering, *Lov og rett* 1964, 26–31.

Cooley, Thomas McIntyre, *A treatise on the constitutional limitations which rest upon the legislative power of the states of the American union* (Little, Brown, and Company 1868).

Council of Europe, *Collected edition of the "travaux préparatoires" of the European Convention on Human Rights* (Nijhoff 1975).

Council of Europe, *Practical Guide on Admissibility Criteria* (CoE 2011).

Coward, Kirsti, Bugge, Helge Olav and Rognlien, Stein, *Festskrift Lovavdelingen – 100 år* (Universitetsforlaget 1986).

d'Entreves, Alexander, Legality and legitimacy, 16 *Review of Metaphysics* 687 (1963).
Dahl, Hans Fredrik, *Norsk presses historie* (Universitetsforlaget 2010).
Dahl, Hans Fredrik and Sørensen, Øystein, *Et rettferdig oppgjør?* (Pax 2004).
Dahl Jacobsen, Knut, *Lojalitet, nøytralitet og faglig uavhengighet i sentraladministrasjonen*, Tidsskrift for samfunnsforskning 1960, 231–248.
Dahl Jacobsen, Knut and Eckhoff, Torstein, *Rationality and responsibility in administrative and judicial decision-making* § V (Munksgaard 1960).
Dahl, Robert A., *A preface to democratic theory* (University of Chicago Press 1956).
Dahl, Ottar, ed., *Makt og motiv: et festskrift til Jens Arup Seip* (Gyldendal 1975).
Danielsen, Per, Injurier verre enn knyttneveslag, *Lov og rett* 2002, 626–627.
De Schutter, Olivier and Tulkens, Françoise, *Rights in conflict: The European Court of Human Rights as a pragmatic institution, in conflicts between fundamental rights* (Intersentia 2006).
Dijk, P. van, Arai, Yukata and Hoof, G. J. H. van, *Theory and practice of the European Convention on Human Rights* (Intersentia 4th edn. 2006).
Dixon, Rosalind, Weak-Form Judicial Review and American Exceptionalism, 32 2012 *Oxford J Legal Studies* 487.
Doublet, David Roland *Rett, vitenskap og fornuft* (Alma Mater 1995).
Doublet, David Roland and Bernt, Jan Fridthjof, *Retten og vitenskapen* (Alma Mater 2 edn. 1993).
Dunoff, Jeffrey L. and Trachtman, Joel P., *Ruling the world?* (Cambridge University Press 2009).
Dworkin, Ronald, *Taking rights seriously* (Duckworth 1977).
Dworkin, Ronald, *A matter of principle* (Clarendon Press 1986).
Dworkin, Ronald, *Freedom's law* (Harvard University Press 1996).
Dworkin, Ronald, *Justice in robes* (Belknap Press 2006).
Dworkin, Ronald, *Justice for hedgehogs* (Belknap Press 2011).
Dyzenhaus, David, *Legality and legitimacy – Carl Schmitt, Hans Kelsen, and Hermann Heller in Weimar* (Clarendon Press, Oxford University Press 1997).
Eckhoff, Torstein, *Rettsvesen og rettsvitenskap i USA* (Akademisk forlag 1953).
Eckhoff, Torstein, Høyesterett som grunnlovens vokter, in *Makt og motiv: et festskrift til Jens Arup Seip* (O. Dahl ed. Gyldendal 1975).
Eckhoff, Torstein and Helgesen, Jan E., *Rettskildelære* (Universitetsforlaget 5th edn. 2001).
Eckhoff, Torstein and Smith, Eivind, *Forvaltningsrett* (Tano Aschehoug 6th edn. 1997).
Eckhoff, Torstein and Wilberg, Ingeborg, *Grunnlov og ekspropriasjonserstatning*, *Lov og rett* 1975, 363–370.
Economist Intelligence Unit, *Democracy index (2012) economist intelligence unit* (The Democracy Index 2012).
Economist Intelligence Unit, *Democracy index (2016) economist intelligence unit* (The Democracy Index 2016).
ECtHR – Procedure for electing judges, *Procedure for electing judges to the European Court of Human Rights* http://assembly.coe.int/CommitteeDocs/2012/ajinfdoc02_2012.pdf (retreived March 26, 2014) (CoE 2010).
Eggen, Kyrre, Ærekrenkende ytringer, *Mennesker og rettigheter* 1994, 353–372.

Eggen, Kyrre, Journalistisk formidling av ærekrenkende ytringer – med særlig vekt på betydningen av Menneskerettighetsdomstolens avgjørelse i Tromsøsaken, *Kritisk juss* 1999, 209–234.
Eggen, Kyrre, Ytringsfrihet, personvern og ærekrenkelser – tre norske saker for EMD, *Kritisk juss* 2000, 223–260.
Eggen, Kyrre, *Ytringsfrihet* (Cappelen akademisk 2002).
Eikefjord, Eirin and Bruaset, Ingvild, *Midlertidig skatteseier, Bergens Tidende* February 13, 2010.
Elgesem, Frode, Ikke dramatisk, *Advokatbladet* 2/2016.
Elster, Jon, *Ulysses and the sirens* (Cambridge University Press 1979).
Elster, Jon, Forces and mechanisms in the constitution-making process, 45 *Duke Law Journal* 364 (1995).
Elster, Jon and Slagstad, Rune, *Constitutionalism and democracy* (Cambridge University Press 1988).
Ely, John Hart, *Democracy and distrust* (Harvard University Press 1980).
Emberland, Marius, Effektivisering av subsidiaritet i EMK, *Lov og rett* 2013, 513–514.
Eng, Svein, *The doctrine of precedent in English and Norwegian law* (Tidsskrift for Rettsvitenskap Foundation 1993).
Eriksen, Christofer, *Prejudikat og prøvelsesrett* (Institutt for offentlig rett, Universitetet i Oslo 2000).
Estlund, David M., Introduction: epistemic approaches to democracy, 5 *Episteme: A Journal of Social Epistemology* 1 (2008).
European Court of Human Rights, *Annual report 2008* (CoE 2008).
European Court of Human Rights, *Dialogue between judges*, 53, (CoE 2011).
European Court of Human Rights, *Analysis of statistics 2012* (CoE 2013).
European Court of Human Rights, *Overview 1959–2016* (CoE 2016).
Falsen, Christian Magnus *Norges Grundlov, gjennemgaaet i Spørgsmaal og Svar* (R. Dahls Enke og Søn 1816).
Falsen, Christian Magnus,*Norge, Norges Grundlov* (R. Dahls Enke og Søn 1818).
Falsen, Christian Magnus, *Bemærkninger i Anledning af Constitutions-Forslaget om Kongens Veto* (Lehmann 1824).
Fauchald, Ole Kristian, Forfatning og miljøvern – en analyse av Grunnloven § 110 B, *Tidsskrift for rettsvitenskap* 2007, 1–84.
Fauchald, Ole Kristian, Jakhelln, Henning, and Syse, Aslak, eds., *Dog fred er ej det bedste. Festskrift til Carl August Fleischer* (Universitetsforlaget 2006).
Feiring, Eli, Demokratiet og rettsliggjøringen av velferdspolitikken, *Tidsskrift for samfunnsforskning* 2006, 575–585.
Fishkin, James S., *Democracy and deliberation* (Yale University Press 1991).
Fjelldal, Stian and Dybfest Dahl, Ingvill SPLITTES – etter ny EU-dom [sic.] Nå blir det lov med politisk TV-reklame, *Verdens Gang*, December 12, 2008.
Flaatten, Sverre, Høyesterett, straffen og tyveriene: straffeutmålingsbegrunnelser i etterkrigstiden, Fagbokforlaget (2017).
Flaatten, Sverre, *Høyesterett, straffen og tyveriene: Straffeutmålingsbegrunnelser i etterkrigstiden* (Fagbokforlaget 2017).
Fleischer, Carl August, *Grunnlovens grenser for lovregulert fastsetting av erstatning ved ekspropriasjon, særlig ved verdistigning som ikke skyldes grunneiers innsats* (Universitetsforlaget 1968).

Fleischer, Carl August, Husaas-komitéens forslag til lovbestemmelser om skjønnsordning og erstatningsfastsettelse ved ekspropriasjon *Lov og rett* 1970, 25–32.
Fleischer, Carl August, Grunnlovens § 105 – foredrag holdt på seminar 4. sept. 1970, *Jussens Venner* 1971, 137–165.
Fleischer, Carl August, Misvisende om den nye ekspropriasjonserstatningslov, *Lov og rett*, 1975, 216–228.
Fleischer, Carl August, Statsrett, oljeskatt og juridiske mistak, *Lov og rett* 1976, 399–413.
Fleischer, Carl August, Om anmelderansvaret – og om retten til fri vurdering, kritikk og karakteristikk *Lov og rett* 1984, 563–578.
Fleischer, Carl August, Gjeldende injuriebestemmelser og strafferettsteoriens faglige svikt, *Lov og rett* 1985, 396–406.
Fleischer, Carl August, Grunnloven 175 år: utvikling, demokratisering, rettskildebruk og "påvirkningsagenter" i forhold til våre i fredstid viktigste grunnlovsbestemmelser §§ 49, 75, 97 og 105, *Jussens Venner* 1989, 153–198.
Foss, Per Kristian, Regjeringens arroganse, *Dagens Næringsliv*, June 23, 2010.
Forst, Rainer, *The right to justification, elements of a constructivist theory of justice* (Colombia University Press 2014).
Frantzen, Torstein, Giertsen, Johan, Thue, Helge J. and Moss, Giuditta Cordero,*Rett og toleranse Festskrift til Helge Johan Thue* (Gyldendal akademisk 2007).
Fredriksen, Halvard H., Betydningen av EUs pakt om grunnleggende rettigheter for EØS-retten, *Jussens Venner* 2013, 371–399.
Friedman, Barry, Dialogue and judicial review, 91 *Michigan Law Review* 577 (1993).
Friedman, Barry, Neutral principles: A retrospective, 50 *Vanderbilt Law Review* 503 (1997).
Friedman, Barry, The history of the countermajoritarian difficulty, part I: The road to judicial supremacy, 73 *New York University Law Review* 101 (1998).
Friedman, Barry, The history of the countermajoritarian difficulty Part III: The lesson of Lochner 76 *New York University Law Review* 1383 (2001).
Friedman, Barry, The birth of an academic obsession: The history of the countermajoritarian difficulty, part IV, 112 *Yale Law Journal* 153 (2002).
Friedman, Barry, The history of the countermajoritarian difficulty, Part II: Reconstruction's political court, 91 *Georgetown Law Journal* 66 (2002).
Friedman, Barry, *The will of the people: How public opinion has influenced the Supreme Court and shaped the meaning of the constitution* (Farrar, Straus and Giroux 2009).
"Front mot frykten," Oslo 1950.
Fuller, Lon L., *The morality of law* (Yale University Press 1964).
Fuller, Lon L., The forms and limits of adjudication 92 *Harvard Law Review* 353 (1978).
Furre, Berge, *Norsk historie 1905–1990* (Samlaget 1992).
Føllesdal, Andreas, The legitimacy of international human rights review: The case of the European Court of Human Rights, 40 *Journal of Social Philosophy* 4 595–607 (2009).
Gaarder, Peder Krabbe, *Fortolkning over Grundloven og de øvrige Love, som danne Norges Riges offentlige Ret* (Kristiania 1845).
Gardbaum, Stephen, The new Commonwealth model of constitutionalism, 49 *American Journal of Comparative Law* 54 (2001).
Gardbaum, Stephen, Reassessing the new Commonwealth model of constitutionalism, 8 *International Journal of Constitutional Law* 167 (2010).
Garner, Bryan A., *Black's Law Dictionary* (West Publishing 1996).

Garner, Bryan A., *A Dictionary of Modern Legal Usage* (Oxford University Press 2001).

Gibson, James L. and Caldeira, Gregory A., The legitimacy of transnational legal institutions: Compliance, support, and the European Court of Justice, *American Journal of Political Science* 31, (1995).

Ginsburg, Tom,. The virtues of evolution in an age of revolution: Norway's enduring constitution in comparative perspective, *Nytt Norsk Tidsskrift* 3/2014, 225–237.

Ginsburg, T., Elkins, Z. and Blount, J., Does the process of constitution-making msatter? *Annual Review of Law and Social Sciences*, Vol. 5, No. 5, 2009, 201–223.

Ginsburg, T. and Melton, J., *Does the constitutional amendment rule matter at all?* University of Chicago, Public Law Working Paper No. 472.

Graber, Mark A., The nonmajoritarian difficulty: Legislative deference to the judiciary, 7 *Studies in American Political Development* 35 (1993).

Gravensteen, Runa, *Hatefulle ytringer: En studie av argumentasjonen om ytringsfrihet og minoritetsvern i norske rettskilder*, Master's thesis (Universitetet i Oslo 2013).

Graver, Hans Petter, Avvik tåles ikke, *Dagbladet* March 26, 2009.

Graver, Hans Petter, *Refleksjoner om rederibeskatningsdommen* Minervanett, April 22, 2010, www.minervanett.no/refleksjoner-om-rederibeskatningsdommen/ (retrieved March 26, 2014).

Greer, Steven, *The European Convention on Human Rights* (Cambridge University Press 2006).

Grendstad, Gunnar, Waltenburg, Eric N. and Shaffer, William R., Revealed preferences of Norwegian supreme court justices, *Tidsskrift for rettsvitenskap* 2010, 73–101.

Grødeland, Åse B., *Perceptions of European supranational courts: The legal insiders' and outsiders' perspective* (Forthcoming).

Habermas, Jürgen, *Between Facts and Norms* (MIT Press 1996).

Habermas, Jürgen, Democracy, solidarity and the European Crisis, Social Europe Journal be cited to "Lecture given in Leuven 4.26.2013, accessible at https://www.scribd.com/document/169207191/Jurgen-HABERMAS-Democracy-Solidarity-and-the-European-Crisis".

Hagerup, Francis, *Nogle Ord om den nyere Retsvidenskabs Karakter* (Kristiania 1888).

Hagstrøm, Viggo, *Ånd og rett – festskrift til Birger Stuevold Lassen* (Universitetsforlaget 1997).

Halvorsen, Marit, Schweigaard, Aschehoug og prøvingsretten som forsvant: bidrag til utviklingen av læren om prøving av skjønnsmessige forvaltningsvedtak, *Tidsskrift for rettsvitenskap* 2011, 56–86.

Hambro, C. J., *Portræter og profiler* (Aschehoug 1937).

Hambro, Edvard, Noen betraktninger om forholdet mellom grunnlov og folkerett, *Lov og rett* 1964, 224–230.

Hanssen, Kjetil, Glad for å bli satt på plass, *Aftenposten*, February 22, 2010.

Haug, Bjørn, *Mange jern i ilden* (Bjørn Haug 2008).

Haugland, Jens, Grunnlov og politikk, *Lov og rett* 1975, 371–374.

Haugland, Jens, Merknader til ekspropriasjonserstatningsloven, *Lov og rett* 1975, 190–191.

Haugland, Jens, *Dagbok frå Kongens råd* (Samlaget 1986).

Haugli, Åsne *Vil la Stortinget utnevne Høyesterett, Dagens Næringsliv*, March 18, 2010.

Helgadóttir, Ragnhildur, *The influence of American theories of judicial review on Nordic constitutional law* (Martinus Nijhoff Publishers 2006).

Helgesen, Jan E., *Teorier om "Folkerettens stilling i norsk rett"* (Aschehoug 1982).

Helgesen, Jan E. Bør vi – anno 2002 – modernisere individets grunnlovsvern in *Lødrup, Rettsteori og rettsliv*, 385 (Universitetsforlaget 2002).

Hirschl, Ran, *Towards juristocracy* (Harvard University Press 2004).

Hirschl, Ran, The Nordic counternarrative: Democracy, human development and judicial review, 9 *International Journal of Constitutional Law* 449 (2011).

Hjelm, Claus Winter, *Om Grundlovens Principer og den Aand, hvori de under gjensidig Begrændsning ere gjennomførte i dens enkelte Bestemmelser* (Feilberg & Landmark. 1863).

Hjort, J. B., Grunnloven, et postulat?, *Jussens Venner* 1962, 1–66.

Hoffman, Leonard (Lord), *The universality of human rights. Judicial Studies Boards Annual Lecture* March 19, 2009.

Holmøyvik, Eirik, Årsaker til utviklinga av prøvingsretten i Noreg og Danmark, *Tidsskrift for rettsvitenskap* 2007, 718–779.

Holmøyvik, Eirik, Dommernes uavhengighet og forholdet til de øvrige statsmakter, in *Dommernes uavhengighet* (B. Tønder, N. A. Engstad and A. L. Frøseth eds., Fagbokforlaget 2012), 99–127.

Holmøyvik, Eirik, *Maktfordeling og 1814* (Fagbokforlaget 2012).

Hurrell, Andrew, Legitimacy and the use of force: can the circle be squared? 31 *Review of International Studies* 18 (2005).

Høgberg, Benedikte Moltumyr, *Forbud mot tilbakevirkende lover* (Universitetsforlaget 2010).

Høgberg, Benedikte Moltumyr, Grunnloven § 97 etter plenumsdommen i Rt. 2010 s. 143, *Tidsskrift for rettsvitenskap* 2010, 694–744.

Høyesterett, Norges, Norges Høyesterett Årsmelding 2013 (2014).

Innstilling fra undersøkelseskommisjonen av 1945 (Bind I, Oslo: Aschehoug, 1946.

Interights, *Judicial Independence: Law and Practice of Appointments to the sEuropean Court of Human Rights* (Interights 2003).

Iversen, Magnus Hoem, *Overtramp eller valgkamp?*, Master's thesis (Universitetet i Bergen 2012).

Jacobs, Francis G., Ovey, Clare and White, Robin C. A., *The European Convention on Human Rights* (Oxford University Press, 5th edn. 2010).

Jakobsen, Uffe, The conception of "Nordic democracy" and European judicial integration, *Nordisk tidsskrift for menneskerettigheter* 2009, 221–241.

Joas, Hans, *Die Sakralität der Person* (Suhrkamp 2011).

Johansen, Per Anders, Får i pose og sekk etter SV-selvmål, *Aftenposten*, February 13, 2010.

Johnsen, Jon T., Menneskerettsvernet i straffeprosessen. Er det behov for en mer aktiv lovgiver?, *Lov og rett* 2002, 585–605.

Judt, Tony, *Postwar – a history of Europe since 1945* (Pimlico 2007).

Kahneman, Daniel, Knetsch, Jack L. and Thaler, Richard H., Anomalies: the endowment effect, loss aversion, and status quo bias, 5 *The Journal of Economic Perspectives* 1, 193–206 (1991).

Kant, Immanuel, *Critique of pure reason* (Scientia Verlag 1982).

Kári, A, Rogvi, *West-Nordic constitutional judicial review* (Djoef Publishing 2013).

Kavanagh, Aileen, Constitutional review, the courts and democratic scepticism, 62 *Current Legal Problems* 102 (2009).

Keller, Helen and Stone Sweet, Alec, *A Europe of rights* (Oxford University Press 2008).

Kelsen, Hans, *La garantie juridictionnelle de la Constitution* (Marcel Girard Librarie 1928).

Kelsen, Hans, Judicial review of legislation – a comparative study of the Austrian and the American constitution 2 *Journal of Politics* 183 (1942).

Kierulf, Anine, Rettsstatens overnasjonale vending: den andre prøvingsretten, *Nytt Norsk Tidsskrift* 2009, 256–270.

Kierulf, Anine, Er internasjonale menneskerettigheter en relevant rettskilde ved grunnlovstolking?, *Retfærd* 2011, 23–48.

Kierulf, Anine, Hvilken rolle spiller Grunnloven § 100 i Høyesteretts ytringsfrihetspraksis?, *Lov og rett* 2012, 131–150.

Kierulf, Anine, Innenfra og utenfra – Grunnloven og menneskerettighetene, in *Tolkingar av Grunnlova* (E. Holmøyvik ed., Pax 2013, 424–449).

Kierulf, Anine, Lite teori om grunnlovstolking, *Advokatbladet* 2/2016.

Kierulf, Anine, Grunnloven som irrelevant rettskilde, *Lov og rett*, 03/2016, 185–189.

Kierulf, Anine and Slagstad, Rune, Historikeres fortellinger om juss, *Tidsskrift for rettsvitenskap* 2012, 421–457.

Kierulf, Anine and Slagstad, Rune, Høyesteretts dommere, in *Lov, sannhet, rett.* (Universitetsforlaget 2015).

Kierulf, Anine and Strømme, Vidar, Tolkning og injurier, *Lov og rett* 2004, 474–491.

Kinander, Morten ed., *Makt og rett* (Universitetsforlaget 2005).

Kinander, Morten, Fra tilbakeholdenhet til aktivisme – Nyere utviklingslinjer i forholdet mellom rett og politikk i Høyesterett, *Lov og rett*, 03/2016, 141–164.

Kjønstad, Asbjørn, Er Høyesterett statsvennlig? *Lov og rett* 1999, 97–122.

Kolberg, Martin and Borten Moe, Ola, *Demokrati, ikke arroganse!*, *Dagens Næringsliv*, July 2, 2010.

Kristjánsson, Mímir, *På tynn is*, *Klassekampen*, March 2, 2010.

Kumm, Mattias, The idea of Socratic contestation and the right to justification: The point of rights-based proportionality review, 4 (2) *Law & Ethics of Human Rights* (2010), 142–175.

Lambertz, Göran, Lindskog, Stefan and Möller, Mikael, eds., *Festskrift till Torgny Håstad* (Iustus Förlag 2010).

Langeland, Nils Rune and Sandmo, Erling, *Siste ord* (Cappelen 2005).

Langholm, Sivert, ed., *Den Kritiske analyse. Festskrift til Ottar Dahl* (Universitetsforlaget 1994).

Lasson, P. C., Supplement og Ord- eller Realregister til det i 1868 trykte Skrift om "Straffeprocessen i dens nyeste Skikkelse m. v." (1869).

Lasson, P. C. and Hurtigkarl, Frederik Theodor, *Haandbog i den norske Processes første Deel* (Cappelen 1843).

Law, David S. and Versteeg, Mila, The declining influence of the United States constitution, 87 *New York University Law Review* 762 (2012).

Lejman, Fritjof and Norback, Lars, *Festskrift tillägnad professor, juris doktor Karl Olivecrona vid hans avgång från professorsämbetet den 30 juni 1964* (Norstedt 1964).

Letsas, George, *Intentionalism and the interpretation of the ECHR* (Nijhoff 2010).

Lewis, Anthony, *Make no law: The Sullivan case and the First Amendment* (Random House 1991).
Lie, Mikael *Betenkning angående grunnlovens §§97 og 105 og om domstolenes myndighet til å prøve loves indre gyldighet* (St. forh. 1923, Dok. 13).
Lien, Marius, *Kaffegildet på Bislet, Morgenbladet*, September 24, 2009.
Lindseth, Peter L., *Power and legitimacy: reconciling Europe and the nation-state* (Oxford University Press 2010).
Locke, John, *Second treatise of government* (Hackett Pub. Co. 1980).
Lord Sumption, *The limits of law (the 27th Sultan Azlan Shah Lecture), the 27th Sultan Azlan Shah Lecture*, 12.20. 2013.
Lorentzen, Pål W., *Ytringsfrihet på norsk, Dagbladet*, September 25, 2004.
Lyng, Jon, Brytningsår. *Erindringer* 1923–1953 (Cappelen, 1972).
Lødrup, Peter, Aarbakke, Magnus, Aasland, Gunnar and Tjomsland, Steinar, *Rettsteori og rettsliv*, (Universitetsforlaget 2002).
Lønning, Inge, Når grunnloven setter grenser, *Kirke og kultur* 2010, 5–11.
MacIntyre, Alasdair C., *Whose justice? Which rationality?* (Duckworth 1988).
Madsen, Mikael Rask, From Cold War instrument to Supreme European Court: The European Court of Human Rights at the crossroads of international and national law and politics, 32 *Law & Social Inquiry* 137–159 (2007).
Mæhle, Synne Sæther, *Grenser for rettsanvendelsesskjønn* (Gyldendal akademisk 2005).
Mæland, Henry John, *Ærekrenkelser* (Universitetsforlaget 1986).
Martí Mármol, José Luis, The sources of legitimacy of political decisions: Between procedure and substance, in *The theory and practice of legislation: essays in legisprudence* (L. Wintgens, P. Thion and M. Carly eds., Ashgate 2005), 259–281.
Matningsdal, Magnus, Kontradiksjon i sivile saker og straffesaker, *Jussens Venner* 2013, 1–115.
Matningsdal, Magnus, Siktedes tilstedeværelse i fengslingsmøtet ved første gangs fengsling, *Lov og rett* 2013, 232–247.
Medlemsblad for Den norske dommerforening (1952), 111.
Meiklejohn, Alexander, *Free Speech and its Relation to Self-Government* (Harper Brother Publishers 1948).
Meling, Ingjerd, *"Privatlivsvern og æresvern": Hva er gjeldende rett og hvilke problemstillinger reiser seg i møte med de endringer som vil finne sted ved ikrafttredelsen av ny straffelov?*, Master's thesis (Universitetet i Oslo 2013).
Melteig, Tilfeldighetsprinsippets betydning for uavhengige domstoler, *Lov og rett* (1992), 425.
Mestad, Ola, and Michalsen, Dag, *Rett, nasjon, union* (Universitetsforlaget 2005).
Mestad, Ola and Michalsen, Dag, *Frihetens forskole: professor Schlegel og eidsvollsmennenes læretid i København* (Pax 2013).
Michalsen, Dag, Ny og gammel rettskildelære, *Tidsskrift for rettsvitenskap* 1994, 192–239.
Michalsen, Dag, *Forfatningsteori møter 1814* (Akademisk publisering 2008).
Michalsen, Dag, *Rett. En internasjonal historie* (Pax 2011).
Michelman, Frank I., *Brennan and democracy* (Princeton University Press 1999).
Michelman, Frank I., Ida's Way: Constructing the Respect-Worthy Governmental System, 72 *Fordham law review* 22 (2003).
Mill, John Stuart, *On liberty* (Cambridge University Press 1989).

Miller, Vaughne, *The European Court of Human Rights: the election of judges* (May 4, 2011): www.parliament.uk/briefing-papers/SN05949 (retrieved March 26, 2014).
Morgenstierne, Bredo, *Betenkning angående spørsmålet om ophevelse av grunnlovens § 97 og dermed sammenhengende spørsmål* (St. forh. 1923 Tillegg til dok. 13).
Morgenstierne, Bredo, *Lærebog i den norske Statsforfatningsret* (T. Steen, 1900).
Morgenstierne, Bredo, *Lærebog i den norske Statsforfatningsret* (Steen 2nd edn. 1909).
Munch-Ræder, Ole, *Den norske Statsforfatnings Historie og Væsen* (Høst 1841).
Møse, Erik, *Menneskerettigheter* (Cappelen akademisk 2002).
Nadim, Morten, Er Høyesterettsdommere politisk farget? – En undersøkelse av 17 dommeres votum i dissenssaker, *Lov og rett* 2013, 655–671.
Neppi-Modona, Guido, The Various Aspects of External and Internal Independence of the Judiciary, Venice Commission, CDL(2012)035.
Nickel, James W., *Making sense of human rights* (Blackwell Publishing 2nd edn. 2007).
Nicol, Danny, Original Intent and the European Convention on Human Rights, *Public law* Spring, (2005), 152–172.
Nissen, Gunnar Brun, Hiorthøy, Finn, and Gaarder, Karsten, *Den dømmende makt* (Universitetsforlaget 1967).
Nolte, Georg, *European and US constitutionalism* (Cambridge University Press 2005).
NTB, *Giske anker trolig dom om politisk TV-reklame* December 11, 2008.
NTB, *Frp mener regjeringen tøver, Nationen*, March 12, 2009.
Opsahl, Torkel, *Delegasjon av Stortingets myndighet* (Tanum 1965).
Opsahl, Torkel, Internasjonale tiltak til fremme av menneskerettighetene, in *Med lov skal land byggjast: heiderskrift til Knut Robberstad 70 år* (Universitetsforlaget 1969), 127–153.
Opsahl, Torkel, Plikt og betingelse, in *Nordisk gjenklang: festskrift til Carl Jacob Arnholm* (K. S. Selmer ed., Tanum 1969), 233–253.
Opsahl, Torkel, Kløfta-saken, dommerkunsten og dens tolkning, *Lov og rett* 1976, 49–50.
Ordskiftet om Beredskapslovene 12 oktober 1950, Norsk Rikskringkasting 1950.
Peter, Fabienne, *Political Legitimacy*, Stanford Encyclopedia of Philosophy: https://plato.stanford.edu/entries/legitimacy/ (2010).
Petersson, Olof, Den sista maktutredningen?, *Nytt Norsk Tidsskrift* 2003, 351–362.
Platou, Oscar, *Forelæsninger over retskildernes theori* (A. W. Brøgger 1915).
Post, Robert C. and Siegel, Reva, Roe rage: Democratic constitutionalism and backlash, 42 *Harvard Civil Rights-Civil Liberties Law Review* 62 (2007).
Rasmussen, Hjalte, *On law and policy in the European Court of Justice* (Nijhoff 1986).
Rawls, John, *Political liberalism* (Columbia University Press 1993).
Raz, Joseph, *The authority of law: essays on law and morality* (Clarendon Press; Oxford University Press 1979).
Raz, Joseph, *Ethics in the public domain – essays in the morality of law and politics* (Clarendon Press 1995).
Ringen, Stein, Wealth and decay: The Norwegian study of power and democracy, 4 *Times Literary Supplement* 2–4, (2004).
Roach, Kent, Dialogic judicial review and its critics, 23 *Supreme Court Law Review* (2d) 49 (2004).

Robberstad, Anne, Mener Høyesterett undergraver demokratiet, *Advokatbladet* 2/2016.

Robberstad, Anne, Viljen til å skape lov og Grunnlov, *Lov og rett*, 01/2016, 49–64.

Rokkan, Stein, Geography, religion and social class: Crosscutting cleavages in Norwegian Politics, in Seymour Martin Lipset and Stein Rokkan, eds, *Party Systems and Voter Alignments* (New York Free Press 1967).

Ross, Alf, *Retskilde- og Metodelære i realistisk Belysning*, Tidsskrift for Retsvidenskap 1931, 242–301.

Rui, Jon Petter, Forbudet mot gjentatt straffeforfølgning (ne bis in idem) i Den europeiske menneskerettighets-konvensjon protokoll 7 artikkel 4 – på ny, *Lov og rett* 2009, 283–298.

Rui, Jon Petter, The Interlaken, Izmir and Brighton Declarations: Towards a paradigm shift in the Strasbourg Court's interpretation of the European Convention of Human Rights?, 31 *Nordic Journal of Human Rights* 28 (2013).

Ryssdal, Rolv, The relationship between the judiciary and the legislative and executive branches of the government in Norway, 57 *North Dakota Law Review* 527–539 (1981).

Sandvik, Hilde and Michalsen, Dag, *Kodifikasjon og konstitusjon: Grunnloven § 94s krav til lovbøker i norsk historie* (Pax 2013).

Scanlon, Thomas, A theory of freedom of expression, 1 *Philosophy and Public Affairs* 204 (1972).

Scharpf, Fritz Wilhelm, *Governing in Europe – effective and democratic* (Oxford University Press 1999).

Schei, Tore, *Tvistemålsloven* (Tano Aschehoug 2nd edn. 1998).

Schei, Tore, Har Høyesterett en politisk funksjon?, *Lov og rett* 2011, 319–335.

Schei, Tore, Uten dekning, *Advokatbladet* 2/2016.

Schiøtz, Cato and Strømme, Vidar, Paradigmeskifte i injurieretten, *Lov og rett* 2002, 401–402.

Schjelderup, Ferdinand, *Fra Norges kamp for retten: 1940 i Høyesterett* (Grøndahl 1945).

Schmitt, Carl, *Verfassungslehre* (Duncker & Humblot 1928).

Schmitt, Carl, *Legality and legitimacy* (Duke University Press 2004).

Schubert, Glendon A., *Judicial decision-making* (Free Press of Glencoe 1963).

Schweigaard, A. M. and Motzfeldt, U. A., *Det juridiske Fakultets Betænkning af 18 Januar 1841 angaaende Ophævelsen af det bergenske Bagerlaugs Privilegier* (Rt. 1895 s. 289).

Seip, Jens Arup, *Fra embedsmannsstat til ettpartistat og andre essays* (Universitetsforlaget 1963).

Seip, Jens Arup, Den norske Høyesterett som politisk organ, *Lov og rett* 1965, 1–21

Seip, Jens Arup, Jus og politikk, *Lov og rett* 1965, 396–323.

Seip, Jens Arup, *Tanke og handling i norsk historie* (Gyldendal 1968).

Seip, Jens Arup, *Utsikt over Norges historie* 2 (Gyldendal 1981).

Sejersted, Francis, *Ideal, teori og virkelighet* (Cappelen 1973).

Sejersted, Francis, *Høyres historie*, 3 (Cappelen, 1984).

Sejersted, Francis, *Demokrati og rettsstat* (Pax 2001).

Sejersted, Francis, Frihetsrevolusjonen, *Nytt norsk tidsskrift* 2007, 256–268.

Sejersted, Francis, Den liberale vending, *Nytt norsk tidsskrift* 2009, 226–239.

Sejersted, Francis, *The age of social democracy* (Princeton University Press 2011).

Sejersted, Fredrik, Misvisende om rett og politikk, *Dagbladet*, June 3, 2009.
Sejersted, Fredrik, Misvisende om rettsstaten, *Dagbladet*, June 6, 2009.
Sejersted, Fredrik, Rett og politikk i europeiseringens tid, *Nytt norsk tidsskrift* 2009, 545–553.
Sejersted, Fredrik, Det elastiske panser, in *Tolkingar av Grunnlova* (E. Holmøyvik ed., Pax 2013),35–109.
Sejersted, Fredrik, *Grunnlovsendring må til, Dagens Næringsliv*, November 26, 2013.
Selmer, Knut, ed., *Nordisk gjenklang: festskrift til Carl Jacob Arnholm* (Tanum 1969).
Shapiro, Martin, The Supreme Court and constitutional adjudication: Of politics and neutral principles, 31 *George Washington Law Review* 587 (1963).
Sigmond, Frithjof B., Lov om erstatning ved ekspropriasjon – forholdet til Grunnlovens § 105, *Lov og rett* 1975, 167–177.
Simpson, A. W. B., Hersch Lauterpacht and the genesis of the age of human rights, 120 *Law Quarterly Review* 49–80 (2004).
Skeie, Jon, *Ang. ot. prp. nr. 43 for 1916: Ændringer i loven av 17de mai 1904 om salg og skjænkning av brændevin m. v.* (St. forh. 1917 dok. 1).
Skeie, Jon, *Om ærekrænkelser efter norsk ret* (Norli 1910).
Skeie, Jon, *Den norske civilproces* (Norli 2 edn. 1940).
Skjerdal, Nicolai V., Relativisering av domstolenes grunnlovskontroll – på tide å forlate tredelingslæren? in Hans Petter Graver, Ida Hjort Kraby and Marius Stub, eds, *Forsker og formidler. Festskrift til Erik Magnus Boe* (Universitetsforlaget 2013, 275–296).
Skoghøy, Jens and Edvin A., Forholdet mellom internasjonale menneskerettigheter og norsk rett, *Kritisk juss* 1998, 111–119.
Skoghøy, Jens and Edvin A., *Tvistemål* (Universitetsforlaget 2nd edn. 2001).
Skoghøy, Jens and Edvin A., Norske domstolers lovkontroll i forhold til inkorporerte menneskerettskonvensjoner, *Lov og rett* 2002, 337–354.
Skoghøy, Jens and Edvin A., Betydningen av Den europeiske menneskerettighetskonvensjon på sivilrettens og sivilprosessens område, in *Rettshjelp fra kyst til vidde* (J. P. Rui ed., Gyldendal 2009).
Skoghøy, Jens and Edvin A. , Praktiseringen av krav til dommerhabilitet i Norges Høyesterett, *Lov og rett* 2009, 323–341.
Skoghøy, Jens and Edvin A., Dommeratferd og dommerbakgrunn, *in Festskrift till Torgny Håstad* (Iustus Förlag 2010), 711–726.
Skoghøy, Jens and Edvin A., Dommerrollen gjennom de siste 50 år – noen utviklingstrekk, *Lov og rett* 2011, 4–24.
Skoghøy, Jens and Edvin A., Nasjonal skjønnsmargin etter EMK, *Lov og rett* 2011, 189–190.
Skoghøy, Jens and Edvin A., Nasjonal EMK-prøving, *Lov og rett* 2012, 170–178.
Skretting, Nils Gunnar, *The Bøhler Doctrine* (University of Oslo – unpublished manuscript).
Slagstad, Rune, Norsk rettsrealisme etter 1945, *Tidsskrift for rettsvitenskap* 1987, 385–403.
Slagstad, Rune, *Rett og politikk: et liberalt tema med variasjoner* (Universitetsforlaget 1987).
Slagstad, Rune, Prøvingsretten i det norske system, *Nytt norsk tidsskrift* 1989, 333–356.

Slagstad, Rune, Breakthrough of judicial review in Norway, in *Constitutional Justice under Old Constitutions* (E. Smith ed., Kluwer 1995), 81–111.
Slagstad, Rune, *De nasjonale strateger* (Pax 1998).
Slagstad, Rune, Shifting knowledge regimes: The metamorphoses of Norwegian reformism, *Thesis Eleven* 2004, 65–83.
Slagstad, Rune, *Rettens ironi* (Pax, 2. edn. 2011).
Slagstad, Rune, Høyesteretts institusjonelle egenart, *Lov og rett* 2015, 637–641.
Smet, Stijn, Freedom of expression and the right to reputation: Human rights in conflict, 26 *American University International Law Review* 183 (2011).
Smith, Carsten, Den internasjonale rettens innvirkning på den nasjonale retten, *Tidsskrift for rettsvitenskap* 1962, 182–204.
Smith, Carsten, Folkerettens stilling ved norske domstoler, *Tidsskrift for rettsvitenskap* 1964, 356–374.
Smith, Carsten, Domstolene og rettsutviklingen, *Lov og rett* 1975, 292–319.
Smith, Carsten, Om internasjonale menneskerettigheter og nasjonale domstoler, *Jussens venner* 1980, 302–314.
Smith, Carsten, Judicial review of parliamentary legislation: Norway as a European pioneer, *Public Law* 45:12 2000, 595–606.
Smith, Carsten, Bør menneskerettigheten styrkes i vår grunnlov? *Jussens Venner* 2006, 235–247.
Smith, Eivind, *Høyesterett og folkestyret* (Universitetsforlaget 1993).
Smith, Eivind, *Constitutional justice under old constitutions* (Kluwer 1995).
Smith, Eivind, Høyesterett – en trussel mot demokratiet?, *Lov og rett* 1999, 451–486.
Smith, Eivind, *Konstitusjonelt demokrati* (Fagbokforlaget 2nd edn. 2012).
Solum, Lawrence, *Legitimacy*, Legal Theory Lexicon http://lsolum.typepad.com/legal_theory_lexicon/2005/06/legal_theory_le_2.html (2010).
Somin, Ilya, Political ignorance and the countermajoritarian difficulty: A new perspective on the central obsession of constitutional theory, 89 *Iowa Law Review* 1287 (2004).
Spano, Robert, Universality or Diversity of Human Rights: Strasbourg in the Age of Subsidiarity, *Human Rights Law Review*, 2014, 487–502,
Stang, Frederik, *Systematisk Fremstilling af Kongeriget Norges constitutionelle eller grundlovbestemte Ret* (D. F. Hoppes forlag 1833).
Stavang, Per, *Parlamentarisme og folkestyre* (Fagbokforlaget 4 edn. 2002).
Steenbuch, Henrik, *Svar paa det fra Lehmanns Bogtrykkerie udkomne Skrift: Nogle Ord om Kongens Veto* (Det Wulfsbergske Bogtrykkerie 1824).
Stein, Friedrich, *Das private Wissen des Richters* (C. L. Hirschfeld 1893).
Stone, Harlan Fiske, The common law in the United States, 50 *Harvard Law Review* 25 (1936).
Story, Joseph, *Commentaries on the Constitution of the United States; with a preliminary review of the constitutional history of the colonies and states, before the adoption of the Constitution* (Hilliard, Gray, and Company 1833).
Strand, Vibeke Blaker, Forholdet mellom den norske Grunnlovens menneskerettigheter, de internasjonale menneskerettighetskonvensjonene og ordinær lovgivning, *Retfærd* 2007, 1–23.
Strauss, David A., Persuasion, autonomy, and freedom of expression, 91 *Columbia Law Review* 334 (1991).

Strauss, David A., The modernizing mission of judicial review, 76 *University of Chicago Law Review* 859 (2009).

Stub, Marius, Om forbudet mot husinkvisisjoner i Grunnloven § 102, *Tidsskrift for rettsvitenskap* 388–444, (2009).

Stub, Marius, Boe, Erik Magnus, Kraby, Ida Hjort and Graver, Hans Petter, Forsker og formidler. *Festskrift til Erik Magnus Boe* (Universitetsforlaget 2013).

Sundby, Nils Kristian, *Om normer* (Universitetsforlaget 1974).

Sunde, Jørn Øyrehagen, "Ansees Hævet" – Føresetandar for utviklinga av den norske prøvingsretten på 1800-talet, in *Forfatningsteori møter 1814* (D. Michalsen ed., Akademisk publisering 2008), 215–267.

Sunde, Jørn Øyrehagen, Andre premiss og anna resultat, *Tidsskrift for rettsvitenskap* 2012, 168–204.

Sunde, Jørn Øyrehagen, Dissenting votes in the Norwegian Supreme Court 1965–2009: A legal cultural analysis, *Rechtskultur – Zeitschrift für Europäische Rechtsgeschichte* 59–73 (2012).

Sunstein, Cass R., Beyond Judicial Minimalism, 43 *Tulsa Law Review* 825 (2013).

Sunstein, Cass R., *One Case at a Time - Judicial Minimalism on the Supreme Court* (Harvard University Press 2001).

Sverdrup Thygeson, Ulrik, *Grunnlovens forbud mot jesuitter og munkeordener: Religionsfrihet og grunnlovskonservatisme 1814–1956* (University Of Oslo 2009).

Taube, Caroline, Lagrådet imorgon: Kan eller bör Lagrådet och lagrådsgranskningen förändras?, *Svensk juristtidning* 2009, 277–281.

Thomson, James A., Review essay: Swimming in the air:sss Melville W. Fuller and the Supreme Court 1888–1910, 27 *Cumberland Law Review* 139 (1996).

Tocqueville, Alexis de, *De la démocratie en Amérique* (Librairie de C. Gosselin 1835).

Torgersen, Ulf, Høyesterett i norsk politikk, *Tidsskrift for samfunnsforskning* 1960, 94–104.

Torgersen, Ulf, *De generelle synspunktene på Grl.* § 97 (Universitetet i Oslo 1955).

Tushnet, Mark, Alternative forms of judicial review, 101 Michigan Law Review 2781–2802 (2003).

Tushnet, Mark, *Weak courts, strong rights – Judicial Review and Social Welfare Rights in Comparative Constitutional Law* (Princeton 2009).

Tverberg, Arnulf, Det graderte grunnlovsvernet ved tolkning av grunnloven og prøving av lovers grunnlovmessighet, in *Tolkingar av Grunnlova* (E. Holmøyvik ed., Pax 2013), 256–303.

Uggerud, Ken, Den andre bølge? Om menneskerettighetenes tilfeldige tilværelse i norsk rett, in *Dog fred er ej det bedste. Festskrift til Carl August Fleischer* (A. Syse, H. Jakhelln and O. K. Fauchald eds., Universitetsforlaget 2006), 577–603.

Ulfstein, Geir, Føllesdal, Andreas and Schaffer, Johan Karlsson, *The Legitimacy of international human rights regimes* (Cambridge University Press 2013).

Unneberg, Bjørn, Professor Andenæs og grunnloven, *Lov og rett* 1975, 374–379.

Valle, Inger Louise, Demokratiet og menneskerettighetene, *Mennesker og rettigheter* 1983, 16–30.

Vermeule, Adrian, Second opinions, 97 *Virginia Law Review* 1435, (2011).

Vislie, Camilla S., *Høyesterett og menneskerettighetene* (Tano Aschehoug 1999).

Waldron, Jeremy, The core of the case against judicial review, 115 *Yale Law Journal* 1346 (2006).

Weber, Max and Parsons, Talcott, *The theory of social and economic organization* (Free Press 1964).
Wechsler, Herbert, Toward neutral principles of constitutional law, 73 *Harvard Law Journal* 35 (1959).
Weiler, J. H. H., *The constitution of Europe* (Cambridge University Press 1999).
Weiler, J. H. H., The geology of international law: governance, democracy and legitimacy, 64 Heidelberg Journal of International Law 547–562 (2004).
Wessel-Aas, Jon, Effektivisering av subsidiaritet i EMK – En replikk til Marius Emberland, *Lov og rett* 2013, 702–704.
Wessel-Aas, Jon, *Giske og politisk reklame: Hadde ett problem – "løser" det ved å lage flere*: http://www.uhuru.biz/?p=4 (2009) (retreived March 26, 2014).
Wold, Terje, Den Europeiske menneskerettskonvensjon og Norge, in *Legal essays: A tribute to Frede Castberg* (Universitetsforlaget 1963).
Wold, Terje, Domstolenes deltakelse i justisforvaltningen (Lecture at the Norwegian Judges' Society's Annual General Meeting, November 7, 1964).
Wolland, Steingrim, Norsk ytringsfrihet i et menneskerettslig perspektiv, *Mennesker og rettigheter* 1994, 337–345.
Wyller, Thomas Chr., Kings Bay-saken: jus, politikk og statsvitenskap, *Lov og rett* 1964, 15–26.
Zürn, Michael, Autorität und Legitimität in der postnationalen Konstellation in *Leviathan Sonderband* 27 (A. Geis, F. Nullmeier and C. Daase eds., Nomos 2012).
Ørsted, Anders Sandøe, Haandbog over den danske og norske Lovkyndighed, Coldin (1822).
Ørsted, Anders Sandøe, *Haandbog over den danske og norske Lovkyndighed* (Kjøbenhavn 1822).
Østerud, Øyvind, Makt og urett – kommentar til en rettsteoretisk kritikk av Makt- og demokratiutredningen, *Lov og rett* 2006, 106–116.
Østerud, Øyvind, Rettsliggjøring og demokrati, *Tidsskrift for samfunnsforskning* 2006, 613–621.
Østerud, Øyvind and Selle, Per, Power and democracy in Norway: The transformation of Norwegian politics, 29 *Scandinavian Political Studies* 25 (2006).
Østlid, Henry, Hvordan offentlige voteringer ble gjennomført i Norges Høyesterett, *Tidsskrift for rettsvitenskap* 1955, 171–207.
Østlid, Henry, *Dommeratferd i dissenssaker* (Universitetforlaget 1988).
Øy, Nils E., Kritisk søkelys på norsk injurielov og domstolspraksis, in *"Ved redaktør forstås-"* (S. Finslo ed., Norsk redaktørforening 1998), 119–173.

Index

Books in the Series

Constitutions, Religion and Politics in Asia: Indonesia, Malaysia and Sri Lanka
Dian A. H.Shah

Proportionality: New Frontiers, New Challenges
edited by Vicki Jackson and Mark Tushnet

Constituents Before Assembly: Participation, Deliberation, and Representation in the Crafting of New Constitutions
Todd A. Eisenstadt, A. Carl LeVan, and Tofigh Maboudi

Assessing Constitutional Performance
Tom Ginsburg and Aziz Huq

Buddhism, Politics and the Limits of Law: The Pyrrhic Constitutionalism of Sri Lanka
Benjamin Schonthal

Engaging with Social Rights
Brian Ray

Constitutional Courts as Mediators
Julio Ríos-Figueroa

Perils of Judicial Self-Government in Transitional Societies
David Kosař

Making We the People
Chaihark Hahm and Sung Ho Kim

Radical Deprivation on Trial
Cesar Rodríguez-Garavito and Diana Rodríguez-Franco

Unstable Constitutionalism
edited by Mark Tushnet and Madhav Khosla

Magna Carta and its Modern Legacy
edited by Robert Hazell and James Melton

Constitutions and Religious Freedom
Frank Cross

International Courts and the Performance of International Agreements: A General Theory with Evidence from the European Union
Clifford Carrubba and Matthew Gabel

Reputation and Judicial Tactics: A Theory of National and International Courts
Shai Dothan

Social Difference and Constitutionalism in Pan-Asia
edited by Susan H. Williams

Constitutionalism in Asia in the Early Twenty-First Century
edited by Albert Chen

Constitutions in Authoritarian Regimes
edited by Tom Ginsburg and Alberto Simpser

Presidential Legislation in India: The Law and Practice of Ordinances
Shubhankar Dam

Social and Political Foundations of Constitutions
edited by Denis J. Galligan and Mila Versteeg

Consequential Courts: Judicial Roles in Global Perspective
edited by Diana Kapiszewski, Gordon Silverstein and Robert A. Kagan

Comparative Constitutional Design
edited by Tom Ginsburg

Judicial Review in Norway
Anine Kierulf